THE PHIL(
ISAIAH BERLIN

ALSO AVAILABLE FROM BLOOMSBURY

In Search of Isaiah Berlin: A Literary Adventure, Henry Hardy
The Tyranny of Opinion: Conformity and the Future of Liberalism,
Russell Blackford

THE PHILOSOPHY OF ISAIAH BERLIN

Johnny Lyons

BLOOMSBURY ACADEMIC
LONDON • NEW YORK • OXFORD • NEW DELHI • SYDNEY

BLOOMSBURY ACADEMIC
Bloomsbury Publishing Plc
50 Bedford Square, London, WC1B 3DP, UK
1385 Broadway, New York, NY 10018, USA

BLOOMSBURY, BLOOMSBURY ACADEMIC and the Diana logo are trademarks of
Bloomsbury Publishing Plc

First published in Great Britain 2020

Copyright © Johnny Lyons, 2020

Johnny Lyons has asserted his right under the Copyright, Designs and Patents Act, 1988,
to be identified as Author of this work.

For legal purposes the Acknowledgements on p. xx constitute an extension
of this copyright page.

Cover image © INTERFOTO / Alamy Stock Photo

All rights reserved. No part of this publication may be reproduced or transmitted
in any form or by any means, electronic or mechanical, including photocopying,
recording, or any information storage or retrieval system, without prior
permission in writing from the publishers.

Bloomsbury Publishing Plc does not have any control over, or responsibility for, any
third-party websites referred to or in this book. All internet addresses given in this book
were correct at the time of going to press. The author and publisher regret any
inconvenience caused if addresses have changed or sites have ceased to exist,
but can accept no responsibility for any such changes.

A catalogue record for this book is available from the British Library.

A catalog record for this book is available from the Library of Congress.

ISBN: HB: 978-1-3501-2142-3
PB: 978-1-3501-2143-0
ePDF: 978-1-3501-2144-7
eBook: 978-1-3501-2145-4

Typeset by Deanta Global Publishing Services, Chennai, India
Printed and bound in Great Britain

To find out more about our authors and books visit www.bloomsbury.com and
sign up for our newsletters.

To Eddie Hyland for daring me to philosophize
To John Simmons for daring me to write
To Henry Hardy for daring me to publish
In memory of my mother, Bernadette, and of my friend, Doug

Be a Philosopher; but amidst all your Philosophy, be still a Man.

David Hume, 'Of the Different Species of Philosophy', section 1 of *Philosophical Essays Concerning Human Understanding* (London, 1748), 7

CONTENTS

Foreword by Henry Hardy ix
Preface xii
Abbreviations xviii
Acknowledgements xx

PART ONE GENERAL INTRODUCTION 1

1 The nature of Berlin's political philosophy 3

PART TWO PHILOSOPHY 21

2 In the beginning … 23
3 Kant's Copernican revolution 36
4 The humanistic turn 53
5 Taking history seriously 65
6 Interlude: Taking stock 79
7 Philosophy, literature and human understanding 101

PART THREE CONTINGENCY 109

8 Philosophy and belief 111
9 The logic-choppers 118
10 The postmodern appropriation 123

11 The hedgehog's revenge 139

12 What we are left with 158

13 Reason, history and liberalism 166

PART FOUR FREEDOM 173

14 Theory versus practice 175

15 The central problem of freedom 180

16 Is belief in determinism liveable? 187

17 Truth, freedom and value pluralism 200

18 Reimagining the nature and authority of philosophy 212

PART FIVE AUTHENTICITY 223

19 Framing the debate 225

20 Three romantic thinkers 231

21 Smashing the jigsaw 240

22 The liberalism of romanticism 243

Epilogue 253
Bibliography 262
Index 273

FOREWORD

In the autumn of 2017 I received an email out of the blue from the author of the book before you, an Irish former academic now working in communications in the banking sector, in Dublin. Johnny Lyons told me he had nearly completed a book on the thought of Isaiah Berlin, adding with commendable lack of self-effacement:

> I have read everything published by Isaiah Berlin [...] and pretty much everything written on Berlin. I think my work is original, significant and interesting. I have attached the preface to my work, which will give you some background on why I have written it. I believe (I may be wrong, of course) it's worthy of publication. I thought I might therefore contact you to help me determine if my belief is correct.

I read the preface and was immediately attracted by Lyons's style and approach. In the course of my lifelong work on Berlin I have read too many reams of pedestrian and unilluminating academic prose, and this was something completely different: fresh, perceptive, warm, natural, ambitious. It is very rarely that I encounter writing on Berlin that stands out so prominently from the drab general background, and I was immediately stimulated, indeed excited. I replied: 'Your preface so whets the appetite: well written, sensible, unhidebound. I am trying to write such a book myself, and you seem to have beaten me to it! I should be fascinated to read the rest, and would be happy to give you my view of it.'

Lyons sent me what he had written (drafts of all but the last chapter). In my response I wrote: 'I am enormously impressed by your range of reading and reference, especially given that you do not work as an academic,' and that my initial reaction to the preface was fully borne out by reading what he had sent.

There followed three months of intensive email correspondence about numerous successive drafts of the chapters, some of which incorporated Lyons's responses to detailed suggestions I had made on previous versions. I have, in effect, been present at the birth of a notable and notably humane study of Berlin's ideas that is utterly distinctive, and certainly 'original, significant and interesting'. These qualities can be measured by the fact that it is not a book one could have remotely pictured to oneself before reading it. It is unlike anything else written on Berlin, and the contribution of its style to the light it throws on Berlin's thought is not to be underestimated. I have also come to know the author personally (though not in person at the time of writing), which helps me to understand why he has been able to write this marvellous book. I count the whole experience a privilege.

I was right to sense at the outset that Lyons had stolen a march on me. Some of what he says captures what I see as Berlin's understanding of humanity so well that it hardly needs restating. But the book also travels well beyond any journey I might have undertaken myself, offering us a whole series of original insights to which I could not have aspired. In particular, Lyons uses his phenomenally wide reading to throw many valuable sidelights on his story, and to place Berlin's work in the context of the intellectual climate against which it stands out so markedly.

Berlin used to refer to 'the sensation – for which there is no substitute – of suddenly sailing in first-class waters', and it was a sensation of this kind that I experienced on first looking into Lyons's Berlin (PI3 123). The sensation has stayed with me, and, indeed, strengthened, during the months in which I have become more closely acquainted with his text. Lyons is a stout Cortez *de nos jours*, looking on Berlin's works not so much for the first time as with a new vision that should enable readers to see them afresh.

Berlin also used to commend the first-handedness of certain authors – what he described as the absence of anything between the person and the object – explaining in one case that 'his vision is direct, not mediated by anything, not framed by categories, preconceptions, a desire to fit things into some framework' (A 513).[1] Something of this kind can be said of Lyons. He sees Berlin plain, and therefore sees more in him than many others. His selection of principal topics is one of which Berlin would surely have approved: the special nature of philosophical questions, the deep contingency of human nature and value, the centrality of full freedom in human self-understanding and the role of personal authenticity in complementing the somewhat barren vision of life offered by some thinkers of the Enlightenment. On all these topics Lyons has arresting things to say, and it is my belief that his account of Berlin will take its place as a permanent milestone in the study of that remarkable thinker.

My own work on Berlin has mainly been of the subterranean kind characteristic of editors. I have laboured in the coal seams of his uncollected and unpublished writings, heaving them to the surface from time to time in what is intended to be a user-friendly form. It has been an enterprise that would have failed if the work I

---

[1] The person referred to is Stephen Spender.

had edited had not been taken up by writers and thinkers who could understand it, see its value and interpret it for Berlin's readers in our own time. Happily a number of such figures have emerged over the years, but none whose writing is more vigorous, seductive and truthful than that of Johnny Lyons. The belief he expressed in his initial email is undoubtedly correct, by a very wide margin.

Henry Hardy

PREFACE

I met Isaiah Berlin twice. Our second meeting turned out better than the earlier one. The first time I met him was in 1994, when he was in Dublin to receive an honorary degree from Trinity College. At the time, I was a graduate student at the same university and was planning to write my PhD on his political thought. I had written to Berlin in advance of his visit asking if he would be prepared to let me interview him. He kindly agreed and so I met him at the American ambassador's residence in the Phoenix Park, where he was staying as a guest. Having arrived at the residence, I was escorted to a large and opulent drawing room in the far corner of which Berlin was already sitting. He was much smaller than I imagined and was wearing a dark three-piece suit, which looked familiar from the photos of him that have appeared on the covers of some of his books. From the moment we shook hands he began talking in the manner he was famous for – feverishly fast and with a deep and lilting tone that sounded luxuriantly Eastern European. Regrettably, I let the occasion get the better of me. When I finally got the chance to ask him a few questions they sounded stilted and superficial, and not even his polite replies of 'Well, not exactly …' or 'If we considered the topic slightly differently …' could assuage my tongue-tied sense of inferiority or my embarrassment. Perhaps sensing my discomfort, he did his best to let our meeting finish on a cheery note by retailing the surreally amusing story of the misunderstanding that led to Winston Churchill hosting the American songwriter Irving Berlin at lunch in Downing Street in 1944 rather than the philosopher and wartime diplomat Isaiah Berlin, whose regular dispatches from Washington during the Second World War he had so much enjoyed.

Although I was already familiar with this well-known anecdote, hearing it told by Berlin himself was hard to beat. His broad smile was infectious when he reached the part of the story in which Irving Berlin responded to Churchill's question (Churchill was still under the misapprehension that he was conversing with Isaiah Berlin) about what his most important piece of work was in recent times with the answer '*White Christmas*, I guess.' After his lunch with Churchill, Irving Berlin went back to the Savoy Hotel, where he was sharing rooms with the film director Alexander Korda, and reportedly said to him, 'You know, Mr Churchill is probably the greatest man in England, or in the world maybe, but I do not know what it was, I somehow felt we didn't click. I do not know what it was. Now she [Winston Churchill's wife, Clementine] is a wonderful woman, I could talk to her always. With him, I do not know, something, something – I just cannot make it out.'[1]

The second occasion on which I met Berlin proved more auspicious. The meeting took place in his own grand Georgian home in Oxford towards the end of 1996. I cannot remember what made me think that a second interview would be a good idea, or, indeed, what possessed Berlin to agree to meet me once more, but I am so glad that he did.[2] For whatever reason, I didn't feel as overwhelmed on this occasion, and our conversation began to flow from the moment he welcomed me into his hallway. I had read his recently published book of essays, *The Sense of Reality*, which perhaps gave me the hook I needed to assert myself a bit more.[3] Anyway, a conversation (he still spoke 99 per cent of the time) ensued that lasted most of the afternoon.

Our talk covered a number of diverse topics, including our shared passion for Diderot's masterpiece *Rameau's Nephew*, our discussion of which led to a lengthy exploration and assessment of Lionel Trilling's *Sincerity and Authenticity*, which he also much admired. On this second occasion he seemed genuinely interested in what I had to say, especially in my view that a deep concern for truth lay at the heart of his world view: he quizzed me about my own interpretation of his philosophical outlook and for a few wonderful moments I felt the unique exhilaration of having a genuine dialogue with an endlessly cultivated and engaging mind. I also got a first-hand sense of what his editor and friend, Henry Hardy, has described as Berlin's 'genius for being human'.[4]

Another thing that struck me on that memorable afternoon was the seemingly effortless ease with which he moved between the various branches of philosophy: one minute he would be referring to the limits of toleration and negative liberty, and the next to the potential significance of Leibniz's distinction between *truths of reason* and *truths of fact*. And there was nothing contrived or arbitrary about the way he shifted from a familiar topic in political theory to much deeper and more recondite areas of epistemology (our understanding of knowledge) or metaphysics (our understanding of reality). Indeed, the seamless and authoritative manner in which he ranged across the various fields of philosophy felt as natural as it did necessary.

---

[1] For a complete telling of this story by Berlin see http://berlin.wolf.ox.ac.uk/tribute/2berlins.htm.
[2] Berlin's authorized biographer, Michael Ignatieff, suggests a generic-type answer: 'He [Berlin] was prodigal with words and time. To an obscure graduate student in Oregon he would expound his distinction between two concepts of liberty with the same gusto that he devoted to sharing gossip with Arthur Schlesinger, Jr.', Michael Ignatieff, *Isaiah Berlin: A Life* (1998: Chatto & Windus, London), 7.
[3] SR: see Abbreviations, 17–18 below.
[4] Henry Hardy, *In Search of Isaiah Berlin: A Literary Adventure* (2018: I.B. Tauris, London), 7.

Berlin died less than twelve months after our second meeting, and my own PhD suffered a similar fate a few years later. While I had the nous to realize that a proper study of Berlin's liberalism needed to be philosophically grounded, I also knew that I did not have the requisite knowledge and skill to fulfil such a brief. I felt that, as a history graduate, I lacked the conceptual depth and acuity needed to do Berlin's liberalism justice, and it was not obvious to me at the time whether I had the intellectual wherewithal to acquire such expertise. In the midst of my unconfident philosophical ignorance I found myself reading Thomas Nagel's then latest collection of essays, *Other Minds*. In the introduction to his book, Nagel remarks:

> Bernard Williams once posed the awkward question, What is the point of doing philosophy if you are not extraordinarily good at it? The problem is that you cannot, by sheer hard work, like a historian of modest gifts, make solid discoveries that others can then rely on in building up larger results. If you are not extraordinary, what you do in philosophy will be either unoriginal (and therefore unnecessary) or inadequately supported (and therefore useless). More likely, it will be both unoriginal and wrong.[5]

Reading these lines effectively finished me off, and there was nothing in Nagel's attempt at a reassuring response to Williams's devastating remarks that I found particularly convincing.[6]

Shortly afterwards, I abruptly gave up my PhD and sought to make my way in the commercial world. But while I abandoned academia (or it abandoned me), I couldn't quite manage to wave goodbye to philosophy. I had developed an addiction to its charms and their power has grown rather than diminished in the intervening years. I have continued to be an avid reader of philosophy, seeking to close the glaring gaps in my knowledge of the subject while also trying to keep abreast of its latest and more significant developments. Highlights along the way have included Plato's dialogues, Hume's *A Treatise of Human Nature*, Kant's *Critique of Pure Reason* and almost everything by Nietzsche, as well as more contemporary works such as Richard Rorty's *Philosophy and the Mirror of Nature*, Hilary Putnam's *Reason, Truth and History* and Thomas Nagel's *The View from Nowhere*. One of the traits that all these works share is something I have touched on briefly above: the manner in which they treat philosophical themes and issues is open and all-embracing as opposed to artificially closed and fragmented. Unlike

---

[5] Thomas Nagel, *Other Minds: Critical Essays 1969–1994* (1995: Oxford University Press, Oxford), 10.

[6] There were also, of course, non-intellectual reasons for deserting my doctoral research, including being fed up with being financially broke, the poverty of decent job prospects as well as chronic indiscipline on my part.

so much of contemporary philosophy, which resembles a kind of bocage landscape in which the various fields of philosophy are studied as if they are entirely discrete and self-contained, these ancient and modern thinkers follow philosophical questions wherever they happen to lead. Their writings amply reveal that most genuine philosophical questions inhabit multiple fields of the subject at once, all of which need to be 'trespassed' by the genuine philosophical explorer. They also testify to there being 'no shallow end to the philosophical pool'.[7] Of course, doing philosophy in this more capacious and ambitious way is much more difficult and precarious than treating it as a siloed subject that one pursues by specializing in a particular branch or even sub-branch of philosophy. But the challenge of difficulty is never a reason to cease pursuing something worthwhile. And there are few intellectual questions more difficult or more worthwhile than the ones philosophy confronts. To paraphrase Paul Valéry, a difficult question resembles the light while an impossible one is like the sun.

My reason for returning to Berlin is not that I believe I have somehow become 'extraordinarily good' at philosophy. Rather, it is because I have become a little better at it. And one of the results of my becoming more adept at it is that I feel I have arrived at a point where I can now finally do Berlin's political thought some justice. Doing Berlin justice means getting under the surface of his thought and excavating its philosophical foundations. This type of excavation is not something that scholars have typically chosen to do. The purpose of this study is to show that it is only by unearthing Berlin's conception of philosophy that we can make sense of his political theory.

The hedgehog and the fox

There is an isolated surviving line by the ancient Greek poet Archilochus that Berlin immortalized in his celebrated essay on Tolstoy: 'The fox knows many things, but the hedgehog knows one big thing' (HF2 1). While Berlin acknowledges that this line can be understood non-metaphorically as meaning no more than that a fox for all his cunning cannot defeat a hedgehog's single defence, he invites us to adopt a less literal reading of the ancient fragment:

> But, taken figuratively, the words can be made to yield a sense in which they mark one of the deepest differences which divide writers and thinkers, and, it may be, human beings in general. For there exists a great chasm between those, on one side, who relate everything to a single central vision, one system, more

---

[7] P. F. Strawson, *Analysis and Metaphysics: An Introduction to Philosophy* (1995: Oxford University Press, Oxford), vii.

or less coherent or articulate, in terms of which they understand, think and feel – a single, universal, organising principle in terms of which alone all that they are and say has significance – and, on the other side, those who pursue many ends, often unrelated and even contradictory, connected, if at all, only in some *de facto* way, for some psychological or physiological cause, related by no moral or aesthetic principle; these last lead lives, perform acts and entertain ideas that are centrifugal rather than centripetal; their thought is scattered and diffused, moving on many levels, seizing upon the essence of a vast variety of experiences and objects for what they are in themselves, without, consciously or unconsciously, seeking to fit them into, or exclude them from, any one unchanging, all-embracing, sometimes self-contradictory and incomplete, at times fanatical, unitary inner vision. The first kind of intellectual and artistic personality belongs to the hedgehogs, the second to the foxes. (RT 24–5)

Berlin is a thinker who fits squarely into the second category. Like Tolstoy, Berlin was by nature a fox, but, unlike the great Russian novelist, he *believed* in being a fox.

It is, of course, possible to turn Berlin's self-description on its head and claim that his celebrated account of value pluralism makes him more of a hedgehog than a fox. This claim is intelligible, but misses the spirit of the distinction, which even he himself admits 'becomes, if pressed, artificial, scholastic and ultimately absurd'. The whole point of the distinction for Berlin is to help differentiate thinkers who 'relate everything to a single central vision' from those 'who pursue many ends, often unrelated and even contradictory'. So while it could be argued that Berlin is a hedgehog because he related everything to value pluralism, this classification fails to register that the 'single vision' of the hedgehog is a monistic one that is diametrically opposed to the idea and sensibility of value pluralism, a viewpoint that not only describes the pluralistic perspective of foxes but celebrates it. Incidentally, the literary critic Edmund Wilson considered Berlin a genuine hedgehog dressed up as a fox. Berlin had the following to say about Wilson's view:

> He [Edmund Wilson] was, in my eyes, a great critic, and a noble and moving human being, whom I loved and respected and wanted to have a good opinion of me; I was deeply touched when, not long before he died, he made me inscribe a line from the Bible with a diamond upon the window-pane of his house in Wellfleet, a privilege reserved for friends. The line was a verse from Isaiah, with whom, he insisted, I had obviously identified myself – another ineradicable fantasy, like his obstinate insistence that I had written as I did about Tolstoy only because I, too, was a fox, longing to be, indeed believing myself to be, a hedgehog. Nothing said to deny this absurdity made the faintest impression on him. He knew that 'like all Jews' I sought unity and a metaphysically integrated

organic world; in fact, I believe the exact opposite. The constructions of his inner world withstood all external evidence (PI3 295–6).

As we shall see, Berlin established his fox-like intellectual credentials with his own world view, which can be described as that of pluralism. Pluralism has a legitimate claim to be regarded as the philosophy of the fox in its purest form. Indeed, it is hard to imagine an outlook that the typical fox would find more agreeable and the hedgehog more disagreeable.

Finally, I would like to highlight at the outset that Berlin's pluralism is not an instance of philosophical theory in the dry and detached sense of the term, by which I mean that it bears little or no connection to how we normally think and act in everyday life. Berlin's philosophy is not intended to be left in the library like Hume's scepticism or Berkeley's immaterialism. Rather, it is close to a creed, albeit a subversive if deeply humane one in the context of the Western intellectual tradition. Indeed, a major concern of what follows will be to show that Berlin's pluralist vision of liberalism is as much a practical guide to human life in all its rich and irreducible variety as it is an attempt to offer a dispassionate account of the human situation. Put slightly differently, my aim is to bring out what makes Berlin's pluralism a philosophy for humans.

ABBREVIATIONS

The abbreviations of Berlin's works listed below, which I have lifted from the superb Isaiah Berlin virtual library http://berlin.wolf.ox.ac.uk/index.html, are used throughout the book. Abbreviations for subsequent editions of Isaiah Berlin's works add the relevant number, so that, for example, RT2 is the 2nd edition of RT. All quotations from these writings are used by courtesy of the trustees of the Isaiah Berlin Literary Trust.

A   *Affirming: Letters 1975–1997*, ed. Henry Hardy and Mark Pottle (2015: London, Chatto and Windus)

AC   *Against the Current: Essays in the History of Ideas*, ed. Henry Hardy, introduction by Roger Hausheer (1979), 2nd ed., foreword by Mark Lilla (2013: Princeton, Princeton University Press)

AE   *The Age of Enlightenment: The Eighteenth-Century Philosophers*, selected with introduction and commentary by IB (1956), 2nd ed., ed. Henry Hardy (2017: Oxford, Isaiah Berlin Literary Trust), online in IBVL

B   *Building: Letters 1960–1975*, ed. Henry Hardy and Mark Pottle (2013: London, Chatto and Windus)

BI   Henry Hardy (ed.), *The Book of Isaiah: Personal Impressions of Isaiah Berlin* (2009: Woodbridge, The Boydell Press in association with Wolfson College, Oxford)

CC   *Concepts and Categories: Philosophical Essays*, ed. Henry Hardy, introduction by Bernard Williams (1978), 2nd. ed., foreword by Alasdair MacIntyre (2013: Princeton, Princeton University Press)

CTH   *The Crooked Timber of Humanity: Chapters in the History of Ideas*, ed. Henry Hardy (1990), 2nd ed., foreword by John Banville (2013: Princeton, Princeton University Press)

E   *Enlightening: Letters 1946–1960*, ed. Henry Hardy and Jennifer Holmes (2009: London, Chatto & Windus)

FEL   *Four Essays on Liberty* (1969), superseded by L

FIB	*Freedom and its Betrayal: Six Enemies of Human Liberty* (1952 lectures), ed. Henry Hardy (2002), 2nd. ed., foreword by Enrique Krauze (2014: Princeton: Princeton University Press)
FL	*The First and the Last* (1999: New York, New York Review Books; London)
HF	*The Hedgehog and the Fox: An Essay on Tolstoy's View of History* (1953), 2nd. ed., ed. Henry Hardy, foreword by Michael Ignatieff (2013: Princeton, Princeton University Press)
IBVL	The Isaiah Berlin Virtual Library
L	*Liberty*, ed. Henry Hardy, essay on 'Berlin and His Critics' by Ian Harris (2002: Oxford and New York, Oxford University Press)
MN	*The Magus of the North: J. G. Hamann and the Origins of Modern Irrationalism*, ed. Henry Hardy (1993), superseded by TCE
PI	*Personal Impressions*, ed. Henry Hardy, introduction by Noel Annan (1980), 3rd ed., foreword by Hermione Lee (2014: Princeton, Princeton University Press)
PIRA	*Political Ideas in the Romantic Age: Their Rise and Influence on Modern Thought*, ed. Henry Hardy, introduction by Joshua L. Cherniss (2006), 2nd. ed. (2014: Princeton, Princeton University Press)
POI	*The Power of Ideas*, ed. Henry Hardy (2000), 2nd. ed., foreword by Avishai Margalit (2013: Princeton, Princeton University Press)
PS	*The Proper Study of Mankind: An Anthology of Essays*, ed. Henry Hardy and Roger Hausheer, foreword by Noel Annan, introduction by Roger Hausheer (1997), 2nd ed., foreword by Andrew Marr (2014: London, Vintage)
RR	*The Roots of Romanticism* (1965 lectures), ed. Henry Hardy (1999), 2nd. ed., foreword by John Gray (2013: Princeton, Princeton University Press)
RT	*Russian Thinkers*, ed. Henry Hardy and Aileen Kelly, introduction by Aileen Kelly (1978), 2nd ed., revised by Henry Hardy, glossary by Jason Ferrell (2008: London, Penguin Classics)
SR	*The Sense of Reality: Studies in Ideas and their History*, ed. Henry Hardy, introduction by Patrick Gardiner (1996: London, Chatto and Windus)
TCE	*Three Critics of the Enlightenment: Vico, Hamann, Herder*, ed. Henry Hardy (2000), 2nd. ed., foreword by Jonathan Israel (2013: Princeton, Princeton University Press)
UD	*Unfinished Dialogue* (with Beata Polanowska-Sygulska), foreword by Henry Hardy (2006: New York, Prometheus Books)
VH	*Vico and Herder: Two Studies in the History of Ideas* (1976), superseded by TCE

ACKNOWLEDGEMENTS

This book was quite a long time in coming. I believe it owes its genesis to my wonderful history teacher in secondary school, Pat Fox, of Christian Brothers College, Monkstown; Bartley Sheehan, a family GP and friend who encouraged my inchoate intellectual self; two great historians of medieval and modern Ireland, James Lydon and Bill Vaughan, respectively, and the literally mind-changing lectures on the history of political theory of James (Eddie) Hyland, all three of Trinity College, Dublin; the tutorials of the subtly knowledgeable Richard Tuck and the captivating lectures on Renaissance political thought of Quentin Skinner, both then of the University of Cambridge; and a number of intellectually curious and often brilliant undergraduate students whom I had the good fortune of teaching at Trinity College, Dublin, in the 1990s. During this incubation period I also learned, in the company of Christiane Voss, that philosophy could be serious fun, and from a modern Socrates of philosophy, the late Fr. Fergal O'Connor OP, that philosophy's form or style can be as telling as its content.

It then went through a phase of prolonged neglect, even if it received the odd wistful gaze. During this time, I was reminded of the unselfish love of my parents and siblings and experienced the luck of meeting the person who would become my wife and the joy of bringing three children into the world. In more recent years, I had the good fortune through my job (I have been working full-time in the commercial world since the late 1990s) to encounter the quietly inspiring John Simmons and others from the writing group, *Dark Angels*, who managed to convince me that I should give writing a go. With their goodwill and encouragement, I began, finally, to pluck up the courage to write a book on my philosophical hero, Isaiah Berlin.

I would like to single out a number of people who have helped me more directly with this book: Eddie Hyland, for so kindly agreeing to provide detailed and informed comments on earlier drafts of this book, after more than twenty years of being out of touch with each other; the late Barry Stroud, for emphasizing that there is no substitute for committing one's philosophical thoughts to paper to discover if you really have something worth saying – a nice variation of Flannery O'Connor's 'I write because I don't know what I think until I read what I write';

Thomas Nagel, for reminding me that Berlin could just as easily be described as a hedgehog as he is a fox; Quentin Skinner, for his unfailingly judicious and encouraging comments on Part Two; Galen Strawson, for his helpful remarks regarding sections of Part Four; John Banville for his typically shrewd and generous-spirited feedback on Part Five; and, most of all, Henry Hardy, Berlin's lifelong editor and chief keeper of his flame, who so kindly and enthusiastically agreed to give my whole work the expert 'Hardy treatment' and who also did me the honour of writing the Foreword to my book, for which I am most grateful; to a number of friends including Paul Barry, Shane Barry and Rowan Manahan who offered to read an earlier draft of this book and, in so doing, proved that the philosophically inclined general reader is not a mere fiction; Robin Baird-Smith, Liza Thompson, Lucy Russell and Joseph Gautham of Bloomsbury for their enthusiasm, support and professionalism in steering my book through the publishing process. All of them, especially Henry Hardy, helped to make this book immeasurably better than it would otherwise be. Needless to say, the responsibility for all remaining errors and inadequacies is entirely my own.

I wish also to take this opportunity to record my appreciation of the late Sir Isaiah Berlin (1909–97), the intellectual love of my life. In addition to providing the world with some of the wisest insights about the human predicament, he showed genuine interest in and kindness towards an obscure young enthusiast for his work. On both counts, I will be forever grateful.

Finally, I express my deepest gratitude to my father and siblings, to my wife, Aisling, and to our children, Ali, Julie and John, who make pretty much everything good in my life possible and worthwhile. I can't thank them enough.

PART ONE

GENERAL INTRODUCTION

1 THE NATURE OF BERLIN'S POLITICAL PHILOSOPHY

Political thinkers are of two types. There are philosophers with an interest in politics, and political theorists with an interest in philosophy. Notable examples of the former are Plato, Hobbes and Popper; of the latter, Cicero, Machiavelli and Tocqueville. Berlin falls squarely into the first category, and I will therefore examine and evaluate his political theory through a philosophical lens.

I begin with some preliminaries. The first is a concise descriptive summary of Berlin's renowned version of liberalism, intended for readers unfamiliar with his political thought. I shall then address head-on a number of influential objections to treating Berlin in any kind of systematically philosophical manner before exploring his abiding scepticism about the value of various forms of absolute rationalism or pure reason in practical affairs. I shall end by providing an explanatory outline of the structure and interpretive spirit of the book. These initial steps will, I hope, begin to vindicate my philosophical approach to Berlin's political thought, and also bring to the surface a number of central themes in his theory, themes that usually receive scant, if any, attention in commentaries on his work.

A summary of Berlin's political philosophy

The best place to start to get to grips with Berlin's political philosophy is his most famous essay, 'Two Concepts of Liberty'.[1] Delivered in 1958 as his inaugural lecture in the Chichele Chair of Social and Political Theory at Oxford University, this paper remains the classic statement of Berlin's liberalism. It begins by making what looks like a purely conceptual distinction between two notions of political liberty. The first of these notions is described as 'negative liberty', since it refers to the extent to which I am free from the interference of other individuals or authorities.

---

[1] Isaiah Berlin, *Two Concepts of Liberty: An Inaugural Lecture Delivered before the University of Oxford on 31 October 1958* (1958: Clarendon Press, Oxford), 57. Republished with revisions in (L 166–217).

The specification of 'other human beings' is important, since being negatively free does not require or entail that I am free from physical or psychological constraints. It simply refers to the degree of freedom from human interference or coercion. Contrasted with it is 'positive liberty', so called because it is the freedom *to* do something rather than the freedom *from* something. In many ways this is a far richer, if more nebulous, notion, which 'derives from the wish on the part of the individual to be his own master'.

So far, one could be forgiven for supposing that Berlin is making a rather obvious distinction between 'the freedom which consists in being one's own master and the freedom which consists in not being prevented from choosing as I do by other men' (L 178). And besides, one might add, are not these distinct notions simply two sides of the same coin? Berlin does not dissent, acknowledging that both concepts appear at 'no great logical distance from each other' (L 178). But what distinguishes his seminal essay is the arresting way in which he proceeds to treat these concepts. Rather than following the conventional philosophical method of analysing them in an empirical vacuum, Berlin treats both concepts normatively and historically, showing not only that there is a substantively significant – not merely a logically valid – distinction to be made between negative and positive liberty, but also that the failure to recognize its significance can cause far more harm than mere conceptual confusion.

Berlin begins the central core of his argument by acknowledging that negative and positive liberty respond to real and legitimate human needs and ideals, and that both are essential in a free and tolerant society. Negative freedom has been the beating heart of political liberalism, with its insistence that individuals be left alone to their own devices as long as their actions do not unduly encroach or harm others. Historically, positive liberty has lain at the heart of emancipatory theories of politics from democratic and republican doctrines to those of nationalism and communism.

But Berlin argues that one of the salient lessons of modern history since the French Revolution, and especially in the twentieth century, is just how catastrophically the concept of positive liberty is vulnerable to or exploitable by the worst types of totalitarianism. History has shown how tragically brief the leap can be from a desire for self-realization to the sense of having discovered a real or rational self and ending in the embrace of oppressive forms of despotism. One of the principal factors that have caused such a deformation over the past two hundred years is the enormously influential assumption that harmony among social values is not merely desirable but possible. So, for example, if I know in my heart of hearts or by the light of unaided reason that my true self is a manifestation of what my political party or my nation or humanity as a whole can or should be, the historical record has shown that it can be a short skip and jump before we find 'the wise' or 'the party leaders' or 'the chosen few' having to force the rest of us to be free to bring about 'the radiant tomorrow'. Experience has shown just how potent this urge can be when it is fuelled by the persistent and still influential belief that the genuine goals of all rational human beings must fit into a single, universal and all-embracing system, a kind of cosmic jigsaw where everything, or at least everything objectively worthwhile, eventually finds its natural, preordained place and fits without remainder.

Philosophically, the most gripping feature of 'Two Concepts of Liberty' is the rejection of what its author calls *moral monism*, a view that he maintains has informed so much of Western philosophy since Plato and which at times has had such an appalling impact on peoples' lives. Berlin counters the 'ancient faith' or what he sometimes calls the 'Ionian fallacy' of moral monism by arguing that our most basic and objective values and ideals such as liberty, equality, justice, compassion, friendship, patriotism do not form part of some integrated and harmonious rational system but are in permanent and often tragic conflict with each other. His contention is not to be conflated with the old bromide that things can never be perfect in an imperfect world, that we are condemned to living in a universe that is morally suboptimal as a result of fundamentally avoidable pragmatic constraints. Rather, it is the far more philosophically radical view which holds that genuine human values and ends conflict in principle, that deep and pervasive ethical disagreement is theoretically as well as practically inescapable. And the reason why our different ideals and divergent ways of life are locked in perpetual conflict is not due to the mere absence of an objective yardstick to measure and balance their relative worth. For even if *per impossibile* there were a magical moral yardstick, it would simply reveal the existence of genuine and irreconcilable conceptions of the good. Furthermore, it would also show that such differences are indeterminate and incommensurable in the sense that they could not be systematically and ordinally ranked on some single scale of value. Berlin calls this unconventional and disruptive view *the pluralism of values* or simply *pluralism*. It stands for his conviction that 'the world we encounter in ordinary experience is one in which we are faced with choices between ends equally ultimate, and claims equally absolute, the realisation of some of which must inevitably involve the sacrifice of others' (L 213–14).

The historical fact and putative philosophical truth of pluralism, the idea that human values and ways of life are in conflict with one another and not reducible to one another or translatable into the terms of some overarching system such as utilitarianism or deontology, forms the basis of Berlin's anti-utopian defence of a tolerant, liberal society. As he states near the end of 'Two Concepts of Liberty':

> Pluralism, with the measure of 'negative' liberty that it entails, seems to me a truer and more humane ideal than the goals of those who seek in the great disciplined, authoritarian structures the ideal of 'positive' self-mastery by classes, or peoples, or the whole of mankind. It is truer, because it does, at least, recognise the fact that human goals are many, not all of them commensurable, and in perpetual rivalry with one another. … It is more humane because it does not (as the system-builders do) deprive men, in the name of some remote, or incoherent, ideal, of much that they have found to be indispensable to their life as unpredictably self-transforming human beings. (L 216–17)

With little exaggeration Berlin's entire philosophical career after the Second World War can be viewed as a prolonged clinical assassination of each of the various elements that combine to form value or moral monism. The main reason why his demolition job could not be completed more efficiently is that moral monism takes many forms, requiring multiple murders. Indeed, moral monism never really dies, as its basic ideals and assumptions rarely if ever cease to prove alluring, particularly among hyper-rationalistically minded souls and their disciples. Philosophers are particularly prone to overestimating the power and reach of reason, which helps explain the persistent attraction and influence of a theory such as moral monism. But it would be wrong to assume that once philosophers are taken out of the equation, Berlin's battle with monism amounts to little more than tilting at windmills. The violent and tragic record of much of the recent past is hardly bereft of evidence that this particular philosophical myth is not limited to the abstract minds of solitary thinkers but exists in various, if largely implicit, guises behind the utopian thoughts and actions of countless dictators and ordinary people.

But there is also a more positive if under-appreciated element informing Berlin's fidelity to liberalism. Underlying his more explicitly political vision that a liberal society is one which safeguards a person's right to be left alone to follow his or her own way of life is the principle that the freedom to be or rather become who we are is an ultimate good in itself. For Berlin, negative liberty derives its value from providing us with a right or opportunity to pursue our own ideals, to freely engage in our own creative experiment of living. In this respect, Berlin has a great deal in common with his like-minded forbear, John Stuart Mill, who also saw liberalism not just as a formal political arrangement but, more fundamentally, as a free way of life, the realization of which is viewed as 'more precious than life itself' (L 251). Both thinkers shared the belief that there must be limits to political authority and power since they were more interested in and put far greater value on what people can do when they are free not to have to concern themselves with the relatively narrow, if necessary, matter of political life. But what gives Berlin's defence of liberalism its real philosophical twist is that individual freedom becomes even more precious in a world where there is a prevalent and irreducible diversity of human values and ways of life without an objective moral hierarchy.[2]

---

[2]John Gray has recently put forward a very interesting, if not entirely convincing, argument that Alexander Herzen's understanding of freedom informs the basis of Berlin's defence of negative liberty:

> One might summarise Berlin's defence of negative freedom in these terms: if freedom is the absence of obstructions to pursuing the discordant ends of existing human beings, positive freedom applies to a type of human being that does not exist. One implication of this account is worth noting: negative freedom is not valuable primarily because it facilitates personal autonomy – a condition in which individuals have achieved a high degree of self-knowledge and independence. For liberal thinkers such as J.S.Mill and more recently Joseph Raz, it is this condition of autonomy that defines a liberal society. Against this, Berlin is suggesting that the autonomy imagined in

In Berlin's account of our situation, the freedom to put our own shape on our own lives derives its vindication not merely from the value we attribute to personal autonomy but from the pluralist insight that there is no uniquely right way of living – though there are surely wrong and wasteful ways of living one's life.

That, in very rough summary, is Berlin's political philosophy. While it encapsulates the bare bones of his argument, it comes nowhere near doing justice to the immense volubility and vitality of his thought. Nor does it convey the conceptual subtlety, historical allusiveness and literary flair that distinguish his approach to political thought and practice. These are virtues of his work that nobody can pretend to imitate or summarize. They can only be appreciated by reading Berlin's writings directly.

Some objections to treating Berlin as a political philosopher

The first and perhaps most common argument against identifying Berlin as primarily a political philosopher is that by his own admission he gave up on philosophy relatively early in his academic career. In the preface to *Concepts and Categories*, the second of four volumes initially published in 1978–80 as *Selected Writings*, Berlin gives a clear and explicit account of his decision to bid farewell to philosophy in favour of a different field of study – namely, the history of ideas. The reason he gives for switching his focus to history is that in contrast to philosophy he felt that it offered at least the possibility of 'know[ing] more at the end of one's life than when one had begun' (CC2 xxvii). But the superficiality of treating him first and foremost as a historian of ideas emerges the moment we start reading 'The Purpose of Philosophy', the very first essay in *Concepts and Categories*. What it makes abundantly clear is that he had simply found a new and more engaging way of doing philosophy. His approach to intellectual history became the pursuit of philosophy by other means.

And yet Berlin's decision to abandon the subject was entirely genuine on one level. He was, indeed, waving goodbye to philosophy, but it was philosophy of a very specific, if dominant, kind. It was the genre of philosophy that enjoyed its high

---

these theories of positive liberty is a fantasy removed from the actualities of any human life. Every human being harbours warring impulses that can lead to tragic loss; becoming an autonomous individual – if such a thing is possible – does not alter this fact. John Gray, *Isaiah Berlin: An Interpretation* (2013 edn: with a new introduction: Princeton University Press, Princeton, NJ), 12.

While I am far more sympathetic than not to the spirit of Gray's reading of Berlin's thought, it eludes me why he feels that personal autonomy must count as a version of positive freedom. One might be more inclined to accept Gray on this matter if personal autonomy is identical with moral autonomy but it isn't or at any rate not inevitably. And I don't believe either Herzen or Berlin thought so too. We shall return to this topic in the final chapter of the book.

noon in Oxbridge in the period directly before and after the Second World War, a style exhibited by logical positivism in the 1930s and by its successor, linguistic analysis, between the 1940s and the early 1960s. While there are important differences between these two philosophical schools, which we will come to shortly, they do share a broadly similar view of the nature and value of political philosophy, a view that proved increasingly uncongenial to Berlin after the war.

According to both logical positivism and linguistic analysis, the only legitimate role for philosophers interested in evaluative thought – to which traditional political philosophy naturally belongs – was to investigate the meaning and status of moral concepts. The general term that was commonly used to describe this particular and essentially piecemeal form of intellectual activity was *meta-ethics*, an expression that was intended to suggest that those engaged in such an enterprise were not so much taking part *in* ethics as engaging in the study *of* ethics. This distinction was crucial, as both logical positivists and linguistic analysts were adamant that meta-ethics should be a value-free intellectual inquiry. They also shared the view that philosophy, like poetry, makes nothing happen in the sense that neither it nor its practitioners possess any kind of special, first-order moral expertise and authority. The main difference between then and now is not so much that meta-ethics has lost its foothold as that it is no longer seen as the only viable way of pursuing ethical enquiry. It is clear from Berlin's writings during this period that he had little patience with this purely second-order, putatively value-neutral analysis of moral and political concepts. It is likely that he would have been sympathetic at the time with the later withering assessment of post-war moral philosophy expressed by his philosophical colleague and friend Bernard Williams (1929–2003), that it had 'found an original way of being boring, which is by not discussing moral issues at all'.[3] Indeed, one is tempted to describe logical positivism and linguistic philosophy as conceptual palette cleansers: they served to remove the metaphysical smog of Hegelianism and other forms of obscurantist thought which still held sway in parts of academic philosophy in the Anglophone world but they were peculiarly incapable of filling the void when their negative (and necessary) project was done.

But what is significant for our purposes is that Berlin managed to break free of the academic straitjacket imposed by the prevailing schools of philosophy of the time, and discovered a new and more engaging way of thinking about our human experience, one which affirmed the possibility of rational debate about substantive moral and political values and ideals. In this respect Berlin fulfilled as indispensable a role as other major thinkers of his time, including Herbert Hart

---

[3] Bernard Williams, *Morality: An Introduction to Ethics* (1972: Cambridge University Press, Cambridge), xvii.

(1907–92), John Rawls (1921–2002) and Robert Nozick (1938–2002), in bringing about the resurgence of evaluative or normative political philosophy.

A second, less obvious, objection to treating Berlin in any kind of stridently philosophical way is that his writings do not lend themselves to such an interpretative approach. According to this influential view, his thought is too opaque and fragmented to warrant a systematic treatment of his writings.[4] Anyone who is familiar with Berlin's writings will have a natural sympathy for this prevailing viewpoint. There is no doubt that Berlin could be demure about stating his political theory in direct form, preferring to present his own ideas indirectly through his treatment of various historical thinkers and their thoughts. The experience of reading Berlin is of a very different kind from that of reading more mainstream exemplars of contemporary analytic political theory. His writings do not conform to the formal and detached style of compressed argumentation that still dominates analytical political theory. Rather, it is happily free of the characteristic vices of the analytic *genre*. Berlin presents his ideas in a far more engaging, loose and impressionistic manner – in a way, he is a non-philosopher's philosopher. He is also the archetypal fox, expressesing his views obliquely and allusively through the accumulation of numerous digressions and subordinate clauses and thereby rendering any definitive interpretation of his position vexatiously elusive.[5]

However, a key objective of this book is to convince the reader that the hegemonic style and standard of analytical political theory do not exhaust the legitimate modes of serious philosophical enquiry into political morality. I shall argue that Berlin developed a very different and more illuminating way of bringing philosophy to bear on our understanding of human affairs. His approach shares several of the virtues of the analytic tradition including a commitment to precise and clear expression, intellectual rigour and a willingness to go where the argument leads. But it also transcends the constricting conventions of that tradition in new and significant ways, not least by showing an appreciation of the central importance of history to moral and political philosophy as well as a commitment to restoring

---

[4]See, for example, the concerns raised by Larry Siedentop in 'The Ionian Fallacy: Isaiah Berlin's Singlemindedness', his review of Claude Galipeau's *Isaiah Berlin's Liberalism* (1994: Clarendon Press, Oxford) in *The Times Literary Supplement*, 23 September 1994, and more pointedly by Brian Barry in 'Isaiah, Israel and Tribal Realism', his review of various books by and on Berlin, *The Times Literary Supplement*, 9 November 2001, 7–8. I should also make clear that my study of Berlin is not the first attempt at a systematic treatment of his thought. Others, including Galipeau's book, John Gray's *Isaiah Berlin* (1995: HarperCollins, London) and George Crowder's *Isaiah Berlin: Liberty and Pluralism* (2004: Polity Press, Cambridge), have been systematic in their elucidation and analysis of the moral and political aspects of Berlin's thought, but I consider my study is the first genuinely sustained treatment of the philosophical foundations of Berlin's normative political thought. My approach is based on the conviction that a thinker's ideas can be unsystematic in style without being unsystematic in substance.

[5]Joseph Brodsky aptly described Berlin's distinctive style as resembling 'the sardonic eloquence of the best of nineteenth-century Russian fiction'. See Joseph Brodsky 'Isaiah Berlin: A Tribute' in Edna and Avishai Margalit eds., *Isaiah Berlin: A Celebration* (1991: The Hogarth Press, London), 212.

philosophy's direct engagement with how we actually live our lives. Indeed, I will be claiming that the intellectual integrity and appeal of Berlin's understanding of humanity reside in his historically minded and steadfastly humanistic conception of the philosophical enterprise.[6]

A third and perhaps more sobering objection is that the world doesn't need another book on Berlin. And, besides, surely it is better to read the writings of a thinker than a book about the thinker's writings. Indeed, it was the nagging force of such misgivings that had been largely responsible for my reluctance to embark on this study for over twenty years. Some version of Maslow's dictum, 'What is not worth doing is not worth doing well,' was holding me back. Moreover, another related inhibiting factor owes something to what Michael Dummett (1925–2011) said about the risk of adding to the mountain of publications that are already there: 'Every learned book, every learned article, adds to the weight of the things for others to read, and thereby reduces the chances of their reading other books and articles.'[7]

Yet the urge to write a book eventually won out against the cogency of these counterveiling pressures. In the end, of course, only the reader can determine for herself or himself if my efforts have produced something of worth. But I would like to think that if my book has some merit, it lies in prompting more people to read the ideas of Isaiah Berlin, a thinker whose ideas have only grown more germane and urgent in our strangely unsteady, insubstantial and menacing times.

Berlin's scepticism about rationalism

As we shall see, a distinctly philosophical interpretation of Berlin is crucial to revealing what makes his political thought so interesting and worthwhile. But whether such an approach manages to show that his political philosophy is objectively true and right is a far more complicated and controversial matter. Interestingly, one of the more notable insights to emerge from a philosophical take on Berlin is his deep scepticism about the unproblematic ways in which we take our ideas to be right and true. Berlin does not just give us cause to doubt the

---

[6]My understanding of Berlin's thought shares something of the view expressed by Roger Hausheer in his introduction to PSM2, where he remarks that 'the sheer scale of his [Berlin's] activity in many prima facie unrelated fields has meant that he will be admired by different readers for apparently disconnected parts of his *oeuvre*, with scarcely any realisation that these are all fragments of a total picture' (PSM2 xxxiv). Broadly speaking, it is also consistent with the interpretations put forward by Jonathan Lieberson and Sidney Morgenbesser in their extended essay on Berlin in J. Lieberson, *Varieties: Essays* (1988: Weidenfeld & Nicolson, New York), 111–47, John Gray, *Isaiah Berlin* (1995: HarperCollins, London) as well as Bernard Williams in his fine introduction to CC2, especially where he says, 'We can perhaps see, too, how the development of his thought from general theory of knowledge to the history of ideas and the philosophy of history was not merely a change of interest; and that his complex sense of history is as deeply involved in his philosophy, even in its more abstract applications, as it is, very evidently, in his other writings, and in his life' (CC2 xxxviii–ix).

[7]Michael Dummett, *Frege: Philosophy of Mathematics* (1991: Duckworth, London), x.

influential idea that all genuine values, including truth, justice and compassion, are compatible with each other, but he also questions whether our deepest and most cherished normative beliefs can be said to be true absolutely and non-contingently. This is not to imply that he is sceptical about the reality or truth of morality or of the value of philosophy in practical human matters. Rather, it is to claim that he questions and to an extent subverts our cosy and complacent understanding of how objectivity applies in the world of human affairs as distinct from the external or physical world.

Berlin's doubts about the basis upon which objectivity is ordinarily attributed to our moral and political beliefs alert us to another sceptical feature of his thought. His main objection to our habit of regarding our most basic and precious evaluative beliefs as straightforwardly true and universally applicable owes less to an intolerance of our naive if deluded tendency of confusing the merely familiar with the objectively correct, and much more to an unwavering opposition to the excessively intellectualist idea that unless our beliefs are underwritten by some overarching and rationally self-sufficient moral theory, they are mere prejudices. Berlin's writings betray a philosophical antipathy to the assumption that our ethical and political ideals are only as good as the degree, if any, to which they can be justified on purely universal and timeless theoretical foundations, something which much of philosophy has traditionally and self-assuredly assumed it is uniquely qualified to provide. This core assumption goes back at least as far as Plato and found one of its most theoretically insistent expressions during the Enlightenment of the seventeenth and eighteenth centuries, an era which paradoxically was responsible for subjecting so many dogmatic and superstitious beliefs and biases to the unforgiving light of unaided, scientific reason. But Berlin's deep sympathy with the spirit and achievement of the Enlightenment did not blind him to its misplaced faith in the power of pure reason to resolve the intellectual and moral tensions that lie deep within the heart of our relations with ourselves and others. His persistent ambivalence concerning the so-called Enlightenment Project is conveyed in the following passage:

> A very great deal of good, undoubtedly, was done, suffering mitigated, injustice avoided or prevented, ignorance exposed, by the conscientious attempt to apply scientific methods to the regulation of human affairs. Dogmas were refuted, prejudices and superstitions were pilloried successfully. The growing conviction that appeals to mystery and darkness and authority to justify arbitrary behaviour were, all too often, so many unworthy alibis concealing self-interest or intellectual indolence or stupidity was often triumphantly vindicated. But the central dream, the demonstration that everything in the world moved by mechanical means, that all evils could be cured by appropriate technological steps, that there could exist engineers both of human souls and of human bodies, proved delusive. (PI2 62)

Berlin's reservations regarding the theoretical claims of universalistic and rationalistic moral and political discourse might suggest that there is a certain tension or even inconsistency in his outlook or, perhaps, *in my view* of his outlook. For, on one hand, I am arguing that we need to read Berlin philosophically, and, on the other, I am saying that he is sceptical of the theoretical assumptions underpinning traditional moral and political philosophy. So let me be clear. Rightly or wrongly, Berlin does not take a forlorn view of the philosophical enterprise. He is adamant that philosophical reflection in the broadest sense of that term is a viable and valuable intellectual project, which has a real and necessary role to play in our lives. But what he is opposed to is the idea that the living, breathing world of human beings is or ought to be answerable to some spuriously complete and systematic set of theoretical principles. Berlin's writings are infused with an anti-reductionist conviction that for moral and political theory to have any meaning and authority, it must abandon the delusion of finding a single, all-embracing and hyper-rational model of the good life that seeks to be acceptable to all human beings at all times. It must, instead, accept the fact that deep down we are creatures of time and chance for whom the promise of moral monism – the notion that there is a uniquely correct and timeless answer to the question of how we should live our lives – has lost its credibility.[8]

But that may be putting things a little too negatively and deflatingly. A more positive way of making the same point is to say that Berlin's vision rests on the notion that philosophical reflection can be trusted only when it confronts the reality of our predicament. That meant, for Berlin, that philosophy must embrace as its raw material the rich but unruly actuality of the human world, deriving whatever philosophical insights can be wrought from the infinitely messy and complex fabric of everyday life. Working out what survives from reflecting on the ineliminable imperfectability and contingency of the human state of affairs is, I shall argue, one of the leitmotifs running through Berlin's *oeuvre*. Berlin offers us an alternative frame for making sense of ourselves and our relation to the world, one that makes room for a more truthful and inclusive appreciation of our individual and social lives while acknowledging that occupying a world that is bereft of cosmic significance does not entail that human life is meaningless. He manages to reverse the dynamic between philosophy and the actual lives of human beings by making the former more accountable to the latter rather than the other

---

[8]The Peruvian writer, Mario Vargas Llosa, captures this apparently contradictory feature of Berlin's thought in his short, shrewd essay. 'Isaiah Berlin: A Hero of Our Time' in his *Making Waves* (1996: Faber, London):

> It is a paradox that someone like Isaiah Berlin, who loves ideas so much and moves among them with such ease, is always convinced that it is ideas that must give way if they come into contradiction with human reality, since if the reverse occurs, the streets are filled with guillotines and firing-squad walls and the reign of the censors and the policemen begins. (147)

way around and thereby allowing us to appreciate what Kant referred to as 'the crooked timber of humanity'.[9]

This approach is the opposite of how most modern and recent moral and political philosophers have pursued their field of study. They have tended to operate, consciously or not, on the basis that an inverted form of anthropomorphism should apply to our understanding of who or what we are, that it is right to make sense of the world of human nature by treating human beings as purely or primarily natural entities. Berlin felt that this approach committed at least one fatal intellectual error. By interpreting who we are in exclusively naturalistic or scientific terms, theorists had not just distorted our view of human nature but ended up denying us of more direct, if empirically less verifiable, sources of knowledge about ourselves. The less scientific roots of human knowledge he was referring to lie mainly in the humanities and arts, in such subjects as history, anthropology, psychology, literature and so forth. As a result, his aim is to try to rebalance the philosophical scales which have, since Newton, favoured the naturalistic model, a perspective that values objectivity over subjectivity, scientific evidence over moral intuition and the view from nowhere over the view from here and now. His intention is not to replace one with the other, for they are both legitimate if often rival and even incommensurable forms of thought, but to remind us that we have more than one source of understanding about ourselves and the world and, moreover, that we ignore non-scientific forms of human insight at our peril. More specifically, he wants to rehabilitate the idea that the humanities can shed light on the more distinctive aspects of human life, aspects that science not only ignores but is incapable of even registering. And one of the main ways in which he urges us to realize how humanism can help us more fully and profoundly comprehend ourselves and others is by ceasing to define what counts as reliable, objective knowledge in strictly scientific and universalist terms. There is, in other words, a recognition of an irreducible duality of perspectives, the scientific and the humanistic, at the core of Berlin's pluralistic outlook – though it is clear where his interests lie. It is worth emphasizing also that Berlin's effort to reorientate philosophy by restoring our belief in the power and pertinence of more anthropocentric forms of intuitive understanding and knowledge does not rely on or imply any kind of anti-scientific prejudice or agenda on his part. Berlin's problem with the scientific outlook is not with science itself but, rather, with the scientistic mindset that has accompanied its rise and which has had such a deleterious effect on so much philosophy as well as on our ordinary, everyday beliefs. One of the great myths of scientism is that science provides the only source

---

[9] The quote is Berlin's translation of the following line from Immanuel Kant's 'Idea for a Universal History with a Cosmopolitan Purpose': 'Idee zu einer allgemeinen Geschichte in weltbürgerlicher Absicht', *Kant's gessammelte Schriften* (1990– : Berlin, Georg Reimer), Vol. viii 23.22.

of truth and reason. Another, of course, is its tendency to deny that we are vastly limited cognitive beings.

It is hardly surprising, therefore, that one of the hallmarks of Berlin's thought is its possession of a distinctively humanistic and imaginative intelligence which knows enough about the fragmented and unresolvable character of human life not to be seduced by the temptations of theoretical tidiness and completeness. This makes for an authentic and gripping account of humanity, one that is far more philosophically nuanced and original than has been appreciated. Furthermore, much of the power and appeal of his thought derive from its capacity to show that philosophical reflection can enjoy a genuine claim to authority when it is serious about grasping our essential contingency or historicity. I suspect this may be what lies behind Michael Ignatieff's (1947–) description of Berlin as 'the most historically minded of twentieth-century liberal philosophers and the most philosophical of historians of ideas'.[10]

For Berlin, realistic moral and political philosophy is necessarily promiscuous, complex and provisional: to fulfil its remit of helping us make sense of the world we inhabit, it has to take notice of a number of distinct but connected fields of enquiry, including those of the natural and social sciences, of history and of literature; it must be historically self-conscious enough to discern the unavoidable and deep-seated contingency of its own biases and concerns; and it must show sufficient intellectual humility to recognize that if the study of human thought has taught us anything it is that there are no eternal and irrefutable moral truths, no unrevisable forms of knowledge and no such thing as a final script when it comes to producing a sufficiently true and truthful account of human nature and the human condition.

In this respect, Berlin's conception of the nature and point of philosophy shows the imprint of David Hume. Like Hume (1711–76), Berlin is suspicious of the arid intellectualism and formalism of ultra-rationalistic moral and political philosophy and of its immodest tendency to claim that it possesses or someday could possess the gospel truth about how we ought to live our lives.[11] There is nothing absolutist or blissfully unreal about Berlin's approach. Nor is there a suggestion that the recognition of our deep contingency renders philosophy worthless. Rather, there is a grown-up Humean recognition that the absence of absolute and complete rational foundations for our beliefs and ideals does not imply that we are left with no reasons to maintain and cherish them. Berlin's thought embraces the world of living, breathing, imperfect human beings, seeing it not as an arena to be fundamentally transformed, but as a phenomenon to be more fully and self-consciously understood and illuminated. In effect, Berlin shows that philosophical

---

[10]Michael Ignatieff, *Isaiah Berlin: A Life* (1998: Chatto & Windus, London), 271.
[11]For an excellent analysis of Hume's non-intellectualist conception of philosophy, see Annette Baier's paper 'Extending the Limits of Moral Theory', *Journal of Philosophy* 83 no. 10 (October 1986): 538–45.

reflection about human situation can be pursued without incurring the cost of practical relevance. He achieves this by revealing that philosophy can be both a foe and a friend, a source of distortion as well as illumination and that the virtues and vices of philosophy are not the exclusive concern of professional philosophers but, rather, of genuine and enduring interest to humankind. For Berlin there is a real sense in which philosophy is or ought to be everyone's business, at least to some extent, since the ideas and assumptions that it is concerned with permeate our lives whether we notice them or not.

This might explain why one of Berlin's favourite definitions of philosophy was that put forward by the relatively obscure eighteenth-century German philosopher, Georg Christoph Lichtenberg (1742–99):

> Philosophy is ever the art of drawing distinctions, look at the matter how you will. The peasant uses all the propositions of the most abstract philosophy, but wrapped up, embedded, tangled, *latent*, as physicists and chemists say; the philosopher gives us the propositions in their pure state. (AE 277)

After quoting this definition, Berlin goes on to say:

> In this aphorism Lichtenberg expresses very succinctly the notion that philosophy is what in our own time came to be called 'analysis' – not an instrument of discovery of new truths about the world, so much as of eliciting, with the greatest possible exactness and rigour, that which is already contained in common speech, in order to discriminate, isolate, study, classify, examine the interrelations and the functions of, types of expression and ways of speech (or thought), the peculiarities of which cannot be observed so well (or at all) in the rich amalgam – vague, blurred, ambiguous and impure – in which ordinary language must of necessity always remain if it is to be useful in the practical conduct of life. The task of the philosopher is to 'unpack' sentences which give rise to philosophical problems into their ingredients, and so disentangle the thick rope of daily talk into its constituent strands, without which the problems cannot be solved or 'dissolved'. This is certainly one of the most original remarks ever made about philosophy. (AE 277)

Finally, the reader might be forgiven for thinking that Berlin's conception of political philosophy is innately conservative, that having what he calls 'a sense of reality' entails the needlessness of a genuinely critical perspective as well as a preference to merely comprehend the world as it happens to be and not to try to change it for the better. One might even be tempted to go a step further and suspect that Berlin's scepticism about the assumptions underlying traditional moral theory is a symptom of a deeper complacency, of an unwarranted satisfaction with the *status quo*. Leaving aside the obvious point that not all forms of conservatism are by definition unphilosophical or uncritical, I think that it would be a mistake to identify Berlin as a conservative, or even a liberal conservative. Those who are doubtful about the use and value of theory – or, in Berlin's case, about monistic or excessively rationalistic and formal conceptions of moral and political theory – are always vulnerable to being labelled as reactionary. But such labels are misguided when applied to Berlin. He is the least *political* political philosopher one can imagine, which might also explain why he had an enduring fondness for the traditional non-doctrinalism of British politics (a feature of British or perhaps English public life that has increasingly disappeared in more recent times). Rather, he is far more interested in what we think and do when we are not having to worry ourselves about politics. It is hardly surprising therefore that Berlin's preoccupation with politics has only a tangential connection with the comparatively narrow and polarizing ideological debate between conservatism and liberalism and so forth; and where it does connect with the cut and thrust of political life, it is clear that Berlin had a fundamentally meliorist view of human affairs. Berlin's abiding concerns operate at a higher (or rather deeper) but no less realistically engaged level. His main interest lies in setting out the topography of the modern human condition in such a way that people more readily perceive the importance and value of being left alone to pursue whatever way of life they choose in a manner that permits all of us to enjoy that same precious freedom of choice. His conviction is that liberalism provides the most reliable route to achieving this state of affairs. One of the reasons why we cannot retire carelessly to a life of largely apolitical or, rather, unpolitical privacy is because a liberal society faces all sorts of recurring and unavoidable risks and dangers from both within and outside that must be confronted and in extremis defeated. For liberal humanists such as Berlin politics may be a necessary evil but there are far greater evils and inconveniences lurking than the necessity of having to continually revise and safeguard the basic principles and practices of a civilized, open and tolerant society. The pursuit of a *summum bonum* may have lost its credibility in a Godless age but there is nothing illusory about the need to protect liberalism from its *summum malum,* which is a totalitarian and capricious state or, more relevantly today, global capitalism in its more nefarious forms.

The structure and spirit of the book

The titles and order of the various parts and chapters that follow are not exactly self-explanatory, so it might help if I provide an outline of the book's organization. This will also serve to amplify my reasons for thinking that the key to unlocking Berlin's ideas is through a philosophical filter.

Part Two is concerned with identifying the philosophical foundations of Berlin's picture of the world. It opens with an account of how Berlin broke away from the analytic school of philosophy and discovered a new way of pursuing the subject, one that eschewed several of the assumptions and biases of the analytic tradition while embracing a much more imaginative and allusive style of philosophical argumentation. His departure from the analytic norm is reflected in his adoption of two major philosophical insights. The first of these is derived from Immanuel Kant's (1724–1804) transformative claim that our understanding of truth and reality is inescapably dependent on the contribution we make through the concepts and categories we ourselves create to interpret and experience the world. Kant's celebrated Copernican revolution reframes our picture of the world in such a way that we become more open to the possibility of non-scientific forms of human understanding and knowledge. The second major insight is the historicist one he gains principally from the work of the barely known Neapolitan thinker, Giambattista Vico (1668–1744), that there are no aspects of our thought that can be said to be non-perspectival and ahistorical, that all patterns of anthropocentric understanding are culturally and historically conditioned, though crucially not entirely without remainder. Another vital lesson that Vico teaches Berlin is the centrality of the faculty of *fantasia* or imaginative understanding in giving us access to long-dead thinkers and the cultures to which they belonged. Berlin's effort to combine these distinct yet humanistically orientated patterns of understanding into his world view produces a philosophically fertile but far from unproblematic perspective.

Part Three examines the implications of Berlin's conception of philosophy for his defence of liberalism. After making some initial remarks on the broad philosophical theme of the relation of theory to practice, I explore the pluralist foundations of Berlin's liberal theory in the light of three types of critique. The first of these is still the most common and, I shall argue, the least serious one. It centres on the complaint that Berlin's liberalism is not only unsupported by his pluralism but unavoidably and fatally contradicted by it. The main problem with what I call the logic-chopping critique is that it exaggerates virtually to the point of parody the place and power of deductive reasoning in the sphere of practical philosophy and, as a consequence, ends up profoundly misunderstanding the essential character of Berlin's justification of liberalism. The other two critiques are far more philosophically penetrating and potentially damaging. One claims that Berlin's liberal vision can succeed perfectly well without relying on what it identifies as its residual and obsolete faith in philosophy. The main idea informing this rather extreme critique is that Berlin's political theory should dispense with what's left of its debt to the sclerotic tradition of foundational philosophy and proudly declare its underlying postmodern or post-philosophical credentials. The final critique, which comes from the opposite end of the philosophical spectrum, contends that the foundation upon which Berlin bases his liberalism is no real foundation at all since pluralism gives a theoretically inadequate and ultimately implausible account of our moral and political state of affairs. The source of this objectivist assessment is rooted in the monistic idea that there are uniquely right answers to the questions of private and public morality, that in the last analysis harmony rather than conflict defines the absolutely true and rationally optimal character of our ethical lives. The main burden of this part of the book is to show that Berlin's position can survive the attacks of his leading postmodernist and monistic liberal critics but not intact – both critiques expose areas of genuine frailty in the Berlinian edifice.

The focus of Part Four is to examine another fundamental feature of Berlin's outlook that rarely gets mentioned by political theorists. I am referring to his view of free will. It is one of the more noticeably bizarre puzzles that so few scholars have discussed this aspect of his thought given that it forms such a cornerstone of his liberal outlook. The main concern here will be to explore why Berlin took the problem of free will so seriously and to examine his reasons for adhering to the still philosophically unfashionable view – most analytical philosophers would say indefensible – that we should maintain our commitment to freedom in the libertarian or ultimate sense of that term, that is, the sense which claims that *I could have acted other than I did*. This will involve situating Berlin's distinctive view of freedom in the context of the wider debate of free will and determinism. As this remains a notoriously thorny topic that shows no sign of yielding to any kind of final solution – the problem of free will is as old and intractable as any in philosophy – I will not be making any bold claims that Berlin's contribution to the fundamental debate is conclusive or even particularly groundbreaking. Berlin himself made no pretensions to solving or significantly advancing the central question of free will: we still seem to be faced with the paradox that there are at the very least two conflicting and recalcitrant views of freedom – on the one hand that we experience ultimate freedom and on the other that ultimate or libertarian freedom makes no naturalistic or even conceptual sense – each of which is supported by what appear to be overwhelming yet conflicting, even incommensurable, reasons. Instead, I want to show that Berlin provides an arresting case both for denying that compatibilism offers a convincing, non-evasive solution to the free will problem and for asserting that a widespread belief in determinism or, more relevantly, in compatibilism would risk annihilating our most basic and cherished ethical concepts and categories, including those underpinning our faith in a liberal, free society. Given the centrality of our strongly held, intuitive belief in our own ultimate freedom and the absence of a definitive answer to the free will problem, Berlin advises that it would be both premature and reckless to give up our everyday notion of freedom on the basis of the terrifically undeveloped and unsatisfactory compatibilist 'solutions' to the problem of free will. The validity of Berlin's recommendation is examined in the light of one of the most perceptive analyses of the free will problem of the last seventy years, an account which was put forward by his long-time Oxford colleague, P.F. Strawson (1919–2006).

The final part of the book examines another strangely neglected feature of Berlin's thought. Anyone familiar with the scholarly literature on his work will be aware that a great deal, arguably far too much, has been written on his renowned concept of negative liberty. But comparatively little has been said about his deeper reasons for prioritizing this essentially political idea. Why did Berlin consider that the legitimacy of the state is so dependent on providing each of us with an inviolable, if necessarily limited, space to live as we choose? What is it about negative liberty that endows it with such pre-eminence in his view of the world of human affairs? The largely untapped source of the answer resides in Berlin's belief that being free to choose how we live our lives is as sacred as life itself, that it is, as he says, what 'makes human life human' (L 52). How he arrives at this conclusion is, I shall argue, far more indebted to romanticism, a movement that contains the core of the modern ideal of individual freedom and authenticity, than scholars have acknowledged. One of the benefits of bringing this aspect of his liberalism to greater light is that it serves to explain why Berlin remained fundamentally ambivalent about the Enlightenment.

In terms of the general spirit informing the book, this is an unapologetically sympathetic account of Berlin's thought. It makes no pretensions to providing a sternly detached analysis of his work. Nor does it seek to iron out all the ambiguities and inconsistencies in his ideas, which a veritable army of scholars have claimed to have exposed. My priority is twofold: firstly, to uncover the often obscure philosophical moorings to which Berlin's well-known political ideas are firmly tied and secondly, to reveal the nature and significance of Berlin's distinctively philosophical understanding of politics and society against the background of a much broader level of philosophical discussion and debate. In short, this is primarily a book which is focused both on excavating hidden layers and on making new and fertile connections rather than one intent on exposing conceptual gaps and pin-pointing logical contradictions.

Those who are disposed to the analytic style of treating thinkers and their thoughts may find my approach theoretically flaccid and frustrating: I don't subject Berlin's ideas to the kind of coercively argumentative method of analysis that tends to go with the analytic territory. Rather, my account has far more in common with what one might say about a fascinating companion. Typically, when we describe our friends we don't feel a relentless desire to focus on their abject failings and shortcomings. And this isn't because we are unaware of or unaffected by their flaws. It is more to do with the sense that what make our friends interesting and valued are the traits they possess rather than the ones they lack. So the interpretive spirit I have adopted towards Berlin's ideas resembles that of a fond but not uncritical or reverential friend and one who is convinced that Berlin's standing as a philosophical thinker deserves to be rehabilitated. This approach feels especially appropriate in respect of Berlin, a genuine intellectual who managed to live his life in a manner that exemplified his highly cultivated, equivocal and generous-spirited convictions.

PART TWO

PHILOSOPHY

2 IN THE BEGINNING ...

The breadth and depth of Plato's (427/8–348/7 BC) influence upon Western thinking can easily blind us to the staggering originality and magnetism of his thought. As one of the major founders of Western philosophy, he created something new that transformed how humankind, or at least its Western variant, makes sense of things. It wasn't for nothing that Whitehead memorably remarked that 'the safest general characterization of the European philosophical tradition is that it consists of a series of footnotes to Plato'.[1] Through a set of captivating dialogues he developed a new and distinctively systematic way of looking at the world and our place in it. My aim here is not to discuss his substantive arguments. Rather, I shall touch on a number of more general and abstract features of his philosophical approach, what we might refer to as his conception of the nature of philosophy itself or meta-philosophy. This will provide a good starting point for a discussion of the relationship between philosophy and practical life before we explore the elements of Berlin's own humanistic conception of philosophy and practical life.

The first aspect of Plato's meta-philosophical outlook is its capaciousness. He is the first and arguably greatest example of a thinker who sought to provide an integrated picture of everything. Unlike so much of contemporary philosophy, in which specialists focus exclusively on highly specific topics within the discrete sub-fields of the discipline, Plato's approach to the subject is all-encompassing. He weaves a complex intellectual tapestry that brings together wide and disparate elements of thought and experience. And he adopts such an ambitiously inclusive methodology because he regards it as philosophically unavoidable. This is most obvious in his masterpiece, *The Republic*, which contends that a genuinely philosophical enquiry into a concept such as justice must go beyond the conventional and superficial understandings of that term. What is most instructive

---

[1] Alfred North Whitehead, *Process and Reality: An Essay in Cosmology* (1929; Free Press, New York), 39.

about this work is not so much its particular substantive claims as the manner in which it shows that a proper investigation of justice necessarily involves a consideration not only of moral and political philosophy but of other branches of philosophy too, especially metaphysics, epistemology and aesthetics.

A related ingredient in Plato's view of the philosophical project concerns the notion of philosophy's authority. Plato argued that there are deep, if hidden, connections between everyday ideas such as justice, courage and love, and more abstract and esoteric concepts such as truth, knowledge and human nature, and, crucially, that gaining awareness of these connections has implications for how we ought to think about and conduct our lives. There is, in other words, a claimed continuity between philosophical reflection and our more diurnal thoughts and actions.

As you read a Platonic dialogue, you are prone to discover how shallow or confused your grasp of something like love or justice or knowledge may be. This initial realization, which might be described as the euphoria (or embarrassment) of ignorance, can then prompt us to question the origins and basis of what we unreflectively accept as true and right. It can also provoke us to start thinking more critically or, at least, non-platitudinously about the meaning and validity of, for example, our current moral values and political ideals, and to develop more considered, precise and independent-minded thoughts about them. The key point here is that philosophical reflection can and should have an effect on how we think and behave in our day-to-day lives. Plato left us with the enduring idea that philosophy matters because only philosophy can adjudicate the merits and demerits of our pre-theoretical intuitions and beliefs. And he conveyed this feature of our situation through his unforgettable analogy of the cave, a place of darkness from which we must escape before we can see the light of reason and grasp life's purpose. Only those assumptions and convictions which survive the most unforgiving filter of philosophical rumination and analysis deserve our assent. Hence the Socratic motto that 'the unexamined human life is not worth living', precisely because it does not partake in or result from genuine and sustained philosophical illumination and, consequently, holds us back from pursuing the good life.[2] Knowledge and virtue are therefore inextricably linked.

Finally, it is worth emphasizing that aside from a handful of letters, all Plato's works are written as dialogues. Rather than presenting his ideas in conventional treatise format, he expresses them through a variety of interlocutors who ask impertinent questions, experience bafflement, perhaps tease out a philosophical distinction or two and puzzle over possible solutions. While there is still much scholarly debate about Plato's motives for choosing the dialogue form to convey his ideas, what is beyond contention is its irresistible power to articulate his distinctive conception of philosophy. The dialogue both reflects and expresses Plato's view

---

[2]Plato, *Apology* 38a. *Plato Complete Works*, ed. John M. Cooper (1997: Hackett, Indiana), 33.

that philosophy is an essentially Socratic activity that must always question itself and that never really arrives at a final conclusion or even a particularly stable set of doctrines. His very deliberate choice of the dialogic form raises the more general question whether style should occupy a more self-consciously central role in philosophy than most thinkers since Plato have been willing to entertain. Plato suggests that *how* we process and articulate our ideas is inseparable from *what* we end up thinking and doing, that philosophical excellence is as much a matter of dialectical engagement as it is about arriving at a substantive vision. It is hardly surprising that he mistrusted writing as much as he did, seeing it as more likely to dull the mind than invigorate it. The written word is a medium that is peculiarly susceptible to enabling shallow cleverness rather than nourishing genuinely intelligent thought.[3]

The contrast between a Platonic dialogue and a typical paper in the latest issue of *Mind* or *The Journal of Philosophy* could not be more pronounced. Indeed, one suspects that the passage of time only goes so far in explaining the difference in a reader's experience. Whereas it is obvious that the former has been written by a recognizably grown-up and uniquely gifted thinker and writer, the latter more often than not provokes the opposite reaction. Admittedly, in certain branches of philosophy, such as symbolic logic or the philosophy of mathematics, this contrast may be legitimate and even inevitable. But when it comes to the more practical branches of philosophy, such as ethics and politics, the gap can become disconcerting, even ludicrously so. And, crucially, we do not feel that our sense of disquiet is attributable to the mere prolixity of so much contemporary philosophical writing. There is also the suspicion that the arid and deadening formality of the writing reflects a sterility and immaturity of sensibility. This in turn raises the legitimate question of why we should take such philosophy seriously in the first place. Style is not insignificant and being clear, precise and unwoolly are not its only or necessarily most vital virtues. As we shall see, Berlin developed a mode of philosophical writing – what might be described without hyperbole as a kind of philosophical literature – that rarely feels remote or removed from the worlds he seeks to bring to our attention.

The 'death' of political philosophy

There are probably few philosophical schools or styles of philosophy more at odds with Plato's than the ones which achieved their heyday in Oxford during

---

[3]In the *Phaedrus* Plato compares writing to poison implying that it is not good for the life of the mind. But he complicates this picture by using the notoriously slippery term *pharmakon* or drug which can mean both a remedy and a poison, a cure for illness or its cause and therefore suggesting that certain forms of writing, primarily the dialogue form, hold out the possibility of being beneficial rather than harmful to the soul.

the decades immediately before and after the Second World War, a place and time which left a lasting impression on Isaiah Berlin. This was the era when logical empiricism and, subsequently, linguistic analysis increasingly ruled the philosophical roost. More relevantly, for our purposes, it was also the period that witnessed the so-called death of political philosophy, or, more precisely, of 'political philosophy of the recommending sort' as one commentator has described it.[4] Perhaps the quickest and surest way of identifying the significance of what happened during this time is to note that its so-called death was viewed as a sign of philosophical progress rather than a symptom of any kind of intellectual malaise. My treatment of this well-trodden episode is limited to its more philosophical aspects as distinct from its sociological causes. The latter story, in any case, has already been expertly told by Brian Barry (1936–2009) in his paper 'The Strange Death of Political Philosophy'. It is also worth mentioning that by the time Barry published his collected papers in 1991 he considered it apt to make the following mordant remark about the whole episode:

> The earlier 'death' of political philosophy was caused to some extent by the view that the activity was impossible. Its fate was reminiscent of that suffered by Algernon's imaginary friend Bunbury: the doctors found out that he could not live, so he died.[5]

From the perspective of logical positivism, political philosophy of the normative or recommending sort does not belong within the domain of rational discourse, and so cannot qualify as a philosophically viable field of study. This is because it does not fall into either of the two putatively exhaustive domains of cognitively meaningful debate which the logical positivists recognized: the realms of the empirical and formal sciences. For the assumptions and claims of normative political thought are neither empirically verifiable nor analytically true, that is, necessarily true in virtue of the meaning of the terms themselves. Traditional political philosophy, they argued, is shot through with subjective judgements and emotionally charged preferences in which reason plays no part. Political philosophy operates within the realm of subjective taste rather than that of reason and truth, rhetorically persuasive in its own way, perhaps, but incapable of contributing in any serious way to the sum of knowledge. And so like other vast swathes of value-laden thought such as theology, ethics and aesthetics, the logical positivists concluded, it must be relegated to the domain of the cognitively

---

[4]This description is one that the philosopher Ted Honderich used in his 1973–4 *Royal Institute of Philosophy* lecture 'Equality and Violence', *Royal Institute of Philosophy Supplement* 8 (March 1974), 46–82.

[5]Brian Barry, *Democracy and Power: Essays in Political Theory 1* (1991: Clarendon Press, Oxford), 2.

meaningless. As one of the leading lights of logical positivism, A. J. Ayer (1910–89), stated:

> The presence of an ethical symbol in a sentence adds nothing to its factual content. Thus if I say to someone, 'You acted wrongly in stealing that money,' I am not stating anything more than if I had simply said, 'You stole that money.' In adding that this action is wrong I am not making any further statement about it. I am simply evincing my moral disapproval of it. It is as if I had said, 'You stole that money,' in a particular tone of horror, or written it with the addition of some special exclamation marks.[6]

The logical positivists, of course, were not denying that value judgements would continue to exert a dominant influence in everyday life – that was never likely to change. They were simply saying that evaluative statements are purely subjective, emotional expressions of preference and aversion – 'hurrah/boo' declarations as they were fond of describing them – devoid of any rational content. For them, all forms of normative or evaluative political philosophy are subjective, arbitrary and strictly meaningless. The positivist dismissal of evaluative thought amounted to an extreme application of Hume's exhortation that unless objects of enquiry are either *relations of ideas* or *matters of fact*, they should be committed to the flames since they contain 'nothing but sophistry and illusion'.[7]

The fortunes of political theory did not fare much better with the advent of linguistic analysis, the immediate successor to logical positivism, which became the most influential Anglophone philosophical movement of the post-war era. While linguistic analysis may have adopted a less explicitly pejorative attitude to normative political theory, its view of the subject was still far removed from anything that the age-old discipline of political thought claimed as its birthright. The only positive and legitimate task that ordinary language philosophy felt it could assign to political theory was the normatively neutral one of the piecemeal analysis of political concepts. The method for carrying out such a stridently non-foundational pursuit was linguistic analysis. This drastically limited remit could take two forms: the negative one of uncovering the linguistic confusions that constitute the subject matter of much of the tradition of political thought; and/or the more positive one of clarifying the meaning and use of putatively meaningful and relevant political concepts. In both cases linguistic analysis was judged to exhaust the legitimate activity and range of the subject. Linguistic philosophers viewed anything more ambitious such as attempting to provide substantive

---

[6]A. J. Ayer, *Language, Truth and Logic* (1936: 2001 edn: Penguin, London), 110.
[7]David Hume, *Enquiries concerning Human Understanding and concerning the Principles of Morals*, Sect. XII, Part III.

foundations for theories of liberalism or socialism, or justifications of conceptions of justice or equality and so forth, as misconceived and worthless. And like their positivist predecessors, they rested this claim on the more basic notion that reason has no intrinsic place in matters of normative ethics. The characteristic tone of the deflationist view that linguistic philosophy took of political theory is captured by one of its leading practitioners of the time:

> The answer to 'Why should I obey *any* law, acknowledge the authority of *any* state or support *any* Government?' is that this is a senseless question. ... For the general question suggests an equally general answer and this is what every political philosopher has tried to give. But no general criterion applies in every instance. ... The political theorists want an answer which is always and infallibly right, just as the epistemologists want a guarantee that there are material objects or that generalisation to the unexamined must be valid. But these are all equally senseless requests, for they result from stretching language beyond the bounds of significance.[8]

The inhibiting and demoralizing effect that logical empiricism and linguistic analysis had upon traditional political philosophy, and the radically restricted view that both philosophical schools shared of political theory's legitimate remit, revolve around roughly four overlapping and connected epistemological claims. Firstly, they were at one in their scepticism about the possibility of rational justification in politics. They both saw normative political philosophy as fatally compromised by its naive faith in the possibility of reason generating an objectively grounded morality. Their core difficulty with the entire tradition of political philosophy is not so much that it went astray at some point as that it has been an intrinsically empty and fruitless enterprise from the very start. Secondly, their shared scepticism about the discipline was in turn founded on the then virtually axiomatic notion that there exists a strict and exhaustive dichotomy between statements of fact and statements of value, or more specifically, between the kind of empirical investigations that political scientists pursue and the emotively charged pronouncements that traditional moral and political philosophers typically indulge in. Their third claim was that, in contrast to empirical statements and analytic statements, all value judgements are ultimately subjective and cannot be objectively grounded. Underpinning these three claims, at least for the logical positivists, is the notorious *verification principle*, which states that only assertions that are in principle verifiable by observation or experience could possess or convey cognitively meaningful information. Statements that could not be verified

---

[8]Margaret MacDonald, 'The Language of Political Theory', in *Logic and Language,* First Series, ed. A. Flew (1951: Oxford University Press, Oxford), 183–4.

in this way must be either analytic or meaningless. The final claim is that the only philosophically defensible role for those choosing to engage in political theory is to restrict their enquiry to the second-order, value-neutral analysis and clarification of moral and political concepts, that the only philosophically respectable form of political theory is value-free political theory. The outcome of this philosophical verdict for traditional normative political philosophy is not difficult to grasp. The parlous state of the subject during the post-war decades was accurately if rather smugly called out by Anthony Quinton (1925–2010) in his introduction to a selection of post-war philosophical papers on political theory:

> It has been widely held, indeed, that there really is no such subject as political philosophy apart from the negative business of revealing the conceptual errors and methodological misunderstandings of those who have addressed themselves in a very general way to political issues. A solid testimony to the width of this conviction has been the near-unanimity with which analytic philosophers have, until very recently, avoided the subject altogether. Of course, the great tradition of political thought remains an important subject of study in its own right. But to study its members is only marginally to continue the work they were doing. Many teachers of political philosophy are in fact students of the history of very general, theoretical, political ideas. But this no more makes them political philosophers than close attendance at the bull-ring makes an aficionado into a bull-fighter.[9]

Looking back on this period, it is tempting to view it too readily from the vantage point of what took place afterwards and characterize it as an unwelcome but mercifully temporary setback in the great onward march of Western political thought. We would do well to resist this temptation. Like most acts of blatant anachronism, it obscures more than it reveals. Not only was there nothing ineluctable about the rebirth of traditional normative political philosophy following rumours of its death in or around the mid-1950s, but there is perhaps the more significant point that its demise was not even seen at the time as a particularly regrettable development by the vast majority of philosophers. Much of the appeal of both logical positivism and linguistic analysis particularly among the new generation of clever and ambitious analytic philosophers lay precisely in the possibility that the traditional problems of philosophy could be solved or rather dissolved. So the decline of orthodox political theory was positively received, at least within mainstream analytic tradition: in fact, its virtual disappearance was generally thought to have eliminated the thick fog of various forms of overblown metaphysical speculation, naive linguistic essentialism and thinly concealed

---

[9]Anthony Quinton, ed. *Political Philosophy* (1967: Oxford University Press, Oxford), 3.

ideology that had infected the age-old tradition of political theory from the beginning and for far too long. More positively and constructively, its death or, at least, effective disappearance was judged to have finally cleared the ground for a methodologically sophisticated, morally neutral analysis of politics to emerge in which solid and uncontroversial facts rather than subjective and arbitrary values would take centre stage. And so the common charge that analytic philosophy had committed some kind of *trahison des clercs* by declaring its abdication from engagement in 'real world' problems tended to be dismissed by the theoretically initiated as bogus and beside the point.[10]

More relevantly, though rumours of the death of the subject may have been exaggerated, it has never been entirely clear on what philosophical basis, if any, its rebirth took place. Granted, John Rawls's *A Theory of Justice*, published in 1971, was a turning point. His book certainly succeeded in resurrecting the possibility of engaging in foundational political theory. But notwithstanding the sheer brilliance of Rawls's masterpiece, and, indeed, Robert Nozick's clever, if unconvincing, rejoinder in *Anarchy, State and Utopia*, we have not exactly reached anything even close to a consensus about the optimal methodology or even subject matter of normative political thought. On the contrary, one could plausibly argue that the flourishing of analytic political philosophy since the early 1970s has only been made possible by the absence of any seriously threatening scepticism about the theoretical feasibility or practical worth of the whole enterprise. What if Rawls's crucial concepts of a reflective equilibrium and of an overlapping consensus amount to no more than hopeful intuitive hunches that are in the end as justifiably deniable to those who don't share his basic liberal assumptions as they may be pre-theoretically appealing to those of us who do? Moreover, what if Nozick's political theory adds up to an ingenuous but practically irrelevant effort at resuscitating Lockean-style, contractarian liberalism? Are we not better advised to take note of the ancient Greek historian, Thucydides, when he observed that in the end political morality comes down to recognizing the unalterable fact that the powerful take what they can and the powerless concede what they must.[11] If Thucydides is right, or at least more right than wrong, about the immoral or amoral nature of politics, it would seem that contemporary political philosophy needs to take a much harder look at itself. Perhaps the most we should realistically expect from normative political theory is an admission that politics is ultimately about the ubiquitous and ineradicable conflicts of interests between the haves and the have-nots and that efforts to come up with anything more philosophically ambitious and ethically

---

[10]On the latter point, see Richard Wollheim's article 'Modern Philosophy and Unreason', *Political Quarterly* XXVII (1953), 246–57.

[11]I am referring, in particular, to chapter XVII of Thucydides *History of the Peloponnesian War* which features the famous Melian Dialogue.

lofty than emphatically pragmatic, modus vivendi justifications of irredeemably partial political arrangements may be as practically pointless as they seem theoretically ungrounded. So the question of whether the renaissance of analytic political thought has flattered to deceive or is based on cogent philosophical reasoning remains a much more contested matter than the vast majority of its current practitioners seem willing to entertain.

Berlin's contribution to political philosophy can help us address this central challenge by showing how political speculation can be both grown-up and ethically engaging. Acquainting ourselves with his conception and style of philosophy provides the key to understanding how such an approach to politics is achieved.

Berlin's non-reductive view of philosophy

The question 'What is philosophy?' is more often asked than answered. The stock response 'It's talking about talking' has the merit of being clear and concise and not untrue.[12] It even manages to indicate something of the second-order dimension of philosophical thinking. But it does not get us much further than this, even if we add 'critical thinking about thinking'. Berlin's attempt at answering what may well be an impossible question is more informative and instructive. It also offers the best place to start to make sense of his own distinctive philosophical outlook.

Berlin never seemed to tire of addressing the large question of the nature of philosophy, sometimes even to the point of self-plagiarism. His starting point is deceptively commonplace. Typically, he begins by introducing a familiar threefold classification of enquiry into those that are factual, those that are analytic or necessarily true, and those that fall into neither of these buckets of enquiry. According to this picture the distinguishing characteristic of both empirical and analytic domains of investigation is that either we already know the answers to the specific questions that belong to them or there exists an agreed and available procedure – namely the inductive or deductive method – that we can use to solve them. For example, answers to the questions 'Where is my coat?' or 'In what country was US President Obama born?' depend on factual knowledge, while answers to analytic questions like 'What is the cube root of 729?' can be answered by carrying out a straightforward mathematical calculation. The key point here is that even if you don't know the answers to these types of questions, there is an agreed, accessible and authoritative way of discovering them or, at the very least, a

---

[12]Anthony Quinton, philosophy entry in Ted Honderich ed. *The Oxford Companion to Philosophy* (1995: Oxford University Press, Oxford), 666.

reliably scientific or common-sense method that might lead to uncontroversially clear and provable answers.

So far not so very different from the sort of analysis one might typically expect from a paid-up member of the positivist school of philosophy. But what differentiates Berlin's tripartite classification is his view of the questions that fall into a third domain of investigation. Where the logical positivists typically reserved this category for all evaluative judgements, which they dismissed as cognitively empty or, at the very least, as non-knowledge, Berlin, on the other hand, insists it is the domain in which all genuinely philosophical questions belong. The examples he typically gives range from the most abstract and metaphysical questions, such as 'What is time?', 'What is a number?', 'What is the nature of reality?', or 'What is knowledge?', to the more concrete and personally urgent, 'What is the meaning of life?', 'What is happiness?', 'Why should I obey the law?', 'Are human rights inalienable?', 'Is freedom more precious than equality?' and so on. There are a number of things about these type of questions that Berlin singles out as immediately arresting: not only are they baffling and likely to induce severe mental cramp for anyone who is prepared to think about them for more than a passing moment, but, even more perplexingly, there seems to be no available means of answering them in any kind of demonstrable and conclusive way. And the final rub is that they do not seem to become any more soluble or dissoluble if we discover more facts about them or develop greater powers of inductive or deductive reasoning. In short, we appear to be in the presence of questions which are deeply meaningful and yet fiendishly intractable. At this point one might think there is much to be said in favour of Wittgenstein's memorable remark near the end of his first masterpiece *Tractatus-Logico-Philosophicus*: 'Whereof one cannot speak, thereof must one be silent.'[13] Berlin chose not to let Wittgenstein's austere (and perhaps valid) strictures regarding the unsayable silence his own views on the subject.

Berlin is quick to point out that not all philosophical questions necessarily remain recalcitrant forever. Even a quick glance at the history of Western thought reveals that in countless cases what were once regarded as philosophical problems have ended up becoming scientific questions, for example, medieval astrology gradually ceased to be considered a branch of philosophy with the arrival of its modern scientific variant: once the link connecting the movement of the planets with observable forces was broken, astronomy quickly became a subject for scientific rather than religious minds. Astrology, in the meantime, has managed to

---

[13] Ludwig Wittgenstein, *Tractatus-Logico-Philosophicus*, trans. by C. K. Ogden (1922: Kegan Paul, London), Sentence 7. Of course, in contrast to logical positivists such as A.J. Ayer, Wittgenstein did not revel in this discovery. For an excellent exploration of Wittgenstein's 'non-revisionary' conception of philosophy, see Jonathan Lear, 'Leaving the World Alone', *The Journal of Philosophy* 79 no. 7 (July 1982), 382–403.

survive in much the same way as all superstitions have. But the key point here is that the history of philosophy can be seen in part as a shedding of certain portions of itself into one or other of the two domains of scientific enquiry, the empirical and the formal sciences. Hence Berlin's remark:

> The history of thought is thus a long series of parricides, in which new disciplines seek to achieve their freedom by killing off the parent subjects and eradicating from within themselves whatever traces still linger there of 'philosophical' problems, that is, the kind of questions that do not carry within their own structure clear indications of the techniques of their own solution. (CC2 6)

As he adds, the sentiment expressed in the above passage echoes the vivid portrayal of philosophy as an endlessly self-perpetuating subject expressed by his Oxford colleague and friend, J. L. Austin (1911–60) (CC2 191):

> In the history of human enquiry, philosophy has the place of the initial sun, seminal and tumultuous; from time to time it throws off some portion of itself to take station as a science, a planet, cool and well regulated, progressing steadily towards a distant final state. This happened long ago at the birth of mathematics, and again at the birth of physics; only in the last century we have witnessed the same process once again, slow and at the same time almost imperceptible, in the birth of the science of mathematical logic, through the joint labours of philosophers and mathematicians. Is it not possible that the next century might see the birth, through the joint labours of philosophers, grammarians and numerous others students of language, of a true and comprehensive science of language. Then we shall have rid of ourselves of one more part of philosophy (there will still be plenty left) in the only way that we can get rid of philosophy, by kicking it upstairs.[14]

Another general and related feature of philosophy that Berlin underscores is our relentless desire to define its problems in scientific terms. While, on one level, he recognizes this tendency as a necessary and legitimate driver of the development and expansion of scientific enquiry and knowledge, he warns that it has often led to efforts to force square philosophical pegs into round and inflexible scientific holes. The Procrustean urge to redefine bona fide philosophical questions so that they can be assigned to one of the other two kinds of scientific, measurable knowledge – deductive or inductive – is more often motivated by temperamental factors such as the need for certainty, or dissatisfaction with large, unanswerable

---

[14] J. L Austin, *Philosophical Papers* (1979 edn: Oxford University Press, Oxford), 232.

questions, than by the dictates of truth and reason. He also makes the point that our systematizing and homogenizing impulses have been behind many of the most misguided attempts to produce a science of humankind, which in turn have informed some of the most potent and repressive political ideologies of modern times:

> What do men do and suffer, and why and how? It is the view that answers to these questions can be provided by formulating general laws, from which the past and future of individuals and societies can be predicted, that has led to misconceptions alike in theory and practice: to fanciful, pseudo-scientific histories and theories of human behaviour, abstract and formal at the expense of the facts, and to revolutions and wars and ideological campaigns conducted on the basis of dogmatic certainty about their outcomes – vast misconceptions which have cost the lives, liberty and happiness of a great many innocent human beings. (POI2 2)

A final characteristic of the philosophical enterprise that Berlin almost ritually highlights is that many of its central preoccupations and problems either presuppose or are inescapably tangled up with value judgements. This largely explains why such subjects as ethics, aesthetics, law and, of course, political theory remain firmly within the philosophical fold. Many of the most basic questions of philosophy involve normatively infused concepts and judgements which, Berlin argues, are 'unable or unwilling to emerge by either the empirical or the formal door' (POI2 2). But again, what chiefly distinguishes Berlin's attitude to evaluative philosophical questions is his refusal to dismiss them as purely emotive and cognitively vacuous. Put more positively, questions of value are, in his view, amenable to rational discussion and objectively informed debate even if they may not lend themselves to uniquely correct and verifiable solutions. We shall shortly examine why he took this view and how it informed his political philosophy. Suffice to say at this point that one of the ways in which Berlin departed from the prevailing philosophical wisdom of his time was in his rejection of ethical subjectivism and other species of ethical non-cognitivism.

What ought to be emerging by now is that Berlin's general view of philosophy is very different to the positivist view of the subject that was dominant in the pre- and post-war Anglophone philosophical world. Unlike his contemporaries but in accordance with the great tradition of philosophy, Berlin adopted a more inclusive appreciation of the philosophical enterprise. Granted his starting point resembles the conventionally positivist classification of knowledge, but he does not share the positivists' narrowly scientific and descriptive view of the subject. Berlin rejected the prevailing idea that philosophy's remit should be restricted to that of 'secretary to science and obituarist of metaphysics' (CC2 xxxii). Nor did he share the view that the questions in the discarded third category all turn out in the end to be gibberish, mere pseudo-problems. Rather, he viewed this last category as containing the deepest concerns of human life, the ones with which philosophy should be most preoccupied. He considered therefore that the notion that genuinely normative political theory could or ought to be buried by its positivist and linguistic undertakers as philosophically incoherent as well as ludicrous. Berlin found the positivist classification useful in providing some initial foothold on the large and notoriously difficult question of defining the philosophical terrain. But it is his basically humanistic understanding of what characterizes genuinely philosophical questions, especially in so far as they may relate to human values and ideals, that anchors his own position and differentiates it from that of his more positivist-minded contemporaries.

It is now finally time to turn our attention to Berlin's own specific philosophical vision and to uncover its underlying connections with his normative political theory and, ultimately, his defence of liberal society. There are three distinct but interlocking philosophical elements that inform his own normative conception of political morality: these include his debt to Kant's transformation of our naive understanding of reality and truth, his insistence on the core insights of historicism and, finally, his emphasis on the unscientific but no less objective sources of reason and understanding. Let's now examine each of them in turn.

3 KANT'S COPERNICAN REVOLUTION

The hope that the intractable questions of philosophy could be solved once and for all – or dissolved in the sense of being exposed as misleading or nonsensical – has been around as long as the subject itself. This hope was especially intensely felt during the European Enlightenment of the seventeenth and eighteenth centuries. Following the transformational and rapid impact of Newton's discoveries in the natural sciences, many of the leading minds of the time became increasingly and not unreasonably optimistic that a similar type of breakthrough could soon be achieved in the so-called *human sciences*, that the seemingly insoluble questions of philosophy or metaphysics could either be reformulated as testable scientific hypotheses and/or valid conceptual questions, or else relegated to the ash heap of nonsense. Either way 'the science of man' like 'the science of nature' seemed destined to transform the world of human affairs for the betterment of mankind. According to Berlin, what the great *philosophes* and the positivists after them failed to appreciate is that their faith in the omniscience and omnipotence of the scientific method with regard to our understanding of ourselves and others is illusory.

Acknowledging, as Berlin does, that the history of philosophy can be depicted as 'a series of parricides' in which what were once conceptual problems eventually get hived off to their proper homes in either the scientific arena (empirical or logical domains of enquiry) or the graveyard of dead ideas was never intended to imply that the logical terminus of philosophy itself is its own progressive and inevitable redundancy and death. Interpreting philosophy in this way – that is, assuming that all its problems and preoccupations are capable of being either outsourced to the sciences or else discarded in the dustbin of empty, irrational beliefs – is to misunderstand its character and the deeper reasons for its persistence. According to Berlin, unless we end up experiencing some kind of far-reaching and wholly unprecedented (though not strictly impossible) transformation in our conceptual repertoire, we can be reasonably certain that there is always likely to be a large and irreducible, if varying and unpredictable, set of philosophical problems that warrant and reward serious discussion and yet resist final resolution. Berlin's justification for subscribing to this view is rooted in what he regarded as the greatest discovery of the eighteenth-century German philosopher Immanuel Kant. And it boils down to the Kantian insight that philosophy cannot expire since it is concerned with the identification and elucidation of the very categories and concepts of thought which all human thinking and understanding, including scientific knowledge and everyday common sense, presuppose and depend upon.

Broadly speaking, Berlin differentiates between categories and concepts of thought by treating the former as the underlying models or 'hidden structures of thought' that shape how we think about certain activities and areas of enquiry and by referring to the latter as the basic ideas and ideals that fall within these patterns of thought permitting us to make sense of ourselves and the world around us. He also felt that certain categories and concepts were more permanent and universal than others; typically but by no means exclusively, the more fixed and common categories included those that underpin our understanding of the inanimate or physical world while the less universal and unchanging ones inform our sense of ourselves as human beings.

Berlin thought that Kant's so-called Copernican revolution – the idea that, although our notion of the world or reality depends at least partly on what is out there, the inescapably innate structuring activities of the human mind shape our understanding of the world as well – permanently and radically redefined the philosophical landscape. Kant himself introduced this basic and literally world-changing idea at the start of his great masterpiece *Critique of Pure Reason*:

> Hitherto it has been assumed that all our knowledge must conform to objects. But all our attempts to extend our knowledge of objects by establishing something in regard to them *a priori*, by means of concepts, have, on this assumption, ended in failure. ... We should then be proceeding precisely on the lines of Copernicus' primary hypothesis. Failing of satisfactory progress in explaining the movements of the heavenly bodies on the supposition that they revolved around the spectator, he tries whether he might not have better success if he had made the spectator to revolve and the stars to remain at rest. A similar experiment can be tried in metaphysics, as regards the *intuition* of objects. If intuition must conform to the constitution of objects, I do not see how we could know anything of the latter *a priori*; but if the object ... must conform to the constitution of our faculty of intuition, I have no difficulty in conceiving such a possibility.[1]

The textbook account of Kant's place in Western philosophy tends to portray his achievement as the navigation of a way between the Scylla of rationalism and

---

[1] Immanuel Kant, *Critique of Pure Reason*, trans, Norman Kemp Smith (1992 edn: Macmillan, London, Bk. Xvi–xvii. Henceforth referred to as CPR.

the Charybdis of empiricism by revealing that the point of philosophy is not so much a matter of deduction or induction as of recognizing that the objects of our experience 'must conform to the constitution of our faculty of intuition'. While there is nothing strictly wrong with this familiar (if slightly cartoonish) version of events, I shall present Kant's seminal contribution differently. Another way of describing his philosophical breakthrough is to see it in less abstract terms as an attempt to respond to the conflict between science and ethics. This way of reading Kant helps bring out the parallels that exist between the philosophical challenge confronting the hermit of Königsberg and the one facing the fox of Oxford without doing undue violence to the historical character of their respective ideas.

Like Berlin, Kant faced a situation in which the very idea of practical philosophy as a coherent intellectual pursuit was under grave threat. For Kant the main source of this threat lay in the conflict between the findings of science and the traditional claims of morality and religion. It seemed clear that if one accepted the tenets of Newtonian science, for which there seemed to be a great deal of incontrovertible and ever-expanding wealth of evidence, then there appeared to be no obvious room for free will, morality or even God. Moreover, the attempts by certain philosophers, most notably Berkeley (1685–1753) and to a lesser extent Leibniz (1646–1716), to characterize the claims of science as inferior to those of metaphysics had largely backfired: the assured and fast-paced progress of science contrasted sharply with the comparatively anarchic battlefield of philosophical debate and disagreement. In the end it was left to the inimitable Hume (1711–76) to declare the death of dogmatic metaphysics, and in so doing raise serious doubts about the credentials of much of traditional philosophy as a feasible and respectable intellectual discipline. For it was by no means obvious what legitimate purpose, if any, was left for the subject to fulfil against the panorama of the apparent superfluousness of metaphysical speculation and of the onward march of science.

Awoken from his self-proclaimed dogmatic slumber, Kant confronted an unpromising vista which displays a striking resemblance to the philosophical landscape that Berlin would face almost two hundred years afterwards. As in Berlin's time, the increasingly dominant naturalistic conception of philosophy associated with Enlightenment rationality held that propositions fall into one of two exhaustive domains of enquiry. Using Leibniz's terminology, there are truths of reason, which correspond roughly to what the logical positivists would later call (using Kant's terminology) analytic or *a priori* truths. These are the kinds of proposition or judgement that are known independently of experience, such as 'All bachelors are unmarried' or 'A square has four sides'. In addition, there are truths of fact, which broadly correspond to what would later be called factual or *a posteriori* truths. Factual truths are the kinds of proposition that are contingent rather than necessary, and largely based upon the inductive sciences. Examples of such synthetic statements might be 'It's raining outside' or 'Leibniz died in 1716'. Once one accepted this general view that all valid propositions can be systematically divided up into these two classes, it did not appear that there was anything left for philosophy to do. After all, the empirical sciences were increasingly showing that their rapid success could be achieved without the guiding hand of philosophy. So unless philosophy was prepared to drastically revise its remit to one of analysing and elucidating analytic propositions, it looked as if its raison d'être had become surplus to requirements. As we have seen, a similar enough fate afflicted the subject during the high noon of logical positivism and linguistic analysis in the mid-twentieth century.

The genius of Kant lay in finding a way beyond this seemingly hopeless philosophical impasse by perceiving, first of all, that the most general propositions of the sciences, including the empirical sciences, do not conform to the seemingly obvious and putatively exhaustive twofold classification of knowledge. He observed that there are core scientific propositions that are neither analytic nor synthetic, but can only be described as synthetic *a priori*. According to Kant, $7 + 5 = 12$ is an example of a synthetic *a priori* statement since it provides us with new knowledge (though many have since considered it an analytic statement). More plausible examples of such propositions include Kant's own example that 'between two points you can only have a straight line' and, indeed, Berlin's personal favourite that 'no object is both red and green all over'.[2]

This in turn led to Kant's broader and more impactful discovery – what Berlin describes as his 'permanent revolution' – that the truth is partially yet inescapably subject- or mind-dependent. In other words, our idea of reality depends both on what there actually is out there independently of us and on the contribution we make through the concepts and categories in terms of which we necessarily and mainly unconsciously interpret and experience the world. The objective and the subjective are intermingled and inextricable when it comes to our apprehension of the world since they both necessarily feed into how we perceive it, how the world appears to us and not just as it is in itself. Hence the distinction between transcendent knowledge and transcendental idealism where the former, according to Kant, refers to the outdated fiction of a mindless or presupposition-less metaphysical picture of reality or what Wilfred Sellars (1912–89) would later call 'the Myth of the Given', and the latter denotes the structure imposed by the human mind on the contents of experience. As Kant states:

> I call all knowledge transcendental if it is occupied, not with objects, but with the way that we can possibly know objects even before we experience them. (CPR B25) [3]

---

[2] See, for example, Berlin's paper, 'Synthetic *A Priori* Propositions', Reply to Sellars (1951). It is available on the Isaiah Berlin Virtual Library (IBVL).

[3] For Kant, the transcendent is defined as that which goes beyond the possible knowledge of a human being, the idea of transcendent knowledge is an illusion of pure reason of which he is giving a critique. The poetry of Wallace Stevens can be particularly helpful in giving us a sense of the nature and

It was on this basis that he introduced his famous distinction between the world as it is in itself, the mind-independent world of *noumena*, and the world as it appears to us, the mind- or subject-dependent world of *phenomena*. Kant, of course, was not denying that reality exists or that the truth is some kind of random fiction invented by us.[4] Rather, he was making the very different claim that the *noumenal* world cannot be directly known to us. The world as it is in itself is unknowable. Correlatively, the phenomenal world in which we make sense of and live our lives is the world of appearance, the necessarily subject- or mind-dependent world of everyday, common-sense experience.

Kant's view of our perception is a bit like imagining that no one can see anything without irremovable pink-tinted spectacles. We find it difficult to imagine what we would see if we tried, *per impossibile*, to remove our human filters: we usually end up speculating (perhaps absurdly) that our sight would resemble something along the lines of the monochrome vision of some animals, or the even cruder vision of, say, a frog – or how we imagine a frog sees. Our lenses give us access only to a heavily filtered world via the connective tissue of our perceptions. So we are both blind and not blind: we cannot see (or know) the *noumenal* world as it is independently of our perception and we certainly can't have knowledge of it, but we do have access to and knowledge of the lens-coloured, mind-dependent world of phenomena or appearance. We like to think that there is a relation between the two, but the challenge of working out the nature of that connection is something that we are, or seem constitutionally, unable to determine. According to Berlin, the chief legacy of Kant's breakthrough rests on his being the first thinker:

> to draw a clear distinction between, on the one hand, questions of fact, and, on the other, questions about the patterns in which these facts presented themselves to us – patterns that were not themselves altered however much the facts themselves, or our knowledge of them, might alter. These patterns or categories or forms of experience were themselves not the subject-matter of any possible natural science. (CC2 9)

Also of crucial significance is the following claim expressed in the Preface to the second edition of the *Critique of Pure Reason*:

---

difference between the transcendent and the transcendental: the final line of one of his most celebrated early poems, 'The Snow Man', captures the distinction nicely: 'Nothing that is not there and the nothing that is.'

[4]According to Kant, our access to the world is unavoidably dependent on our categories of understanding that in turn are dependent on our subjective perception, which explains why he thought that 'the transcendental idealist is, therefore, an empirical realist'. CPR, A371.

> I have therefore found it necessary to deny *knowledge* in order to make room for *faith*. The dogmatism of metaphysics, that is, the pre-conception that it is possible to make headway in metaphysics without a previous criticism of pure reason, is the source of all that unbelief, always very dogmatic, which wars against morality. (CPR B 30)

Kant's decision that he had to repudiate metaphysical certainty to accommodate belief or faith, which marks another step in his broader effort to bring metaphysics down to epistemological earth, is particularly relevant for our purposes. For the result of this highly original claim is that several crucial but imperilled entities were given a philosophical lifeline. The matter of God's existence together with the related questions of the existence of free will and the reality of morality could no longer be dismissed as meaningless. It's not that Kant could prove or disprove the existence of God or free will or morality but, rather, that his metaphysical innovation provided the requisite elbow room to protect them from the encroaching threat of science. Once we accept that science operates within the world of appearances, the natural world of space and time and cause and effect, and not in the unknowable world as it is in itself, then we are left with legitimate room to consider how we are in ourselves, which includes our faith or belief that we are free agents susceptible to the rules of morality.

It is hard to overestimate the significance of this philosophical breakthrough. In a way Kant single-handedly kept philosophy alive by showing that natural science could not overwhelm it, that there can exist a space for a certain type of metaphysical speculation to breathe, which in turn gave much needed oxygen to other basic concepts and beliefs such as those concerned with freedom, morality and the meaning of life to reassert themselves, albeit in a radically altered way. This helps explain why Kant still remains so unignorable. It also serves to underwrite how much Kant's basic conception of philosophy is echoed in Berlin's view of the subject, the spirit of which is encapsulated in the following remark from the Preface to the first edition of his *Critique of Pure Reason*:

> Human reason has this peculiar fate, that in one species of its knowledge it is burdened by questions which, as prescribed by the nature of reason itself, it is not able to ignore, but which, as transcending all its powers, it is also not able to answer. (CRP 7)

Berlin's debt to Kant's conception of the nature of philosophy is most evident in his various attempts to explain the meaning and durability of the subject and, more specifically, in his unshakable conviction that a problem can be 'perfectly meaningful without being strictly verifiable' (POI2 2). But for our purposes we are more concerned with the specific matter of how Berlin deployed Kant's transcendental argument to found his own conception of philosophical anthropology. A brief word about transcendental-type arguments is necessary before we engage this topic directly.

Typically, since Kant, transcendental arguments have been deployed by philosophers in an effort to refute scepticism about the external world. They endeavour to do this by seeking to reveal that even the most exacting forms of scepticism presuppose that we have experiences of a certain type, and that the possibility of having such experiences can be explained only by the existence of the very objects of experience that the sceptic calls into doubt. Not surprisingly, transcendental arguments of this kind have not gone unchallenged by sceptics. One of the more notable sceptical objections was put forward in an important paper published in 1968 by Barry Stroud (1935–2019).[5] Stroud claimed that the main problem with the transcendental argument is that even if we admit that it may, indeed, be extremely difficult, if not impossible, for us to avoid believing that there is an external world, that in itself is not sufficient to justify the claim that there actually is one. In other words, to acknowledge that we must believe something to be true is not the same as the separate and epistemologically more ambitious claim that our seemingly non-optional belief in the existence of the world must, in fact, be true. Stroud's objection has proved remarkably difficult to refute. Several commentators have asserted, quite plausibly, that it loads the dice too heavily against the transcendental argument. But even this response does not really deflect Stroud's core challenge, which is that beliefs, even beliefs of an apparently unavoidable kind, do not make things necessarily so. My main reason for mentioning this influential argument is that while Stroud's challenge may well be decisive in refuting the classic transcendental argument against scepticism about the external world, it does not follow that it applies to Berlin's deployment of the same form of argument for more philosophically practical purposes. His use and application of the argument operates firmly within the world of appearances in which we live our everyday lives. So rather than seeking to achieve the grand task of establishing some form of necessary relation between the world of appearance (the *phenomenal* world) and the external, perspectiveless world (the *noumenal* world), Berlin's version of the argument is both metaphysically and epistemologically more modest. It is an internally generated form of the transcendental argument which aims to establish human self-understanding on firm phenomenological grounds. But, as we shall see, even internalizing the transcendental argument is not without its own philosophical challenges.

Much of the underlying unity and scope of Berlin's distinctive model of philosophy derive from his interpretation and application of Kant's *Critique of Pure Reason*. What primarily interests Berlin about Kant is not the familiar patterns

---

[5]Barry Stroud, 'Transcendental Arguments', *Journal of Philosophy* 65 (1968): 241–56. Republished in Barry Stroud, *Understanding Human Knowledge* (2000: Oxford University Press, Oxford).

of thought associated with our apprehension of the natural world such as time, space, number and so forth, but the central categories and concepts undergirding and articulating our understanding of ourselves as human beings. It is these more anthropological or humanistic categories of thought, many of which, as he admits, are less fixed and universal than those that relate to and shape our view of the external world which largely explain the nature and persistence of philosophy and provide the conceptual basis of his normative political ideas. As he states:

> There exist central features of our experience that are invariant and omnipresent, or at least much less variable than the vast variety of its empirical characteristics, and for that reason deserve to be distinguished by the name of categories. This is evident enough in the case of the external world. … Such permanent features are to be found in the moral and political and social worlds too: less stable and universal, perhaps, than in the physical one, but just as indispensable for any kind of intersubjective communication, and therefore for thought and action. An enquiry that proceeds by examples, and is therefore not scientific, but not formal, that is not deductive, either, is most likely to be philosophical. (CC2 215–16)

So what, we may ask, are these putative concepts and categories of thought that are indispensable to our own self-understanding? And secondly, how do we access them? Berlin's handling of both these questions begins, predictably enough, with the caveat that they are themselves irreducibly philosophical problems, by which he means that empirical research and/or deductive logic cannot answer them since they themselves presuppose the very patterns of thought requiring scrutiny. He also emphasizes that because we take many of these quasi-primordial, human-centred concepts and categories of thought for granted, they are virtually too ubiquitous and obvious for us to notice them. The final general feature about these very abstract thought patterns is that they resist straightforward, let alone systematic analysis given their inherently opaque, often hidden and ambiguous meanings and uses. However, Berlin does not let these challenges prevent him from giving us at least some tangible picture of the entities we are dealing with here. Specific examples of these general categories and concepts include

> such notions as society, freedom, sense of time and change, suffering, happiness, productivity, good and bad, right and wrong, choice, effort, truth, illusion (to take them wholly at random). (CC2 217)

While this list is hardly exhaustive – Berlin emphasizes that it could not be otherwise as there is no mechanical rule or convenient algorithm capable of producing a reliable and complete list – it does put some flesh on the bones of the mental apparatus which Berlin considers essential to comprehending ourselves as recognizable members of the human species. These more humanistically minded thought spectacles reflect as much as they shape our everyday understanding of ourselves. They are less stable than the more fixed and uncontested concepts and categories that are, in some way, both shaped by and shape the physical world. Where the latter perhaps have a stronger claim to reflect how things really are *sub specie aeternitatis* (from the perspective of eternity), the former frame the world far more *sub specie temporis nostri* (from the perspective of our own time). In any case, it is the human-oriented patterns of thought which make possible and at the same time constrain our mental picture of ourselves and of the social world we inhabit.

Berlin's emphasis on the more humanistic categories and concepts of thought is not the only way in which he diverged from Kant. A second and more basic departure centres on his claim that the fundamental categories that mould our understanding of the physical as well as the human world are, as he says himself, 'brute facts and not *a priori* truths' (CC2 216). His reason for claiming that the categories are contingent (or *a posteriori*) rather than necessary (or *a priori*) is never fully explained, but is no doubt based on a version of the originally Humean idea that it's not absurd or beyond the bounds of strict possibility to imagine their absence.[6] To assert otherwise would be to indulge in a form of unsubstantiated, non-contextual metaphysical certitude, something to which Berlin remained philosophically allergic: his deep empirical bent meant he was sceptical of the power of *a priori* reasoning, in so far as it relates to our more anthropocentric concepts and categories of thought.

But acknowledging that even our deepest and most common categories of thought are contingent does not mean that they are merely subjective in the arbitrary sense of that term. For one of the lessons of both history and social anthropology is that our ultimately contingent patterns of thinking can prove remarkably resilient and last a very long time indeed. Moreover, it would seem that our ability to communicate with and make sense of long-dead thinkers and their thoughts as well as distant and strange societies would be rendered impossible without their persistent, if necessarily contingent, presence. As Berlin remarks:

> The basic categories (with their corresponding concepts) in terms of which we define men ... are not matters of induction or hypothesis. To think of someone

---

[6]Berlin does elaborate on the concept of brute facts in his commentary on one of the aphorisms of the obscure German philosopher Georg Christoph Lichtenberg: 'Man is a cause-seeking creature; in the spiritual order he could be called the cause-seeker. Other minds perhaps think things in other – to us inconceivable – categories.' He then adds:

> These words have a Kantian flavour, especially the implication that the category of causality is so deeply rooted in us as to act as a defining characteristic of mankind; but that nevertheless it is only a 'brute' fact (and not an a priori 'necessity') that we think of things in exclusively causal terms; for other beings might think and sense within other frames of reference, but what these experiences could be is beyond our ken, because we are as we are, and cannot see beyond our own – evidently unalterable – horizon (AE 276–77).

as a human being is *ipso facto* to bring all these notions into play: so that to say of someone that he is a man, but that choice, or the notion of truth, mean nothing to him, would be eccentric: it would clash with what we mean by 'man' not as a matter of verbal definition (which is alterable at will), but as intrinsic to the way in which we think, and (as a matter of 'brute' fact) evidently cannot but think. (CC2 217)

Clearly, Berlin's application of the transcendental argument is not without its own challenges. For a start, there is the thorny issue of how to tell the difference between the concepts and categories of thought which are *brute facts* (a concept that can hardly be accused of precision and transparency) and therefore beyond explanation and those that are susceptible, at least in principle, to further explanation and justification. It also lacks any clear and uncontroversial criteria for determining the difference between our so-called more fixed and shared categories and concepts of the self and those that are interpreted as more parochial and transient. Without such an objectively reliable standard there is always the risk of conflating what happen to be our own historically and culturally situated assumptions and preferences with those of 'humanity' writ large, assuming, of course, that such an entity as humanity can be said to have any objective meaning or basis in the first place. As we shall see in the next chapter, Berlin had good reasons for thinking that any attempt to provide a complete and unrevisable account of our most basic categories and concepts of thought is futile since it would require that we occupy some God-like view from nowhere, of transcending our own historically contingent and un-transcendable condition. No such perspective-independent or discourse-independent standpoint exists. But even if we accept the unavailability of an Archimedean perspective from which we can objectively cast judgement on the nature and validity of our mental picture of the world, especially the world of human affairs, that doesn't mean we can somehow escape the implications of its absence: in other words, discovering that one is lost in a forest may be better than not knowing one is lost in a forest but it doesn't solve the basic predicament one is left in. As we shall see, both of these concerns will be partly addressed when we explore the more specific issue in Berlin's thought between what he claims are recognizable human values and ideals and those which he judges are beyond 'the human horizon' (CTH2 12). Needless to say, the deeper question of whether some form of a correspondence theory of truth in which it makes sense to claim that we can access or track the natural world as it is anyway or mindlessly can survive the Kantian challenge is beyond the scope of this book.

A third basic way in which Berlin moves beyond Kant is in his emphasis of the basic value-ladenness of the mental structures that shape our view of human nature. This aspect of his philosophical outlook is, I believe, much more important than has been appreciated. For it is not just that Berlin is arguing that our more humanistically oriented concepts and categories are ethically charged, but largely implicit in this view is a more basic rejection of any absolute dichotomy between facts and values. The positivist idea that values cannot be derived from facts is one that remains hugely influential among philosophers and, indeed, beyond, in our everyday, common-sense understanding. Berlin is not opposed to Hume's well-known distinction as long as it is not interpreted too literally or pushed to the point where it becomes a false and constricting dichotomy. However, he affirms that most, if not all, of the underlying patterns of thought which are presupposed by and applicable to our understanding of ourselves are inherently value-laden. Examples of the more basic value-laden categories and concepts include suffering, happiness, sanity, cruelty, survival and so forth as well as the more intellectually centred ideas of truth, knowledge and objectivity. The key point is that we cannot understand human nature in a value-neutral way since such an approach betrays an ignorance of the normatively charged nature of the very models of thought that make possible human self-understanding and social interaction in the first place. Berlin articulates this point most explicitly in the following passage, which deserves quoting at length:

> This will hold of values too (among them political ones) in terms of which men are defined. Thus, if I say of someone that he is kind or cruel, loves truth or is indifferent to it, he remains human in either case. But if I find a man to whom it literally makes no difference whether he kicks a pebble or kills his family, since either would be an antidote to ennui or inactivity, I shall not be disposed, like consistent relativists, to attribute to him merely a different code of morality from my own or that of most men, or declare that we disagree on essentials, but shall begin to speak of insanity and inhumanity; I shall be inclined to consider him mad, as a man who thinks he is Napoleon is mad; which is a way of saying that I do not regard such a being as being fully a man at all. It is cases of this kind, which seem to make it clear that ability to recognise universal – or almost universal – values enters into our analysis of such fundamental concepts as 'man', 'rational', 'sane', 'natural' etc. – which are usually thought of as descriptive and not evaluative – that lie at the basis of modern translations into empirical terms of the kernel of truth in the old *a priori* natural law doctrines. (CC2 217)

What this extract helps bring out is why Berlin felt that self-assured declarations of the death of traditional political philosophy were misguided to the point of absurdity. All such declarations rested on the common fallacy that making sense of the world of human affairs can be carried out in a value-free, narrowly scientific manner.

As an aside, it is likely that Berlin had the work of his colleague and friend H. L. A. Hart in mind in the final sentence of the above passage. Hart, a renowned philosopher of law, produced his seminal work, *The Concept of Law* (1961), at roughly the same time as Berlin's essay 'Does Political Theory Still Exist?' was published.[7]

---

[7] H. L. A. Hart, *The Concept of Law* (1961: Clarendon Press, Oxford), hereafter referred to as COL. For an excellent philosophical discussion of the normative foundations of Hart's jurisprudence which

What is noteworthy about Hart's positivist conception of law is the extent to which it explicitly argues for ethical foundations or, as he states, a 'minimum content of natural law'. 'It is a truth', Hart asserts, 'of some importance that for the adequate description not only of law but of many other social institutions, a place must be reserved, besides definitions and ordinary statements of fact, for a third category of statements: those the truth of which is contingent on human beings and the world they live in retaining the salient characteristics which they have' (COL 165). Hart lists the following five traits of our nature as constituting the minimum content of natural law: human vulnerability, approximate equality, limited altruism, limited resources and limited understanding and strength of will. Their inclusion in his jurisprudential outlook raises the philosophically intriguing question of the extent to which a coherent and compelling theory of law is dependent on an irreducible set of elementary values and norms. In addition, Hart's derivation of the five aspects of humanity is a classic, if unheralded, instance of an another transcendental argument in action.[8]

According to Berlin, whatever we may think about the possibility of philosophy being value-neutral in its more formal and recondite fields of enquiry such as logic, metaphysics and epistemology, the assumption made absolutely no sense when it came to the practical sphere of political morality. The basic ideas underpinning our very notion of human nature and social interaction, such as the desire for survival and security, the sense of right and wrong, the demands of basic sanity and reason, and the need for companionship and sociality, and less elementary and ethically thicker ethical and political concepts such as justice, liberty, mercy, murder, cruelty, and so forth, are inextricably value-laden *all the way through*. This

---

acknowledges, albeit implicitly, the transcendental derivation of the 'minimum content of natural law', see W.G. Runciman, *Social Science and Political Theory* (1963: 1971 edn: Cambridge University Press, Cambridge), chapter viii:

> Hart lists five particular truisms which provide the basis of such a set of assertions: [assertions that are best described as the minimum content of natural law] human vulnerability, approximate equality, limited altruism, limited resources, and limited understanding and strength of will. Because of these facts, which Hart emphasizes to be contingent facts, there are certain rules or principles which must be embodied in any social organization which is to be viable. Of course, it can always be argued that there may be political philosophies which deny the value of social organization altogether or which set up the life of the hermit as the only and overriding ideal. But it is surely reasonable, with Hart, to dismiss such notions without argument; we need no more take seriously the political philosophy of (to take Hart's own example) a suicide club than we did the flat-earthers' geography. (169)

[8] In a letter to Michael Walzer in 1986, Berlin wrote:

> Common ground is, I suppose, what Herbert Hart tried to formulate as a kind of empirical version of natural law, that is, those laws without which no society can survive – if everybody lied, killed (or even, I suppose, if the majority did), no society could survive and this is therefore almost a kind of biological necessity, however the word 'necessity' is interpreted. But clearly this is not enough as a minimal code – even if sufficiently universal (A 276).

doesn't mean, of course, that it is not possible to engage in relatively value-free, empirically based analyses of concepts such as democracy, liberty or equality; as we have noted, Berlin is perfectly happy to accept the ordinary, common-sense distinction between facts and values or, more specifically, between, for example, an empirical account of democratic forms of government and a normative defence of democracy. But it is to claim that empirical inquiries can provide at best only a partial account of the nature and significance of such central and inherently value-laden concepts. For example, a formal linguistic analysis of a concept like democracy will not get you very far without at some point engaging in substantive and inescapably contested normative argument.[9] Similarly, a purely empirical investigation of the same political concept cannot even begin to answer the most basic normative question of whether it is a good or justified form of government. Again, this is not to imply that formal or empirical enquiries performed by social and political scientists do not have a legitimate and worthwhile role to play in our understanding of human nature and society. But for Berlin it is emphatically to deny that such forms of enquiry have within their power the capacity to exhaust our understanding of intrapersonal and interpersonal matters. It also amounts to an affirmation that any political theory worth its salt necessarily engages in normative judgements. As Berlin remarks:

> To suppose, then, that there have been or could be ages without political philosophy is like supposing that, as there are ages of faith, so there could have be ages of total disbelief. But this is an absurd notion: there is no human activity without some kind of general outlook. Scepticism, cynicism, refusal to dabble in abstract issues or to question values, hard-boiled opportunism, contempt for theorising, all the varieties of nihilism are, of course, themselves metaphysical and ethical positions, committal attitudes. Whatever else the existentialists have taught us, they have made this fact plain. The idea of a completely *wertfrei* theory (or model) of human action (as contrasted, say, with animal behaviour) rests on a naive misconception of what objectivity or neutrality in the social studies must be. (CC2 206)

Another way in which Berlin's transcendentalism deviates from Kant is its emphasis on history or, more precisely, on the influence of history and historical consciousness on the genesis and variation of our assumptions and beliefs. As we

---

[9]Another aspect of Berlin's transcendentalism is that it is entirely different from the philosophically uninteresting if occasionally rhetorically effective forms of moral universalism. I am referring here to tautologies such as 'murder is wrong' where murder means unlawful killing as well as moral generalizations like those found in the US Declaration of Independence concerning 'We hold these truths to be self-evident, that all men are created equal,' where the self-evidence of the putatively timeless and universal moral claim is very much in the historically situated and depressingly unselfconscious mind of the beholder.

have noted already, Berlin denies that our categories of thought exist *a priori*, and, as a consequence, rejects the idea that they can be understood in boldly ahistorical and ultra-rationalistic terms, including those associated with our apprehension of the external world such as space, time and cause. Berlin is in many ways a Humean empiricist to his very fingertips. As a general rule the furthest he will go in describing our most fundamental patterns of thought is to classify them as 'permanent or semi-permanent', 'stable' or 'fixed'. These are the predicates he tends to reserve for the categories of thought associated with the external world together with what he regards as the more basic and invariant aspects of human nature. But he also claims that there is a necessarily changing set of categories and concepts, albeit far more evident in the sphere of our self-understanding, that is much more susceptible to variation and change. These are the categories of thought he typically describes as 'malleable', 'fluid', 'less permanent' or 'less fixed'. The main point here is that while all our patterns of thought (scientific and non-scientific) are necessarily contingent rather than logically necessary, some are far more ephemeral and situated than others. And the two key determining factors at play here are history and culture. As he states:

> Kant, in his doctrine of our knowledge of the external world, taught that the categories through which we saw it were identical for all sentient beings, permanent and unalterable; and indeed this is what made our world one, and communication possible. But some of those who thought about history, morals, aesthetics did see change and difference: what differed was not so much the empirical content of what these successive civilisations saw or heard or thought as the basic patterns in which they perceived them, the models in terms of which they conceived them, the category-spectacles through which they viewed them. ... Some of these [models, spectacles, categories] are as old as human experience itself; others are more transient. With the more transient, the philosopher's problem takes on a more dynamic and historical aspect. (CC2 10–11)

This passage provides a clear window into Berlin's historicized view of our more permanent and not so permanent patterns of thought. It draws our attention, in particular, to his conviction that the task of the philosopher is not just to register the more stable and universal concepts and categories that shape our grasp of the external and human world, but also to pay close attention to more malleable and normatively contested patterns of thought that are in turn more susceptible to historical change and cultural variation. For example, the ancient Athenians may have invented democracy, but their understanding of that particular form of government is very different from ours. Being sensitive to the possible historical and normative continuities and discontinuities between ancient and modern democracies is one of the principal tasks of the political philosopher. The same applies, of course, to other basic and general concepts and values such as justice, love, freedom, wisdom, mercy and so forth. Given the vicissitudes of time and chance and the interaction between our patterns of thought and history, we can never just assume that long-past epochs or remote cultures use similar concepts in the same way. Semantic equivalence does not denote substantive continuity.

Philosophers, particularly moral and political philosophers, need to be acutely aware when they are analysing ethically rich concepts like piety, honour, natural rights, freedom, toleration, sincerity, nationalism and so on, that their meaning and relevance may not only be peculiar to certain historical epochs and cultures but that their very possibility may not have even entered the moral or imaginative consciousness of earlier forms of Western society, let alone non-Western cultures. In other words, there is no reason to assume – and many reasons and much historical and anthropological evidence to doubt – that our concepts and categories, especially the more ethically loaded ideals and values, possess some vital and invariable essence that persists through time and space. This insight inevitably raises the concern that Berlin's philosophical anthropology is vulnerable to relativism. Again, we will discuss this specific matter in more detail later on, but it may be helpful at this juncture to say something of a preliminary nature on the matter.

Berlin's philosophical anthropology recognizes and accommodates the more uncontroversial insights of cultural and historical relativism. Among these is the virtual bromide that we are products of our time and place. But Berlin's thought also incorporates the less obvious relativist lesson that history and culture have an immeasurable impact on the very concepts and categories found in our own and other times and cultures. This is hardly surprising, once we give up the hyper-rationalist yet still widespread view that human nature can be understood ahistorically. It also explains why the past can be such a foreign and unassimilable country, and why the ways of other cultures, including cultures or subcultures within our own society, can often seem both strange and even impenetrable. How could things be otherwise when we consider the porousness of human life to the peculiar forces of whatever cultural and historical milieu in which it finds itself? But Berlin would also want to insist that there are non-relativist limits to the difference that history and culture make. And the reason why he felt there are such limits is based largely on his transcendental conception of the categories of human understanding. At the very bedrock of our more anthropocentrically centred patterns of thought is, he argues, a minimal conception of human nature without which the idea of what it means to be human would vanish and never get off the ground. These are the elemental and elementary traits, that we have referred to already, such as a desire for self-preservation and avoidance of danger and pain, a sense of vulnerability and need for solidarity, a basic understanding of right and wrong, strength of will, limited altruism, a minimal level of sanity, and so forth, without which we would remain mutually unintelligible. As he remarks in one of his less well-known papers, 'Is a Philosophy of History Possible?':

> The categories and concepts in terms of which situations and events and processes are described and explained in such [historical] accounts are, to a large extent, imprecise; they have a so-called 'open texture'. They are the everyday notions common to mankind at large, related to the permanent interests of men as such. They may be modified at particular periods, in particular countries, by particular circumstances, but all of them are species of basic human attitudes, outlooks, goals, beliefs. Without some degree of understanding – indeed sharing of – these concepts, it would not be possible to understand either men or history at all. (CC2 320–1) [10]

Does this preclude the possibility of societies emerging without even these apparently minimal elements? Of course not. No such contingent possibilities can be ruled out. But Berlin felt that it is unlikely that such societies have been very numerous, or if they have, that they would have survived for very long. And if and where they did or could exist, such phenomena would hardly be a reason to abandon the notion of humanity, just as the discovery of a community of flat-earthers would hardly give us reason to give up our trust in the inductive method of science. The more significant challenge facing Berlin is whether his normative theory of human nature is persuasive enough for his claim that there are objective or non-arbitrary limits to what counts as failing within 'the human horizon'. Either way, the spirit and rationale of Berlin's opposition to wholesale cultural and historical relativism is captured in the following excerpt from his essay 'Alleged Relativism in Eighteenth-Century Thought':

> The last possibility is an all-pervasive scepticism: what is beyond the ken of our culture cannot be known or speculated about; *ignoramus et ignorabimus* [We do not know and we shall never know]; history and anthropology may be pure culture-conditioned fictions. So, indeed, they may; but why should we attend to this wild piece of subjective idealism? The onus of proof is on the sceptics; to say that the past is completely unknowable robs the concept of the past of all meaning: it is thus a strictly self-annihilating notion. (CTH2 90)

The next step in our excavation of Berlin's philosophical outlook involves an exploration of his debt to another long-dead thinker, in this case the

---

[10] This paper was originally published as part of Isaiah Berlin and others, 'Is a Philosophy of History Possible?' in Yirmiahu Yovel ed. *Philosophy of History and Action* (1978: Magnes Press, Dordrecht, Boston, London and Jerusalem) and then republished in CC2 318–25.

comparatively obscure pre-Kantian Neapolitan thinker, Giambattista Vico (1668–1744). Familiarizing ourselves with Vico's influence on Berlin will deepen our understanding of Berlin's philosophical vision in a number of ways. In the first place, it will serve to explain why Berlin became convinced that the sources of knowledge available to us are not limited to the exact and empirical sciences. This insight helped reinforce and deepen Berlin's belief that positivism relies on an oversimplified and, in the end, crudely reductionist view of knowledge and objectivity. In addition, Vico's writings revealed to Berlin that the humanities, and especially history, provide us with a fertile and largely untapped source of understanding and truth. There is a deep sense in which Berlin's outlook finds a distinct echo in Hayden White's remark that 'when you want to ask the question … "what is man?" all you've got is history'.[11] And finally, Berlin himself explicitly singled out Vico's importance in his intellectual autobiography, 'The Pursuit of the Ideal', for the discovery of historical or cultural pluralism, that is, the idea that the past cannot be understood properly if we view it in terms of existing in some eternal present (CTH2 17–18). Put more positively, Vico showed that long-distant epochs and societies possessed their own unique and often incommensurable conceptions of the world and that therefore one of the chief lessons of history is to recognize the ineliminable but not necessarily inaccessible otherness of the past.

---

[11]Hayden White and Erlend Rogne, 'The Aims of Interpretation Is to Create Perplexity in the Face of the Real: Hayden White in conversation with Erlend Rogne', *History and Theory* 48 (2009): 71.

4 THE HUMANISTIC TURN

It has become something of a commonplace within analytic philosophy that there exists a serious and arguably unresolvable tension between the traditional notion of truth and the supposed insights of historicism. Put simply, how can the putatively timeless objectivity and universality of truth be reconciled with the competing idea that the truth is itself historically contingent? Unless we are willing to accept some variant of the Hegelian notion that Truth or Spirit (*Geist*) is literally unfolding in harmony with the inexorable and triumphal march of history, we seem to be left with one of two mutually exclusive options: either we argue that truth or rationality is in some way immune to the vagaries of time and place or we accept that everything, including truth and reason, is historically conditioned through and through. The former has an unerring tendency to lead to positivism while the latter invites unqualified relativism and self-defeating epistemological chaos.

The seemingly endless debate between positivism and relativism since the time of Hegel (1770–1831) has by now become distinctly stale and, as one distinguished philosopher remarked, it is a debate that we seem doomed to repeat like some sort of neurotic symptom.[1] However, I believe Berlin is among a number of notable thinkers who point the way beyond this unsatisfactory conceptual impasse. He articulates his suggestion most clearly and grippingly in his essay 'The Divorce between the Sciences and the Humanities' (AC2 101–39). It is an approach that builds on his reading of Kant but which has its roots in the ideas of the earlier Neapolitan thinker, Giambattista Vico.

As we have observed briefly already, Berlin is deeply sceptical of several core assumptions undergirding the Western philosophical tradition. These include the ideas that every genuine and important question has a uniquely true answer,

---

[1] Hilary Putnam 'Beyond Historicism', in his *Realism and Reason: Philosophical Papers*, Vol. 3 (1983: Cambridge University Press, Cambridge), 287–303.

that the method of discovering the answer to each and every genuine question is ultimately the same across all cognitive fields of human enquiry and, finally, that the answers once discovered hold true eternally and universally. While these three assumptions have informed the mainstream philosophical tradition in one shape or another since Plato, they were especially intensely felt and articulated during the European Enlightenment of the seventeenth and eighteenth centuries. This was the era in which the naturalistic world view came into its ascendency and in which its claims to knowledge and truth seemed as infallible as its path to progress appeared irresistible.

An assumption that acquired particular force and prestige during this period centred on the idea that, as Berlin puts it, 'the method which leads to correct solutions to all genuine problems is rational in character; and is, in essence, if not in detailed application, identical in all fields' (AC2 102). The method being referred to encompasses that of induction and deduction. Moreover, the development and incremental progress of this new, seemingly all-conquering way of making sense of the physical world was so rapid that most informed contemporary thinkers felt that it was only a matter of time before the same level of progress could be made in the world of human affairs.

It was precisely this conviction, the idea that human nature could be fully and objectively comprehended, analysed, measured and, if necessary, manipulated in much the same way as the physical world that Berlin judges as one of the great intellectual errors of Enlightenment thinking. The error has two major sides. In the first place, it suffers from a peculiar but fatal kind of inverted anthropomorphism. In its understandable and well-intended urge to apply the scientific method to the sphere of human thought and action, it makes the basic mistake of supposing that we could and should be treated, as Berlin states, 'on a par with rivers and plants and stones' (PSM 343). What the Enlightenment forgot or missed was that, notwithstanding the fact that we are physical objects that form part of the natural world and are interpretable as such, we also possess inherent traits that are not reducible to or even registered by the physicalist world view. It is hardly surprising therefore that the so-called science of man ended up producing a hopelessly partial and impoverished model of the self, not least the optimistic belief in the perfectibility of humankind.

But it's the other side or dimension of this severely non-anthropocentric and hyper-rationalistic error that is far more telling for our purposes. In fact, it wasn't so much a factual or descriptive error as a failure of the imagination. The fatal flaw lies in being blind to the non-scientific sources of understanding and knowledge. These sources spring primarily from our own internally generated thoughts and feelings about ourselves and others rather than from our cool and clinical ideas and observations about the external world of physical objects, including, of course, the purely physical manifestations of human beings. Rather paradoxically, our own internally driven view of ourselves and others is more direct and has the sense of being more intuitively sure-footed and even objective than the more empirical and measurable type of knowledge concerned with the natural world which science prides itself in producing incrementally. For instance, we may not be able to demonstrably prove or quantify a person's love or hatred towards someone or something but we know or have an intuitive sense of what love and hatred feel and look like. Similarly, our capacity or motivation to provide a scientific theory of music, literature or art may be limited and error prone but that doesn't inhibit our appreciation of a sonata, poem or painting. And our relative ignorance concerning the internal workings of the brain does not prevent us from having deeply complex and nuanced conscious and self-conscious experiences. As Berlin comments:

> A man could understand fully his own intellectual or poetical construction, a work of art or a plan, because he had himself made it, and that it was therefore transparent to him: everything in it had been created by his intellect and his imagination. ... But the world – nature – had not been made by men: therefore only God, who had made it, could know it through and through. ... Men could know 'from the inside' only what they had made themselves, and nothing else. The greater the man-made element in any object of knowledge, the more transparent to human vision it will be; the greater the ingredient of external nature, the more opaque and impenetrable to human understanding. There was an impassable gulf between the man-made and the natural: the constructed and the given. All provinces of knowledge could be classified along this scale of relative intelligibility. (PSM 341–2)

According to Berlin, what marks out Vico as 'a man of genius' is his discovery that history provides us with a domain of knowledge which we can only know internally or humanistically, something that he says St. Augustine (354–430 AD) had implicitly acknowledged when he said 'one could know fully only what one had oneself made' (PSM 341). The following passage gives a clear impression of what exactly Berlin thought Vico's bold step adds up to:

> Human history did nor consist merely of things and events and their compresences and sequences (including of human organisms viewed as natural objects), as the external world did; it was the story of human activities, of what men did and thought and suffered, of what they strove for and aimed at, accepted, rejected, conceived, imagined, of what their feelings were directed at. It was concerned, therefore, with motives, purposes, hopes fears, loves, and hatreds, jealousies, ambitions, outlooks and visions of reality; with the ways of seeing, the ways of acting and creating, of individuals and groups. These activities we knew directly because we were involved in them as actors, not spectators. There was a sense, therefore, in which we knew more about ourselves

than we knew about the external world; when we studied, let us say, Roman law, or Roman institutions, we were not contemplating objects in nature, of whose purposes, or whether they had any, we could know nothing. We had to ask ourselves what these Romans were at, what they strove to do, how they lived and thought, what kind of relationship with other men they were anxious to promote or frustrate. ... There was, therefore, a clear sense in which our knowledge was superior, at least in kind, about intentional behaviours – that is, action – to our knowledge of the movement and position of bodies in space, the field of the magnificent triumphs of the seventeenth-century science. What was opaque to us when we contemplated the external world was, if not wholly transparent, yet surely far more so when we contemplated ourselves. It was therefore a perverse kind of self-denial to apply the rules and laws of physics or of the other natural sciences to the world of mind and will and feeling; for by doing this we would be gratuitously debarring ourselves from much that we could know. (PSM 342–3)

My reason for quoting this passage at length is that it contains several insights that Berlin took to heart and let inform his own philosophical outlook. The main one centres on something we have already alluded to, that there are rich and reliable sources of knowledge beyond those of the exact (e.g. logic, mathematics) and empirical (e.g. physics, chemistry, biology) sciences. Moreover, our understanding of ourselves and others is more directly and objectively felt than our understanding of the natural world, most of which is learned and accepted on the basis of testimony. There is even a sense in which our awareness as well as our knowledge of ourselves may strike us as superior to our knowledge of the external world. What Vico therefore manages to do is to offer us a fresh perspective that not only liberates us from the still influential scientistic idea that scientific knowledge is the only form of knowledge available but also points us in the direction of where to find other compelling forms of understanding and truth, namely, in the past. But before we explore the other substantive lessons that Berlin derives from Vico's interpretation of the past, it is worth pausing briefly to consider the philosophical significance of Vico's discovery.

The assertion that that there are various sources of knowledge is more significant than it may at first seem. We may well find the view that our non-scientific understanding of ourselves and others can qualify as knowledge reassuring but it does raise a number of puzzling questions: How do we acquire such knowledge? How do we differentiate between real, objective knowledge and mere prejudice in the sphere of human affairs? What do we do when the insights of humanistic understanding conflict with the findings of natural science? While these questions raise a host of difficult metaphysical, epistemological and moral problems, what is perhaps most striking about them is that they can be legitimately asked at all. No doubt many philosophers would dismiss such questions as pseudo-questions on the grounds that our own internally focused understanding of ourselves and others does not qualify as knowledge in any objective or scientifically demonstrable sense of that term. They may have a point but what's instructive about Vico's allegedly 'radical step' is that it doesn't confront us as self-evidently wrong or implausible. Indeed, the moment we are prepared to recognize that Vico may have been onto something, Berlin's pluralist view of philosophy makes a great deal more sense. For it opens up the possibility of seeing philosophy as primarily a humanistic rather than a quasi-scientific discipline, a subject that is or rather should be more concerned with what Socrates regarded as the large and vital questions of human life. The other thing about Vico's emphasis on the internal, emphatically subjective sources of knowledge is that it coheres with Kant's later conception of the philosophical enterprise. One of the core aspects of Kant's Copernican edifice hinges on the principle that our understanding of the world contains an unavoidably subjective dimension, which has the effect of making philosophical room for our freedom and morality and, more generally, for how we interpret ourselves independently of (but not necessarily in contradiction with) the particular findings of natural science.

Returning to the question of what other specific insights can be derived from Vico's view of history, the answer for Berlin is essentially twofold. The first prong relates to the Vichian concept of *fantasia* or imagination and the second focuses on his account of the radical difference and often incommensurability of past societies and cultures.

Briefly, *fantasia* or imagination – what Gottfried Herder (1744–1803) would later call *einfühlung* (empathy) and Wilhelm Dilthey (1833–1911), later still, refer to as *verstehen* (understanding) – is what brings the past and long-dead thinkers to historical life. It refers to our capacity for imaginative insight, to a certain empathic understanding that we normally associate with novelists and poets than with scientifically minded thinkers. It is, Vico felt, only by self-consciously entering into the *mentalité* of a distant culture or the haecceity of a long-dead thinker and his thoughts and then endevouring to reconstitute how they thought and felt that we learn not just how strange much of the past is but what the ties, however tenuous, are that bind us together. As Berlin remarks, '[Vico's] deepest belief was that what men have made, other men can understand' (TCE2 62). The understanding we derive from reading or writing imaginative – but not imagined – reconstructions of the past, including what the French historian, Marc Bloch (1886–1944), called 'the thrill of learning singular things', amounts to a form of knowledge, albeit not one that is a species of scientific knowledge. What we have here is a way of grasping aspects of our lives that are not just neglected by scientific forms of explanation but have no real place in their world view. Vico distinguished between what he called *verum* and *certum*, where the former refers to knowledge that can be logically demonstrated while the latter denotes a different type of knowledge that is based on mankind's direct subjective experience of the world; the former can produce an X-ray but only the latter can give us a portrait of an individual (TCE2 138). Berlin was fond of elucidating the meaning and significance of Vico's distinction by comparing and contrasting it with one introduced much later by his Oxford colleague, Gilbert Ryle, namely, between 'knowing that' and 'knowing how':

> Vico's *fantasia* is indispensable to his conception of historical knowledge; it is unlike the knowledge that Caesar is dead, or that Rome was not built in a day, or that thirteen is a prime number, or that a week has seven days; nor yet is it like knowledge of how to ride a bicycle or engage in statistical research or win a battle. It is more like knowing what it is to be poor, to belong to a nation, to be a revolutionary, to be converted to a religion, to fall in love, to be seized by nameless terror, to be delighted by a work of art. (CTH2 65)[2]

He is even prepared to interpret Vico's concept of *fantasia* as a precursor of Kant's transcendental method on the basis that it enables

> a kind of transcendental deduction ... of historical truth. It is a method of arriving not, as hitherto, at an unchanging reality via its changing appearances, but at a changing reality – men's history – through its systematically changing modes of expression. (TCE2 15)

Vico's proto-Kantian recognition of the deep subjectivity of our perceptions of reality, the idea that the key to unlocking the past lies in imaginatively appreciating how the basic patterns of thought peculiar to distant cultures generated their own distinctive yet intelligible conceptions of the world, brings us to the third major aspect of Vico's significance for Berlin. It relates to something which emerges from the type of history conducted by Vico in his *Nuovo Scienza*.

One of the great, if unintentional, discoveries to emerge from Vico's boldly imaginative reconstruction of the past is centred on what Berlin refers to as cultural

---

[2] Here the allusion to Gilbert Ryle is implicit, but Berlin refers explicitly to Ryle's distinction in relation to Vico in his earlier essay, 'Vico's Theory of Knowledge and its Sources' (TCE2 163). There is also a passage in Berlin's essay 'The Concept of Scientific History' which vividly articulates his understanding of this third dimension of knowledge resulting from *fantasia*: Capacity for understanding people's characters, knowledge of ways in which they are likely to react to one another, ability to 'enter into' their motives, their principles, the movement of their thoughts and feelings (and this applies to the behaviour of masses or to the growth of cultures) – these are the talents that are indispensable to historians, but not (or not to such a degree) to natural scientists. The capacity for knowing which is like knowing someone's character or face, is as essential to historians as knowledge of facts. (CC2 174–5)For a perceptive and balanced account of the influence of Vico's ideas on the evolution of Berlin's thought, see Joseph Mali, *The Legacy of Vico in Modern Cultural History* (2012: Cambridge University Press, Cambridge), 195–256.

pluralism – 'a panorama of a variety of cultures, the pursuit of different, and sometimes incompatible, ways of life, ideals, standards of value' (CTH2 68). Berlin thought that Vico's highly original account of Homer's genius provided a particularly vivid example of the pluralistic perceptions that could be gleaned from reading his *Nuovo Scienza*. Unlike his contemporaries, who were fond of debating among themselves ad nauseam that the ancients were better poets than the moderns, or vice versa, but who all shared the common assumption that there exist timeless and universal criteria of aesthetic excellence, Vico developed a very different and prescient take on the matter, one that sought to combine the specificity and concreteness of philology with the more abstract, seemingly free-floating insights of historical and imaginative speculation. Rather than indulge in chauvinistic and crudely anachronistic judgements about the past, Vico displayed his genius by considering what makes Homer's epic poems such singularly sublime works of art. The verdict that emerges is that only a society as peculiarly violent and yet densely imaginative as pre-Socratic Greece could have produced a poet of the unique calibre and range of Homer: 'No placid, refined, or meek philosopher could have naturally produced Homer's statements, similes, and descriptions.'[3] Vico's analysis suggests that the parlour game of comparing the poetry of the ancient world with that of the modern on the basis of some ahistorical scale of value made no sense whatsoever since each culture gives birth to masterpieces that belong to it and it alone. What struck Berlin most forcibly about Vico's work is the sense that history is the story of unredeemable loss as well as undeniable gain. As Berlin observes, Vico may have lived in a far more humane, knowledgeable and rational age than Homer, but for those very reasons the modern self has lost its power to produce or convincingly revive the kind of elemental poetry characteristic of the *Iliad* and the *Odyssey*. As Berlin then adds:

> There is something boldly original about a thinker who, in so self-satisfied a civilisation as that into which Vico was born, one which saw itself as a vast improvement on the brutality, absurdity, ignorance of earlier times, dared maintain that an unapproachably sublime poem [Homer's] could have been produced only by a cruel, savage and, to later generations, morally repellent age. This amounts to a denial of the very possibility of a harmony of all the excellences in an ideal world. From this it follows that to judge the attainments of any one age by applying to them a single absolute criterion – that of the critics and theorists of a later period – not only is unhistorical and anachronistic, but rests on a fallacy, the assumption of the existence of timeless standards – the ideal values of an ideal world – when in fact some of the most admired works of

---

[3] From Chapter 5: 'Philosophical Proofs for the Discovery of the True Homer', Giambattista Vico, *New Science* (1999 edn: Penguin, London), 366–72.

men are organically bound up with a culture some aspects of which we may – perhaps cannot help but – condemn, even while claiming to understand why it is that men situated as these must have felt, thought and acted as they did. (CTH2 70–1)

What this commentary brings out is arguably Berlin's greatest debt to Vico, notably, the discovery that the ideal of a timelessly perfect society makes little or no philosophical or historical sense. What's abundantly evident in Vico's exposure of the radical discontinuities between the past and present is the implicit avowal that utopia is not just de facto unattainable, but conceptually and morally bankrupt. Of course, Vico's alleged uncovering of the truth of deep cultural incommensurability or pluralism goes against one of the main currents of Western thought, namely, the outlook associated with what Berlin refers to as *philosophia perennis*. This term stands for the notion that there is some unchanging and ahistorical perspective to which we can appeal in determining the nature of truth, knowledge and moral goodness and that, in the final analysis, all objective human values and ideals form part of an intellectually coherent and ethically harmonious system of thought. The notion of perennial philosophy was very much embraced by the Enlightenment, which helps explain why the *philosophes* looked down on the genre of historical writings exemplified in Vico's *Nuovo Scienza* as 'a vermin that kills great works' since it served to conceal and distract us from what they regarded as the timeless and more profound truths of human nature.[4] According to Berlin, Vico was instrumental in challenging this hitherto sacred – and still very influential – philosophical assumption by pointing out that genuine engagement with the past revealed the opposite is the case. There are no eternally and universally true answers to the so-called perennial questions of human life. Rather, different epochs and cultures have different views about what count as philosophical problems and which ones are more significant than others with the result that the deeper as well as the less permanent traits of humankind must be understood historically and not statically or in any kind of narrowly a priori fashion.

Vico's alleged uncovering of cultural pluralism raises the spectre of relativism, and the more specific question of whether there is anything that separates cultural pluralism from ethical relativism. Berlin is adamant that cultural and, indeed, value pluralism are not variants of relativism. He distinguishes pluralism from relativism on epistemological, historical and ethical levels, a distinction that is permitted and even required by his conception of the transcendental categories and concepts that he argues form the basis of our understanding of humanity. As we have seen, the underlying patterns of thought associated with our grasp of the

---

[4] Quoted (from Voltaire) in Anthony Grafton's introduction to Giambattista Vico's, *New Science* (1999 edn: Penguin, London), xii.

human world are necessarily subject-dependent and value-laden just as the very concept of our own being is. And our concept of the self is ultimately made up of epistemological, ethical and anthropological presuppositions and values which are inextricably commingled with each other. Berlin's version of pluralism embraces this more capacious and value-rich concept of the self in a way that most versions of relativism cannot, if they are to remain faithful to their own core meta-ethical position. As a result, Berlin is not blocked from arguing that pluralism leaves open the possibility of inter- and intra-cultural communication and understanding without postulating any form of moral authoritarianism or uniformity. He makes this point eloquently in his late essay 'The Pursuit of the Ideal':

> Communities may resemble each other in many respects, but the Greeks differ from Lutheran Germans, the Chinese differ from both; what they strive after, and what they fear or worship are scarcely ever similar. This view has been called cultural or moral relativism. … It is not relativism. Members of one culture can, by the force of imaginative insight, understand (what Vico called *entrare*) the values, the ideals, the forms of life of another culture or society, even those remote in time or space. They may find these values unacceptable, but if they open their minds sufficiently they can grasp how one might be a full human being, with whom one could communicate, and at the same time live in the light of values widely different from one's own, but which nevertheless one can see to be values, ends of life, by the realisation of which men could be fulfilled. (CTH2 10–11)

For Berlin there is a coherent if messy middle ground between the simplicities and distortions of the rather bloodless concept of man imagined by Platonic and Enlightenment rationalism and the uncompromisingly ethnocentric idea of 'other mores, other beasts' or, more politely, 'one radically incommensurable tribe among others' canvassed by cultural, historical and moral relativists. In this respect, his version of cultural pluralism has much in common with Clifford Geertz's notion of interpretive anthropology.[5] Berlin is at one with Geertz in his view that while there is no such thing as human nature without culture or history, it is also the case that culture (or history) does not exhaust our humanity. Geertz articulates this more plausible, hybrid position as well as the absurdity of facile moral and cultural universalism (and relativism) pithily in his classic work *The Interpretation of Cultures*:

> The notion that unless a cultural phenomenon is empirically universal it cannot reflect anything about the nature of man is about as logical as the notion that

---

[5]Berlin was clearly impressed with Geertz's work *The Interpretation of Cultures* (1983: Fontana Press, London) (hereafter TIC) which he explicitly mentions and endorses in his essay 'Alleged Relativism in Eighteenth-Century European Thought' (CTH2 73 & 86).

because sickle-cell anaemia is, fortunately, not universal, it cannot tell us anything about human genetic processes. (TIC 44)

What both Berlin's cultural pluralism and Geertz's interpretive anthropology share is a tacit acknowledgement that there is no inherent contradiction between the claim that there is such a thing as a common humanity and the equally valid claim that our concept of humanity is sufficiently permeable and inclusive to allow of a very large but not unlimited variety. Whether Berlin provides a coherent and sustainable *via media* between moral universalism on the one hand and ethical relativism on the other will be discussed in more detail further on. Suffice to say at this point that a great deal hinges on whether his conception of pluralism and the version of liberalism he believes it engenders can be historically and philosophically vindicated.

A final and often overlooked feature of Berlin's debt to Vico is the recognition that the goal of providing an exhaustive and value-neutral account of ourselves and of the past is unreachable. And the reason is that we ourselves, like our ancestors, are culturally and historically situated beings whose understanding of the world we are a part of is and can only ever be deeply partial and limited. As participative and fallible actors on the world's stage rather than impartial and omniscient spectators we remain at best only partly and imperfectly conscious of the deep and largely hidden mental frameworks that enable but also colour – and inevitably constrain – our view of the world. As one of Berlin's commentators states, trying to analyse our categories of thought in any kind of absolute and scientific way 'is like trying to make the base of the mountain balance on its summit; it lies several levels below and beyond the reach of causal concepts' (PSM2 xxviii).

Berlin's argument that we are unable to fully fathom let alone validate our most basic mental frameworks prefigures much of the postmodern preoccupation with the seemingly ineradicable fact that we have no way of occupying some ahistorical or non-situational space beyond our own world view for the simple reason that no such space exists. This is what Berlin means when he says that the Archimedean perspective is permanently unavailable to us:

> Most of the certainties on which our lives are founded … the vast majority of the types of reasoning on which our beliefs rest, or by which we should seek to justify them … are not reducible to formal deductive or inductive schemata, or a combination of them. … The web is too complex, the elements too many and not, to say the least, easily isolated and tested one by one … we accept the total texture, compounded as it is out of literally countless strands … without the possibility, even in principle, of any test for it in its totality. For the total texture is what we begin and end with. There is no Archimedean point outside it whence we can survey the whole and pronounce upon it … the sense of the

general texture of experience … is itself not open to inductive or deductive reasoning: for both these methods rest upon it. (CC2 149–50)

One cannot separate or sufficiently distance the explanans from the explanandum, which is precisely what would need to happen to sit in Solomonic judgement on our own conceptual framework, let alone on those of the distant past. In summary, the view from nowhere is forever beyond the powers of human reason even if we can't help ourselves from believing we can and should strive to reach it.

In the final paragraph of his essay 'The Divorce between the Sciences and the Humanities', Berlin makes the following bold claim:

> The great cleavage between the provinces of natural sciences and the humanities was, for the first time, made, or at least revealed, for better or for worse, by Giambattista Vico. Thereby he started a great debate of which the end is not in sight.
>
> Where did this central insight originate? Did the idea of what a culture is, and what it is to understand it in its unity and variety, and its likeness, but, above all, its unlikeness, to other cultures, which undermines the doctrine of the identity of civilization and scientific progress conceived as the cumulative growth of knowledge – did this spring fully armed like Pallas Athene out of his head? Who, before 1725, had such thoughts? … These are problems on which, even now, not enough research has been done by historians of ideas. Yet, fascinating as they are, their solution seems to me to be less important than the central discoveries themselves; most of all, the notion that the only way of achieving any degree of self-understanding is by systematically retracing our steps, historically, psychologically and above all, anthropologically, through the stages of social growth that follow empirically discoverable paths, or, if that is too absolute a term, trends or tendencies with whose workings we are acquainted in our own mental life, but moving to no single, universal goal; each a world on its own, yet having enough in common with its successors, with whom it forms a continuous line of recognisably human experience, not to be unintelligible to their inhabitants. Only in this fashion, if Vico is right, can we hope to understand the unity of human history – the links that connect our own 'magnificent times' to our squalid beginnings in the 'the greatest forest of life'. (AC2 139)

Berlin's interpretation of Vico's originality raises a number of basic questions about the historical and philosophical basis of his own outlook. The first of these concerns the epistemological status of his claims about Vico's 'originality' or 'discovery'. More specifically, is it sustainable or even possible to distinguish between the historical identity and philosophical validity of past 'discoveries' such as Vico's claimed cultural pluralism? And if it is coherent, is there not a straightforward tension between such a distinction and Berlin's acknowledgement that our assumptions and beliefs are historically and culturally conditioned? Another question centres on the plausibility of Berlin's appropriation of Vico as a forerunner of cultural pluralism. How seriously should we take Berlin's claim that 'my political pluralism is a product of reading Vico'? For while we may well grant that Berlin read Vico as a proto-pluralist, can we really believe that this is how Vico saw himself? In other words, is there any real historical accountability and substance at work in Berlin's approach to the history of ideas? And finally, does Berlin's interpretation of Vico and of other past thinkers reveal a genuinely historically minded view of philosophy or does it have more in common with the sort of ahistorical and anachronistic readings of past thinkers characteristic of so much Anglophone 'histories' of philosophy?

Rather than address these questions by considering Berlin's treatment of Vico, we shall change focus and seek to answer them by analysing Berlin's celebrated interpretation of the infamous Renaissance political theorist, Niccolò Machiavelli. My reason for focusing on Machiavelli rather than Vico is threefold. Firstly, Berlin states that Machiavelli was even more central to his philosophical formation since he felt that it was the Florentine thinker who discovered the even deeper truth of value pluralism. Secondly, one of the most eminent historians of early modern European intellectual history, Quentin Skinner (1940), has devoted much of his professional life to the study of Machiavelli and his thought. Moreover, Skinner is among the founders of the Cambridge school of intellectual history which is dedicated to recovering the contextual meaning of the ideas of past thinkers. So investigating Berlin's view of Machiavelli's alleged originality in the light of Skinner's pioneering work on Renaissance political thought should give us an authoritative perspective from which to judge its historical accuracy and philosophical coherence. Thirdly, carrying out such an analysis forms a crucial step in our ultimate goal of identifying the validity of Berlin's pluralist defence of liberalism.

5 TAKING HISTORY SERIOUSLY

The idea that philosophy can flourish without having to bother about its past – let alone the vastly broader non-philosophical past – is one that has proved remarkably robust and prevalent within the analytic tradition of philosophy. Roughly from the outset of the twentieth-century analytical philosophers have tended to operate on the assumption that doing philosophy and studying the history of the subject are two separate, or at least eminently separable, intellectual pursuits. This attitude is nicely captured by Willard van Orman Quine's (1908–2000) jibe that 'there are two sorts of people interested in philosophy, those interested in philosophy and those interested in the history of philosophy'.[1] In other words, real philosophy, the sort that is serious about solving live philosophical issues, can and ideally should be done without referring to the works of previous philosophers, especially long-dead, obscure ones. Those who wish to devote their professional lives to studying the history of the subject, the argument goes, are welcome to do so, but they should be under no illusions that their activity is any other than a primarily antiquarian pursuit that has no significant bearing on the genuine work of contemporary philosophy.

Berlin's philosophical outlook deviates sharply from this dismissive attitude to history. He does not share the view that philosophy, and particularly practical philosophy, can be coherently pursued independently of history or, more specifically, of a certain historical self-awareness which springs from a knowledge and appreciation of the past. But nor is he interested in reading long-dead philosophers in a strictly antiquarian manner. He argues that since so much of our mental architecture is prone to change, and since these changes inform not just what we

---

[1] Attributed to Quine in Alasdair Macintyre 'The Relationship of Philosophy to its Past', in *Philosophy in History: Essays on the Historiography of Philosophy*, ed. Richard Rorty, Quentin Skinner and J. B. Schneewind (1984: Cambridge University Press, Cambridge), 39–40.

believe but how and why we believe the things we do, it is hard to see how philosophy could responsibly view history as superfluous. Once you take Kant's Copernican revolution seriously and then add the Vichian, historicist twist that our regulative categories of thought reflect to a greater or lesser extent the indelible imprint of time and place, the very notion that history could form anything less than a large and indispensable part of the philosophical enterprise becomes unsustainable.

Berlin's method could be described therefore as *doing philosophy historically* or *historically minded philosophy*. As we have seen, he does not see the past as an entirely foreign country without remainder: while acknowledging and even celebrating the pastness of the past, his view of history operates on the basis that long-dead thinkers and their cultures are penetrable in virtue of our most basic and enduring patterns of thought. This is not some bland middle way between the naivety of perennial philosophy and the aridity of antiquarianism. On the contrary, Berlin's approach reflects and exemplifies a commitment to gaining philosophical insight through genuine engagement with the past. Underlying this approach is the idea that history constitutes a necessary, not merely an optional, ingredient of the humanistic philosophical enterprise and, more broadly, of what Alexander Pope called the 'conversation of mankind'.

It is now time to convey in more detail the historical dimension of Berlin's thought. I will do so by focusing on his treatment of a specific thinker, one who was instrumental in the formation of Berlin's own political philosophy. I am referring to the notorious Renaissance political theorist, Niccolò Machiavelli (1469–1527). My reason for taking this approach is twofold: it allows us to grasp the nature and implications of Berlin's version of the history of ideas in more concrete terms. And, secondly, it helps us to get a deeper understanding of the strengths and limitations of his historically minded philosophy by situating it within the wider debate about philosophy's relation, if any, to the past.

Berlin's essay 'The Originality of Machiavelli' sets out to identify the enduring meaning and significance of Machiavelli's political thought: what he originally meant, what he means for us, and the relationship, if any, between the two. According to Berlin's account, the key to interpreting Machiavelli lies in his juxtaposition of pagan and Christian thought. What emerges from seeing him in this light, Berlin argues, is the realization that Machiavelli's originality only partly rests on his decision to side unambiguously and unblushingly with the outlook of the ancients over that of Christianity. By reasserting the heroic values and worldly ideals of classical Rome at the cost of the prevailing God-filled morality of the day, Machiavelli was free to advise rulers to follow the priorities of their principality or state even if this requires violating the dictates of conventional, Christian morality. An aspiring prince or republican government must think and act in accordance with the classical, worldly virtues of courage, ambition, glory, practical wisdom and so forth that are more suited to the arena of politics, and not be unduly hamstrung by compassion, honesty, kindness and what David Hume would later call the 'monkish virtues' of piety, humility and self-denial that are bound up with the Christian morality of individual conscience.² It is precisely the way Machiavelli laid bare the objective and brutal conflict between these distinct and conflicting moral codes or systems of thought, those of ancient Rome and of Christendom, that chiefly distinguishes his contribution to the Western tradition of political thought. The crucial breakthrough being attributed to Machiavelli is not the traditional one that he separated politics from morality but that he favoured the worldly ethic of the ancients over the divine morality of Christianity on the grounds that it was far more suitable to the concerns and priorities of a successful ruler.

Berlin then proceeds to make the much stronger claim that Machiavelli's writings gave birth, albeit unintentionally, to the idea that ethical values do not live in objective harmony with each other. As he remarks:

> But the question that his writings have dramatised, if not for himself, then for others in the centuries that followed, is this: what reason have we for supposing that justice and mercy, humility and *virtù*, happiness and knowledge, glory and liberty, magnificence and sanctity, will always coincide, or indeed be compatible at all? (AC2 90)

Berlin gradually expands this far more ambitious and contestable line of interpretation by identifying what he sees as the truly iconoclastic dimension of Machiavelli's originality:

> Machiavelli's cardinal achievement is his uncovering of an insoluble dilemma, the planting of a permanent question mark in the path of posterity. It stems from the *de facto* recognition that ends equally ultimate, equally sacred, may contradict each other, that entire systems of value may come into collision without possibility of rational arbitration, and that this happens not merely in exceptional circumstances, as a result of abnormality or accident or error – the clash of Antigone and Creon or the story of Tristan – but (this was surely new) as part of the normal human situation. (AC2 94)

Berlin is careful not to push the argument too far by seeking to enlist Machiavelli as a conscious forerunner of moral or value pluralism:

> I do not mean that Machiavelli explicitly asserts that there is a pluralism or even dualism of values between which conscious choices must be made. But this follows from the contrast he draws between the conduct he admires and that

---

²*An Enquiry Concerning the Principles of Morals*, § 9, Conclusion, Part I, 219, ed. L.A. Selby-Bigge and P.H. Nidditch (1975 edn: Oxford University Press, Oxford).

which he condemns. He seems to take for granted the obvious superiority of classical civic virtue, and brushes aside Christian values, as well as conventional morality, with a disparaging or patronising sentence or two. (AC2 95)

But he is adamant that, unwittingly or not, Machiavelli hit upon a deep and pervasive truth not just about political life but about the state of human existence as a whole, a truth that is diametrically opposed to one of the more sacred and potent assumptions of Western thought,

> namely, that somewhere in the past or the future, in this world or the next, in the church or the laboratory, in the speculations of the metaphysicians or the findings of the social scientist, or in the uncorrupted heart of the simple good man, there is to be found the final solution of the question of how men should live. (AC2 95-6)

According to Berlin, the philosophical significance of Machiavelli's thought thus resides in his sowing the seed of a permanent, potentially shattering doubt about the theoretical coherence as well as the practical feasibility of the underlying monistic credo of Western civilization. Berlin ends his essay by arguing that two key implications – one negative and one positive – follow from Machiavelli's unleashing, albeit unwittingly, a hugely destructive salvo against the unquestioned acceptance and philosophical force of moral monism. The negative one consists in undermining

> the sense of certainty that there is somewhere a hidden treasure – a final solution to our ills – and that some path must lead to it (for, in principle, it must be discoverable); or else, to alter the image, the conviction that the fragments constituted by our beliefs and habits are all pieces of a jigsaw puzzle, which (since there is an *a priori* guarantee for this) can, in principle, be solved, so that it is only because of lack of skill or stupidity or bad fortune that we have not so far succeeded in discovering the solution, whereby all interests will be brought into harmony – this fundamental belief of Western political thought has been severely shaken. (AC2 97-8)

And there is the more positive effect of Machiavelli's work, namely, its unwitting opening of the path to empiricism, pluralism and toleration in the wake of its irreverent doubts about the prevailing assumption that every ethical conflict is in principle, if not in practice, rationally resolvable and that all objective moral values are ultimately compatible and commensurable. For if this age-old and hitherto untouchable tenet of Western thought is not just unattainable in practice but also indefensible in principle, as Berlin is convinced it is, we are faced with a very different vista. Machiavelli's 'scandalous' writings begin the process of awakening humankind to the possibility of an ethically principled rather than a merely pragmatic foundation for moral diversity, toleration and liberalism:

> This was a major turning point, and its intellectual consequences, wholly unintended by its originator, were, by a fortunate irony of history (which some call dialectic), the basis of the very liberalism that Machiavelli would surely have condemned as feeble and characterless, lacking in single-minded pursuit of power, in splendour, in organisation, in *virtù*, in power to discipline the unruly against huge odds into one energetic whole. Yet he is, in spite of himself, one of the makers of pluralism, and of its – to him perilous – acceptance of toleration. (AC2 99)

Berlin's essay on Machiavelli provides a particularly vivid and detailed illustration of how he interprets the thought of a past thinker in a way that illuminates a major plank of his own outlook. As one acute commentator has stated: 'His [Berlin's] encounter with Machiavelli is a philosophical conversation, rather than a historical exhumation.'[3] Yet a legitimate question to ask at this point is: Why bother with history in making what looks like a purely philosophical point? Following Ockham's rule of theoretical parsimony, would it not be more efficient to dispense with the historical frills and serve up one's own philosophy as plainly, directly and analytically as possible? What crucial difference or authority, if any, is history supposed to lend to Berlin's method of political thought? Asking the question in this blunt way at least focuses our attention on why Berlin took history so seriously, and forces us to explore some of the themes mentioned at the beginning of this section. For Berlin, doing philosophy and studying its history are not activities that should be, or really can be, kept separate from each other. They are essentially two sides of the same coin. But saying this is far from saying enough. A good way to start getting underneath this complex matter is to consider how the distinction between the historical meaning of Machiavelli's ideas and their significance for us operates in Berlin's essay.

The first thing to emphasize is that Berlin seems genuinely concerned with recovering the actual meaning of Machiavelli's thought. Having reviewed the mountainous and frequently conflicting interpretations of the thinker who managed to even give Satan the sobriquet 'Old Nick', he finds them all wanting to a greater or lesser extent. Perhaps taking his cue from the great Renaissance scholar Felix Gilbert, he argues that the only way to unlock the enigma of Machiavelli's heterodox thought is to situate it in relation to the classical world, and more specifically to the ancient Roman republic and its moralists. This led

---

[3] Alan Ryan, 'Wise Man', *New York Review of Books* (17 December 1998).

him to conclude that what Machiavelli was seeking to achieve was not so much to divorce politics from morality or even to cast an unashamedly cold eye on the ruthless, amoral reality of high politics, but rather to reassert the political ideals and civic values of a more worldly and heroic age. Machiavelli's political morality is derived from the thought of republican Rome rather than from Christendom, which in turn meant that it was public rather than private, situational rather than ideal, active rather than contemplative.

Berlin's interpretation of Machiavelli's originality has been partly vindicated by one of the most distinguished historians of early modern political thought and an acknowledged expert on Machiavelli, Quentin Skinner. In his own major work on the foundations of modern political thought, Skinner commends Berlin for perceiving what so many others missed:

> Thus the difference between Machiavelli and his contemporaries cannot adequately be characterised as a difference between a moral view of politics and a view of politics as divorced from morality. The essential contrast is rather between two different moralities – two rival and incompatible accounts of what ought ultimately to be done.[4]

While there is no doubt that Skinner is more exclusively concerned than Berlin with situating the author of *The Prince* and the *Discourses* in his historical context, he explicitly endorses Berlin's main conclusion that a defining aspect of Machiavelli's revolution is his uncompromising commitment to the pagan values of civic honour, glory and fame and, more controversially, his unbuttoned, unchristian backing of the conventionally immoral methods that are practised by certain rulers to maintain their state.[5] Skinner shows in sedulous detail how Machiavelli departed from the traditional wisdom of his time by repudiating the regulative humanist assumption that the only legitimate way of securing and sustaining political stability as well as achieving the time-honoured goals of honour, glory and fame is by following the dictates of conventional morality. Indeed, he goes one step further by claiming that Machiavelli's advice to rulers regarding the necessary methods for attaining and maintaining their power was

---

[4]Quentin Skinner, *The Foundations of Modern Political Thought*, Vol. 1 (1978: Cambridge University Press, Cambridge), 135. The footnote accompanying the above quotation states, 'For a recent and extremely eloquent statement of this interpretation of Machiavelli's originality, see the important essay by Berlin, 1972.'

[5]See Richard Tuck, 'Humanism and Political Thought', in *The Impact of Humanism on Western Europe*, ed. Anthony Goodman and Angus MacKay (1990: Longman, London), 43–65 as well as Marcia Colish's earlier article in the same vein, 'Cicero's *De officiis* and Machiavelli's *The Prince*', Sixteenth Century Journal 9 no. 4 (1978), 81–93. Both Tuck and Colish imply that what makes Machiavelli Machiavellian is his unadulterated and unabashed Ciceronianism.

also opposed to the traditional counsel provided by the classical Roman moralists, most notably, by Cicero (106–43 BC) in his hugely influential *De officiis (On Moral Duties)*.

Skinner may, of course, be going one step too far here. His former Cambridge colleague, Richard Tuck (1949), has argued that the assumptions informing Cicero's treatise on moral obligations are far more subversive of Christian values than Skinner is willing to acknowledge. Tuck adds that the overlap between the pagan and Christian ethical codes should not blind us to the deeper truth that for Cicero the glory of the Roman *res publica* was the *summum bonum*, whereas for Christianity the ultimate good was distinctly non-secular and achievable only beyond our merely mortal world. The implication of Tuck's argument is that Machiavelli saw all too clearly what his own contemporaries and, indeed, Skinner seem to have overlooked, that Machiavelli's undiluted and unappeasable Ciceronianism may have been the real source and inspiration of his heretical advice to rulers and that therefore Machiavelli's insistence on describing a conventionally immoral ruler as a virtuous one was not in this instance a matter of hypocrisy being the tribute vice pays to virtue.

But there is also a deeper and more relevant sense in which Skinner is undeniably right to highlight the unabashed irreverence at the core of Machiavelli's political thought, that is, his redefinition or rather inversion of the Christian *and* classical concept of *virtù*. His intervention involved a rejection of the age-old and undisputed principle that the legitimate aims of the ruler could only be achieved through following the dictates of traditional morality, a morality that reflected the undisputed consensus of Christian and classical normative prescriptions. For example, it is an inviolable axiom of the *De officiis* that good faith must be observed as a method of being a virtuous statesman ('fidesque iuris iurandi saepe cum hoste servanda': 3. 29). So it must surely have been one of the most shocking moments for Machiavelli's original readers to come upon the title of chapter 18, in which the author asks how far good faith should be kept ('Quomodo fides a principibus sit servanda'). This example forms part of Machiavelli's repudiation of one of the most inviolable precept of both pagan virtue and Christian providence – that a ruler must obey the dictates of morality if he wishes to maintain his state and achieve glory, or in the language of the classical moralists, that *utile* or expediency cannot be in genuine conflict with *honestum* or moral rectitude. Machiavelli declared that there is no guarantee that following such a sacred moral precept will help bring political stability and glory. Moreover, he crucially added that an honest and dispassionate analysis of the facts of political life shows that, more often than not, the very opposite applies, and that therefore a ruler must be willing to subordinate the rules of conventional morality to the overriding demands of political expediency on a regular basis if he wishes to protect his kingdom or principality, that he has no choice but to engage in what one contemporary philosopher has aptly and paradoxically called 'admirable immorality'.[6]

Accordingly, Machiavelli's realpolitik would appear to have been entirely new and revolutionary. Where his contemporaries and ancient predecessors may have been prepared to grant that in exceptional circumstances political necessity can override normal, everyday morality, Machiavelli argued that since a ruler finds himself in a virtually permanent state of political necessity, a truly virtuous prince will be prepared and willing to resort frequently to deceit, violence, treachery and so forth since he is committed to the priority of maintaining his state and of pursuing the traditional goals of honour, glory and fame. But the critically relevant point for our purpose is that Berlin's more philosophical interpretation of Machiavelli's originality, namely, that the Florentine author uncovered an unbridgeable gulf between two conceptions of the good, is supported and amplified by both Cambridge contextualists, albeit in different ways: whereas Skinner sees Machiavelli's concept of *virtù* as signalling a bifurcation between traditional morality (classical and Christian) and a new political morality, Tuck believes that Machiavelli is the pure face of unadulterated Ciceronianism in a Christian world.

Even before Skinner completed his magisterial work on the foundations of modern political thought, Berlin's essay had been singled out as one of the impressive works of scholarship published to mark the quincentenary in 1969 of Machiavelli's birth in 1469.[7] In a comprehensive review of more than 500 scholarly items written about the Florentine's life and writings in 1969 and its immediate aftermath, the intellectual historian John Geerken judged that Berlin's paper was the most outstanding contribution on 'the aspect of his thought that has triggered all other interest in him, that lies at the hub from which all other concerns radiate

---

[6]See Michael Slote, *Goods and Virtues* (1983: Clarendon Press, Oxford). It is worth noting in this context the parallel between Berlin's Machiavelli and the contrast he makes between Christian or private morality and pagan or public morality and Max Weber's account of the vocation of the politician with its distinction between 'the ethics of intention' and 'the ethics of responsibility'. The following passage towards the end of Weber's essay, 'The Politics of Vocation', is particularly pertinent: But it is enormously impressive if a *more mature* man (whether old or young in years) who feels his responsibility for the consequences genuinely and with all his heart and acts according to the ethics of responsibility, says at whatever point it may be: 'Here I stand: I can no other.' That is the expression of authentic humanity and stirs one's feelings. For the possibility of this sort of situation occurring at some time or other must indeed exist for *any one* of us who is not inwardly dead. To that extent, the ethics of intention and the ethics of responsibility are not diametrically opposed, but complementary: together they make the true man, the man who can have 'the vocation of politics'. Weber, *Selections in Translation*, ed. W. G. Runciman (1978: Cambridge University Press, Cambridge), 224. The extent to which Machiavelli's prince of virtù resembles Weber's politician with a vocation is striking.

[7]John H. Geerken, 'Machiavelli Studies since 1969', *Journal of the History of Ideas* 37 no. 2 (1976), 351–68, henceforth referred to as MS. For a philosophically sophisticated account of the contemporary significance of Machiavelli's originality or 'problem', see the work of Berlin's close friend and colleague, Stuart Hampshire, *Innocence and Experience* (1989: Allen Lane, London), 159–89.

... his reflection on the relationship of politics and ethics' (MS 365). Geerken also mentions that Berlin's essay supplanted the previously dominant view that Machiavelli's novelty lay in divorcing politics from morality with the far more historically and philosophically plausible claim that Machiavelli subscribed to 'morality' as well as 'politics', though his morality was not a Christian one but, rather, a pagan and heroic moral outlook with its own independent scale of civic values and ultimate moral ends. As Geerken concludes:

> And to Machiavelli must go the credit for perceiving the misalignment between private, Christian ethics and public, political practice – a misalignment he not only exposed but sought to repair by referring the political enterprise not to an intrinsically hostile and historically compromised Christianity, but to a congenial tradition of secular, classical antiquity. It was the first step in building a proper understanding of politics. (MS 368)

But apart from seeking to identify the historical meaning of Machiavelli's thought, Berlin is clearly more concerned with the task of determining the wider philosophical significance of the Renaissance thinker's ideas, a significance that somehow outlives its specific historical context. And this is where things get more historically controversial and philosophically complex. For Berlin wants to claim that the substance of Machiavelli's originality possesses an identity and significance that transcend his own peculiar time and place:

> Anyone who believes in Christian morality, and regards the Christian commonwealth as its embodiment, but at the same time largely accepts the validity of Machiavelli's political and psychological analysis and does not reject the secular heritage of Rome – a man in this predicament is faced with a dilemma which, if Machiavelli is right, is not merely unsolved but insoluble. This is the Gordian knot which, according to Vanini and Leibniz, the author of *The Prince* had tied – a knot which can be cut but not undone. (AC2 97)

What is it for Machiavelli's alleged discovery to be true in the way that Berlin is demanding here? Is he arguing that Machiavelli stumbled on a truth that applies to all men at all times? And if so, is he therefore vulnerable to the charge of committing an act of blatant anachronism, as some historians have argued, by seeking to appropriate the sixteenth-century Florentine author as an unlikely forerunner of modernity and even liberalism?[8] Or is Berlin, in fact, up to

---

[8] See, for example, Mark Hulliung's *Citizen Machiavelli* (1983: Princeton University Press, Princeton, NJ), 249–54. The view that Berlin lets his pluralist preconceptions anachronistically colour his interpretation of the past was articulated by Ernest Gellner with his usual acerbic if overblown wit:

something else here? And let's be clear that how we answer this question is of the utmost importance since Berlin is not just saying that Machiavelli's originality is limited to the discovery that rulers are required to violate the demands of ordinary morality in order to fulfil their ethically legitimate political obligations and goals. He also wants to argue that Machiavelli discovered or uncovered a truth of far more profound normative significance, that is, the truth of value pluralism. In other words, the politician's problem of dirty hands is only the tip of the pluralist iceberg: the ubiquitous and irreducible nature of disagreement within and between objective human values and ideals goes far wider and deeper than anything Machiavelli could have imagined even if he did succeed in shining an unforgiving light on one aspect of our pluralistic moral universe. As Berlin states:

> After Machiavelli, doubt is liable to infect all monistic constructions. The sense of certainty that there is somewhere a hidden treasure – the final solution to our ills – and that some path must lead to it (for, in principle, it must be discoverable); or else, to alter the image, all the pieces of the jigsaw puzzle, which (since there is an *a priori* guarantee for this) can, in principle, be solved, so that it is only because of lack of skill or stupidity or bad fortune that we have not so far succeeded in discovering the solution, whereby all interests will be brought into harmony – this fundamental belief of Western political thought has been severely shaken. Surely, in an age that looks for certainties, this is sufficient to account for the unending efforts, more numerous today than ever, to explain *The Prince* and the *Discourses*, or to explain them away? (AC2 97–8)

Let's take the charge of anachronism first. For a start, Berlin repeatedly states that his claim that Machiavelli dealt the first major blow to moral monism – the belief that all genuine moral values and ideals are ultimately compatible and harmonious – does not in any way entail that we are warranted in identifying him as some kind of proto-pluralist, not to mention early modern liberal. In fact, he insists that Machiavelli never affirms moral dualism, still less moral pluralism. Rather, for Berlin, Machiavelli's dramatic juxtaposition of ancient Roman *virtù* and Christian virtue was largely an unwitting testimony to an ineradicable conflict that always existed between these competing conceptions of the good life. He simply laid

---

'Machiavelli, Vico, Herder, Tolstoy ... come out looking suspiciously alike – Niccolò Berlini, Gianbattista Berlino, Johann Gottfried Berliner, and Lev Nicolaievich Berlinov', Ernest Gellner, *Prospect*, November 1995, 56. There is no doubt that Berlin can be guilty of exaggerating the degree to which past thinkers may have anticipated his theory of the plurality of values, but we should not take such caricatures of his anachronism too seriously either. Broadly speaking, Gellner had a sharp polemical pen but a frequently superficial and tiresomely narrow philosophical mind which only retained the appearance of cleverness as long as debate stayed on a complacently rhetorical level.

bare something Christianity had succeeded in keeping a firm lid on for over a millennium and a half.

Berlin is also careful to stress that Machiavelli's inadvertent discovery of moral dualism before its time did not in the least diminish his belief in the absolute superiority of the worldly ideals of ancient Rome. This hints at something more fundamental in Berlin's view of the past: his central belief in the historicity or contingency of moral truths. Once we recognize that these truths and the concepts and ideals associated with them have an inherently historical dimension and that our contingent awareness of and respect or contempt for these concepts and truths in turn develop and change over time, then our understanding of the nature and task of moral and political philosophy is or should be radically transformed too. No longer can we study the so-called canonical texts of long-dead philosophers in the hope that we may discover timeless truths that are straightforwardly applicable to all men at all times. Nor can we naively and condescendingly impose our current notions of what is morally right and laudable on past thinkers or epochs and judge them serenely by our own lights. The lesson of historicity renders both of these perspectives untenable. In short, the option of ahistorically plundering the piggy bank of long-dead philosophers to buttress one's argument or, alternatively, to make past thinkers look silly or quaint, is no longer available. Instead, the proper study of mankind must proceed on the basis of a historically informed and fitful intellectual diffidence which acknowledges the inevitable contingency of even our most fundamental and precious values and ideals while taking on board the genuine and unassimilable pastness of the past. It is possible to convey this point more concretely if we return once again to Berlin's essay on Machiavelli.

We have seen that, for Berlin, Machiavelli's 'cardinal achievement' is:

> his de facto recognition that ends equally ultimate, equally sacred, may contradict each other, that entire systems of value may come into collision without the possibility of rational arbitration and that this happens not merely in exceptional circumstances, as a result of accident or abnormality or error … but … as part of the normal human situation. (AC2 94)

So, Machiavelli's central if unintended accomplishment was the unearthing of a genuine meta-ethical truth, the notion that there is more than one conception of the good life, and even more heterodoxically, that there exists no moral common denominator or yardstick against which distinct and competing ways of life and ideals can be impartially compared or conflicts between them rationally resolved. We shall be returning to this defining idea in more detail further on, but for now let us consider the philosophical status of value pluralism in the context of the implacable historicity of human life and moral ends.

What is instructive about Berlin's reading of Machiavelli is its appreciation of how certain putative ethical truths may or may not be appreciated or even recognized by past thinkers. Machiavelli's stumbling upon the alleged truth of moral dualism did not prompt a conversion on his part to anything remotely approaching a respect for moral diversity or the virtue of toleration. Nor could it in the sense that such reactions were not even notional options, let alone real ones. The historical record shows that it was only after the Renaissance and primarily in the wake of the wars of religion that the idea and, indeed, reality of toleration gradually gained acceptance in Western society. Political toleration was to a very large extent the pragmatic child of the widespread and increasingly intolerable violence of religious conflict rather than the outcome of any implausibly popular intellectual conversion to the truth of value pluralism. And yet Berlin wants to claim that Machiavelli's significance lies in raising a permanent and lethal question mark concerning one of the most sacred and enduring assumptions of Western thought, namely, that all genuine moral values are ultimately compatible, and its corollary, that all moral conflict can be rationally resolved. For Machiavelli, we are told, left to posterity the original and subversive insight that there is not one, but at least two if not more, answers to the question of how we should live our lives, and that the various competing answers to this question all have their own moral integrity and legitimacy even though they are in irreducible conflict with one another.

The significance of what Machiavelli dramatized is variously described by Berlin as 'the planting of a permanent question mark in the path of posterity', 'a profoundly upsetting conclusion', an 'uncomfortable truth' and 'the dilemma [that] has never given men peace since it came to light' (AC2 94, 87, 89, 99). What we appear to be dealing with here is a very distinctive type of truth that was not, and probably could not be, understood, let alone acted upon, in Renaissance Europe or, indeed, in the centuries immediately following. This does not mean that value pluralism was necessarily any less true – or, correspondingly, that moral monism any less false – in Machiavelli's time than it is today. Rather, it is to suggest that different historical periods and cultures are not only more sensitive to and respectful of certain truths than others, but that the consciousness and flourishing of certain insights or truths are also crucially dependent on the peculiar contingencies of our historical and cultural make-up and self-awareness. The emergence of the idea that there are valid but conflicting conceptions of the good, and that the legitimacy of the state is partly derived from protecting its citizens' right to freely choose their own way of life, is historically and culturally unique and was by no means an inexorable feature of the modern Western age.

Berlin's central argument, therefore, is that Machiavelli's importance lay in lighting a fuse that helped lead to the rise of modernity and its gradual endorsement of liberal toleration. It is clear that Berlin's argument is not meant to imply that the significance of Machiavelli's *idée maîtresse* allows us to postulate any kind of direct or even observable historical cause and effect. Nor is it designed to suggest that Machiavelli's originality paved the way to the belated recognition of pluralism and the inevitable rise of liberalism. Rather, Berlin claims that Machiavelli ended up planting a seed of scepticism in the Western mind, which in turn raised serious and undeniable doubts about the validity of the long-held and pervasive idea that since all objectively good things are ultimately compatible, mankind is rationally and morally required to continue its quest for a perfect, harmonious society, if not in this world then in the next. As Berlin concludes:

> If there is only one solution to the puzzle, then the problems are, firstly how to find it, then how to realise it, and finally how to convert others to the solution by persuasion or by force. But if this is not so (Machiavelli contrasts two ways of life, but there could be more than two), then the path is open to empiricism, pluralism, toleration, compromise. Toleration is historically the product of the realization of the irreconcilability of equally dogmatic faiths, and the practical improbability of complete victory of one over the other. Those who wished to survive realised that they had to tolerate error. They gradually came to see merits in diversity, and so became sceptical about definitive solutions in human affairs.
>
> But it is one thing to accept something in practice, another to justify it rationally. Machiavelli's 'scandalous' writings begin the latter process. 'This was a major turning-point, and its intellectual consequences, wholly unintended by its originator, were, by a fortunate irony of history (which some call its dialectic), the bases of the very liberalism that Machiavelli would surely have condemned as feeble and characterless. ... Yet he is, in spite of himself, one of the makers of pluralism and of its – to him – perilous acceptance of toleration' (AC2 98–9).

What historians tend to find historically doubtful, if not flatly implausible, about Berlin's bold interpretations of long-deceased thinkers such as Machiavelli and Vico is that they seem to bear little or no correspondence with the actual historical record. It is felt that there is an unmistakable sense in which his view of Machiavelli's significance conspicuously loses contact with historical reality, that it lacks what the Cambridge school of contextualism regard as historical accountability. And arguing that Berlin's treatment of Machiavelli and other historically remote thinkers is more of an exercise in the history of philosophy than it is in the history of ideas, that it is philosophy *first* and not history in the strictly contextual sense of that term, doesn't really get Berlin off the hook. Any hard and fast distinction between philosophically motivated accounts of past thinkers and historically centred interpretations of canonical theorists cannot be accepted willy-nilly since Berlin then runs the risk of becoming indistinguishable from the flock of ahistorically minded and chronically anachronistic analytic philosophers. But while there may be no clean or definitive solution to the matter of the philosophical and historical status of Berlin's claim regarding Machiavelli's 'discovery', it is, I think, possible to show that his own distinctive version of philosophical history is far more sophisticated and cogent than conventional analytic 'histories' of philosophy than contextualists allow. The next chapter will begin to explain why and thereby serve to support one of the main arguments of this book, namely, that Berlin's philosophical outlook shows that acknowledging the historicity of liberalism does not disqualify it from generating a philosophically and historically vindicatory account of itself.

6 INTERLUDE: TAKING STOCK

We are finally in a position to make a number of interim generalizations and judgements about Berlin's philosophical vision. The purpose of what follows is to try to distil the significance of certain salient aspects of his outlook while also looking at some of the major questions raised in the preceding chapters and, where necessary, highlighting a number of unresolved issues.

Berlin's understanding of what constitutes philosophy derives from his own meta-philosophical view of the subject. Unlike, on the one hand, positivists who felt that philosophical problems are meaningless unless they are empirically verifiable, or, on the other hand, linguistic philosophers, who believed that virtually all philosophical problems reflect a confused grasp of the underlying meaning and use of our ordinary language, Berlin holds what appears at first to be a rather conventional, if nebulous, view of the nature of philosophy, one that identifies it primarily with the intractable questions it asks. But, of course, if this was all he said about the subject he would be open to the charge of stating the blindingly obvious or perhaps, more culpably, of confusing the merely unanswerable with the sublime. Rather, what differentiates his world view is that it gives us a glimpse of what philosophy can be when it sheds its heavy and constricting layers of naturalistic clothing. Once philosophy ceases to regard itself as the handmaiden of science, significantly new and liberating possibilities emerge. Reading Berlin is like opening a door to a new yet strangely familiar vista that transforms our understanding and appreciation of the landscape, especially when it comes to our view of human affairs. Whereas before we might have dismissed or derided certain unanswerable questions as gibberish, now their existence and meaning start to make more sense and their persistence a cause for wonder. Similarly, where before we might have been suspicious or even intolerant of the suggestion that genuine questions do not necessarily possess uniquely right answers, we become more susceptible to seeing their absence as natural as leaves to a tree. The methods and success of natural science cease to overshadow a different but arguably no less important source of non-scientific understanding. Berlin's humanistic and pluralistic view of the subject also underscores his conviction that the primary aim of philosophy is less about trying to reach some idealized form of universal consensus than about deepening and refining our self-understanding. In short, philosophy is more about identifying and exploring meaningful problems than trying to produce definitive and final solutions. A philosopher who thinks that the purpose of philosophy is purely or primarily to solve or dissolve its problems or, more immodestly, to create a philosophy (or an anti-philosophy) to end all philosophy is, more likely than not, under the illusion that he or she has reached the conceptual equivalent of ground zero.

A key part of what Berlin wants us to perceive is that we never really arrive at such a bedrock, not simply because it is always possible to peel away what we think is the final layer of our conceptual understanding – consider, for example, the difference between a pre-Freudian and Freudian perspective – but also on account of the deep though unmystical fact that no such non-perspectival place exists. It is not just that we can always ask the next question in philosophy, which in turn prompts us to explore and add new and hidden layers of thinking and understanding. It is the more basic point that the questions we ask and how we seek to answer them will always and necessarily be a function of the perspectival peculiarities of our historically and culturally formed circumstances. In this respect, Berlin stays true to the kernel of Kant's revolutionary discovery that we can only make sense of the world when we accept that it is inescapably our own creation. But none of this should imply that such enquiries are ultimately meaningless or futile. On the contrary, by exploring the multiple sources of human understanding, philosophy helps us to become more self-aware of the various and varying patterns of thought that underpin our comprehension of both the world and ourselves and thereby fulfil one of the original and vital goals of philosophy, which is 'to assist men to understand themselves and thus operate in the open, and not wildly, in the dark' (CC2 114).

This raises the fundamental question of whether there can be any real progress in practical or normative philosophy, or more specifically, whether there is such a thing as a rationally grounded convergence or growth of non-scientific understanding and even knowledge over time? This is a fiendishly difficult question that is in a way the underlying question of this book. My central claim is that Berlin's writings provide us with an original and illuminating account of what human understanding can amount to in the only way that such understanding tends to disclose itself – through the application of a highly imaginative, sharp and morally engaged intelligence that helps us to see ourselves and the world in a richer, truer and more generous light.

One of the delights of reading Berlin is that he shares something of the grand intellectual sweep that typifies the ambition of the Western philosophical tradition. In common with that tradition, which goes back to the ancient Greek thinkers, Berlin's work reflects a genuine Socratic curiosity and willingness to engage with real, complex, living problems. A typical Berlin essay begins with a deceptively simple and narrow question, which in turn provokes an investigation into a series of other philosophical questions ranging across virtually all branches of the subject from metaphysics and epistemology through to aesthetics and moral and political philosophy. In this respect, Berlin's writings have far more in common with, for example, Plato's dialogues or Hobbes's *Leviathan* than it does with much of contemporary professional philosophy, which is defined by an almost crippling division of labour that renders the treatment of topics frustratingly truncated and shallow – not to mention its ceaselessly, and mainly, destructive negativity. One of Berlin's former students, David Pears, sought to capture this free-flowing and multilayered character of Berlin's thought by comparing his philosophical approach to that of an artist:

> Listening to him [Berlin] is like watching an artist painting a picture with breathtaking rapidity. You want to say, 'Wait a minute, I do not quite understand what is going on in that corner,' but each brush-stroke immediately helps and is helped by the next one. This is not just a stylistic trait but an essential feature of his thought.[1]

Another defining element of Berlin's philosophical vision rests on his distinctive account of the value-ladenness as well as historicity of the philosophical enterprise, especially insofar as it is concerned with our understanding of the human as distinct from the physical world. By historicizing and extending the scope of Kant's transcendental idealism, he sought to show that our own necessarily subjective view of the world, especially the world of distinctly human affairs, is moulded by historically persistent as well as varying categories and concepts of thought.

A basic feature of Berlin's internally focused application of the transcendental argument is its rejection of the fact–value dichotomy, a dichotomy that has been all too influential since the rise of positivism in the nineteenth century. Let's recall that this is the view that empirical statements are capable of being objectively true while value judgements are incapable of aspiring to such status and, indeed, lie beyond or, rather, below the lofty domain of reason. We have seen that one of the main ways in which he declared his departure from the emotivism of positivism was by insisting that value judgements constitute some of the most fundamental and common categories and concepts of thought that shape our understanding of ourselves and others. This, of course, does not mean that our values cannot

---

[1]David Pears, 'Philosophy and the History of Philosophy', in *Isaiah Berlin: A Celebration*, eds. Edna Ullmann-Margalit and Avishai Margalit (1991: Hogarth Press, London), 38.

be revised, transformed or forgotten about, but it does imply that any attempt to dismiss values and, indeed, normative debate as cognitively meaningless is unsustainable. Quine's remark, therefore, that 'philosophy of science is philosophy enough' would have struck Berlin as absurd, just like he considered talk of the death of political theory as unserious.[2] The superficiality of both judgments does not lie in their descriptive waywardness: analytic philosophy was for quite a while the midwife of the sciences and Peter Laslett's observation that normative political theory had officially died by 1953 was by no means sociologically inaccurate. The error resides, rather, in their view of what practical or evaluative philosophy, more correctly understood, is or should be. As Berlin consistently reminds us, our urge to transform philosophy and history into something they are not, that is, into quasi-scientific disciplines, an urge that has become particularly pronounced since the Enlightenment, is virtually limitless. This scientific impulse has been responsible for some of the Western world's greatest accomplishments, but that does not make its appropriation of philosophy any more necessary or defensible. Nor should we let it suggest that evaluative discourse can be displaced by descriptive discourse. The very concept of the self is soaked in values all the way through, which renders any serious attempt to disentangle the so-called factual aspects of our nature from its value-laden traits hopelessly flawed.

Berlin's insistence that political philosophy is an inherently normative discipline does not mean that he is therefore committed to some foundational and implausibly comprehensive conception of the good life. In this respect, his own moral and political philosophy contrasts sharply with that of a thinker like Plato. Plato founded a highly influential intellectual tradition that was built on the central claim that only philosophy could provide the key to defining the objectively good life. This basic assumption underpinned Western thought until modern times – Christianity simply provided theological foundations to justify its own conception of what constituted the morally good life for mankind. The story of how the foundational ambition of our intellectual tradition declined with the rise of modernity is a complex one. The relevant point for our purposes is that Berlin shares the modern view, which is profoundly and irreversibly sceptical of the capacity of philosophy (or theology) to ground an absolute, all-encompassing conception of the human good. In short, given what we know, we cannot turn the clock black unless we deny or somehow spectacularly forget what we have come to believe and claim we know. And one of the central insights of modernity is that we are what we have contingently become and are neither the product of an unfolding, teleological historical process nor the chosen species of some cosmically transcendent Being.

---

[2] W. V. Quine, 'Mr Strawson on Logical Theory', *Mind* 62 no. 248 (October 1953), 433–51.

Another major and related feature of Berlin's philosophical outlook centres on his historicist claim that the transcendental categories and concepts of human nature are themselves sensitive to and transformed by historical change. While it's clear he felt that the patterns of thought relating to the physical world were far less prone to the impact of cultural and historical variation (Berlin is no Kuhnian), he never appears to let his implicit and unobtrusive scientific realism prejudice or undermine the conceptual and moral integrity of his account of human beings. But it should also be said that he never really tackles, let alone seeks to reconcile, the deeply problematic duality of our understanding of the external world and that of the human world. His version of pluralism operates very much in the human rather than the physical world.

The historicist turn in Berlin's thought is driven by a recognition that the basic conceptual spectacles through which we interpret the world of human affairs are ultimately contingent – some, admittedly, being more historically variant than others. This in turn allows Berlin to more readily accommodate the fact that history leaves a large and indelible stamp not only on the various contingent aspects and verities of our nature but also on the way in which different societies at different times understand and value them. One commentator has recently described Berlin's outlook as 'sensibility philosophy', to amplify the fact that his conception of philosophy is 'attuned to history and historical shifts' without becoming a conventional 'history of ideas' in the antiquarian sense of the term (POI2 xv). For Berlin, the critical task of philosophy is to identify and elucidate the underlying categories that shape our experience and thought and how these categories develop and change throughout history so that we are not operating in the dark any more than we need to be.

This aspect of Berlin's humanistic viewpoint is not without its own internal tensions. There are occasions when he appears committed to a fairly strong and universalistic philosophical anthropology which suggests that there are relatively fixed, if minimal, limits to the variability of our values and ideals. There are also as many occasions where he appears to deny any presupposition or commitment to anything as empirically and normatively ambitious as a conception of universal human nature. This tension or oscillation may well be an instance of what his colleague, J. L. Austin, described thus: 'There's the bit where you say it and the bit where you take it back.'[3] Being in two minds about a mere detail or peripheral feature of one's thought might be excusable but holding such divergent views about human nature hardly qualifies as a trivial concern. I don't think there is any uncontroversial way of resolving this tension in Berlin's thought since there is ample textual evidence and sufficient looseness of expression in his pluralism to suggest that he wavered between two competing positions.

---

[3] J. L. Austin, *Sense and Sensibilia* (1962: Oxford University Press, Oxford), 2.

However, we can perhaps soften the sharpness of this inconsistency in his thought by suggesting that human nature is a scalar rather than a sortal concept. This move would also seem to comport with Berlin's largely tacit view of the matter. In the field of logic, sortal concepts define a class, which allows us, for example, to distinguish between cats and dogs, whereas scalar concepts identify a characteristic such as solidity or warmth that objects can possess to a greater or lesser extent. It seems to make more sense to treat human nature as a scalar rather than a sortal concept for the simple reason that human nature is too promiscuous, slippery and contested a concept to define in anything other than a 'more or less' sense.[4] In certain moments, Berlin claims that human beings possess a shared nucleus of needs, 'a minimum of moral ground', that revolves around such overriding goals as sanity, reason, life, liberty and happiness. At other times, he exhibits a deep scepticism about the existence of any kind of universal human nature, and a disinclination to commit himself to anything more than the rather amorphous and unsubstantiated claim about human beings' capacity to communicate with each other across time and space. Which version of Berlin are we to believe? While most scholars have decided to plump one way or the other, it seems wiser to resist such a binary interpretive strategy.[5] We end up selling Berlin short if we categorize him either as some kind of universalistic liberal rationalist or, in contrast, as a proto-postmodern ethnocentric liberal. The truth lies somewhere in the messy middle ground. Berlin knows enough about humanity to affirm that featherless bipeds do, indeed, share something in common but not enough to ground any kind of grand and substantive theory of human nature and of the human good.

There is evidence that Berlin holds a middle-ground position on the knotty matter of human nature, one that is at least compatible with my suggestion that the notion of human nature is best interpreted as a scalar rather than a sortal concept. In his extended correspondence with the Polish philosopher, Beata Polanowska-Sygulska, he explicitly entertains the idea that Wittgenstein's concept of 'family

---

[4] I am indebted to James. L. Hyland for highlighting the relevance of this aspect of logic to political philosophy. See J. L. Hyland, *Democratic Theory: The Philosophical Foundations* (1995: Manchester University Press, Manchester), 49–50.

[5] Among the more notable commentators who have identified Berlin at the more universalist end of the spectrum include Perry Anderson, 'England's Isaiah' in the *London Review of Books* (20 December 1990), 3–7. Claude Galipeau, *Isaiah Berlin's Liberalism* (1994: Oxford University Press, Oxford); Steven Lukes, *Liberals and Cannibals* (2003: Verso, London), ch. 6; George Crowder, *Isaiah Berlin* (2004: Polity Press, Cambridge); John Riley, 'Isaiah Berlin's "Minimum of Common Moral Ground"', in *Political Theory* 41 (2013), 61–89. Those who have read Berlin in a more ethnocentric spirit include Richard Rorty, *Contingency, Irony and Solidarity* (1989: Cambridge University Press, Cambridge) (hereafter CIS), ch. 3; John Gray, *Isaiah Berlin* (1995: HarperCollins, London) and *Two Faces of Liberalism* (2000: Polity Press, Cambridge), ch. 1. Berlin provides the most lucid yet still ambiguous statement of his position in 'Reply to Robert Kocis', *Political Studies* XXXI (1983), 388–93. And later in his 'Reply to Ronald H. McKinney, "Towards a Postmodern Ethics: Sir Isaiah Berlin and John Caputo", *The Journal of Value Inquiry* 26 (1992), 557–60.

resemblance', or what Berlin refers to as his idea of 'family face', provides a kind of spectrum solution to the question of the validity or otherwise of the idea of a shared human nature. As he says:

> Wittgenstein once explained the concept of 'family face' – that is, among the portraits of ancestors, face A resembles face B, face B resembles face C, face C resembles face D etc., but there is not a central face, 'the family face', of which these are identifiable modifications; nevertheless, when I say 'family face' I do not mean nothing, I mean precisely that A resembles B, B resembles C and so on, in various respects, and that they form a continuum, a series, which can be attributed to family X, not to family Y. So with the various natures of various cultures, societies, groups etc.
>
> This is what I mean – that there is not a fixed, and yet there is a common, human nature: without the latter there would be no possibility of talking about human beings or, indeed, of intercommunication, on which all thought depends – and not only thought, but feeling, imagination, action. (UD 41)

It might be helpful to readers who are unfamiliar with Wittgenstein's concept of 'family resemblances' if we quote the relevant passage from his *Philosophical Investigations* where he outlines the nature and relevance of this concept by giving an account of the similarities and differences between various kinds of games:

> 66. Consider for example the proceedings that we call 'games'. I mean board-games, card-games, ball-games, Olympic games, and so on. What is common to them all? – Do not say: 'There must be something common, or they would not be called "games"' – but *look & see* whether there is anything common to all. – For if you look at them you will not see something that is common to *all*, but similarities, relationships, and a whole series of them at that. To repeat: do not think but look! – Look for example at board-games with the multifarious relationships. Now pass to card-games; here you find many correspondences with the first group, but many common features drop out, and others appear. When we pass next to ball-games, much that is common is retained, but much is lost. – Are they all 'amusing'? Compare chess with noughts and crosses. Or is there always winning and losing, or competition between players? Think of patience. In ball-games there is winning and losing; but when a child throws his ball at the wall and catches it again, this feature has disappeared. Look at the parts played by skill and luck; and at the difference between skill in chess & skill in tennis. Think now of games like ring-a-ring-a-roses; here is the element of amusement, but how many other characteristic features have disappeared! And we can go through the many, many other groups of games in the same way; can see how similarities crop up and disappear. And the result of this examination is: we see a complicated network of similarities overlapping & criss-crossing:

sometimes overall similarities, sometimes similarities of detail.67. I can think of no better expression to characterise these similarities than family resemblances; for the various resemblances between the members of a family; build, features, colour of eyes, gait, temperament, etc. etc. overlap and criss-cross in the same way – And I shall say: 'games' form a family.[6]

Wittgenstein's non-trivial analysis of 'game' serves to undermine the myth of linguistic essentialism but whether the application of the idea of 'family resemblances' retains its explanatory power when it comes to analysing the more normatively laden and essentially contested concepts like selfhood, agency, equality, love, sanity, justice and so on. remains a moot point.

Richard Wollheim (1923–2003) is one of the few commentators on Berlin's thought who seem to share something akin to my view that there is a refreshing candidness about Berlin's lack of consistency on this matter. Where others may see an unforgiveable tension or even contradiction at the heart of this aspect of Berlin's thought, Wollheim sees signs of a genuine Humean thinker instead: someone, in other words, who knows too much about life to allow the hobgoblin of strict consistency to be his overriding philosophical touchstone. As Wollheim states:

> Berlin is the kind of Humean Hume was …. Berlin's concern with observation, with what I call the surface of life, is something that he might well be ready to justify as preparing the ground for theory, for explanation, but, as to the chances of our ever finding theories, at any rate about the human world, that are likely to retain their hold over us after the first flush of excitement, I believe that his most encouraging response would be: Wait and see. Perhaps, but who knows? Maybe, maybe not.[7]

Wollheim's interpretation seems more sensitive and faithful to Berlin's stance than one typically finds among his academic critics. It touches on something mentioned in the introduction, where I highlighted the Humean anti-intellectualism at the heart of Berlin's view of philosophy, the sense that reason should not demand more of life than is reasonable and realistic. In this vein it also recognizes that occasionally there is more profundity to be found on the surface of life. Not everything *deep* is necessarily un-shallow. But none of this really vitiates the central problem of whether there is anything that can be said about human nature either

---

[6]Ludwig Wittgenstein, *Philosophical Investigations*, trans. G. E. M. Anscombe (1953: Blackwell, Oxford).
[7]Richard Wollheim, 'The Idea of a Common Human Nature', in *Isaiah Berlin: A Celebration,* eds. Edna and Avishai Margalit (1991: Hogarth Press, London), 78–79. Another distinguished commentator who has emphasized this aspect of Berlin's thought is Berlin's lifelong editor, Henry Hardy. Hardy discusses what he describes as 'the depth in his [Berlin's] concern with surface' in the introduction to his book, *In Search of Isaiah Berlin: A Literary Adventure* (2018: I. B. Tauris, London).

minimally or maximally which is more than platitudinously true about how we see human beings in any particular time and place. We will, therefore, be exploring this question more fully in the next chapter.

The third general point about Berlin's philosophical view of the world concerns the nature and status of his conception of value and cultural pluralism. As we saw, his interest in history and particularly in thinkers who went against the current of Platonic and Enlightenment rationalism such as Machiavelli, Vico and Herder, awakened him to what he saw as their most significant and permanent contribution to human thought, namely, that there is more than one way of living a good life and among the various and often conflicting conceptions of the good there exists no moral barometer or algorithm to calculate which is the best. Similarly, on a larger societal level, various cultures at different times and in different places have developed their own distinct ethical ideals and ways of living that are not transferable in any authentic or commensurable way from one culture to another. It is precisely this aspect of cultural pluralism that goes against the grain of the prevailing assumption in Western thought that the pursuit of a perfect society in which moral disagreement would finally be resolved and replaced by a morally harmonious state of affairs is achievable and therefore worth pursuing. What is particularly noteworthy about Berlin's conception of moral and cultural pluralism is that it is as much an epistemological and ethical claim as it is a historical or anthropological observation. The epistemological dimension is crucial for a number of reasons: most obviously, it serves to differentiate value pluralism from the bromide that we just happen to live in an imperfect world of moral uncertainty and disagreement. More often than not, this anodyne observation takes it for granted that uncertainty and conflict would vanish if human beings were capable of being a little more rational and/or altruistic. But Berlin is saying that moral diversity and disagreement are necessary and pervasive features of modern human life and not symptoms of an imperfect but perfectible world. He thereby also raises an important point about the relation between truth and historicity. Normally, we assume that truth and historicity (or contingency) pull in opposite directions, that truth is necessarily timeless and universal whereas the contingent is strictly ephemeral and local. But Berlin's version of pluralism does not conform to the conventional way of seeing things. He wants to claim that value and cultural pluralism amount to quasi-historical or quasi-contingent discoveries, discoveries that certain historical periods, most notably, modernity, are more open to acknowledging and accommodating than others.

This last point relates to another aspect of Berlin's conception of value pluralism that is noteworthy. It concerns his view about the nature and limits of human understanding. Berlin, it may be recalled, denies the availability of an Archimedean or God's-eye perspective, on the grounds that we can neither escape the Kantian hermeneutic circle nor our Vichian historical situatedness. And this raises an interesting question: Is it more accurate to describe our inability to get outside our own conceptual skin as a contingent truth or a necessary one? Similarly, should we categorize the alleged insight of value pluralism as a historical truth or as a necessary truth? Berlin's writings do not answer either of these questions in any kind of direct and systematic way. But the main reason for asking them is that his claim that value pluralism is true both in theory and in practice (and, correlatively, that value monism is similarly incoherent in practice and in principle) does not exactly mirror our normal understanding of the distinction between contingent and necessary truth. Perhaps the best way to characterize the epistemological status of value pluralism (and value monism) is to suggest that value pluralism is a contingent or contextual truth about the human predicament. In other words, the empirical fact as well as the philosophical truth of value pluralism resides in the world of contingency, not of necessity. One might even describe value pluralism therefore as a contingent or contextual necessity. But even then, as Berlin's account of the German thinker Hamann's insightful remarks on a similar topic intimates, we need to be mindful of not pushing the distinction between the contingent and the necessary to breaking point:

> No bridge is needed between necessary and contingent truths because the laws of the world in which man lives are as contingent as the 'facts' in it. All that exists could have been otherwise if God had so chosen, and can be so still. God's creative powers are unlimited, man's are limited; nothing is eternally fixed, at least nothing in the human world – outside it we know nothing, at any rate in this life. The 'necessary' is relatively stable, the 'contingent' is relatively changing, but this is a matter of degree, not kind. (TCE2, 363)

A fourth and related aspect of Berlin's philosophical perspective is his distinctive approach to the history of ideas. Within the broadly analytic philosophical tradition of the last hundred years or so the academic study of the history of philosophy has been dominated by two very different and competing genres. The earlier and still more prevalent genre tends to treat past philosophers as if they were our permanent contemporaries whereas the more recent, contextual school of intellectual thought is inclined to interpret long-dead thinkers in the directly opposite fashion. While exemplifying several of the virtues and vices evident in both of these genres, Berlin navigates his own unique form of philosophical history. Unlike the traditionalists, he takes a far more historically nuanced approach to long-dead thinkers, which does not naively assume that present and past philosophers form part of some deep and fundamentally unchanging discussion about philosophy's perennial questions. And unlike the contextualists, he does not believe that the history of philosophy cannot be comparable and relevant to present-day problems. Alasdair MacIntyre nicely encapsulates the essence of Berlin's position when he says: 'History is neither a prison nor a museum, nor is it a set of materials for self-congratulation.'[8]

Berlin does not deny that it is possible to treat the thought of a historical figure as germane to a present debate as long as it is done with self-conscious care and does not impose ahistorical assumptions that would be entirely alien, inconceivable or absurd to past thinkers and their times. So, for example, he would no doubt agree that we need to avoid the kind of crudely anachronistic readings that R. G. Collingwood felt analytic – or whom he disparagingly baptized as 'minute' – philosophers are characteristically guilty of. Reading a typically analytic history of philosophy was, Collingwood acerbically remarked, like meeting someone who insisted on translating the Greek word for a trireme as 'steamship' and then complaining that the ancient Greeks had a defective conception of a steamship.[9] But such patently ludicrous 'historical' interpretations should not lead us to deduce that the historical context necessarily exhausts the great texts of the past without remainder. A common assumption is that there must be aspects of a text that can in part transcend their specific historical context or intention and that these aspects tend to be more obvious and arresting when it comes to the great canonical texts of the past. After all, this is surely one of the primary reasons why they are seen as canonical: they have an irreducible quality or set of qualities that somehow surpass any single interpretation no matter how comprehensive and sophisticated an interpretation may be.

It is also worth bearing in mind that the seemingly interminable debate between contextualists and their critics reflects a deeper conflict between history and philosophy from which there is unlikely to emerge a final and harmonious resolution. This is the disagreement that centres on the question of whether philosophical history is legitimate or even possible. For if we are serious about taking on the fact

---

[8] Alasdair MacIntyre, *A Short History of Ethics* (1967: Routledge & Kegan Paul, London), 4.

[9] R. J. Collingwood, *An Autobiography* (1939: Oxford University Press, Oxford), 63. It should be noted that the putative validity of the historicist or contextualist critique of characteristically analytic 'histories' of philosophy is not thought to be restricted to such ludicrous examples. The spirit of astringency that informs the contextual critique of analytic history of philosophy is conveyed by Raymond Geuss and Richard Bourke in the following passage:

> 'Property' did not mean 'the same thing' for Locke as it did for Hayek, and 'democracy' very definitely did not 'mean', or even designate, 'the same thing' for fifth-century Athenians as it does for any of the European societies of the early twenty first century. In order to resolve the resulting semantic confusion, the strategy that comes naturally to much contemporary analytic philosophy is that of distinguishing conceptually between the 'direct democracy' of the ancients and the 'representative democracy' associated with much modern political practice. Each of these might be supplied with some kind of 'Socratic' definition, but neither has anything inherently to do with the other. From this perspective, the fact that both phrases contain the same component (democracy) is no more relevant than the fact that 'cat' and 'catapult' share their first three letters. Richard Bourke and Raymond Geuss eds. *Political Judgement: Essays for John Dunn* (2009: Cambridge University Press, Cambridge), 5.

that we are historically situated beings, then it would seem that we come under pressure to work out whether we can attribute any ultimate moral significance to how we got to where we are. Underlying this question is a virtually infinite number of answers ranging from the conviction, at one extreme, that any effort to provide a vindicatory account of our historical formation is a philosophical non-starter to the affirmation, and at the other extreme, that only a genuinely philosophical history has the power to unlock the inscrutable secret of the past (and the future) and thereby disclose, in Hegelian style, the objective meaning of our lives.[10]

So, notwithstanding the highly original and distinguished contribution of historians such as John Pocock, Quentin Skinner and John Dunn to our understanding of early modern intellectual history, one suspects that Berlin would have considered the reaction of the contextualist school to the anachronistic tendencies of traditional analytic history of philosophy as not a little tendentious and excessive. Indeed, the debate between contextualists and their detractors more often than not deteriorates to the level of *Punch & Judy* caricature where the former describe the latter as fatally ahistorical or anti-historical while the latter reciprocate by referring to their opponents as historical fundamentalists. Interestingly, the doyen of the contextual school of history, Quentin Skinner, chose the occasion of his inaugural lecture as Regius Professor of History at the University of Cambridge to revise, or at least moderate, his earlier stern repudiation of the 'classic texts' approach to the history of political thought. In his book *Liberty before Liberalism* (which is the published version of his inaugural lecture) Skinner explicitly argues that the neo-Roman theory of liberty has something to offer the contemporary world by providing a theory of freedom that rivals or complements the prevailing liberal conception of negative liberty advocated by Berlin.[11] One suspects that Skinner may have come to the realization that the war between the contextualists and their critics has been, at least in part, a phoney one and that his own methodological strictures may have been too demanding in practice even for himself. It might also be the case that a more illuminating way of characterizing the debate between Skinner and his main critics is to see it in terms of a difference between historical purism and historical impurism rather than an opposition between historical contextualism and analytic non-contextualism.[12] The advantage of viewing the debate in terms of the former distinction is that it is more suggestive of where the actual disagreement resides and, moreover, that it may not be as intractable as its chief participants claim. Incidentally, it is more likely to reveal

---

[10]For a sophisticated and refreshingly open-minded analysis of the viability of philosophical history in the context of the analytic philosophical tradition, see chapter one of Gordon Graham's *The Shape of History: A Philosophical Approach to History* (1997: Oxford University Press, Oxford), 14–44.

[11]Quentin Skinner, *Liberty before Liberalism* (1998: Cambridge University Press, Cambridge).

[12]See David Boucher, 'New Histories of Political Thought for Old?' *Political Studies* XXXI (1983), 112–21.

that Skinner's work is often at its most philosophically provocative and historically oecumenical when it prompts us to consider that since the past could have taken many possible paths from the one it ended up taking, it is worth looking back and trying to reconstruct the various and very different forms of life and perspectives that were neglected and that we lost out on. This type of historical or genealogical investigation can become particularly revealing when it leads us to consider what the alternative possibilities were that might have been taken in the past. It also serves remind us of the deep contingency of the past and the present.

Nonetheless, there is no denying that Berlin walks a precarious tightrope in pursuing what he referred to as *the history of ideas*. On a general level, his aim is to carry out a genuinely historical enquiry into the past, but always with an eye to seeking to enrich our understanding of our own contemporary situation. Berlin's interest in history is more fundamentally motivated by the question of whether past thinkers and their thoughts expressed something that is significant and possibly true than it is by a purely disinterested historical preoccupation with the specific intentions and linguistic practices of past thinkers and their times. More specifically, following his discovery, which 'came as something of a shock' through reading Machiavelli that moral monism may be false, the focus of much of his interest in history lay in interrogating more obscure, anti-Enlightenment thinkers such as Vico, Hamann and Herder, who for him helped confirm the alleged fallacy of monism while also vindicating the supposed truth of pluralism (CTH2 8). The question is, however, does Berlin succeed in carrying this off? Does he manage to reconcile the dictates of genuine history and the concerns of humanistic philosophy? Or are we witnessing a series of ingeniously sustained instances of legerdemain at work?

As we have observed already, Berlin's approach to intellectual history has led a number of scholars to contend that he tailors his readings of past thinkers to support his preconceived pluralist and liberal agenda.[13] If we are to judge Berlin by the stern standards of disinterested historical scholarship then it is difficult to exonerate him entirely from the charge of anachronism. It is undeniable that he does occasionally show signs of what one commentator has labelled rather acerbically the 'pen-pal approach' to the history of ideas.[14] For the result of such a 'method' is that the past runs the risk of losing its authentic otherness and of becoming a mere plaything in the service of some thinly disguised, self-fulfilling narrative. In Berlin's case, the argument goes, the past takes on the appearance

---

[13] See, for example, Mark Hulliung, *Citizen Machiavelli* (1983: Princeton University Press, Princeton, NJ); Peter Burke, *Vico* (1985: Oxford University Press, Oxford) and Morton White, 'Tolstoy the Empirical Fox', *Raritan* 22 (2003), 110–26; Perry Anderson, 'England's Isaiah' in the *London Review of Books* (20 December 1990), 3–7.

[14] This is a phrase that Ian Hacking applied to anachronistic readings of the history of philosophy in his essay 'Five Parables' in his *Historical Ontology* (2003: Harvard University Press, Cambridge, Mass), 27.

of a pitched battle between pluralism and monism in which the former ends up eventually but inevitably vanquishing the latter, at least polemically.

But there is an important sense in which such a charge misses the main point of what Berlin is up to. For while it is undeniable that his interest in the past is primarily driven by a concern to elicit some insight about the present human situation, his approach to the history of ideas combines an authentic commitment to historical understanding, what he once referred to as 'detective work', with a pursuit of philosophical enlightenment. In fact, there is a real sense in which these distinct and often rival pursuits manage somehow to meld seamlessly into one in Berlin's writings in a way that mirrors Vico's method of imaginative reconstruction. Underlying Berlin's own disinterment of the ideas of long-deceased thinkers is a key assumption, namely, the notion that the human past is not a hermetically sealed and impenetrable world but a distant and perhaps strange mental landscape that can still be accessed by virtue of our shared humanity, evidenced by our common, if often tenuously linked, patterns of thought. His view of history operates on the basis that we can and should proceed as if we are having a conversation with the long-dead but always with the proviso that we declare as sedulously and truthfully as we can our own distinctive beliefs, values and interests in that conversation. Moreover, as we saw in the previous chapter, our interaction with the past requires a leap of imaginative empathy given the radically different and often incommensurable character of past thinkers and distant cultures. Such an approach prompts us to broaden our minds by seeing ourselves for what we are, as one contingent but not incommunicable form of human life among others. This last point is critical, since it serves to inhibit rather than encourage our habitual but unwarranted belief that history is a story of progress or, indeed, that the past is locked in some form of eternal present. Indeed, Berlin's perspective invites us to view the past through a Vichian lens as a matter of inevitable gains and losses or perhaps just changes that fall into neither category. He conveys this point in an interview he gave in 1979:

> Every kind of new departure of the human spirit undoubtedly gives one an insight into aspects of the past which might not have been noticed before, and to that extent, if you like to call it progress, it is progress. But in the course of this we also lose certain things. I do not believe that there is such a thing as direct progress. There are certain things which people in the nineteenth century saw clearly which we probably see a little less clearly, because we think differently; there's loss and gain. (CC2 304–5)[15]

---

[15] From an interview on *Concepts and Categories* and *Russian Thinkers* which was broadcast in 1979 on Belgian Radio and published in Flemish in 1980. The first two parts of the interview are republished in CC2 284–305.

This, of course, raises a more fundamental question about whether Berlin's view of the past relies on an implausible conception of its accessibility and potential relevance to our own contingently formed way of life. Again, I don't believe there is an easy and definitive answer to this question. However, I shall offer the following tentative suggestion.

Even hard contextualists such as Quentin Skinner have occasionally – but only very occasionally and even then very briefly and amorphously – entertained the idea that there may be certain very general features of human nature and reason that persist through time, permitting us to make claims of a transhistorical nature.[16] But one gets the unmistakable impression from their various writings that even if we acknowledge the possibility of some relatively timeless core of human nature and/or of moral intuition, there is nothing of pivotal historical importance that we should assume can be derived from or attributed to their possible existence. In Skinner's case, one suspects that he is too much of a Wittgensteinian to allow himself to believe that any meaningful, thick conceptions of human nature, truth or rationality etc. could survive beyond the specific form of life or tradition from which they arose and evolved and then almost magically persist in some kind of suspended vacuum. Contextualism is not merely saying it provides the key to recovering the authentic historical meaning of past ideas but that one of the main insights of its mode of inquiry is the disconfirmation rather than confirmation of the validity of transhistorical truth and rationality. Accordingly, if previous forms of life or ideological traditions are as radically variant as Skinner and his disciples suggest then it is difficult to see how the notion of comparability can survive. However, Berlin would no doubt argue that such scepticism is unfounded and that the very survival of a subject like history presupposes the continuity of some minimal yet meaningful core of humanity. In this respect, Berlin's rebuttal of historical or cultural relativists resembles the form of argument that transcendentalism deploys against sceptics, that is, that the possibility of engaging in historical investigations that go beyond mere names and dates relies on the existence of certain common and transhistorical concepts and categories of human thought that historical purists or relativists largely deny. He believed the denial of some level of shared humanity, 'some common ground', across time and space led to self-defeating forms of historical and epistemological relativism.

---

[16]For an interesting analysis of Skinner's supposed 'concessions to those who regard the history of political thought as the study of perennial problems' (275), see Gordon J. Schochet, 'Quentin Skinner's Method', *Political Theory* 2, no. 3 (1974), 261–76. Something that commentators have not mentioned in this regard is the more obvious point that the slippery slope is surely never far from Skinner's mind. Having dedicated much of his professional life to putting historicist manners on the history of political thought he must be understandably reluctant to concede anything that might let the anachronistic genie out of the bottle.

This common ground is what is correctly called objective – that which enables us to identify other men and other civilisations as human and civilised at all. When this breaks down we do cease to understand, and, *ex hypothesi*, we misjudge; but since by the same hypothesis we cannot be sure how far communication has broken down, how far we are being deluded by historical mirages, we cannot always take steps to avert this or discount its consequences. We seek to understand by putting together as much as we can out of the fragments of the past, make out the best, most plausible cases for persons and ages remote from or unsympathetic or for some reason inaccessible to us; we do our utmost to extend the frontiers of knowledge and imagination; as to what happens beyond all possible frontiers, we cannot tell and consequently cannot care; for it is nothing to us. What we can discern we seek to describe as accurately and fully as possible; as for the darkness which surrounds the field of our vision, it is opaque to us, concerning it our judgements are neither subjective nor objective; what is beyond the horizon of vision cannot disturb us in what we are able to see or seek to know; what we can never know cannot make us doubt or reject that which we do. Some of our judgements are, no doubt, relative and subjective, but others are not; for if none were so, if objectivity were in principle inconceivable, the terms 'subjective' and 'objective' no longer contrasted, would mean nothing; for all correlatives stand and fall together. (L 152–3)

Rhetorically compelling though the above passage reads, I think we are still left in something of a quandary. Part of us may find ourselves in agreement with Berlin's view that some nucleus of common humanity and historical continuity is a precondition of thinking and writing about the past, and that the idea that our forebears are so fundamentally unintelligible as to leave no room for some level of meaningful comparability is intuitively implausible. But I suspect that in other moments we are more likely to judge that our putative common humanity may not have as much purchase as Berlin would like us to believe. My main reason for scepticism regarding the prospects for a shared, transhistorical human nature is based on what in the end might also be a mere intuition, namely, that believing in such things can deprive the past of its undeniable and radical otherness. Insisting on the deep and incorrigible pastness of the past still strikes me as a 'truth' or at least an undeniably plausible viewpoint that we would be ill-advised to abandon.[17] To accept the idea that we share some common moral core along the lines

---

[17] The nature of the relationship between our intuitions and philosophical argument is a fascinating one. Working out when and how philosophy ought to respect or reject our intuitive beliefs, especially our strongly held ones, forms a central task of the philosophical enterprise. My own view of the power and importance of intuitive beliefs shares something of the following remark of Saul Kripke:

> Some philosophers think that something's having intuitive content is very inconclusive evidence in favor of it. I think it is very heavy evidence in favor of anything, myself. I really don't know,

advocated by Berlin suggests that some undemonstrable and incredible kind of anthropological or quasi-moral constraint is operating on or within human beings and human society through time and space. Berlin would, of course, resist such a metaphysically loaded and implausible notion but his failure to produce a more robust and detailed justification of his faith in a common core of human values leaves him exposed. There is, of course, the related problem that Berlin's account of morality 'doesn't exclude enough'.[18]

However, it is difficult to avoid being left without serious misgivings on this matter, regardless of what position one takes. For while it appears that Berlin's seemingly minimal common ground may be more maximal than warranted, it also seems clear that Skinner's methodological writings suffer from an excessive reluctance to entertain the feasibility that there might be more weight behind Berlinian notions of a common, transhistorical human nature. In fact, it's hard to see how Skinner can reasonably claim that one of the main motives for studying the past ought to be about helping us to identify untapped treasures and untaken paths, exemplified most brilliantly in his account of how early modern notions of republican liberty possess contemporary normative relevance, without relying on some not insubstantial conception of a shared human nature and rationality. Perhaps past forms of life and the languages that defined them are more porous and interlocking than relativistically inclined Wittgensteinians are prepared to acknowledge.[19] At any rate, it would seem that we are faced with an irresolvable dilemma, which may in turn be a symptom of what one acute commentator has

---

in a way, what more conclusive evidence one can have about anything, ultimately speaking. Saul Kripke, Naming and Necessity (1980 edn: Blackwell, Oxford), 42.

[18] This is the verdict of Roger Hausheer according to Berlin's principal editor, Henry Hardy. See Henry Hardy, *In Search of Isaiah Berlin: A Literary Adventure* (2018: I.B. Tauris, London), 253.

[19] Skinner's more recent writings show a greater willingness to view certain past ideas as relevant to contemporary normative problems which in turn suggests that he may be more hospitable to the idea of transhistorical rationality than before. For example, towards the end of *Liberty before Liberalism*, he makes the following revealing statement:

> If the study of intellectual history is to have the kind of use I am claiming for it, there must be some deeper level at which our present values and the seemingly alien assumptions of our forebears match up. (117)

The above sentence is accompanied by the following, even more revealing footnote:

> I draw here on Donald Davidson's theory of radical interpretation. ... There is unquestionably a deeper level of continuity underlying the dispute I have been examining over the understanding of individual liberty. The dispute revolves, in effect, around the question of whether dependence should be recognised as a species of constraint; but both sides assume that the concept of liberty must basically be construed as absence of constraint on some interpretation of that term. The point of considering this example is not to plead for the adoption of an alien value from a world we have lost; it has been to uncover a lost reading of a value common to us and the vanished world. (117–18)

defined as a deeper conflict between history and philosophy, where both disciplines 'cannot be reduced to or eliminated in terms of one another'.[20] Nonetheless, one thing seems certain: that it is unlikely that the validity or otherwise of transhistorical rationality or truth can be demonstrated *a priori* and that therefore the opposing philosophical claims about intellectual history associated with Berlin and Skinner can perhaps only be established in practice. But the more fundamental legacy of both distinguished thinkers must surely rest on their shared commitment to the indispensability of a rich and lively dialogue between history and philosophy and, more generally, between the past and the present.[21]

The fifth and final feature of Berlin's conception of philosophy that merits special attention is its commitment to truth and truthfulness. At first glance, the attribution of a commitment to truth to Berlin might provoke more puzzlement than anything else. For while we are familiar with the notion that philosophy is among the intellectual disciplines concerned with the pursuit of universal and eternal truth, surely Berlin's conception of the philosophical enterprise suggests that such truth or knowledge is unavailable? How, in other words, can we reconcile Berlin's threefold classification of human enquiry, which distinguishes between the empirical, the *a priori* and the philosophical, the third category consisting, at least in part, of all genuinely unanswered and intractable questions, with the claim that his philosophical outlook is defined by an allegiance to truth? What sort of truth or knowledge, if any, could he be referring to here? This question, and, indeed, Berlin's answer to it, are far more complex and illuminating than critics have acknowledged.

To begin with, Berlin's commitment to truth denotes a certain sensibility which is distinct from any immodest claim that he has uncovered some irrefutable and all-encompassing philosophical truth. Perhaps a better term to adopt here would be truthfulness, or better still, a phrase Berlin himself was fond of using, 'the sense of reality'. In his essay of the same title, Berlin admits that this quality is elusive, not because it is intrinsically transcendent or mystical but because we find it difficult if not impossible to say something of a general nature about it that avoids sounding like either a mere platitude or pretentious nonsense. Berlin suggests that it is not

---

Skinner's concession or rather affirmation regarding possible normative continuities between the past and the present is fascinating and can be seen as a narrowing of the gap between his position and Berlin's belief that there are limits in relation to what he termed 'the human horizon'.

[20]Schochet, 'Quentin Skinner's Method', 276. There is, of course, the possibility that the dilemma is a false one and that it only seems real because we are naively assuming that there must be some elusive but meaningful relationship between history and philosophy. However, to argue that philosophers should stick to philosophy and, similarly, that historians should restrict themselves to history seems to me intolerably myopic and wrongheaded. The fact that it may be extremely difficult to produce convincing philosophical history does not mean that it is an incoherent project.

[21]A convincing if methodologically undeveloped *via media* along the lines suggested above can be found in Margaret Leslie, 'In Defence of Anachronism', *Political Studies* 18, no. 4 (1970), 433–47.

unlike the experience of encountering a new and wonderful painting or piece of music or a novel of genius. And those of us who are better at perceiving or appreciating such matters have what Berlin calls 'that capacity called imaginative insight, at its highest point genius' (SR 25). More specifically, Berlin defines this largely opaque sense of reality as

> a kind of semi-instinctive integration of the unaccountable infinitesimals of which individual and social life is composed, in which all kinds of skills are involved – the powers of observation, knowledge of facts, above all experience – in connection with which we speak of a sense of timing, sensitiveness to the needs and capacities of human beings, political and historical genius, in short the kind of human wisdom, ability to conduct one's life or fit means to ends which, as Faust found, mere knowledge of facts – learning, science – was not at all identical. (SR 33)

Berlin felt that certain thinkers possessed this quality in abundance, including among Russian writers, the political activist and thinker Alexander Herzen (1812–70) and the novelists Leo Tolstoy (1828–1910) and Ivan Turgenev (1818–83), and that having this quality endowed their view of the human world with a profundity and authority that declares itself in the difference between

> the application of laws and rules based on observed uniformities, and beliefs based on coherence with experience, whether one's own and that of one's society, or that of other men and other cultures. All experience embodies what Collingwood called the 'absolute presuppositions' of an age or culture. They are not incorrigible, but it is the grasp of these that distinguishes serious historians from bright storytellers and journalists: it is a faculty which historians require to have in common with imaginative writers. (CC2 322)

Berlin is perhaps more explicit about the meaning of this 'coherence with experience' or 'sense of reality' when he identifies it *in concreto* rather than trying to define it *in abstracto*. The following passage from one of his most celebrated essays gives us a better illustration of what Berlin means by this amorphous but no less objectively real quality:

> No author who has ever lived has shown such powers of insight into the variety of life – the differences, the contrasts, the collisions of persons and things and situations, each apprehended in its absolute uniqueness and conveyed with a degree of directness and a precision of concrete imagery to be found in no other writer. No one has ever excelled Tolstoy in expressing the specific flavour, the exact quality of a feeling – the degree of its 'oscillation', the ebb and flow, the minute movements … – the inner and outer texture and 'feel' of a look, a

thought, a pang of sentiment, no less than of a specific situation, of an entire period, of the lives of individuals, families, communities, entire nations. The celebrated lifelikeness of every object and every person in his world derives from this astonishing capacity of presenting every ingredient of it in its fullest individual essence, in all its many dimensions, as it were. (HF2 43–4)

This way of answering the question about the nature of Berlin's commitment to truth aligns readily enough with the influential idea, especially within analytic circles, that philosophy does not so much contribute to human knowledge as plumb the depths of human thought and understanding. The main appeal of seeing philosophy's task in this way is that it would appear to have the weight of evidence on its side. For one of the few things that we feel can be said with a certain degree of confidence about philosophy is that not many, if any, substantial philosophical truths have survived since the subject got going in earnest over two and a half millennia ago. Interpreting philosophy as the quest for understanding rather than the gradual and incremental growth of knowledge would seem to provide the appropriate framework for interpreting and assessing Berlin's own philosophical outlook.

But that is not saying quite enough in my view. There is also the possibility of deriving something more philosophically concrete and telling from Berlin's world view. It requires us to consider the more cognitively ambitious claim that Berlin's philosophical vision does not only deepen our understanding but that it may contain an important and far from insubstantial philosophical insight. I am not suggesting that his alleged philosophical discovery is of the same character as those of previous major philosophers who have confidently but vainly believed they had finally revealed the key to unlocking the secrets of philosophy, such as Plato with his theory of the *Forms*, Descartes (1596–1650) with his *cogito ergo sum* or even the Vienna Circle with their principle of verification. The philosophical insight that we can attribute to Berlin is more modest than the vaunted intellectual breakthroughs of previous long-deceased thinkers but no less profound. I am, of course, referring to his idea of value pluralism. I think there is an important sense in which if we accept that Berlin's conception of value pluralism does capture or correspond to something important about human life then we have not just increased our understanding of the world but we may also be in possession of an indispensable fact, even truth about our current predicament, a truth that genuinely matters even if it is far from generally accepted, let alone celebrated.

In this respect, there is an especially noteworthy parallel between how we might view the historico-philosophical meaning of Berlin's discovery of the truth of value pluralism and Hans Blumenberg's (1920–96) interpretation of the intellectual roots and evolution of modernity in his magisterial work *The Legitimacy of the Modern Age*. Like Berlin, Blumenberg highlights the illusory nature of the Enlightenment belief in an ahistorical science of human nature without abandoning a commitment to its ideals of unaided reason, freedom of thought and tolerance. And like Berlin, he argues that our gradual recognition that the modern age lacks absolute, non-contingent foundations is not a reason to view its emergence as a purely accidental affair. Indeed, both thinkers seem to share the conviction, albeit via separate intellectual paths, that acknowledging the contingency of modernity is an act of intellectual honesty and maturity rather than grounds for existential anxiety and despair.[22] They also intimate that there is a real sense in which our increasing self-consciousness about modernity's historically contingent rise constitutes a form of epistemological and ethical progress. Whether we call this consciousness a form of understanding or knowledge may ultimately be beside the point.

There are a number of things about modernity that we can still be justifiably and un-metaphysically proud of. They include the most obvious ones of freedom, toleration, democracy, the rule of law and civil liberties. But underlying these achievements are the less visible but no less important inheritances and traits of our culture. These include the idea that human reason is forever fallible and that even our most confident scientific and ethical beliefs must therefore be open to revision, that we no longer need to believe in a transcendent or cosmic Being or a version of the Whig view of history to defend our most cherished values and ideals, and that our Western way of life is not necessarily ethically superior in any absolute sense than those of non-Western societies and cultures but is no less precious and defensible for that. It is these less obvious but more basic and largely sceptically infused and historically self-conscious principles combined with his own distinctive account of ethical and cultural pluralism which explain much of the appeal and wisdom of Berlin's thought. The result is a humanistic and indeed pluralistic conception of philosophy and a justification of liberalism that is at once moderate, unparochial, undoctrinaire, fallible, meliorist, truthful and stridently non-perfectionist. Berlin's essay on Turgenev and the liberal predicament conveys his own unique version of the liberal temperament more personally and tellingly than his more explicitly political writings:

> Civilisation, humane culture, meant more to the Russians, latecomers to Hegel's feast of the spirit, than to the blasé natives of the West. Turgenev clung to it more passionately, was more conscious of its precariousness, than even his friends Flaubert and Renan. ... Chekhov once said that a writer's business was not to provide solutions, only to describe a situation so truthfully, to do such justice to all sides of the question, that the reader could no longer evade it. The doubts that Turgenev raised have not been stilled. The dilemma of morally sensitive, honest, and intellectually responsible men at a time of acute polarisation of opinion has, since his time, grown acute and worldwide. ... He recognised it in

---

[22]Hans Blumenberg, *The Legitimacy of the Modern Age* (1982: MIT Press, Boston, Mass).

its earlier beginnings, and described it with incomparable sharpness of vision, poetry and truth. (RT2 349–50)

What is especially perceptive about this passage and, indeed, Berlin's philosophical perspective as a whole, is the unswerving yet undeluded trust in truth and the concomitant idea that the values of truth and truthfulness themselves have normative implications. But, crucially, it is a moral and political philosophy anchored in the implacable realities and insights of ordinary, everyday human experience. In the above passage Berlin seems to be saying that liberalism may even stand above other ideologies not because it represents the pinnacle of human progress and civilization but on the grounds that it can remain truer to the objective diversity and imperfectability of human life. This suggests that his defence of liberalism is at once ethical *and* epistemological: it combines the epistemological or meta-ethical claim that our values and conceptions of the good are substantively and not just pragmatically in conflict with each other with the moral claim that a more civil and tolerant society is one that coheres with and respects the rich plurality of our values and ways of life. In a way, it is a vision of liberalism that knows too much about its own limits to affirm itself in any kind of self-consciously absolute and dogmatically universal way and yet has seen enough of our humanity and inhumanity to consider itself worth defending tooth and nail. To paraphrase the American jurist, Learned Hand (1872–1961), the spirit of liberalism is the spirit that 'is not too sure that it is right', the spirit that can make it peculiarly difficult for a liberal to take his or her own side in an argument. But it is this self-same spirit whose neglect or even possible demise we are certain would leave us irrevocably demoralized and diminished.

7 PHILOSOPHY, LITERATURE AND HUMAN UNDERSTANDING

The type of insights gained from reading Isaiah Berlin are not unlike those that can be derived from reading a great novel, even one as great as Tolstoy's *War and Peace*. While not wishing to deny the valid and important distinctions between philosophy and literature, there is a sense in which reading both writers can leave readers more open to becoming perceptive, knowledgeable and even wise about themselves and others. And I think one of the reasons why their writings can have this effect on us is their shared commitment to conveying human life in its concrete complexity and variety. As we have seen, Berlin argues that one of the ways philosophy has the capacity to deepen our understanding of human thought and experience is by adopting a more anthropocentric and historicized view of the world. Great imaginative literature also provides us with ways of accessing the elemental but often hidden patterns of thought that help us make better sense of the natural, meaning and limits of human life. And for Berlin, there were few more gifted imaginative writers than Tolstoy when it came to capturing what he refers variously as 'the universal texture', 'the ultimate framework', and 'the sense of reality' associated with human life (HF2 71, 76, 85, 90; 74; 75). His justly celebrated essay on Tolstoy, 'The Hedgehog and the Fox', conveys in a uniquely impressive and memorable way what the great Russian novelist is doing when he is tapping into what he refers to as this mysterious but no less objective 'sense of reality':

> To do this is, above all, to grasp what human will and human reason can do, and what they cannot. How can this be known? Not by a specific enquiry and discovery, but by an awareness, not necessarily explicit or conscious, of certain general characteristics of human life and experience. And the most important and most pervasive of these is the crucial line that divides the 'surface' from

the 'depths' – on the one hand the world of perceptible, describable, analysable data, both physical and psychological, both 'external' and 'inner', both public and private, with which the sciences can deal …; and, on the other hand, the order which, as it were, 'contains' and determines the structure of experience, the framework in which it – that is, we and all that we experience – must be conceived as being set, that which enters into our habits of thought, action, feeling, our emotions, hopes, wishes, our ways of talking, believing, reacting, being. We – sentient creatures – are in part living in a world the constituents of which we can discover, classify and act upon by rational, scientific, deliberately planned methods: but in part … we are immersed and submerged in a medium that, precisely to the degree to which we inevitably take it for granted as part of ourselves, we do not and cannot observe as if from the outside …. It – the medium in which we are – determines our most permanent categories, our standards of truth and falsehood, of reality and appearance, of the good and the bad, of the central and the peripheral, of the subjective and the objective …; hence neither these, nor any other explicitly conceived categories or concepts, can be applied to it – for it is itself but a vague name for the totality that includes these categories, these concepts, the ultimate framework, the basic presuppositions wherewith we function. (HF2 74–5)

This passage helps make clear that Berlin is not suggesting that 'the sense of reality' is peculiarly mysterious and largely ineffable on account of being mystical or transcendent. Rather, he is arguing that while there exists no non-perspectival or Archimedean vantage point from which we can omnisciently survey and adjudicate the human world (and the inanimate world, for that matter), it has, on the whole, taken thinkers and writers of genius to have shown us that the seemingly unreachable depths of human thought can be plumbed, that 'the basic presuppositions wherewith we function' can be unearthed and brought to some semblance of light. Apart from philosophers like Hume and Kant, Berlin judged that this capacity to grasp the underlying thought and, more especially, *flow* of human life was possessed by such novelists as Ivan Turgenev and Boris Pasternak, cultural historians of the calibre of Vico and Herder, his own unclassifiable hero, Alexander Herzen, and, of course, Tolstoy himself. Each of these writers succeeded in their own inimitable manner in transmuting or *getting* what is distinctive about a person, a feeling, a glance or the zeitgeist of a particular age. Two features are especially striking about such sensers or truth-tellers of reality. The first is that their own unique sense of reality is necessarily, if gloriously, finite, partial and imperfect. The second is that the imaginative gift they are endowed with and have nurtured over their lives is incapable of being either learned or applied like some technical skill or causal theory: rather it is rooted in and faithful to the contingent medium of human experience rather than to the exigencies of some independently formal theory or absolute doctrine.

Interestingly, even the famously austere philosopher, Ludwig Wittgenstein, reached something of a comparable view of our non-scientific understanding in his later philosophy, that is, the type of attitude typically associated with the arts and humanities and concerned with portraying the elusive texture and meaning of ordinary, quotidian, often unregarded moments of our existence. In his *Philosophical Investigations*, Wittgenstein considers the matter of how this sort of understanding or insight is acquired:

> Is there such a thing as 'expert judgement' about the genuineness of expressions of feeling? – Even here there are those whose judgement is 'better' and those whose judgement is 'worse'. Correcter prognoses will generally issue from the judgement of those with better knowledge of mankind. Can one learn this knowledge? Yes, some can. Not however by taking a course in it, but through 'experience' …. What can be most difficult here is to put this indefiniteness, correctly and unfalsified, into words …. It is certainly possible to be convinced by evidence that someone is in such and such a state of mind, that, for instance, he is not pretending. But 'evidence' here includes 'imponderable' evidence …. Imponderable evidence includes subtleties of glance, of gesture, of tone. Ask yourself: How does a man learn to get a 'nose' for something? And how can this nose be used?[1]

One of Wittgenstein's most accomplished biographers, Ray Monk (1957), relates a conversation that Wittgenstein had about his favourite novel, *The Brothers Karamazov*, with his friend Maurice Drury (1907–76) where the latter commented on the vivid impressiveness of the central character of Father Zosima. In the novel, Dostoevsky (1821–81) says of Zosima:

> It was said that, by permitting everyone for so many years to come to bare their hearts and beg his advice and healing words, he had absorbed so many secrets, sorrows, and avowals into his soul that in the end he had acquired so fine a perception that he could tell at first glance from the face of a stranger what he had come for, what he wanted and what kind of torment racked his conscience.

When Drury read this passage out, Wittgenstein said: 'Yes there really have been people like that, who could see directly into the souls of other people and advise them.'[2]

---

[1] Ludwig Wittgenstein, *Philosophical Investigations* (1953: Blackwell, Oxford), Part II.
[2] Quoted in Ray Monk, *Ludwig Wittgenstein: The Duty of Genius* (1990: Chatto & Windus, London), 549. Incidentally, Monk exemplifies the true art of biography by presenting us with an authentically compelling version of what Lytton Strachey called 'a point of view' of two of the greatest philosophers

Berlin, it would appear, shares a similar view of Tolstoy's powers of human understanding and empathy:

> Tolstoy is incapable of supressing, or falsifying, or explaining away by reference to dialectical or other 'deeper' levels of thought, any truth when it presents itself to him, no matter what this entails, where it leads, how much it destroys of what he most passionately longs to believe. Everyone knows that Tolstoy placed truth highest of all the virtues. Others have said this too, and have celebrated her no less memorably. But Tolstoy is among the few who have truly earned that rare right: for he sacrificed all he had upon her altar – happiness, friendship, love, peace, moral and intellectual certainty, and, in the end, his life. And all she gave him in return was doubt, insecurity, self-contempt and insoluble contradictions. (RT2 298)

There is an episode towards the end of *War and Peace* where Napoleon says on the eve of the Battle of Borodino: 'The board's set up. The game begins tomorrow.' But just a few pages earlier Pierre Bezukhov had also compared war to a game of chess only to provoke Prince Andrey's sardonic reply: 'Yes, it is ... but there's one little difference. In chess you can take as long as you want over every move. You are beyond the limits of time.'[3] This 'little difference' is, of course, the big and crucial one. And it is this same refusal to move beyond 'the limits of time' or of real, experiential life – only the reader possesses the relative omniscience of hindsight – that informs Tolstoy's novels and which impressed Berlin.

After reading *War and Peace*, the Russian short-story writer and journalist, Isaac Babel concluded: 'If life could write, it would write like Tolstoy.' And it is precisely this feature of Tolstoy's fiction that Berlin most valued and described so perceptively in his landmark study of him. In his autobiographical essay, 'The Pursuit of the Ideal', Berlin mentions that *War and Peace* (along with the works of other great Russian writers) had an immense influence in shaping his outlook:

> Their approach seemed to me essentially moral: they were concerned most deeply with what was responsible for injustice, oppression, falsity in human

---

of the last century, Ludwig Wittgenstein and Bertrand Russell, that enables us to understand them and their respective ideas in more convincing ways.

[3] Leo Tolstoy, *War and Peace*, trans. Anthony Briggs (2005: Penguin, London), 872 and 858 respectively. I am indebted to James Wood's characteristically shrewd essay 'Tolstoy's *War and Peace*' in his *The Fun Stuff* (2012: Farrar, Straus & Giroux, New York) for highlighting the significant link between these passages, 145–61. But I am more generally indebted to Vladimir Nabokov's brilliant essay on Tolstoy for pointing out Tolstoy's 'endowing his fiction with such time-values as correspond exactly to our sense of time'. See his *Essays on Russian Literature*, ed. Fredson Powers (1981: Harcourt, New York), 141.

relations, imprisonment whether by stone walls or conformism – unprotesting submission to man-made yokes – moral blindness, egoism, cruelty, humiliation, servility, poverty, helplessness, bitter indignation, despair, on the part of so many. In short, they were concerned with the nature of these experiences and their roots in the human condition of Russia in the first place, but, by implication, of all mankind. And conversely, they wished to know what would bring about the opposite of this, a reign of truth, love, honesty, justice, security, personally relations based on the possibility of human dignity, decency, independence, freedom, spiritual fulfilment. (CTH2 3)

Passages such as this raise the intriguing question of whether imaginative fiction rather than philosophy is better qualified to answer the Socratic problem of how we should live our lives. The pertinence of this question becomes even more pressing when one observes just how oblivious so much of contemporary moral and political philosophy is of real, living, breathing human beings. It is at least arguable that the more realistic and engaging contemporary moral and political philosophers are those who have shown evidence of something approaching the kind of imaginative understanding of the self that we witness among accomplished novelists and indeed other types of creative minds. This suggestion still strikes many professional philosophers, especially analytic ones, as heresy: they are apt to remind us that philosophy is in the sober business of dispassionately and systematically seeking the unvarnished truth whereas literature operates primarily within the fictional or creative realm and is therefore not answerable to Reality, Truth and Reason. Yet the result of reading Berlin and Tolstoy does not invite such a response and, if anything, prompts us to be sceptical of the basis and bias of such 'philosophical' fears. Berlin's thought raises legitimate qualms about the validity of the now common dichotomies we accept as gospel truth between such things as facts and values, knowledge and opinion, rationality and emotion, history and truth in the realms of philosophical discussion as well as normal, everyday speech. Indeed, nobody familiar with Tolstoy's fiction can ignore the serious doubts it raises about the limitations of theoretical truth or the emphasis it puts on the far more palpable existential truths which can only be derived from actually experiencing the difficulty and ultimate loneliness of life, from being 'confronted with life'.[4] In

---

[4]Leo Tolstoy, *Anna Karenina* (1992 edn: Everyman Library, London), Part 2, Ch. 8:

> Now, though his conviction that jealousy is a shameful feeling, and that one ought to have confidence, had not been destroyed, he felt that he was face to face with something illogical and stupid, and he did not know what to do. Karenin was being confronted with life – with the possibility of his wife's loving somebody else, and this seemed stupid and incomprehensible to him, because it was life itself. He lived and worked all his days in official spheres, which deal with reflections of life, and every time he had knocked up against life itself he had stepped out of its way. He now experienced the sensation such as a man might feel who, while quietly crossing a

any case, Berlin opens up and exemplifies the possibility of interpreting the world of human relations in a fresh and more penetrating light.

Another noteworthy parallel between Tolstoy and Berlin in this context is their shared appreciation of what has been described as the art of defamiliarization. Tolstoy uses the technique of defamiliarization, which consists in rendering something familiar in an unexpectedly new and provocative way 'by removing objects from the automatism of perception', in his novels to prompt us to look at the world differently and see it afresh.[5] His portrayal of the opera scene as well as the various battles in *War and Peace* provide classic instances of this technique in action. Berlin felt that the same kind of defamiliarization effect happened when children ask certain types of questions, the sort of basic and disruptive questions that philosophy typically concerns itself with such as, 'What is a number?' or 'Why can't I go back in time and meet Napoleon at the Battle of Austerlitz?' Berlin felt that there is something fundamentally childlike (but far from childish) about philosophical questions in the way that they can provoke us to look behind, beyond and underneath our conventional and often constricting ways of perceiving the world and make us more aware of the limits and possible distortions of our habitual and predominantly unself-conscious ways of seeing the world. In fact, he considered that one of the hallmarks of a true philosopher is a willingness and ability to appreciate that cross-examining such childlike questions is what philosophy is fundamentally about (PI3 174). Berlin made the following comment on the matter in an interview he gave with Bryan Magee which was screened by the BBC in 1978:

> What sort of 'can't' answers 'May I see the Battle of Austerlitz, please?' We are plunged into philosophy straight away. Someone may tell the child 'You can't because of the nature of time.' But then some philosophically-minded persons will say: 'No, no, there aren't such things as time or its nature. Statements about time can be translated into statements about what occurs "before" or "after" and "simultaneously with". To talk about time as if it were a kind of thing is a metaphysical trap.' We are now launched. Most fathers don't want to answer the questions of their importunate children in that way. They just tell them to shut up, not to ask silly questions, to go away and stop being a nuisance. But this is the type of question which constantly recurs; and philosophers are people who are not bored or irritated by them, or terrified of them, and are prepared to

---

bridge over an abyss, suddenly sees that the bridge is being taken to pieces and that he is facing the abyss. The abyss was real life; the bridge was the artificial life Karenin had been living. (168)

See William Barrett, *Irrational Man: A Study in Existential Philosophy* (1958: Doubleday, New York) for a philosophically engaging treatment of existentialism as well as an intimation of what philosophy might look like if it freed itself from its current professional deformation.

[5]Viktor Shklovsky, 'Art as Technique' (1917) in Lee T. Lemon and Marion Reis trans. *Russian Formalist Criticism* (1965: University of Nebraska Press, Lincoln, Nebr).

deal with them. Children, of course, are conditioned in the end to repress these questions. More's the pity. The children who are not wholly so conditioned sometimes turn into philosophers.[6]

This amounts to an invitation to philosophy to become more grown-up in its outlook than it currently is, to dare to be more than what much of it has regrettably and all too routinely become. Berlin's example of being philosophically, historically and imaginatively responsive to the genuine and enduring thoughts and experiences of human beings surely has more to be said for it than engaging in the quasi-mechanical production of bizarrely formal, spuriously systematic and mind-numbingly unconvincing theories of 'morality' and 'politics'. Chekhov said of Tolstoy's career that it vindicated 'the hopes and expectations reposed in literature'.[7] One could justifiably say the same of the spirit if not the substance of Berlin's contribution to moral and political philosophy.

A tantalizing question

One of the themes that has kept cropping up in one form or another over the course of our discussion is a certain tension that may be said to exist at the heart of Berlin's conception of philosophy. It touches on the old conceptual chestnut of whether there actually exists such a thing as non-scientific truth and knowledge. There is a great deal of consensus both within and outside the philosophical tradition that the quest for such knowledge or truth is nothing more than a fool's errand. The history of philosophy is strewn with the withered remains of what were once confidently and unequivocally proclaimed as substantial and everlasting philosophical truths. One of the central questions that Berlin prompts us to confront is this: Does the declaration of the truth of value pluralism amount ultimately to anything more than another will-o'-the-wisp? Is saying that value pluralism is not merely a historical fact but a philosophical truth akin to saying that Tolstoy, for example, is a writer of genius? It may well be true that many of us happen to find Berlin's theory of value pluralism and/or Tolstoy's novels ethically and imaginatively captivating but can we also say that they provide us with what might be described as actual knowledge?

Our response to this question can only be provisional at this point in our discussion. Berlin's Kantianism commits him to the view that our concepts and categories, including those associated with self-understanding, can transcend – but not in any supernatural or Archimedean sense – at least in part our particular

---

[6]Bryan Magee, *Men of Ideas: some creators of contemporary philosophy* (1978: BBC, London), 28–9.
[7]Quoted in Leo Tolstoy, *A Critical Anthology*, ed. Henry Gifford (1971: Penguin, London), 111.

place and time. But, on the other hand, the historicist or Vichian dimension of his thought has the result of raising serious doubts about the philosophical validity and even possibility of such a quasi-transcendent perspective. Once we start taking our contingency seriously, as Berlin's conception of philosophy suggests we should, it becomes more and more difficult to give credence to the view that our concepts and categories can rise above the historicity of our particular situation in any obviously non-circular, objective way. It is not hard to fall prey to the deflationary doubt that our so-called transcendental categories of thought are themselves nothing more than the dressed-up but basically arbitrary preferences cherished by our own postmodern age. So we are still left with the fundamental question of whether Berlin's defence of liberalism operates ultimately at the level of rhetoric or reason, of ideology or truth. The next chapter will be concerned with addressing this central and tantalizing poser.

PART THREE

CONTINGENCY

8 PHILOSOPHY AND BELIEF

We shall now confront the large and fundamental question left unresolved at the end of the previous chapter, namely, the problem of what, if any, is the relationship between contingency and truth in Berlin's political philosophy. How we answer this question has a crucial bearing on how we interpret and assess his justification of liberalism. If it emerges that there is little or no genuine connection between truth and liberalism in Berlin's thought then we are left with having to treat his moral and political theory through a largely ideological and rhetorical frame. If, on the other hand, it transpires that there is a philosophically significant relation between truth and historicity in his defence of a liberal society, a very different panorama opens up. But before we address the heart of the matter a few general remarks about the relationship between philosophy and belief are in order.

It is a fine question how one's philosophical outlook relates to one's own particular normative views or, more simply, how one's philosophy connects with one's ordinary beliefs. Put more technically, what, if any, is the relation between meta-ethics and normative ethics, the former being a second-order philosophical theory about the nature of ethics, and the latter a first-order, substantive ethical belief. Views about the nature and status of meta-ethics and of normative ethics have varied a great deal since the time Berlin entered the philosophical scene. It may be helpful therefore if we describe how the meta-ethical/normative debate within analytic philosophy has evolved over the last hundred years or so.

Broadly speaking, we can identify three relatively discrete phases in the development of this particular philosophical debate since the 1930s. During the initial phase the default position within Anglophone philosophy was that the business of moral philosophy was very much restricted to the second-order, meta-ethical discussion about morality as distinct from any first-order engagement in substantive ethics. For reasons outlined in the previous chapter we saw that the two prevailing schools of philosophy during this initial phase – logical positivism and linguistic analysis – held that it was impossible for philosophy to provide substantive moral and political beliefs with anything even approaching a cognitive foundation. Meta-ethics was one thing and normative ethics quite another. Philosophers were, of course, not precluded from pontificating on the great moral and political questions of the day as long as they did not commit the error of thinking that their own particular views held any special philosophical weight. The received wisdom of the time was articulated by the philosopher C. D. Broad (1887–1971): 'It is not part of the professional business of moral philosophers to tell people what they ought or ought not to do …. Moral philosophers, as such, have no special information not available to the general public, about what is right and what is wrong.'[1]

For a number of reasons, not all of which were strictly philosophical, this initial phase gradually gave way to a more theoretically ecumenical period. Serious doubts had been raised about the claimed value-freeness of meta-ethical discourse, which in turn led to growing scepticism about the validity of denying the possibility and legitimacy of substantive moral philosophy. The upshot was essentially twofold. In the first place, meta-ethical analysis ceased to be regarded as an entirely value-free or morally neutral activity. And secondly, normative ethics began to reassert itself as a theoretically valid form of moral discussion. This was reflected in the wave of articles and books that began to appear from the late 1960s: the publication in the early 1970s of John Rawls's *Theory of Justice* and the launch of journals such as *Philosophy and Public Affairs* and *Political Theory*, testified to the resurgence of work in the areas of normative political philosophy as well as applied ethics. And while meta-ethics did not exactly go the way of all flesh it certainly ceased to be regarded as the one and only form of legitimate moral enquiry.

And then finally, in more recent years, we have begun to observe the emergence of a new and radical development in which there is a growing suspicion that meta-ethics may not be a particularly significant or even viable philosophical pursuit. This latest twist in the tale centres on the claim that while normative moral philosophy may choose to include or refer to meta-ethical considerations, it need not work on the basis that such considerations are in any way theoretically decisive or even especially germane. The basic argument in this case is that normative philosophy is not required to worry itself unduly about meta-ethics, since the latter has no real moral skin in the game and is therefore largely irrelevant to substantive normative debates. The leading exponents of this view are the late Ronald Dworkin (1931–2013) and, less stridently and unequivocally, Thomas Nagel (1937) and Tim Scanlon (1940).[2] They all share a scepticism about the capacity of conventional 'value-free'

---

[1] C. D. Broad, *Ethics and the History of Philosophy* (1952: Routledge, London), 244.

[2] Ronald Dworkin's view about meta-ethics and normative ethics is conveyed most systematically and eloquently in his penultimate book *Justice for Hedgehogs* (2011: Harvard University Press, Cambridge, Mass), 23–96. Thomas Nagel explicitly acknowledges the influence not just of Dworkin but also Saul Kripke in leading him to this view: where Dworkin convinced him that normative ethical theory rather than meta-ethics holds the key to refuting or at least responding to various forms of moral scepticism,

meta-ethics to deal with the challenge of ethical relativism in its various forms. If Dworkin's views in particular end up gaining further influence we could be seeing the beginning of the end of traditional meta-ethics as a philosophically serious form of enquiry and its possible relegation to a sub-species of ethical enquiry at risk of imminent extinction.

At this point, a legitimate question to ask is 'So what?' What difference does it make whether or not our moral and political beliefs are or can be backed up by philosophy? Surely our ordinary, everyday normative beliefs can survive perfectly well without the need for any theoretical support or endorsement. This type of complaint can emerge from a variety of sources including the philistine one that philosophy is a complete waste of time. Another is the more interesting objection that philosophy as it is currently practised is largely sterile and superfluous and should therefore be ignored. And finally there is the view that while certain branches of philosophy may not be a waste of time, moral and political philosophy certainly is. The philosopher Simon Blackburn (1944) has produced a neat response to these various kinds of complaint and it might be helpful if we survey his treatment of them before moving to a consideration of the central topic of this chapter, that is, how Berlin's defence of liberalism fits into the core debate about the relationship of philosophy to belief.[3]

Blackburn thinks there are three ways of responding to scepticism about philosophy. He labels these the high-ground, the middle-ground and the low-ground responses. The high-ground approach claims that philosophical reflection is an intrinsically worthwhile activity independently of any practical human use it may have. This is a version of the familiar idea about knowledge for knowledge's sake. Its pure-minded defence of the subject may be fine and laudable as far as it goes but its critical weakness is that it does not go very far at all. And, as Blackburn acknowledges, it is unlikely to prove persuasive to more than the converted (who are in a minority of a minority!). The middle-ground response takes less for granted and pins its colours to the argument that reflection matters because it is continuous with practice. According to this view, self-reflexive thought affects how you conduct your life. For example, if reflection has led you to believe in life after death, you may be more prepared to suffer the injustices of this world than a person who does not share your belief in transcendence. In other words, given the power that our thoughts have over our actions, it makes sense to invest some

---

Kripke persuaded him even earlier that the only way to reply to various forms of scepticism about logic is from within classical logic itself. See Thomas Nagel, *The Last Word* (1997: Oxford University Press, Oxford), vii. Finally, the recent work of Tim Scanlon reflects a more qualified but explicit readiness to give up on the idea that meta-ethical enquiry can be value free and devoid of at least some minimal normative implications. See T. M. Scanlon, 'The Aims and Authority of Moral Theory', in *The Oxford Journal of Legal Studies* 12 (1992): 1–23.

[3]Simon Blackburn, *Think* (1999: Oxford University Press, Oxford), 6–13.

time in thinking about the quality of our reflections, to minimize the risk that they are misleading us. The third and final defence of philosophy is essentially an extension of the middle-ground response, a response that is driven by what it sees as the need to descend into 'the basement where human life is a little less polite' (p.10). The need for the low-ground response is perhaps best captured in the celebrated lines from W. B. Yeats' (1865–1939) *The Second Coming*: 'The best lack all conviction, while the worst / Are full of passionate intensity.' By prompting us to step back from our own particular perspective and view it in a more detached light, philosophical reflection can serve two key benefits: it can help reveal that our own language games or folkways may not be as infallible or superior as our pre-reflective biases might indicate, and, secondly, it leaves us less vulnerable to the superficial charms and half-truths of the demagogue. Two notable developments in 2016, the conduct of the Brexit referendum in the United Kingdom as well as the presidential election in the United States, provided us with alarming reminders of just how susceptible even established liberal-democratic societies are to such dangers. What was most disturbing about each of these events was not so much the mendacity of certain politicians, but the fact that their blatant bullshit and downright lies were greeted with seemingly gleeful indifference by so many people. I am using the term 'bullshit' here in the sense defined by Harry Frankfurt (1929) in his perceptive and prescient pamphlet, *On Bullshit*:

> [The bullshitter] is neither on the side of the true nor on the side of the false. His eye is not on the facts at all, as the eyes of the honest man and of the liar are, except insofar as they may be pertinent to his interest in getting away with what he says. He does not care whether the things he says describe reality correctly. He just picks them out, makes them up, to suit his purpose.[4]

It is hardly surprising that the Oxford dictionary chose 'post-truth' as its word of the year in 2016.[5]

Blackburn's typology is instructive in a number of ways. At a general level, it brings out the salient point that philosophy can have consequences for our beliefs and conduct. It also serves to highlight the central question of the continuity

---

[4] Harry Frankfurt, *On Bullshit* (2005: Princeton University Press, Princeton, NJ), 56. His essay was originally published in *Raritan* VI no. 2 (1986).

[5] See Matthew d'Ancona's, *Post-Truth* (2017: Penguin, London) for a good journalistic analysis of how both the 2016 US election and the earlier Brexit referendum reflected the startling decline of respect for truth in public life. We have yet to see if these developments represent more than a temporary collapse in our commitment to as well as our ability to defend the centrality of truth, the rule of law and basic civic decency in Western politics and society. For a perceptive analysis that the future of such epistemic and social norms hangs in the balance far more than we may care to admit, see the recent writings of the historian, Timothy Snyder, *On Tyranny* (2017: Bodley Head, London) and *The Road to Unfreedom* (2018: Bodley Head, London).

between reflection and practice, a theme which will inform much of the discussion that follows. The final point worth noting is one that does not strictly fall within Blackburn's threefold analysis but which he refers to shortly after introducing his typology. This is the theoretically generated notion that philosophy itself has passed its expiry date along with its obsolete bedfellows Truth, Knowledge and Objectivity. This may strike the uninitiated as a strange form of intellectual masochism, but it is a challenge that philosophy has continually faced since its inception. From the time of the ancient Greek Sophists there has never been a shortage of philosophers – or, more accurately, philosophical anti-philosophers – who have questioned the very possibility and use of philosophical reflection itself. This form of radical scepticism about the subject is entirely different from the kind of philistine dismissiveness of all forms of intellectualism that Blackburn is referring to when he offers his low-ground defence of the subject. Its core idea is that philosophy's primary quest to transcend our ordinary beliefs or conventions or ideology is, in the final analysis, an inherently fatuous one. As one of today's more sophisticated anti-philosophical thinkers puts it:

> In short, the very essentials that are in foundationalist discourse opposed to the local, the historical, the contingent, the variable, and the rhetorical, turn out to be irreducibly dependent on, and indeed to be functions of, the local, the historical, the variable and the rhetorical. Foundationalist theory fails, lies in ruins, because it is from the very first implicated in everything it claims to transcend.[6]

This type of root-and-branch scepticism about philosophy brings us close to where we started the chapter. We saw that during the first phase of the analytic tradition, roughly from the 1930s to the 1960s, the predominant response to the question of the relationship of philosophy to evaluative beliefs was deflationary. Philosophy was thought to have nothing of substance to say about our normative beliefs and practices. But it would be a mistake to assume we have merely come full circle with what looks like a contemporary postmodern variation on an earlier analytic theme. For while anti-philosophical thinkers like Stanley Fish (1938), and more famously Richard Rorty (1931–2007), certainly share similar views with their logical positivist forbears about the practical irrelevance of traditional philosophy to our ordinary moral beliefs, their scepticism is global, applying as much to science as to ethics. So whereas Quine felt that 'philosophy of science is philosophy enough', today's postmodern, post-philosophical thinkers go one step further and argue that all forms of foundational philosophy are inescapably empty and should therefore be promptly discontinued.

---

[6]Stanley Fish, 'Antifoundationalism, Theory Hope and the Teaching of Composition', in *Doing What Comes Naturally* (1989: Oxford University Press, Oxford and New York), 345.

The problem stated

Having briefly delineated the main contours of the relationship of philosophy to belief and correspondingly of meta-ethics to normative ethics, we can now focus attention on the relevance of this discussion to Berlin's outlook. More specifically, we are now in a position to examine the nature of the connection between Berlin's meta-ethics and his normative beliefs or, rather, the relation between his value pluralism and his liberalism. That in turn will help to uncover the philosophical roots of his liberalism and to address the deeper matter of the link between truth and contingency (or historicity) in his thought.

At first glance, Berlin's pluralist vision of liberalism can strike us as somewhat puzzling. The puzzle has been identified and expressed most forcibly by the American political philosopher, Michael Sandel (1953). In his introduction to an anthology of writings on liberalism by various contemporary political philosophers, Sandel provides a clear and engaging account of the debate between liberalism and its critics.[7] He begins by rehearsing the familiar liberal distinction between permission and praise, a distinction that informs the paradigmatic liberal view that, for example, pornography or abortion should be legally permitted without necessarily being morally endorsed. Underlying this distinction is the more basic liberal principle that the law of the land should not impose a substantive moral code and preferred way of life but should leave its citizens as free as possible to choose their own ethical ideals and way of living. Sandel argues quite persuasively that the liberal justification of toleration and freedom is far more vulnerable than its proponents are willing to acknowledge. As he provocatively remarks:

> Why should toleration and freedom of choice prevail when other important values are also at stake? Too often the answer implies some version of moral relativism, the idea that it is wrong to 'legislate morality' because all morality is merely subjective. ... Relativism usually appears less as a claim than as a question. ('Who is to judge?') But it is a question that can also be asked of the values that liberals defend. Toleration and freedom and fairness are values too, and they can hardly be defended by the claim that no values can be defended. (LC 1)

According to Sandel, the relativist defence of liberalism does not amount to much of a defence at all. But it is his next move that makes this argument particularly relevant for our purposes. For Sandel claims that Berlin's version of liberalism is 'perilously close to foundering on the relativist predicament':

---

[7]Michael Sandel ed. *Liberalism and its Critics* (1984: Blackwell, Oxford). Henceforth referred to as LC.

In view of the ultimate plurality of ends, Berlin concludes, freedom of choice is 'a truer and more humane ideal' than the alternatives. And he quotes with approval the view of Joseph Schumpeter that 'to realise the relative validity of one's convictions and yet stand for them unflinchingly is what distinguishes a civilised man from a barbarian.' ... If one's convictions are only relatively valid, why stand for them unflinchingly? In a tragically-configured moral universe, such as Berlin assumes, is the ideal of freedom any less subject than competing ideals to the ultimate incommensurability of values? If so, in what can its privileged status consist? And if freedom has no morally privileged status, if it is just one value among many, then what can be said for liberalism? (LC 8)

Sandel's critique offers a notably incisive statement of what looks like a serious problem at the heart of Berlin's justification of liberalism. For, if we accept Sandel's seemingly commonsensical and uncontestable premise, it would appear that we are being asked, on the one hand, to recognize that the moral universe is made up of diverse, conflicting and even incommensurable moral values and ideals, while, on the other hand, accepting the liberal priority of freedom over all other values and ends. This leaves us with the question: Does Berlin's pluralist account of liberalism commit itself to some sort of crippling contradiction, or is the contradiction more apparent than real? The purpose of what follows is to answer this question in a way that helps us address the more fundamental matter concerning the deeper paradox in Berlin's thought stemming from its adherence to both truth and contingency.

9 THE LOGIC-CHOPPERS

The most common way of responding to the alleged paradox at the heart of Berlin's liberalism is also the least revealing and significant. Indeed, when one considers the immense amount of scholarly effort expended on this prevailing response, one is tempted to observe that never has so much been written by so many about such a small and relatively unserious matter.[1] Accordingly, we will not detain ourselves too long on this rejoinder as it does not hold anywhere near as much philosophical water as it supposes.

The kernel of what may be described as the logic-chopping response to Berlin's pluralist defence of liberalism can be stated briefly. Given Berlin's thesis that human values and conceptions of the good life are not just incompatible but also incommensurable, his account of liberalism is left vulnerable to an inescapable inconsistency. For if the incommensurability thesis that forms a core element of Berlin's value pluralism denies the availability of a moral yardstick that can objectively compare and rank diverse and conflicting objective values and moral ends, then we are left with a straightforward logical contradiction between a

---

[1] The following only covers a selection of the ever-expanding cottage industry that has emerged around this specific topic: Steven Lukes, 'Making Sense of Moral Conflict', in his *Moral Conflict and Politics* (1991: Clarendon Press, Oxford); John Kekes, *The Morality of Pluralism* (1994: Princeton University Press, Princeton, NJ), 119–217; George Crowder, 'Pluralism and Liberalism', *Political Studies* XLII (1994), 293–305; Michael Ignatieff, *Isaiah Berlin: A Life* (1998: Chatto & Windus, London), 286; William Galston, *Liberal Pluralism-The Implications of Value Pluralism for Political Theory and Practice* (2002: Cambridge University Press, Cambridge), 48–64; George Crowder, *Isaiah Berlin: Liberty and Pluralism* (2004: Polity Press, Cambridge), 125–47; Robert Talisse, 'Does Value Pluralism Entail Liberalism?', in *Journal of Moral Philosophy* 7 (2010): 303–30.

I should also highlight that there are a number of notable exceptions to the logic-chopping critique of Berlin's pluralist defence of liberalism. In addition to Bernard Williams's Introduction to CC2, there are also the contributions of Jonathan Lieberson & Sidney Morgenbesser in their essay on Berlin in J. Lieberson, *Varieties: Essays* (1988: Weidenfeld & Nicolson, New York), 111–14; John Gray, *Isaiah Berlin* (1995: HarperCollins, London); Michael Walzer, 'Are There Limits to Liberalism?', *New York Review of Books* (19 October 1995); and Jason Ferrell, 'Isaiah Berlin: Pluralism and Liberalism in Theory and Practice', *Contemporary Political Theory* 8 no. 3 (2008): 295–316.

recognition of pluralism and a commitment to liberalism. In short, because pluralism rules out the logical possibility of prioritizing and privileging liberalism, Berlin's pluralist theory of liberalism is self-contradictory and therefore seriously, if not fatally, flawed

It is remarkable how much ink has been spilt in the service of this argument even if we allow for the fact that Berlin is not entirely blameless with regard to this matter.[2] While it may not be as absurd as the (largely made-up) medieval scholastic preoccupation with how many angels can dance on the head of a pin, it is not very far off either. The assertion that the laws of necessity and entailment are decisive or even apply in some morally consequential way within the field of practical philosophy is to betray a staggering ignorance of the subject. The nature and relevance of this point was highlighted by Aristotle over two and a half millennia ago in the *Nicomachean Ethics*:

> For it is the mark of an educated man to look for precision in each class of thing in so far as its nature admits; it is evidently equally foolish to accept probable reasoning from a mathematician and to demand from a rhetorician demonstrative proofs.[3]

This is clearly a lesson that seems to have been lost on a veritable army of contemporary political theorists.

Conveniently, Berlin and his colleague, Bernard Williams, co-wrote a brief reply to this sort of jejune logic-chopping objection to his liberalism. In less than four pages they seek to defuse the various complaints raised by this particular critical perspective.[4] Their rebuttal can be summarized as follows:

- To the objection that pluralism does not uniquely support the values of toleration, freedom of choice, diversity and personal autonomy that are favoured by liberalism, Berlin and Williams respond by saying, 'So what?' It is simply irrelevant and certainly not a serious objection that views other than pluralism support these values.

---

[2] Berlin committed the cardinal error of making the rash and misleading statement that pluralism *entails* negative liberty near the end of 'Two Concepts of Liberty' (L 216). Although he clarified later in his life that he does not claim there is a logical connection between pluralism and liberalism, this does not seem to have put any brakes on the large and flourishing academic production line that owes its existence to his unguarded statement. See Ramin Jahanbegloo, *Conversations with Isaiah Berlin* (1992: Halban, London), 44.

[3] Aristotle, *Ethica Nicomachea*, Vol. 9 of *The Works of Aristotle Translated into English*, ed. W. D. Ross (1910–52: Oxford University Press, Oxford), 1.

[4] Isaiah Berlin and Bernard Williams, 'Pluralism and Liberalism: A Reply' in *Political Studies* 42 (1994): 306–9. This paper shows the imprint of Williams more than of Berlin and therefore must be treated with a degree of caution. Henceforth referred to as PL.

- To the charge that each of the above values are on pluralism's account only one among many others, they respond by questioning why this is considered an objection. All that needs to be said in response is that pluralism can urge the claims of each of the above values more effectively than the enemies of liberalism.

- And finally, to the objection that pluralism undermines the liberal's case by leaving open the question 'Why not the illiberal option?' they respond by simply stating that such a question is not just open to the pluralist but to anybody including the liberal. 'What matters', they argue, 'is whether pluralism must find the question peculiarly difficult to answer'.

Berlin and Williams conclude their joint response by suggesting that the kind of objections raised above, which reflect a preoccupation with formal symmetry and logical consistency, are far from damaging. The charge of inconsistency or contradiction only holds if we allow ourselves to believe, wrongly, that deductive reasoning provides a critical perspective on Berlin's political thought. One gets the distinct impression from the tone of Berlin's and William's dismissal of these objections that they judged them as not just superficial but, to borrow a phrase from the physicist, Wolfgang Pauli, *not even wrong*. They end their paper by urging these political theorists to abandon the formal style and arid obsession with highly abstract and unilluminating argumentation, and, instead, focus their attention on 'the well-known and very important issues about the social and political stability of liberalism and of the outlooks historically associated with it' (PL 309).

While I agree with the underlying spirit of Berlin's and Williams's rejection of this group of concerns, there is a lingering suspicion that they short-change the critique of the logic-choppers. Interpreted more generously, some of the complaints raised by the geometrically minded political theorists may be more valid than Berlin and Williams are willing to admit. The complainants raise at least two legitimate points regarding a distinctly pluralist version of liberalism. The first of these centres on the non-trivial question of whether liberalism would be better served by a different normative or meta-ethical theory, one which might provide it with a more secure foundation. In other words, are there not better ways to justify liberal toleration than to rely on what strikes many as the excessive agnosticism of value pluralism? The second objection is not so much that pluralism does not have any logical connection to liberalism, as that it is incompatible with liberalism, since liberalism overstates the value of liberty in a way that a consistent pluralist would appear to be committed to precluding. Neither of these objections can be disregarded as easily as Berlin and Williams suggest, and I shall therefore seek to address both of them in the chapters that follow.

My own approach, however, will not take the form of analysing the purely logical structure and status of Berlin's political thought. An enquiry of that kind is fuelled by a strong but un-argued assumption that unless some logical link can be established between pluralism and liberalism, then Berlin's political philosophy is in deep trouble. Too many commentators have indulged in what has deteriorated into an almost ritualistic asphyxiation of Berlin's thought by logical nitpicking. Yet what is conspicuously absent in these endless displays of spurious and soporific logic-chopping is a compelling account of why anything of normative substance is thought to hang on the discovery of such logical inconsistencies or contradictions in the field of practical philosophy. I have a strong suspicion that no decisive reason can be given for asserting that the laws of logic possess some pivotal normative significance in the context of this debate. It is hardly difficult to show that pluralism does not logically entail liberalism or even that there may exist some form of logical contradiction between pluralism and liberalism. Yet nothing of any real consequence follows from such deductive argumentation in the area of normative political thought. To claim that pluralism logically entails liberalism or, conversely, that pluralism may logically contradict liberalism is about as close as one can get to engaging in a trivial, smart-alecky intellectual quarrel. As a result, it is hard to see why the rules of deductive reasoning and logical analysis should be thought to possess some vital evaluative authority in relation to the viability or otherwise of Berlin's liberal thought. The analytic tradition lost the philosophical plot when it began thinking that such things as the logical rules of entailment and non-contradiction hold some kind of critical sway outside of the exact sciences of mathematics and logic. Unfortunately, much of Anglophone moral and political philosophy is still in thrall to the spurious power of this geometric model of reason. To show that a principle or argument in moral and political theory is not necessarily logical or logically watertight is to show next to nothing of philosophical importance.

The core of Berlin's and Williams's rebuttal of the logic-chopping critique is essentially the Aristotelian argument that a choice can be rationally defensible without it being the case that we can deduce with logical necessity which choice must be made. They are also suggesting that the mode of argument deployed by Crowder and others against Berlin's defence of a liberal society does not consider the fact that in choosing liberalism (rather than some illiberal option), a value pluralist can reasonably argue that the absence of a logically necessary relationship between pluralism and liberalism does not imply that the choice of a liberal option is arbitrary or unfounded; there can in practical affairs be a multiplicity of good reasons for our preferences that do not fulfil the formal criteria of logical consistency and entailment. Determining the nature and power of these other reasons is the locus of where the real action occurs.

For this reason, it does not seem particularly productive to explore Berlin's pluralist justification of liberalism from a purely logical perspective; incidentally, such an approach also has the effect of draining the life out of Berlin's thought. Instead, we shall adopt a different way of looking at the basis of Berlin's advocacy of liberalism, which seeks to reveal and enfranchise a more complex and cogent relationship between his meta-ethical pluralism and his commitment to diversity, freedom and toleration. My argument will proceed on the basis that something other than a logical relationship (or, conversely, the lack of it) between pluralism and liberalism provides the key to making sense of Berlin's normative political philosophy. Again, this is not to assert that logic is redundant when it comes to evaluative thought. There is an obvious sense in which we cannot dispense with deductive reasoning when it comes to any type of philosophical enquiry, practical or theoretical. But it is to assert that the domain of logic is limited and that the laws of logical consistency and the claims of algorithmic rationality are far from sufficient with regard to establishing the validity or otherwise of the connection between meta-ethics and normative recommendations and, more specifically, between Berlin's affirmation of pluralism and his advocacy of liberalism.[5] So there is, in short, no real reason to take the logic-choppers' critique of Berlin's defence of liberalism seriously since in the end it is not a serious critique.

---

[5]For a critique of the philosophically naive and narrowly dogmatic conviction that consistency must always be an indispensable element of rationality, see Graham Priest, 'Why It's Irrational to Believe in Consistency', in *Rationality and Irrationality: Proceedings of the 23rd International Wittgenstein Symposium*, Berit Brogaard and Barry Smith eds. (2001: Verlagsgesellschaft, Vienna), 284–93. For a much broader and historically informed critique of 'geometric rationality', see Martin Warner, *Philosophical Finesse: Studies in the Art of Rational Persuasion* (1989: Clarendon Pres, Oxford). Warner champions a Pascalian model of argument which is not unsympathetic to the type of philosophical argument adopted by Berlin.

10 THE POSTMODERN APPROPRIATION

We will now look at what is a far more philosophically substantial and radical rejoinder to the alleged contradiction at the heart of Berlin's liberalism. It is the response of one of the most influential thinkers of the last fifty years, Richard Rorty. And, as it conveniently happens, Rorty also takes his lead from Sandel's critique of Berlin but gives a far more original and disarming response than Sandel's rhetorical question would suggest is even possible. Rorty's reading of Berlin manages to get much closer to what is the basic paradox at the heart of Berlin's thought, which centres on the tension between his twin commitment to the claims of truth and to those of contingency or historicity (I shall be using these terms interchangeably). But before we explore Rorty's resolution of Berlin's paradox, let me declare my own position in relation to 'end of philosophy' thinkers such as Rorty.

I am prone to a certain partiality to anti-philosophical thinkers who are honest enough to admit that philosophy may well be a fool's game, that it may, in the end, amount to little more than whistling in the wind. There is something refreshingly liberating as well as disquieting about such a diagnosis. At any rate, there has been no shortage of philosophical thinkers since the time of Protagoras who have been prepared to declare the death of philosophy. And yet the subject has a stubborn habit of outliving its countless obituarists. As the Polish philosopher and one-time colleague of Isaiah Berlin, Leszek Kołakowski (1927–2009), remarked, 'The farewell to philosophy, like the "bye-bye" in a famous Laurel and Hardy scene, never ends.'[1] I am far from sure if Rorty is correct in his diagnosis of what is terminally wrong with the Western tradition of philosophy or in his recommendation of what should replace it. But I am more certain that he makes a number of captivating if

---

[1] Leszek Kołakowski, *Metaphysical Horror* (1988 edn: Penguin, London), 8.

highly subversive observations about the philosophical enterprise, and that even if they are misguided, they are misguided in interesting and non-trivial ways. It is on this basis that I shall be reading Rorty on Berlin.

As we have seen already, the implication of Sandel's critique of Berlin is that his pluralist version of liberalism breaks down as a result of privileging the value of freedom above rival and incommensurable values and ideals. His political theory is thus vulnerable to the charge of self-contradiction or, at the very least, indefensible arbitrariness. Rorty proves his originality by ingeniously turning this charge on its head and then summarily dispensing with it. He detects an implicit but potent assumption underlying Sandel's critique, one which has its roots in Enlightenment rationalism and, ultimately, in Platonism. This is the deeply ingrained notion that only beliefs that can in theory, if not in practice, be rationally justified to everyone, everywhere, warrant our assent. This notion in turn rests on the premise that there exists an Olympian perspective or 'view from nowhere', from which we can somehow escape our own skin and impartially adjudicate our various and competing perspectives and opinions.[2] It is worth emphasizing that the terms 'our' and 'everyone' refer in this case to humanity at large as distinct from a more parochial, historically situated modern Western society. Armed with his invincible, if tacit, rationalist assumptions, Sandel appears to possess all he needs to impugn Berlin's liberal theory: for he can claim that unless Berlin can provide an objective, non-question-begging justification for prioritizing freedom in a pluralist moral world, his theory of liberalism is rendered conceptually and ethically incoherent.

Once Rorty has laid bare the set of mainly hidden but ultra-rational absolutist assumptions informing Sandel's critique, he proceeds to challenge these very assumptions themselves. His argument hinges on a characteristically penetrating and provocative distinction between objectivity and solidarity.[3] Broadly speaking, Rorty claims, there are two ways that more reflective souls have tried to make sense of their lives: the first revolves around the idea of objectivity or Truth (capital 'T' intended) while the latter focuses on the notion of solidarity or community. Those, he says, who strive to get meaning in their lives from our relationship with objectivity or Truth are 'realists' while those of us who derive sense in our lives from our relationship with our own community (actual, historical or imaginary) are 'pragmatists'. Realists want to define their identity and meaning by reference to a universal notion of human nature whereas pragmatists are content to define themselves in relation to a particular contingent community of featherless bipeds.

---

[2]Thomas Nagel coined the phrase in his book of the same name *The View from Nowhere* (1982: Oxford University Press, Oxford). It is, of course, a translation of the Latin phrase *sub specie aeternitatis* or 'under the aspect of eternity'.

[3]His clearest statement of this distinction is found in 'Solidarity or Objectivity' in Richard Rorty, *Objectivity, Relativism, and Truth: Philosophical Papers*, Vol. 1 (1991: Cambridge University Press, Cambridge), 21–34. Henceforth referred to as ORT.

Underpinning the realist's self-image are a set of metaphysical and epistemological assumptions: realists typically rely on a world view that incorporates a privileged relation between beliefs and objects that enables them to discriminate between objectively true and false beliefs. They also rely on a theory of knowledge that provides ways of justifying beliefs that are universal and not merely local, that track the Truth rather than simply reflect local convention. On the other hand, pragmatists are comfortable dispensing with such realist metaphysics and epistemology, since they do not feel the need to commit themselves to a concept of truth as correspondence to reality or, indeed, to a concept of rationality that assumes we need to transcend the limits of our own particular time and place. According to Rorty, pragmatists see truth, as 'what is good for us to believe', and view the distinction between knowledge and opinion as one between 'topics on which agreement is relatively easy to get and topics on which agreement is relatively hard to get' (ORT 22–3).

Rorty believes that the argument for pragmatist solidarity has a lot more going for it than anything the partisans of realist objectivity can offer. For a start, he contends, the latter have had more than two and a half millennia to vindicate their vaulted claims and yet, like the great statue of King Ozymandias, 'nothing beside remains'.[4] Is it not time, Rorty asks, that we follow Nietzsche's (1844–1900) advice and finally give up trying to base our beliefs on purportedly universalist but actually non-existent philosophical foundations? More constructively, he urges that the pragmatist perspective offers a far more candid and convincing account of how we can make sense of our actual lives. Recognizing the hollowness of the Enlightenment quest for some absolute and perspectiveless objectivity, the pragmatist is content to make do with all that is left – which, of course, was all there ever was from the very start – which is that 'we think of our sense of community as having no foundation except shared hope and the trust created by such sharing' (ORT 33).

Relating this back to Sandel's original critique of Berlin, Rorty claims that pragmatists can defend liberalism perfectly well without having to tie themselves in philosophical knots. By making their peace with the unalterable fact that we cannot provide a non-circular, transcendent justification for our moral and political preferences, Rortian pragmatists simply defend their liberalism by 'insisting that the beliefs and desires they hold most dear should come first in the order of discussion. This is not arbitrariness, but sincerity.'[5]

Rorty's ingenious response to Sandel leaves us with a number of pressing questions. The first of these is whether Rorty has any grounds for enlisting Berlin as a proto-postmodernist bourgeois liberal. I think we are on pretty secure

---

[4] From Percy Bysshe Shelley's poem 'Ozymandias'.

[5] 'The Priority of Democracy to Philosophy', in R. Rorty, *Objectivity, Relativism and Truth: Philosophical Papers*, Vol. 1 (1991: Cambridge University Press, Cambridge), 195.

ground by answering this specific question with an unambiguous 'No'. While it is undeniable that there may well be a few isolated passages in Berlin's writings that could plausibly invite a pragmatist or postmodernist reading, it is equally clear that Rorty's attempt to appropriate Berlin as a precursor of his own brand of pragmatic liberalism doesn't stack up. Even someone who has only a passing acquaintance with Berlin's thought would see that its resemblance to Rorty's post-philosophical, postmodern outlook is superficial at best. Indeed, Rorty's version of Berlin provides further evidence in support of Daniel Dennett's (1942) theory of the *Rorty Factor*: 'Take whatever Rorty says about anyone's views and multiply it by .742' to work out what they really said.[6] In this instance, Dennett's calculation of the 'Rorty Factor' would seem excessively generous.

But a more relevant and fundamental question is whether Rorty's response to Sandel is valid. In other words, even if Rorty is wrong to identify Berlin as an early liberal postmodernist, is his underlying claim that liberalism can do perfectly well without philosophical foundations basically correct? I am less sure about the right answer to this bigger question. However, there exist enough serious doubts about Rorty's neo-pragmatism to suspect that his justification of liberalism is ultimately unsuccessful. My problem with Rorty's post-philosophical position is threefold.

The first issue revolves around his wholesale ethical relativism, which rests on the claim that different cultures and their concomitant language games are best understood as self-contained and mutually exclusive bubbles. This strikes me as a rather extreme and unjustified reaction to the genuine challenge of cultural difference and ethical incommensurability. As we observed in the previous chapter, one can reject the Enlightenment belief in the existence of an ahistorical human nature undergirded by transcendent theories of truth, rationality and morality without having to sign up to the view that reason or truth have no purchase beyond our own lights. There are, in other words, more options available than Rorty's distinction between objectivity and solidarity allows. By adopting the principle of interpretive charity and thereby amplifying the commonality of other cultures, it is possible to make even the most exotic or long-dead societies intelligible, if perhaps not always ethically agreeable. As Berlin was fond of saying, *tout comprendre* is not necessarily *tout pardonner*. And independently of Berlin, one of the more salient insights to emerge from Donald Davidson's seminal work on conceptual schemes and translation is that interpretive practice requires that 'whether we like it or not, if we want to understand others, we must count them right in most matters'. It should be noted that Davidson's contribution to our understanding of conceptual schemes happens at such a high level of abstraction that it is difficult to

---

[6]Quoted by Michael David Rohr in his entry on Richard Rorty in Edward Craig, ed. *The Routledge Encylopaedia of Philosophy*, Vol. 8 (1998: Routledge, London & New York), 353.

determine if it really does have implications for the comparatively concrete debate concerning cultural and historical relativism. It is also unclear whether there is more to his principle of interpretive charity beyond the observation that we seem to have a built-in susceptibility to thinking we can understand other conceptual schemes or ways of life.[7]

And yet it is not even clear if these type of considerations are particularly telling in relation to the core challenge posed by Rorty's sophisticated version of ethnocentrism. The temptation to indulge in moralistic shrugs can be overwhelming for those of us who dislike or feel threatened by Rorty's brand of ethnocentric relativism. But self-satisfied gestures are no substitute for sober argument. The need to resist the temptation of falling back on consoling pieties is particularly necessary in this instance since Rorty is usually two or more steps ahead of his critics and can spot a dressed-up platitude a mile off. That said, it is possible to identify at least one major flaw in Rorty's relativism. And it is a flaw that Berlin's work helps us to expose.

In his Oxford Amnesty Lecture, delivered in 1993, Rorty makes the typically startling claim that our growing commitment to universal human rights over the last two hundred years or so is best explained by our capacity to be moved by 'sad and sentimental stories' rather than by anything to do with our 'deepening understanding of the nature of rationality or of morality'.[8] By sad and sentimental stories, Rorty means the type of stories found in morally inspirational works of fiction such as *Uncle Tom's Cabin* or in emotionally gripping TV reports from journalists in war-torn parts of the globe. He argues that it is edifying writers like Harriet Beecher Stowe (1811–96) and heart-tugging journalists who are responsible for broadening our moral imagination rather than anything attributable to the philosophical and universalist writings of the likes of Plato, Kant or Mill (1806–73). His conclusion is:

> If it seems that most of the work of changing moral intuitions is being done by manipulating our feelings rather than by increasing our knowledge, that is a reason to think that there is no knowledge of the sort that philosophers like Plato, Aquinas, and Kant hoped to get. (TP 172)

The immediately striking thing about this conclusion is its reliance on a spuriously sharp and absolutist juxtaposition of philosophy and literature (and journalism). It appears Rorty is so keen to deny there is such a thing as objective philosophical

---

[7] Donald Davidson, 'On the Very Idea of a Conceptual Scheme', *Inquiries into Truth and Interpretation* (1984: Oxford University Press, Oxford), 197.
[8] Richard Rorty, 'Human Rights, Rationality and Sentimentality', *Truth and Progress: Philosophical Papers*, Vol. 3 (1998: Cambridge University Press, Cambridge), 185.

knowledge that it completely blinds him to more humanistic and realistic conceptions of reason and morality. One suspects that, like many relativists, he is deep down an objectivist *malgré lui*. But let us leave this suspicion aside for the moment. Berlin offers a possible path out of the seemingly unavoidable Rortian dichotomy between an insipid and baseless foundationalism and a wholesale and complacent ethnocentrism. His argument is articulated most effectively in a short and little known paper he wrote towards the end of his life.[9] The article, which was written in response to a critique of his conception of cultural pluralism, provides the most explicit version of Berlin's argument in favour of a non-relativist 'a minimum of common values'. For Berlin, relativism is the doctrine according to which

> the values embodied in a given vision or form of life, in particular of entire societies, are not merely incompatible, but are such that the motives for holding them, for living in the light of such values, are seen as totally arbitrary, or, at best, opaque, though not necessarily unintelligible. (CTH2 313)

In contrast, he argues that the doctrine of pluralism states:

> I can imaginatively enter into the situation, outlook, constellation of values, ways of life, of societies not my own. ... I am bound, given my general view, to deny the possibility of some overarching criterion which objectively determines what, in a given situation, all men at all times in all places are required to pursue. ... But I believe that a good many ultimate values have been pursued in common by a great many people in very many places, over very long periods of time; and that it is these alone that we call human values. But that is nevertheless an empirical fact – basic, but still only empirical. The condition of recognising ultimate values, whether my own or those of other cultures or persons, is that I must be able to imagine myself in a situation in which I could myself pursue them, even though they may in fact repel me. (CTH2 313–14)

Berlin then elaborates the implications of his pluralism in ways that are directly relevant to the ethnocentric challenge posed by Rorty. One of the more pertinent points is pluralism's reasons for avoiding extremes of suffering and mitigating the frequency of moral collision. Berlin imagines confronting someone who takes a Nietzschean or Raskolnikovian tragic-romantic view of life expressing a preference for a world where heroism, violence and ruthless self-assertion are valued over

---

[9]"Reply to Ronald H. McKinney, 'Towards a Postmodern Ethics: Sir Isaiah Berlin and John Caputo', *Journal of Value Inquiry* 26 (1992): 395–407', Isaiah Berlin, 'Reply to Ronald H. McKinney', *Journal of Value Inquiry* 26 (1992) no.3, 557–60 and reprinted in CTH2 313–18.

a peaceful, compromise-addicted, decent society. He asks himself what we can objectively say to such a person. He concedes that we can no longer rely on any kind of Platonic argument capable of demonstrating objectively, absolutely and ahistorically the unique rightness of one way of life. But he denies that the absence of such foundational moral philosophies entails that we must accept willy-nilly some form of moral subjectivism or sentimentalism of the type advocated by Rorty. We still have available to us resources of rational and critical argumentation, and, of course, our historically generated and informed, if necessarily provisional and fallible, moral intuitions. As Berlin states:

> My reason for saying that the variety of values that human beings are able to pursue and have pursued and are likely to pursue is limited, and not, even in theory, infinitely great, is that I believe that it is a matter of empirical fact that in so far as communication between human beings is possible, across time and space as well as within single communities, this is based on a common human nature (or outlook) which alone makes this possible. (CTH2 316–17)

What is interesting about this passage is that it serves to reveal that Berlin's version of value pluralism neither presupposes nor affirms an absolute universalism but, instead, adopts a certain universalistic *outlook* that is based on the possibility (rather than an a priori requirement) of meaningful intercultural and transhistorical communication as well as of the reach of reason beyond specific cultures and forms of life. This distinction is more significant than it might look at first. One can feel a certain solidarity with thinkers such as Rorty and John Gray who must reach for their earplugs when they hear terms such as universalism, humanity and human rights being ritually relied on in political philosophy. But if we interpret universalism as an outlook rather than a given, as I believe Berlin did, the moral landscape changes. The possibility of understanding and communicating with other cultures is approached in hope rather than expectation. And that hope is based on nothing more or less than an un-metaphysical motivation to seek out common or communicable patterns of thought and reason in other societies in the not unfounded hope that such possibilities objectively exist.

There is still the very real possibility that none of these objections really undermines Rorty's ethnocentrism, that Berlin's weak form of universalism is itself deeply ethnocentric and largely empty.[10] What if Berlin merely suffered from a failure of nerve or even bad faith in wishfully thinking that his minimal notion of

---

[10] For a more conventionally academic consideration of this aspect of Berlin's thought, see Steven Lukes 'Is Universalism Ethnocentric?', in his *Liberals and Cannibals: The Implications of Diversity* (2003: Verso, London), 10–26.

a shared human nature can magically survive the insight of contingency? But one suspects that postmodernists like Rorty sacrifice too much and too unqualifiedly in an effort to render their precious relativism bulletproof. Besides, this type of extreme relativism was not unfamiliar to Berlin, especially from his own direct exposure to the ideas and doctrines put forward by radical sociologists of knowledge such as Karl Mannheim (1893–1947). Berlin pinpointed the conceptual chaos as well as the moral anarchy that results from accepting such wholesale relativism. His most eloquent articulation of the case against the deep confusion and potential chaos of unfettered relativism is found in his essay 'Historical Inevitability'. The following statement from that paper is as relevant to Rorty as it is to the epistemological and historical relativism it was originally directed against:

> We may reject as empty those general warnings which beg us to remember that all norms and criteria, factual, logical, ethical, political, aesthetic, are hopelessly infected by historical or social or some other kind of conditioning; that all are but temporary makeshifts, none are stable or reliable; for time and chance will bear them all away. But if all judgements are thus infected, there is nothing whereby we can discriminate between various degrees of infection, and if everything is relative, subjective, accidental, biased, nothing can be judged to be more so than anything else. If words like 'subjective' and 'relative', 'prejudiced' and 'biased', are terms not of comparison and contrast – if they do not imply the possibility of their own opposites, of 'objective' (or at least 'less subjective') or 'unbiased' (or at least 'less biased') – what meaning have they for us? To use them in order to refer to everything whatever, to use them as absolute terms, and not as correlatives, is a rhetorical perversion of their normal sense, a kind of general *memento mori*, an invocation to all of us to remember how weak and ignorant and trivial we are, a stern and virtuous maxim, and merited perhaps, but not a serious doctrine concerned with the question of the attribution of responsibility in history, relevant to any particular group of moralists or statesmen or human beings. (L 149–50)

There is, of course, a certain inexorable sense that the philosophical debate regarding relativism will probably never end as long as there are people who reflect on this topic. In fact, given the persistence and intensity of the debate, one cannot help thinking that there must be something non-trivially true in the relativist thesis, just as one finds it hard to deny that moral objectivism (as distinct from moral absolutism) must possess some extra-intuitive validity too. Is it possible that some form of coherent ethical relativism is compatible with a plausible version of ethical cognitivism? The answer to that poser remains notoriously complex and elusive. But it is at least plausible that something along the lines of Berlin's humane and bounded pluralism is a step in the right direction for it points towards an insight that seems both plausible and important – the sense that being members of a particular culture with our own contingent web of beliefs neither precludes the possibility of our understanding other specific cultures or discovering that we even share common traits of a non-trivial nature. This might explain why the following passage from Vico's *Nuovo Scienza* meant so much to Berlin:

> In the night of thick darkness enveloping the earliest antiquity, so remote from ourselves, there shines the eternal and never failing light of a truth beyond all questions: that the world of civil society has certainly been made by men, and that its principles are therefore to be found within the modifications of our own human mind.[11]

J. L. Austin's acute remark that in philosophy 'enough is enough: it does not mean everything' is apt here too.[12] If one applies its spirit to the philosophical debate about the pros and cons of relativism and objectivism, it invites us to avoid the all-or-nothing, simplistic arguments that tend to dominate this age-old debate. To be sceptical of the chimera that insists that everything we say is untrue because everything we say does not amount to everything that could be said is surely right. Clifford Geertz echoes this sensible, grown-up perspective too when he says about cultural and historical relativism:

> I have never been impressed by the argument that, as complete objectivity is impossible in these matters (as, of course, it is), one might as well let one's sentiments run loose. As Robert Solow has remarked, that is like saying that as a perfectly aseptic environment is impossible, one might as well conduct surgery in the sewer. (TIC 30)

Geertz's attitude to cultural relativism is more nuanced and, in certain ways, more ethically insouciant than Berlin's. Geertz argues that the so-called objectivist fears about cultural relativism are frequently based on a bogeyman, and that the much greater threat to an intellectually healthy climate is the sort of moral and cultural provincialism that often underlies and/or fuels anti-relativist thought. But Geertz is entirely at one with Berlin in his opposition to all forms of wholesale cognitive, moral, historical relativism as well as vulgar and uncritical forms of cultural relativism.[13]

---

[11] *The New Science of Giambattista Vico*, trans. Thomas Goddard Bergin and Max Harold Fisch, revised edn (1968: Cornell University Press, New York), paragraph 331.

[12] J. L. Austin, 'Other Minds' in his *Philosophical Papers*, 3rd edn (1979: Oxford University Press, Oxford), 84.

[13] See his superb essay 'Anti Anti-Relativism' in *Available Light* (2000: Princeton University Press, New Jersey), 43–67. Geertz's and Berlin's treatments of this topic also find a revealing and cogent echo in

And it is in the light of both Austin's and Geertz's salutary comments that I would like to leave Berlin with the closing word before moving on to my next main objection to Rorty:

> I do indeed say 'that there are a "minimum" of such values "without which societies could scarcely survive"'. This is an empirical fact – if people were allowed to murder each other indiscriminately, of if truth were never observed in people's statements, or if the means of human subsistence or security were destroyed, and the like, human society would not be able to survive. That is also an empirical fact of a very wide application. But it does not follow that someone could not reject them, and doom human societies to perdition, or at any rate try to do so – that would certainly place someone attempting to do it beyond the horizon of common human values. (RRM 559-60)

This brings us to the second main problem with Rorty's response. In fact, it is not so much a problem as a deep suspicion. It is prompted by something Hilary Putnam (1926–2016) says about Rorty in his paper 'Realism with a Human Face'. Part of Putnam's aim in that essay is to clarify where he disagrees with Rorty. He felt that one of their main areas of disagreement centred on their differing attitudes to metaphysical philosophy – where Putnam himself believed that the task of philosophy is on one level to overcome metaphysics and on another to continue metaphysical discussion, by which he meant that there is a sense in which the philosophical enterprise is 'vain, frivolous, crazy – we must say "Stop!"' and a sense in which it is also 'simply reflection at the most general and the most abstract level; to put a stop to it would be a crime against reason'.[14] But he argues that underlying Rorty's wholesale and nonchalant relativism is a deep conviction that 'metaphysical realism is *wrong*' (RHF 25), a conviction that he cannot really hold if he wishes to stay true to his relativism. Putnam then makes the following telling comment in relation to Rorty: 'I think, in short, that the attempt to say that *from a God's eye view there's no God's eye view* is still there, under all the wrapping' (ibid.). What this observation alerts us to is the suspicion that with Rorty we may well be dealing with a philosopher who suffered from the 'God that failed' syndrome. Further credence is given to this conjecture after reading Rorty's candid and at

---

the more recent writings of Amartya Sen. See in particular his essays 'Our Culture, Their Culture' and 'The Reach of Reason', in his *The Argumentative Indian: Writings on Indian History, Culture and Identity* (2005: Allen Lane, London), 121–38 and 273–300. Sen's essays are particularly instructive in challenging the chauvinistic and complacent views that Western writers holds of non-Western ways of thinking as well as revealing the highly sophisticated, tolerant and open traditions of reason, choice and diversity that exist within the Indian religious and secular traditions.

[14] Hilary Putnam, *Realism with a Human Face* (1992: Harvard University Press, Cambridge, Mass), 19. Henceforth referred to as RHF.

times very moving autobiographical essay *Trotsky and the Wild Orchids*. What emerges clearly from his intellectual self-portrait is a thinker who as a young man literally believed he could personally achieve the quest for philosophical certainty and then gradually reached the deeply disillusioning epiphany that the Platonic ideal of 'holding reality and justice in a single vision had been a mistake'. As he says himself:

> More specifically, I decided that only religion – only a nonargumentative faith in a surrogate parent who, unlike any real parent, embodied love, power and justice in equal measure – could do the trick Plato wanted done. Since I could not imagine becoming religious, and indeed had gotten more and more raucously secularist, I decided the hope of getting a single vision by becoming a philosopher had been a self-deceptive atheist's way out.[15]

Even though he convinced himself that he had overcome his initial disillusion, there is an unmistakable sense that he may never have gotten over the disappointment of failing to become a Platonic mastermind. The purpose of highlighting this point is that it would appear to inform his entire post-epiphanic perspective on the world, including his response to Sandel and his desire to enlist political philosophers like Berlin as fellow postmodern liberal travellers. The problem is that thinkers like Berlin s well as Rawls – whom he also seeks to recruit as a post-metaphysical bourgeois liberal – do not share Rorty's 'strenuous unbelief', and one of the reasons they don't is that they do not share his devil-may-care, all-or-nothing view of philosophy.[16] It is hard to resist the temptation of seeing a resemblance between Alyosha's famous remark in *The Brothers Karamazov*, 'Without God and the future life? It means everything is permitted now, one can do anything?' and Rorty's (over)reaction to his loss of faith in Platonic intellectual self-mastery. But, of course, nihilism or its first cousin, relentless and unchastened irony, are not the only options in a world bereft of God or the Philosopher-King, especially for those of us who never felt the transcendent need to indulge such metaphysical fantasies in the first place.

My final reservation regarding Rorty relates to his views about the implications of contingency. While his treatment of this topic is the most impressive feature of his thought and raises fundamental questions for how liberalism should interpret itself, it is, I believe, ultimately unpersuasive. Let's begin by briefly summarizing Rorty's position on the relation between contingency and liberalism. Like Berlin, Rorty believes that Enlightenment rationalism no longer provides us with a plausible

---

[15]Richard Rorty, 'Trotsky and the Wild Orchids', in his *Philosophy and Social Hope* (1999: Penguin, London), 12–13.

[16]This apt description was coined by the philosopher Jonathan Rée in his review of Rorty in the *London Review of Books* 20 no. 20 (October 1998).

philosophical justification for liberalism: they share the view that such rationalism relies on a metaphysical world view – one which Rorty follows Berlin in describing as 'the jigsaw puzzle approach to vocabularies, practices and values' – which is simply no longer credible. They both reject the Enlightenment view that there exist ahistorical and universal principles from which liberalism or any other political philosophy can derive its legitimacy. There is also a strong affinity in their view that liberal values and practices can survive and flourish without the support of their original Enlightenment rationalistic foundations. This, of course, is the view encapsulated in the closing lines of Berlin's essay 'Two Concepts of Liberty', a view Rorty entirely endorses:

> Indeed, the very desire for guarantees that our values are eternal and secure in some objective heaven is perhaps only a craving for the certainties of childhood or the absolute values of our primitive past. 'To realise the relative validity of one's convictions', said an admirable writer of our time [Joseph Schumpeter], 'and yet stand for them unflinchingly is what distinguishes a civilised man from a barbarian'. To demand more than this is perhaps a deep and incurable metaphysical need but to allow such a need to determine one's practice is a symptom of an equally deep, and more dangerous, moral and political immaturity'. (L 217)

But if we are prepared to accept their shared view that liberalism can jettison its original philosophical moorings without sinking to the bottom, we are quickly faced with a new question: How should post-Enlightenment liberalism understand itself? Rorty's answer has the virtue of being crystal clear:

> In the jargon I have been developing, Schumpeter's claim that this is the mark of a civilised person translates into the claim that the liberal societies of our century have produced more and more people who are able to recognise the contingency of the vocabulary in which they state their highest hopes – the contingency of their own consciences – and yet have remained faithful to those consciences. Figures like Nietzsche, William James, Freud, Proust and Wittgenstein illustrate what I have called 'freedom as the recognition of contingency'. ... I shall claim that such recognition is the chief virtue of the members of a liberal society, and that the culture of such a society should aim at curing us of our 'deep metaphysical need'.(CIS 46)

The most striking thing about this passage is that Rorty views the admission of our own contingency as something to be unequivocally celebrated rather than lamented. This contrasts with the typical philosophical reaction that one would expect from such a discovery, which tends to be either fight or flight: either try to defuse the view that our beliefs are merely contingent or admit defeat and quietly leave the stage. For there are few things more jarring for a moral and political philosopher than to be told that his or her most cherished beliefs and moral ideals may *just* be our own or our culture's beliefs. It is the inclusion of the all-important caveat 'just' that gives contingency its sting (and Sandel's critique its bite). The problem with Rorty is that his own response to the recognition of contingency – what he describes as 'freedom as recognition of contingency' – implies that we can effectively dispense with a concern for truth and reason, even with a small 't' and 'r':

> It is central to the idea of a liberal society that, in respect to words as opposed to deeds, persuasion as opposed to force, anything goes. This open-mindedness should not be fostered because, as Scriptures teach, Truth is great and will prevail, or because, as Milton suggests, Truth will always win in a free and open encounter. It should be fostered for its own sake. *A liberal society is one which is content to call 'true' whatever the upshot of such encounters turns out to be.* That is why a liberal society is badly served by an attempt to supply it with 'philosophical foundations'. (CIS 51–2)

The conviction that contingency must be accepted at the cost of truth and reason strikes me as both unnecessary and undesirable, and further evidence that Rorty remains firmly in the grip of the very metaphysical need he claims we must overcome: he seems to presuppose the counterfactual thesis that only a version of truth that is universal and unchanging could support rationalist or foundational political thought, but since it does not and cannot exist, truth (or 'Truth') is itself rendered irrelevant to politics. As we saw in the previous chapter, Berlin's conception of the epistemological status of value pluralism prompts us to question the philosophical assumption that contingency and truth pull in opposite directions.

Berlin's defence of liberalism invites us to rethink our understanding of truth and reason in response to our modern consciousness of the happenstance of the human predicament. So the only way I believe we can make sense of his pluralist justification of liberalism is by seeing it as a contingent but at the same time a truth-based justification too. This corresponds with the fact that for Berlin value pluralism is not merely a social fact but a deep and important meta-ethical truth, albeit one that modernity is perhaps uniquely conscious of and partial to. It is worth mentioning en passant that Berlin's emphasis on the truth of value pluralism constitutes one of the principal ways in which his theory of liberalism differentiates itself clearly from that of John Rawls, especially the later Rawls. Rawls's defence of the neutral liberal state is based on the conviction that there is not sufficient overlapping consensus to generate a thick conception of the good which all relevant citizens could willingly agree to – hence his revised, quasi-postmodern claim that his theory of justice is 'political not metaphysical'.[17] In contrast, Berlin's

---

[17] See 'Justice as Fairness: Political not Metaphysical' in *Philosophy and Public Affairs* 14 (1985).

justification of liberalism is primarily philosophical rather than political. Berlin is prepared to defend liberalism on the basis that there is a plurality of rationally grounded but incommensurable conceptions of the good and therefore no single conception of the good is owed the allegiance of all persons on any rational grounds. Berlin sees the absence of an overlapping consensus as a symptom of the truth of value pluralism rather than as a merely pragmatic fact that people don't happen to agree about the objectively best form of life.

This requires us to cease interpreting truth insofar as it applies to the world of human affairs as timeless and unchanging and to begin thinking about how we might reconcile a commitment to that epistemological concept with a recognition of our own contingency. In other words, we need not conclude from the failure of Enlightenment rationalism that truth and reason themselves are redundant notions and that some form of postmodern quietism – that is, the view that denies that all significant ontological and epistemological debate is either possible or desirable – is the only viable option available.

Berlin did not produce a systematic or even explicit theory of truth that incorporates and reconciles itself with the historicity of human existence but his various writings – philosophical, historical and biographical – are richly suggestive of what such a theory would look like and how it might work in practice. For implicit in virtually all his works is not simply an engagement with what it means to be human and what it means for someone to live truthfully but an awareness that it is virtually impossible to do justice to one independently of the other.

A philosopher who has produced a highly sophisticated account of truth's relation to contingency is Richard Campbell in his work, *Truth and Historicity*.[18] The main claim of Campbell's book, which does not refer to the writings of Berlin, is that there is a deep and unacknowledged connection between truth and historicity (he also refers to the latter term as contingency) and that a recognition of this connection provides the key to making sense of our existential condition. He also reveals how our contemporary understanding of truth is still largely shaped by the absolutist conviction that that truth must be timeless and universal. His own enquiry into the history of truth intimates that not only is there no need to define truth as timeless and universal but also the only notion of truth that can survive philosophical and historical reflection is one that both acknowledges and adjusts to the awareness of its and our own historicity. Impressively, he manages to defend a non-relativist notion of truth while recognizing the unavoidability of our historicity. His book brings to our attention a wonderfully suggestive quotation from the introduction to Hegel's *Lectures on the Philosophy of Religion*, where the great German thinker makes the following deeply un-Hegelian remark:

---

[18]Richard Campbell, *Truth and Historicity* (1992: Clarendon Press, Oxford).

In thinking, I raise myself above all that is finite to the absolute and am infinite consciousness, while at the same time I am finite self-consciousness, indeed to the full extent of my empirical condition. Both sides, as well as their relation, exist for me in the essential unity of my infinite knowing and my finitude. Those two sides seek each other and flee from each other. I am this conflict and this conciliation.[19]

This passage insinuates what might just qualify as a truth about the human situation, a truth that Hegel later chose to deny, by making the infinite the solvent of the finite. The passage is also less abstract than it may seem: for if we substitute 'historicity' for 'finite' and 'truth' for 'infinite', the meaning and relevance of Hegel's observation become more apparent (without radically changing his intended meaning). What Hegel seems to be touching on here is the irresolvable tension between historicity and truth or, more specifically, between the claim that we are nothing but historically embedded beings and the rival claim that we somehow possess the potential to transcend our own historicity or contingency. It is clear that Campbell is implicitly if underivatively sympathetic to much of Berlin's philosophical sensibility, especially in the way in which both share a desire to liberate philosophy from some of its more constricting and scientifically inspired dichotomies and consequently cease seeing many of its problems as ultimately zero sum, binary ones as Rorty and his detractors would have us believe.

So when Sandel asks 'If one's convictions are only relatively valid, why stand for them unflinchingly?' Berlin's defence of liberalism is not nearly as vacuous as that question haughtily assumes. To start with, Rorty is entirely correct in attributing the rhetorical force of Sandel's question to the assumptions underlying the rationalistic metaphysics of morality that both he and Berlin oppose. But where Berlin diverges from Rorty is in his refusal to accept that the only way to defuse Enlightenment rationalism is by giving up on truth. What Berlin is saying is that the death of the Enlightenment notion of Reason and Truth does not spell the death of reason and truth themselves. More positively, he is suggesting that some of our deepest and most precious truths may also be our most contingent and frail, yet far from random and fickle. As he states himself in the closing paragraph of *Two Concepts of Liberty*:

> It may be that the ideal of freedom to choose ends without claiming eternal validity for them, and the pluralism of values connected with this, is only the late fruit of our declining capitalist civilisation: an ideal that remote ages and primitive societies have not recognised, and one which posterity may regard

---

[19]G. W. F. Hegel, *Lectures on the Philosophy of Religion*, ed. P. C. Hodgson (1985, University of California Press, Berkeley, CA), 212.

with curiosity, even sympathy, but little comprehension. This may be so; but no sceptical conclusions seem to me to follow. Principles are not less sacred because their duration cannot be guaranteed. (L 217)

These few lines amount to what is virtually a philosophical credo, especially if we replace 'truth' for 'principles'. They invite us to reimagine the basis of our allegiance to liberalism, not as something that must derive its appeal from the holy grail of some eternal and universal normative bedrock, but as a grown-up, unmelodramatic and realistic acknowledgement that, even though it arrived only yesterday and may be gone tomorrow, liberalism is not necessarily diminished by the inevitable contingency and fragility of its existence. Saying this, of course, is not saying quite enough, for the next obvious question is: Why is it not necessarily diminished? More specifically, even if we accept that truth and contingency do not necessarily resist one another, why should we think that this is especially germane to, let alone good news for, liberalism? Are we not succumbing either to a version of the old Whig view of history and interpreting the past as an inevitable progression to liberalism or to a variation of the age-old myth which claims that the world is in some cosmically loaded sense our home or a vital staging post to our final destination? I accept that this question is a legitimate one that deserves a more adequate response. However, we will not be in a position to do so until the final section of this chapter.

11 THE HEDGEHOG'S REVENGE

It is now time to switch our focus to a very different way of interpreting Sandel's critique of Berlin. Indeed, the perspective we are about to discuss reflects the essence of Sandel's objection to Berlin's justification of liberalism. This, in short, is the objection from the standpoint of value or moral monism. Value monism is arguably the more formidable challenge to Berlin's pluralist liberalism not just because of its critique of the problematic relation between his meta-ethics and his normative liberalism but for the concerns it raises about the deeper matter of the connection between truth and historicity. Out of respect for the intellectual integrity of both ethical perspectives, we will be examining Berlin's pluralist liberalism in the light of what is one of the most philosophically sophisticated and noteworthy theories of value monism, that is, the work of the distinguished American liberal political philosopher and jurist Ronald Dworkin. Our discussion of Dworkin's thought will be limited to his celebrated article on truth and objectivity from 1996, his direct attack on Berlin's value pluralism in a much shorter paper published in 2001 and, finally, his penultimate and finest work, which was published in 2011 (he died in 2013). The first article, 'Objectivity and Truth: You Had Better Believe It' contains his critique of value pluralism or what he calls the 'indeterminacy' position, while his paper on Berlin as well as his last book are more concerned with formulating his positive theory of moral monism or what he prefers to describe as 'the unity of moral value' thesis.[1]

---

[1] Ronald Dworkin, 'Objectivity and Truth: You had better believe it', *Philosophy and Public Affairs* 25 no. 2 (Spring 1996): 87–139 (hereafter referred to as OT), 'Do Liberal Values Conflict' (hereafter LVC) in R. Dworkin, M. Lilla and R. Silvers eds. *The Legacy of Isaiah Berlin* (2001: New York Review of Books, New York), 73–90 (hereafter DLVC) and R. Dworkin *Justice for Hedgehogs* (2011: Harvard University Press, Cambridge, Mass) (hereafter JH).

Before we examine his critique of Berlin's pluralist version of liberalism, it is worth identifying Dworkin's position with regard to the opening question of this chapter – the nature, if any, of the connection between philosophy and belief. Dworkin is one of the leading proponents of the view that there is no external or Archimedean point from which we can impartially survey and assess our moral and political beliefs (this is a version of the third standpoint I outlined at the start of the chapter). Dworkin's core thesis amounts to the claim that only first-order normative reflection is relevant to addressing our everyday moral and political disagreements. He applies his anti-Archimedean razor with devastating effect, claiming that much of what sees itself as serious moral and political theory does not have a philosophical leg to stand on. His principal target is all forms of what he calls external or global scepticism which seek to deflate the objectivist pretensions of our most fundamental and cherished evaluative beliefs by showing that they lack the metaphysical and/or epistemological properties required to give them the objective status they claim. He provides a persuasive set of arguments to show that no variety of external scepticism possesses the lethal philosophical or rhetorical sting they assert on their own behalf. By arguing that 'morality is a distinct, independent dimension of our experience' and one that 'exercises its own sovereignty', he concludes that we can defuse or simply refute the various objections raised by the external sceptic who thinks he can *per impossibile* stand outside our human perspective and sit in splendid Solomonic judgement on our ordinary ethical beliefs and practices (OT 128).[2]

Dworkin does not share the view that the internal sceptic can be as easily refuted as his external equivalent. On the contrary, he takes internal scepticism far more seriously, especially its most disturbing version, which he describes in the following vivid terms:

> The chilling internal skepticism that grips us in a dark night, when we suddenly cannot help thinking that human lives signify nothing, that nothing we do can matter when we and our whole world will in any case perish in a cosmic instant or two. This kind of skepticism cannot be owned or disowned by semantic reclassifications or meta-ethical refinement. It takes hold as a terrifying, overwhelming, substantive fact, and until its grip is loosened by competing conviction we cannot be sophisticated or ironic, or anything else but hollow or paralysed or sad. (OT 129)

---

[2] Dworkin considers all forms of second-order or meta-ethical discourse, not just of the sceptical variety, as theoretically incoherent and substantively pointless. His rejection of meta-ethics can be found in *Justice for Hedgehogs*, 23–68, as well as in his response to Russ Shafer-Landau and Daniel Star in 'Symposium: Justice for Hedgehogs: A Conference on Dworkin's Forthcoming Book (special issue), *Boston University Law Review* 90, no. 2 (April 2010).

While Dworkin acknowledges that not all forms of internal evaluative scepticism are as extreme and comfortless as the one that prompts us to experience the proverbial dark night of the soul, he nevertheless identifies value pluralism as falling within the category of internal moral scepticism.

We have now finally arrived at the point where we can describe Dworkin's argument against the kind of value pluralism that Berlin holds. In the final section of his paper 'Objectivity and Truth', he takes aim at what he calls the 'indeterminacy' thesis, which he identifies with the 'value pluralist' thesis. He opens up his critique by shrewdly distinguishing indeterminacy from uncertainty and then proceeds to consider a number of moral questions from a first and third person perspective, including 'Do we think that it is neither true nor false that Sophocles' Antigone did the right thing in burying her brother?' and 'Do we deem that the question of abortion is indeterminate and that there is no right answer to that question but only different answers?' We tend to assume that if we do not suppose that Antigone's treatment of her brother was either right or wrong or that the right to have an abortion is either evil or sacred, the default position is indeterminacy. But Dworkin reminds us that *uncertainty* rather than *indeterminacy* is the only genuine default position for those of us who cannot in all honesty make up our minds in cases of moral and political disagreement. In other words, if I cannot decide whether or not abortion should be permitted (or whether Antigone's treatment of her brother was right), then my position is one of uncertainty about what to believe, which is distinct from the position of indeterminacy or value pluralism, which claims that there is no right or wrong, or alternatively no better or worse, answer in such cases. The other crucial point here is that indeterminacy is not *true* by default: this is not to say that indeterminacy or value pluralism cannot be true (although Dworkin is convinced that it is false) but it is to claim that it is in need of as much argument as any other serious and competing moral theory. As he says:

> If (as a matter of their ordinary, everyday moral convictions) one person holds that abortion is wicked, a second that it is not, and a third that the issue is indeterminate, there are three, not two, substantive positions in the field, and a fourth-party observer needs as much or as little argument for siding with any one of the three as with either of the others. (OT 131)

Having asserted with good reason that value pluralism must meet the same criteria of theoretical argumentation and normative persuasiveness required of other substantive moral positions, he then formulates a number of cogent observations and criticisms. The first of these, which was already hinted at above, is that value pluralism is, and should be regarded, as an internal moral position as much as any other internal moral theory such as utilitarianism or deontology. And once we treat it in this way, that is, as holding as morally robust a position as any other rival ethical theory, we are less likely to fall into the trap of assuming that indeterminacy or value pluralism holds by default in cases of moral and political disagreement.

Dworkin's next observation is that once the thesis of value pluralism is correctly identified as occupying the field of moral debate as an substantive participant rather than an agnostic observer, its prima facie appeal diminishes, as it can no longer rely on vague and seemingly impartial statements such as 'There's no right answer' or 'There's no fact of the matter'. These wistful but indolent avowals can hardly be relied upon once it ceases to occupy the default position. Instead, like all internal substantive moral positions, value pluralism must fall back on whatever arguments it has at its disposal to try to convince people of the independent merits of its own perspective. The clear implication of Dworkin's analysis is that once value pluralism loses its thin veneer of neutrality and is required to play on a level moral playing field, its position emerges as far more complacent and consequently far less invulnerable than its proponents have led us to believe.

His final observation is concerned with the way value pluralism fails to do justice to the phenomenology of our actual experience of moral decision-making, especially in times of ethical conflict and doubt. When we face ethical decisions or dilemmas which have a large or even defining bearing on how we lead our lives, typically we do not say to ourselves that there is 'no right answer' to the choices we face. Rather, we normally try to tease out which option is the best, all things considered. Typically, what we don't do is stoically submit to the view that since more than one option is compelling, there is nothing to do but plump for one over the other.

The conclusion that Dworkin draws is that once indeterminacy or value pluralism ceases to be regarded as the normative theory of natural default, and is forced to argue the merits of its own case in the marketplace of moral and political ideas and doctrines, it begins to resemble the philosophical equivalent of the emperor without his clothes. As he acerbically remarks, trying to dress up value pluralism 'in the modest clothes of common sense or practicality is more comic than persuasive' (OT 139).

Dworkin's paper 'Do Liberal Values Conflict?', which articulates his specific views on Berlin's value pluralism, can be read for our purposes as a kind of staging post on his way to formulating his own definitive account of ethical monism a decade later. There are two key points that emerge from his comparatively short essay on Berlin. The first is a reiteration of his view that while value pluralism may not be fatally broken, it is in desperate need of much repair. More specifically, he argues that Berlin's theory needs to 'show, in the case of each of the values it takes to be in some kind of conceptual conflict with one another, why the understanding of that value that produces the conflict is the most appropriate one' (DLVC 90).

More positively, Dworkin also declares his allegiance to the ideal of moral unity or moral monism to which Berlin is diametrically opposed. The basis upon which he rests his allegiance is outlined in only a very brief and sketchy way but its principal idea is sufficiently clear. He wants to argue that there is a deeper coherence and unity underlying our liberal values. And he claims that the key to recognizing the truth of such objective moral harmony derives from understanding the force and appeal of the more basic value of equality of respect.

Finally, we come to the argument of Dworkin's late and last masterpiece, *Justice for Hedgehogs*. I am not going to try to summarize the thesis of this enormously ambitious and sophisticated tome – no summary could come close to doing this work justice. Rather, I will mention some of the key themes in it, which are pertinent to our discussion. The first of these is the historically ironic one that the moral monist or metaphorical hedgehog is now in a minority struggling against the great tide of foxy pluralists. Dworkin believes it is time for the hedgehog, suitably reconstructed, to regain its rightful and pre-eminent place within contemporary moral and political philosophy. The book is informed by his unshakable belief in the truth of 'the unity of value', which is the grand and, as he admits himself, highly unfashionable view that moral truth is unique, objective, consistent and coherent. His conviction that our values are 'not only coherent but mutually supporting' is undergirded by a normative theory of interpretation which acts as a kind cement joining up the various elements of his theory of justice (JH 1). What is particularly noteworthy about his moral monism is that its putative objectivity is not based on any elaborate metaphysical theory. Instead, Dworkin defends the objectivity of moral values on an emphatically non-metaphysical and largely phenomenological theory: he argues that value judgements are objectively true not because they represent non-natural or natural properties 'out there' in the fabric of the universe but because they are true in themselves. According to Dworkin, nothing can make a value judgement true except another value judgement. Supporting this view is a fascinating and self-consciously impressionistic history of philosophy or what he describes as 'a just so story' (JH 15–19). Dworkin's thought-provoking historical–moral tale is worth summarizing: it acts as a convenient thumbnail sketch of the core argument of the entire book, and serves to raise a number of interesting and relevant points for our subsequent discussion.

Dworkin begins his story of Western thought by asserting his affinity with Plato and Aristotle, whom he labels the philosophers of self-affirmation. Like them, he sees the heart of our experience in unabashedly ethical terms: 'We have lives to live and we should want to live those lives well.' The 'God-intoxicated philosophers' of Christianity who succeeded them adhered to the same ethical goal of self-affirmation but with the crucial difference that it was created and endorsed by a transcendent deity. One of the key advantages of the Christian formula was that it fused 'two conceptually distinct issues: how people have come to hold their ethical and moral beliefs, and why those ethical and moral beliefs are correct'. However, the morality of self-affirmation was dealt a near fatal blow with the arrival of the Enlightenment: the new philosophical regime insisted that moral values and moral judgements cannot be deemed true unless they either are empirically vindicated or required by pure reason. The outcome of this new epistemological paradigm was the emergence of 'the Gibraltar of all mental blocks: that something other than value must underwrite value if we are to take value itself seriously'. Dworkin then introduces a wonderful twist into his *just so* story by claiming that Hume of all thinkers shattered the Enlightenment's epistemological code 'in favour of the moral domain'. How exactly? Well, by asserting that an *ought* could not be derived from an *is*, Hume ended up supporting the idea of 'the independence of morality as a separate department of knowledge with its own standards of enquiry and justification'. In the meantime, however, modernity was doing untold damage to the idea of self-interest. Starting with Hobbes, the ancient and religious ethical conception of self-interest was replaced with a much bleaker, amoral account concerned with the pursuit and satisfaction of whatever desires individuals happen to have. The excesses of this modern version of self-interest prompted two major reactions: the Victorian morality of self-denial and the existential ethic of self-assertion. It is clear Dworkin has little time for either of these moral perspectives, as neither shares the ancient and normatively superior idea of self-interest according to which living well meant more than simply satisfying one's desires, and living a good life involves more than just taking an instrumental interest in the lives of others. As he remarks himself: 'Modern moral philosophy seems to have abandoned the idea of ethical and moral integrity.' The final part of Dworkin's conjectural and thought-provoking account of Western philosophy is reserved for Kant. While acknowledging that Kant strikes us as the moralist of self-denial in its purest form, he wants to argue that once you scratch the hard shell of Kant's self-abnegation, you find a moralist of self-affirmation wanting to get out. This final twist (which may be one twist too many even for a 'just so' story) provides Dworkin with what he labels 'Kant's Principle', which is that 'a person can achieve the dignity and self-respect which are indispensable to a successful life only if he shows respect for humanity itself in all its forms' (JH 19).

Having familiarized ourselves with the gist of Dworkin's 'just so' story, we are now in a better position to discuss the implications of his critique of Berlin's liberalism. Compared with Rorty, Dworkin occupies the opposite end of the relativist/objectivist spectrum. The objections he raises with regard to Berlin's political theory are, therefore, of a very different kind and, in a way, more challenging. For the purposes of clarity and convenience I shall divide these questions into three types: the first relates to the alleged theoretical complacency of value pluralism, the second concerns the claim that Berlin's value pluralism is much more morally ambitious than is theoretically warranted, and the final one consists in the belief or, at the very least, the strong suspicion that value pluralism or indeterminacy as a substantive moral argument is just plain wrong. Let's discuss each of these in turn.

Dworkin's charge of theoretical insouciance is well made and perhaps even true. There is much to be said for his account of how the thesis of indeterminacy or value pluralism has regarded itself, not just seeing itself as the strategically default position in cases of moral and political disagreement, but also as epistemologically and morally true by default, too – a kind of principled modus vivendi justification of liberalism. Dworkin may even be more right than wrong in arguing that value pluralism is as much a substantive ethical position as other contemporary moral and political theories such as utilitarianism, Kantianism or communitarianism. And his account no doubt explains what may have caused Sandel's barely concealed annoyance when he asked: 'If freedom has no morally privileged status, if it is just one value among many, then what can be said for liberalism?' (DLVC 8). It might have been considered permissible for indeterminacy to be the default position when evaluative discourse was considered empty and effectively moribund in the 1950s and 1960s but not since then. This mirrors a typically perceptive (and candid) observation that Bernard Williams made in his review of John Rawls's *A Theory of Justice* shortly after it was published:

> Nevertheless, those of us who have felt rather hopelessly that only an untidy pluralism could get anywhere near the complexities of social value must be led to wonder whether what they took for an insightful pessimism may not have been in some part just laziness.[3]

Value pluralism is in for a more challenging ride once it is forced to defend its position in a more rigorous and systematic way. For the form of moral monism that Berlin is fond of opposing can often take on the appearance of a straw man or even a parody. His rejection of the Ionian fallacy tends to be based on a Platonic or at least metaphysically loaded and therefore by now more implausible version of moral monism. In contrast, Dworkin's account of value monism constitutes a far more formidable contemporary and subtle foe, one that bases its account of moral unity not on some metaphysically bizarre 'moral quaverings or *noumenal* entities' but on a rigorous and determinedly un-metaphysical moral theory. Another pertinent point that Dworkin makes is that Berlin has a habit of overexploiting the contingent fact that monistic ways of thinking have often provided theoretical grist to the cruel and oppressive mill of totalitarian regimes. As Dworkin quite reasonably retorts, pluralism can be similarly accused of providing succour to the most appalling forms of political indifference and inertia. While this does not mean that Berlin's value pluralism is left defenceless in the company of Dworkin's objections, it is fair to say that Berlin's justification of liberalism may have enjoyed more theoretically complacent comfort than it deserves and that it has certainly

---

[3] From Bernard Williams, 'Rawls's Principles and the Demands of Justice' *The Spectator*, June 1972, republished in Bernard Williams, *Essays and Reviews 1959-2002* (2014: Princeton University Press, Princeton, NJ), 82–87.

met its philosophical match in the form of Dworkin's hedgehogian theory of justice.

But underlying the charge of complacency, there is Dworkin's more philosophically significant claim that value pluralism needs to regard itself, and be regarded as, a full-blooded, moral theory. He describes pluralism in such terms not just because it occupies a moral position with real and significant implications for ethical and political theory and practice but also for the reason that he denies that it can credibly view itself as a morally neutral meta-ethical theory. These two points are closely connected in Dworkin's critique. He thinks that the whole philosophical enterprise of meta-ethics is conceptually and morally incoherent since its proponents make either confused and irrelevant external observations about values and/or their so-called normatively neutral meta-ethical assumptions presuppose substantive moral convictions themselves. Dworkin is no doubt on to something in his negative assessment of meta-ethics but it hardly represents an insuperable problem for Berlin's defence of liberalism. We know already that Berlin rejected the idea that meta-ethics could and should have no implications for normative theory and practice.[4] Although Berlin is more theoretically sympathetic to maintaining a distinction between meta-ethics and substantive ethics, it is not clear that conceding the substance of Dworkin's critique of meta-ethics does any decisive damage to the foundations of Berlin's liberal theory. For if we acknowledge, as we should, that pluralism amounts to more than a descriptive claim, we are still effectively left with the same questions of whether or not it gives a true account of our moral thought and experience and, secondly, whether it is more compatible with liberalism rather than with other competing moral and political doctrines. So the substantive moral debate simply gets reframed rather than transformed even if we choose to take Dworkin's advice and dispense with meta-ethics altogether.

The second main challenge raised by Dworkin is that Berlin's value pluralism suffers from being unduly normatively ambitious. His central claim here is that the pluralist view that 'there is no right answer' to the various and pervasive conflicts of values is not supported by a sufficiently comprehensive and robust normative argument. In brief, pluralism's core thesis exceeds its theoretical and evaluative reach. Let's look briefly at how he arrives at this conclusion.

After carefully and correctly differentiating Berlin's version of value pluralism from its platitudinous versions, for example, 'that in an imperfect world we cannot have everything we want' or the equally banal one that 'different societies in different times and places are organised around different values', Dworkin

---

[4] For a revealing insight into Berlin's explicit position on the relation between philosophy and moral and political beliefs, see his contribution to a debate that was published in *The Twentieth Century*, Vol. CLVII, Jan–Jun, 1955, 495–521. The debate was named 'Philosophy and Beliefs' and its four participants included Anthony Quinton, Stuart Hampshire, Iris Murdoch and Isaiah Berlin.

succeeds in getting close to identifying its conceptual core. He describes Berlin's pluralism as asserting

1. that values are objective;
2. that there are irresolvable conflicts among objective values;
3. that genuine or objective value conflict is conceptual not contingent;
4. that the ideal of harmony between values is incoherent, not just practically impossible;
5. that securing or protecting one value necessarily involves abandoning or compromising other values;
6. that conflict of values involves some genuine and important damage so that we cannot bring into a single life everything that we think makes a life defective not to have;
7. that we often or may never know what is the right decision when confronted with moral or value conflict;
8. that we often do know that no decision is right because, whatever we do, we do something wrong, we inevitably suffer or commit some injury – is this a summary or a quotation? Either way, a reference is needed. (DLVC 77–80)

Apart from no.3, which is not sufficiently clear or nuanced, Dworkin provides one of the clearest and concise conceptual summaries of value pluralism as an interpretation of morality. But matters rapidly deteriorate once he starts critiquing Berlin's meta-ethical outlook. His first line of attack is to argue that the two liberal values of liberty and equality which Berlin was fond of describing as paradigmatic examples of competing and conflicting values are not necessarily in deep and irresolvable conflict after all. He argues that the perceived conflict between these two values only arises if we accept Berlin's conception of liberty as freedom from the interference of others in your doing whatever it is you wish to do. Dworkin asserts that the notion of 'freedom as non-interference' is implausible on the basis that it is not compatible with even 'minimal egalitarian commitments'.

There are at least two major problems with this objection. On the one hand, it relies on emptying Berlin's conception of negative liberty of all of its historical and moral content so that it becomes virtually indistinguishable from mere licence, which it self-evidently isn't. On the other hand, it tries to make liberty answerable to equality without acknowledging that such a move requires a radical overhaul of our intuitive sense of the meaning and value of the former. It is one thing to argue that equality is a more fundamental or precious value than liberty, but to claim that only a true understanding of liberty is identifiable or compatible with the allegedly more fundamental value of equality of respect is to commit what Berlin saw as a cardinal philosophical error, that is, equating or assimilating one objective value with another. As he never tired of reminding us, 'Everything is what it is: liberty is liberty, not equality or fairness or justice or culture, or human happiness or a quiet conscience' (L 172). Dworkin's commitment to his doctrine of the unity of value leads him to deny the deep and objective differences and conflicts between our most basic values and ideals.

Matters go from bad to worse for Dworkin when he puts forward his more central complaint that Berlin's notion of value pluralism is unsustainable. In his attempt to justify this point he raises the hypothetical question of whether it would be a violation of Dworkin's own liberty if 'he was stopped from murdering his critics' and he then responds by claiming that 'nothing wrong is done in forbidding him (Dworkin) from murdering his critics' and that therefore 'we have reason for rejecting Berlin's conception of (negative) freedom' (DLVC 88-9). The problem with this type of criticism is that it delivers its punch at the cost of relevance. For his hypothetical argument to work as intended it must at the very least bear some passing resemblance to reality or alternatively to the core conceptual issue at hand. It fails on both counts and therefore its charge that Berlin's value pluralism overextends itself fails too. Berlin's theory would have little problem accommodating Dworkin's request that in certain circumstances equality may trump liberty, and to suggest otherwise requires us to accept a mere caricature of Berlin's position.

The other point to emphasize is that Berlin's value pluralism does not operate in a cognitive no man's land where reason is left powerless to help us choose between competing and conflicting values. The claim that we cannot objectively measure the relative worth of human values and ideals and lexically prioritize one over others is not the same as saying that reason is impotent or redundant when it comes to evaluative discourse. One of the more obvious ways that pluralism demonstrates its divergence and distinctiveness from other moral theories is in the nature of its response to moral disagreement. For example, a genuine pluralist will typically argue that there does not exist an objectively right answer to the question of whether the legitimation of pornography damages women more or less than censorship of it might end up harming society. But, at the same time, the authentic pluralist is precluded from arguing that it makes no real objective difference whether children or adults are exposed to pornography or that the need to set limits on censorship is a matter of arbitrary or merely subjective taste. Put more generally, one can believe in moral objectivity without subscribing to the monistic view – or the common, pre-theoretically intuitive view – that there must exist an objectively and uniquely right solution to every moral question. Unfortunately, Berlin does not provide us with a theoretically systematic and precise statement of the moral boundaries or constraints of value pluralism, preferring, instead, to insist on the need for reasonable and humane compromise. This was not the type of abstract argument that appealed to him nor the one he wished to rely on. As a general rule, he tends to treat this topic obliquely and illustratively through his discussion of the works of past thinkers, especially those belonging to the Counter-Enlightenment tradition.

On one level, this is regrettable as theoretical vagueness, even insouciance, does not help Berlin's pluralist cause, especially when his version of liberalism is being confronted by such a formidable philosophical and forensic opponent as Dworkin. One suspects that Dworkin is frustrated with what he no doubt sees as Berlin's philosophical overconfidence about the scope and validity of value pluralism. This is where I think the work of certain contemporary moral philosophers can be of assistance. The contribution of Susan Wolff is particularly relevant here. In her paper 'Two Levels of Pluralism', Wolff shows in an impressively clear and convincing way how value pluralism is a discrete meta-ethical position, distinguishable from both moral absolutism and moral subjectivism.[5] Her paper clarifies that it is possible to think about and respond to ethical questions without assuming that they must possess a uniquely right answer or, alternatively, that they are merely expressions of non-rational preference. Rather, pluralism offers a coherent and intuitively appealing middle road by making sense of moral disagreement without either denying moral objectivism or affirming moral subjectivism and/or relativism. Moral pluralism is compatible with moral objectivism once we free ourselves from the assumption that the only valid form of moral objectivism is moral absolutism. In other words, we can justifiably claim that there are no uniquely right answers to certain questions such as whether justice is superior to compassion or whether euthanasia should be legalized and yet, at the same time, argue that justice and compassion are objectively better than injustice and cruelty. Moreover, a moral pluralist is not theoretically precluded from rejecting the idea, for example, that the right to euthanasia should only be enjoyed by whites and not blacks on the basis that such discrimination is objectively wrong. Similarly, moral pluralism makes far more sense of our moral experience and of the reality and persistence of moral conflict than either moral relativism or moral subjectivism. In contrast to moral subjectivism and moral relativism, moral pluralism does not deny the objectivity of moral truth. It simply says that moral truth is a complicated matter and that one of the central truths of our human predicament is the irreducible plurality and conflict between objective ethical values and ideals. As Wolff says in the closing section of her paper:

---

[5]Susan Wolff, 'Two Levels of Pluralism' in *Ethics* 102 (July 1992), 785–98. The two levels of pluralism referred to in the title of Wolff's paper centre on her idea that, on one level, pluralism is compatible with persistent ethical conflict but incompatible with wholesale moral relativism and, on another level, pluralism is compatible with a more reasonable and qualified form of moral relativism but incompatible with moral subjectivism.

> Pluralism offers an answer to the question of how a commitment to objectivity in ethics can be reconciled with pervasive and persistent disagreements, given the very significant possibility that rational reflection and empirical fact may never be sufficient to resolve them. (TLP 798)

Before we leave this topic, it is worth mentioning the more philosophically weighty contribution of David Wiggins (1933) to this debate. In her article, Wolff refers to the term 'indeterminacy' to describe situations in which 'there are good reasons for one moral position and good reasons for an incompatible moral position but no decisive, overarching principle which can be applied to resolve the difference in any kind of objective sense'. These are cases where we are faced with right versus right. Wiggins is a thinker who has thought deeply about this matter, perhaps most impressively in his article 'Truth, Invention and the Meaning of Life'.[6] While resuscitating the unfashionable idea that the question of life's meaning remains a question that merits philosophical consideration (the paper was originally delivered in 1976), Wiggins ends up concluding that one of the truths we must face when seeking to find meaning in our lives is that we are more in the realm of invention than of discovery. To think that we can find a meaning in our lives in any kind of literal or straightforward sense is naive. The matter of life's meaning, according to Wiggins, does not or, rather, cannot work like that anymore. The meaning of life can no longer be thought to depend on its having an external source and vindication. When we engage in a quest to find meaning in our lives, it is not comparable to the type of quest that seeks to determine the kind of true belief about the natural world as it objectively is in which 'everything true must be consistent with everything else that is true' (TIM 125). The search for life's meaning operates in the realm of the human world not in that of the scientifically objective universe, where there exist few, if any, self-evident, transcendent moral truths to track or aim at. The challenge of finding meaning in life is, Wiggins argues, about realizing and respecting 'a long and incomplete or open-ended list of concerns which are always at the limit conflicting' (TIML 125). Wiggins describes this practical, everyday realm in which we search for meaning as *cognitively underdetermined*, in the sense that there is an absence or lack of a cognitively determinate or conclusive answer to the question of life's meaning. He describes what he means by this term most clearly when he contrasts it with naive moral cognitivism:

> Aristotle wrote (*NE* 109a29): 'Will not knowledge of the good have a great influence on life? Shall we not, like archers who have a mark to aim at, be more likely to hit upon the right thing?' But in reality there is no such thing as

---

[6]Reprinted in David Wiggins, *Needs, Vales and Truth* (1998: Clarendon Press, Oxford), 87–137, henceforth referred to as TIML

> *The Good*, no such thing as knowledge of it, and nothing fixed independently of ourselves to aim at. Or that is what is implied by the thesis of cognitive underdetermination. (TIML 126)

Interestingly and relevantly, Wiggins refers to the work of Isaiah Berlin and others immediately after the passage quoted above. He goes on to state:

> What philosophers, even philosophers of objectivist formation, have constantly stressed is the absence of the unique solutions and unique determinations of the practical that naive cognitivism would have predicted. They have thus supplied the theoretical basis for what modern writers have felt rather as a void in our experience of the apprehension of value, and have expressed not so much in terms of the plurality and mutual irreducibility of the goods as in terms of the need for an organising focus or meaning or purpose that we ourselves bring to life. (TIML 127)

As we shall see in the final part of the book, Berlin felt that the late eighteenth- and nineteenth-century romantic movement performed a large and pivotal role in providing us with the resources to justify and meet the need to give our own lives meaning.

The idea that there is a uniquely correct answer to the question of life's meaning and the nature of 'The Good' has largely vanished since Darwin's discovery of evolution and our growing godlessness. This is essentially consistent with Berlin's view of the matter too, even if he is less theoretically thorough and precise than Wiggins in his argument that whatever meaning we give to our lives must be created in some way by ourselves rather than found in some 'cosmic libretto'. In a letter to a friend dated 1984 Berlin writes:

> As for the meaning of life, I do not believe it has any: I do not ask what it is, for I suspect it has none, and this is the source of great comfort to me – we make of it what we can, and that is all there is about it. Those who seek for some deep, cosmic, all-embracing, teleologically arguable libretto or god are, believe me, pathetically mistaken. (A 246)

But Wiggins is less concerned with exploring the specific implications of our godlessness and more focused on seeking to refute the view that the question of life's meaning and, indeed, of morality is cognitively meaningless. Roughly speaking, Wiggins's argument against unqualified moral non-cognitivism goes along the following lines: Non-cognitivists strangle our understanding of such central and worthy questions as life's meaning with a highly naturalistic and distorted picture of our inner or immersive sense of day-to-day life. They operate on the assumption that the external view of the world is the only view that warrants genuine epistemological status and that the inner world of the self is one of merely subjective attitudes and feelings. One of the ingenious ways that Wiggins points out the absurdity of this viewpoint is by exposing the sheer poverty of its response to suggested variations on the ancient myth of Sisyphus, in which a character (the eternally suffering Sisyphus) was condemned to roll a stone to the top of a hill, only to see it roll down again for him to recommence the task of rolling it up the hill and see it rolling back down ad infinitum. The fundamentally undifferentiated view that non-cognitivists have towards our inner lives means that they cannot really make, let alone justify, qualitative, subjective distinctions between different ways of alleviating Sisyphus' predicament. The basis of their response to different possible ways of assuaging Sisyphus, from injecting him with a magic drug that would make him feel content with his laborious and meaningless life to allowing him to assemble a beautiful and permanent temple, is crudely psychological: their recommendations end up being variations on Bentham's view that 'prejudice aside, pushpin is as good as poetry', where our preferences are seen as emotive and arbitrary (with a seemingly inbuilt bias towards maximizing our hedonic levels). The chief problem with such a view is that it falsifies and cheapens the reality of our moral consciousness. Wiggins theory of cognitive under-determination tries to navigate a coherent path between the negation of moral subjectivism and the naivety of moral cognitivism. His theory, which bears important similarities to Isaiah Berlin's pluralism, puts forward the following theses:

- Practical questions might have more than one answer and that there is not always an ordering of better or worse answers is no reason to conclude that good and bad answers cannot be argumentatively distinguished.
- It is either false or senseless to deny that what valuational predicates stand for are properties in a world. It is neither here nor there that these value properties are not primary qualities.
- Individual human lives can have more or less point in a manner partially dependent upon the disposition in the world of these value properties.
- In as much as invention and discovery are distinguishable, and in so far as either of these ideas properly belongs here, life's having a point may depend as much upon something contributed by the person whose life it is as it depends upon something discovered. (TIML 131–2)

As we noted above, Berlin did not tend to engage in notably formal and robust theoretical justifications of his meta-ethical position. But the relative absence of such theoretically systematic statements of his brand of value pluralism should not imply, as Dworkin claims, that it is virtually indistinguishable from moral scepticism. Berlin makes this point most explicitly in a response he published in the early 1980s to a critique of his pluralism. The relevant section is worth quoting in full:

> It is true that I have argued against the idea that it must be possible, at least in principle, to conceive a state of affairs in which all human problems find their complete solution, that is, the ideal of total and universal human perfection. I believe that this notion is incoherent because it presupposes the possibility of a perfect harmony between values that are, so far as I can see, in principle incompatible, any of which (or any combinations of which) may be final ends for particular individuals or societies. But it is a very far cry from this to say that there are no rational grounds for preferring one value over any other. Of course one can give excellent reasons (that is what I regard as being rational) – to take Hume's famous example – for rejecting an act that would destroy the universe in order to end the pain in my little finger. These reasons would be based both on empirical knowledge and on moral convictions shared with the great majority of mankind. I can give equally good reasons for refusing to take someone's life rather than adding to my own comfort, or choosing to resist those who are bent on the destruction of my family, my friends, my country, rather than seeking my own personal safety, and so on. What rationality means here is that my choices are not arbitrary, incapable of rational defence, but can be explained in terms of my scale of values – my plan or way of life, an entire outlook which cannot but be to a high degree connected with that of others who form the society, nation, party, Church, class, species to which I belong. Of course, in terms of an entire outlook some values are higher than others, so that a 'lower' value will be set aside in favour of a 'higher' one; and, in cases of serious conflict, 'trade-offs' or compromises can constitute rational solutions. But this does not entail the belief that there can be no rational choice of ends save within a single scheme of life valid for all men. Men, because they are men, have enough in common biologically, psychologically, socially, however this comes about, to make social life and social morality possible. But this does not entail the necessity of a single universally valid hierarchy of ends, even as an ideal, with corresponding differences of status, or rights, or duties, or privileges, or permitted ways of life, such as genuine ethical or political monists seem to me to be committed to. (CTH2 308–9)

This brings us to Dworkin's final and most basic criticism of Berlin's value pluralism, namely, that it is philosophically unconvincing and that it gives a flawed pictured of our moral experience. The vindication of this aspect of Dworkin's argument is crucially dependent on the truth of moral monism rather than the alleged falsity of moral pluralism. I shall therefore focus on the former. But before doing so, I should like to reiterate that Dworkin's last masterpiece, *Justice for Hedgehogs*, is immeasurably superior to most contemporary moral and political philosophy, and therefore it would be arrogant of me to venture a verdict that its core argument is conclusively wrong. It is not necessarily irrational or naive to have high hopes for substantive moral and political philosophy, as Dworkin clearly did, and to suggest otherwise is mere close-minded dogmatism. What I will do, instead, is briefly offer two broad reasons for believing that we have some basis to be deeply sceptical about Dworkin's monism.

The first reason to be doubtful derives from the fact that his theory betrays a facile appreciation of the importance of history to philosophy and, more damagingly, to an understanding of ourselves. While his 'just so story' may be full of genuinely perceptive and provocative insights, it also shows that Dworkin has not even come close to a recognition of the deep and inescapable historicity of the human condition. In this respect, his work largely conforms to the conventional perspective that analytic philosophy has towards the past. As indicated in preceding sections of the book, the overwhelming inclination of the analytic tradition has been to view the past as either optional or irrelevant: its exposure to and concern for the actual past could be likened to the experience of a perpetual passenger on a jet plane at high altitude (and on virtual autopilot) who is vaguely conscious of but essentially unhampered by the goings-on in the world below. This proclivity has proved remarkably ubiquitous and persistent to this day. Unlike the Continental philosophical tradition, the vast majority of contemporary analytic philosophy is pursued in a manner that is blissfully untroubled by *the historical turn*. While Dworkin's position may not be as extreme as that of Gilbert Harman, who (in) famously posted above his office door in Princeton 'Just say no to the history of philosophy', it is also clear that his understanding of the relevance of history for philosophy is superficial at best.[7] It is pretty obvious from the casual sweep and tone of his 'just so story' that he too sees history as an optional rather than an integral feature of philosophy, something that can be indulged in to embellish one's argument. Where Rorty felt that the admission of contingency marks the end of foundational political philosophy *tout court*, Dworkin barely registers its presence, let alone its implications for a viable moral and political theory. He rather carelessly exposes his complacent view of the past in his critique of Berlin's pluralism in *Do Liberal Values Conflict?* Towards the end of that essay, where he is seeking to show that there exists an underlying unity as distinct from the irreducible conflict between liberty and equality, he tellingly remarks:

> I agree that the history of ideas is often crucial, and of course I agree that it was of the first importance for Berlin. But we must go beyond simply stating that history is crucial. I do not quite see how history can be decisive at this point

---

[7] Quoted in Tom Sorrell, 'On Saying No to the History of Philosophy', in *Analytic Philosophy and History of Philosophy*, Tom Sorrell and G. A. J. Rogers eds. (2005: Oxford University Press, Oxford), 43–59.

of the argument. History may of course teach us that many societies whose reigning ideology denied any conflict among important values ended in some form of disaster, and that should no doubt put us on our guard. But history cannot, it seems to me, help us further. We are trying to decide how better to understand the value of liberty – in order to see whether we do wrong when, for example, we tax the well-off to redistribute to the poor. I see no substitute for treating that, at least in the main, as a moral rather than an historical issue. (DLVC 86)

Leaving aside Dworkin's thinly veiled impatience with the suggestion that history plays any constitutive and substantive part in solving specific ethical problems, what is most revealing about this passage is the much more profound level of unawareness that history has the power to undermine much of the theoretical foundation of his entire monistic citadel. It is not just that thinkers like Dworkin are obviously, if perhaps innocuously, wrong in their anachronistic readings of the canonical texts of the past; it is their more serious failure to perceive history's imprint on everything we do and think, on the very concepts and categories that are presupposed by and fundamental to human experience and thought. For once we appreciate this latter point, it is no longer possible – unless we let ourselves become subject to some form of deluded denial – to see our central patterns and concepts of thought in some unproblematically pure and contemporaneous way. This is not to assert that historicity or contingency must necessarily overwhelm or displace moral theory but it is to claim that philosophical reflection about how we make sense of ourselves and our normative – and to a lesser extent our scientific – values and ideals cannot be carried out in any realistic and convincing way independently of history.

Once we begin reflecting on the historical origins and relevance of how we came to value the ideals like liberty, equality, democracy and privacy, we also start realizing that there was nothing inevitable about their genesis and eventual (and no doubt, ephemeral) triumph. In this way, historical reflection and self-consciousness can be hugely self-undermining. It forces us to ask to what extent the very idea of providing a philosophical justification of our moral and political ideas makes any coherent sense at all. Put slightly differently, why should we necessarily think that the very idea of or need for a philosophical defence of our normative preferences should survive the consciousness of our contingency? We have already seen how Rorty concluded that a growing awareness about our historicity is or should be literally devastating for traditional or foundational philosophy. We also saw that Rorty's (over)reaction is too extreme and that he ends up sacrificing conceptual coherence at the price of the recognition of contingency. Dworkin, I believe, suffers a similarly undesirable fate but in reverse. By remaining in comfortable ignorance of the deeper reality of contingency – in a way, by showing that he possesses something resembling an eighteenth-century faith in ahistorical, transcendent reason – he ends up formulating a theory of justice that buys universal and moral unity at the price of historical credibility and, ultimately, philosophical and practical relevance.

The second point on which to conclude our critique of Dworkin is by way of highlighting something of a general nature that J. L. Austin said about monistic, or what he referred to as 'totalising', theories akin to Dworkin's. In his essay *A Plea for Excuses*, Austin discusses how the meaning of certain words can change so much over time that our present use of these same words bears only a tenuous and often misleading relation to what they meant in their original or model sense. The example he gives of such a word is the term 'cause': he suggests that primitive man would have interpreted this word as implying that every event has a cause, by which he would have meant that 'every event is an action done by somebody – if not by a man, then by a quasi-man, a spirit'. Since then, we have come to see that events or causes are not actions in this earlier or primitive sense. But, as Austin argues, we still describe events as 'caused' and so the word still 'snares us', by which he means that 'we are struggling to ascribe to it a new, unanthropomorphic meaning, yet constantly, in searching for its analysis, we unearth and incorporate the lineaments of the ancient model'. He alerts us to the trap of using words like 'cause' that invoke outmoded models, reminding us in the process that there is no reason for thinking that the various models used in creating our vocabulary should form part of 'one single, total model'. On the contrary, he argues, it is far more likely that 'our assortment of models will include some, or many, that are overlapping, conflicting, or more generally, simply *disparate*'. The footnote he adds to conclude this point deserves quoting in full:

> This is by way of a general warning in philosophy. It seems to be too readily assumed that if we can only discover the true meanings of each of a cluster of terms, usually historic terms, that we use in some particular field (as, for example, 'right', 'good', and the rest in morals), then it must without question transpire that each will fit into place in some single, interlocking, consistent conceptual scheme. Not only is there no reason to assume this, but all historical probability is against it, especially in the case of language derived from such various civilizations as ours is. We may cheerfully use, and with weight, terms which are not so much head-on incompatible as simply disparate, which just do not fit in or even on. Just as we cheerfully subscribe to, or have the grace to be torn between, simply disparate ideals – why *must* there be a conceivable amalgam, the Good Life for Man?[8]

---

[8] J. L. Austin, 'A Plea for Excuses' originally published in Proceedings of the Aristotelian Society, 1956–57 and later in J. L. Austin, *Philosophical Papers* (1979: Oxford University Press, Oxford), 203. As an aside, it is interesting to speculate whether Austin's view of the 'Good Life of Man' was formed during

This is one of the best short arguments against the type of moral monism that informs theories of justice such as Dworkin's. As Austin states in his characteristically dry and lapidary prose, there is no reason to assume that our values and ideals form a coherent and harmonious unity while there are an abundance of reasons, especially historical ones, for thinking they are necessarily unrelated, conflicting and incommensurable. So, while there is much to applaud in Dworkin's general approach to moral and political philosophy, especially in his insistence which he shares with Berlin, that human values must be understood primarily from an internal, non-naturalistic perspective and in his conclusive demonstration that pluralistic liberalism must fight its own philosophical corner as much as any other rival normative moral theory, he falls critically short of showing not just that his theory of the objective unity of value is true but that we have any real reason to expect it to be true or, correlatively, to be filled with despair by its falsity or indeed by the truth of pluralism.

---

the weekly conversations in which he participated with Berlin, A. J. Ayer, Stuart Hampshire et al. in Oxford before the war. It is also rather fascinating that Austin was happy to limit the articulation of his insight to little more than a footnote whereas Berlin virtually built his intellectual reputation on roughly the same philosophical insight.

12 WHAT WE ARE LEFT WITH

It's time to tie up some loose ends, to the extent that such ends can be tied up, with regard to the question that prompted this third part of the book. Building on the arguments and insights from the preceding chapters, we can now confront the thorny issue of the relation between truth and history in Berlin's thought.

Our starting point is Elizabeth Anscombe's (1919–2001) article 'Modern Moral Philosophy'.[1] First published in 1958, this paper raises a fascinating poser for contemporary philosophy. Anscombe asks how modern moral thought can retain its power and authority if it can no longer rely on the very foundations from which it originated. More specifically, she asks how modern moral theory and practice can maintain their purchase on society given their dependence on a conception of morality derived from God. Anscombe's answer (Anscombe was a Roman Catholic convert) is that once God, or belief in God, disappears along with the corresponding concepts of moral obligation and moral responsibility that form an inherent part of the Christian world view, the meaning and power of our inherited morality can hardly survive unaffected. To suppose that we can continue willy-nilly to rely on the legalistic account of ethics without God as the law-giver, as Anscombe remarks, is to carry on 'as if the notion of "criminal" were to remain when criminal law and criminal courts have been abolished and forgotten'. Her recommendation is that we should dispense with the concepts of moral obligation and moral rightness and wrongness if this is at all psychologically possible since they are remnants of a bygone moral code that no longer generally applies and are only confused and confusing without it.

Even a cursory glance at the current state of moral theory and practice shows that Anscombe's recommendation has not been seriously attempted, let alone realized. Indeed, much of contemporary moral and political philosophy as well as

---

[1] Elizabeth Anscombe, 'Modern Moral Philosophy', from the journal *Philosophy* 33 (1958): 1–19. Anscombe's article helped inspire the contemporary resurgence of interest in virtue ethics by suggesting that the idea of virtue rather than duty should provide the normative basis for contemporary ethics.

everyday moral practice continues in apparently blissful ignorance – or perhaps determined denial – of the enormous extent to which our ethical inheritance is made up of elements that no longer bear any relation to their foundational and, in this case, theological origins. We are, in effect, continuing to live off the moral capital of a religious world view we have officially forsaken. Nietzsche (and arguably Schopenhauer before him) was among the first modern philosophers to shine a bright and unforgiving torch on the hollowness and hypocrisy of our continuing belief in the sort of transcendent morality that should have expired in the wake of God's death or, rather, since the notion of God ceased to be credible. As he says in *Twilight of the Idols*:

> They are rid of the Christian God and now believe all the more firmly that they must cling to Christian morality. That is an English consistency ... . When the English actually believe that they know 'intuitively' what is good and evil, when they therefore suppose that they no longer require Christianity as a guarantee of morality, we merely witness the *effects* of the dominion of the Christian value-judgement and an expression of the depth and strength of this dominion: such that the origin of English morality has been forgotten, such that the very conditional character of its right to existence is no longer felt. For the English, morality is not yet a problem.[2]

As one commentator has remarked, replace 'the English' with 'the West' and you have a virtually unanswerable diagnosis of our modern moral situation.[3] One of the few contemporary philosophers to take Nietzsche's verdict seriously is Alasdair MacIntyre (1929). He begins his original and justly acclaimed book *After Virtue* with the following 'disquieting suggestion': he asks us to imagine a catastrophic decline and fall story affecting the natural sciences. In summary, scientists are blamed by the public for a series of environmental disasters, which result in their being murdered and in the destruction and abolition of all scientific knowledge. Years later, a more enlightened era emerges, which seeks to restore science even though it has largely forgotten what it means. All it possesses are random fragments of scientific texts detached from their original context of meaning. Yet it somehow manages to reassemble these fragments into a set of quasi-theories and practices that go under the revived names of physics, chemistry and biology. Adults debate the relative merits of phlogiston theory and evolutionary theory and children are taught Euclid while memorizing the surviving parts of the periodic table. In

---

[2] Friedrich Nietzsche, *Twilight of the Idols* (1998 edn: Oxford University Press, Oxford), *Reconnaissance* Raids of a UnTimely Man, Section 5, 45.
[3] Michael Tanner, *Nietzsche* (1994: Oxford University Press, Oxford), 34. I am indebted to Tanner's book for highlighting the similarity between Anscombe's and Nietzsche's analysis of the predicament of modern morality.

this hypothetical scenario, 'nobody, or almost nobody', realizes that what they are doing is not natural science in any proper sense at all. For everything that they do and say conforms to certain canons of consistency and coherence, and those contexts which would be needed to make sense of what they are doing have been lost, perhaps irretrievably.[4] Having introduced this hypothesis, MacIntyre then delivers his killer blow. He suggests that 'in the actual world which we inhabit the language of morality is in the same state of grave disorder as the language of natural science in the imaginary world' he has just described. And one of the ways in which contemporary moral and political philosophy manifests its state of disorder, according to MacIntyre, is by its pervasive and interminable moral disagreement. Echoing Anscombe, but in far greater and more systematic detail, MacIntyre reckons that the language of current moral discourse is largely and necessarily meaningless because it consists of miscellaneous fragments of ancient cultures (largely Greek) to which modern theories of natural rights and utility have been arbitrarily and incoherently bolted on. The net result is that we carry on as if moral disputes could in principle be objectively resolved. But, of course, we have long since lost and forgotten the essential moral ingredient necessary for genuine moral dialogue and agreement, which is the idea of a human *telos*, that is, an objective moral goal for which all men have reason to strive. By discarding or simply forgetting about our debt to Aristotelian ethics, MacIntyre argues, we have deprived ourselves of the capacity and therefore possibility of reaching a meaningful consensus on how we should live our lives. And to exacerbate our tower of Babel predicament, we have largely replaced a much richer and coherent ethic of virtue with an anaemic and self-contradictory morality of rules.

The purpose of the last few pages is to remind ourselves of the reality and force of what Nietzsche described as 'the problem of morality'. The point of introducing Anscombe and MacIntyre is that in contrast to the vast majority of contemporary moral and political philosophers, they at least register an awareness of the reality and significance of this problem. Their radical strategies also reflect the very real challenge that this problem poses – rather revealingly, neither tries to defuse it by arguing that it is susceptible to some form of the genetic fallacy. And it is in the context of this central, if relatively neglected, problem of moral and political philosophy that I have chosen to frame Berlin's pluralist defence of liberalism.

If we are willing to accept that the question posed by Nietzsche is among the defining questions for contemporary evaluative philosophy, then we must ask to what extent Berlin's political philosophy meets the challenge. Berlin at least holds out the possibility that liberalism does not need to regard itself as entirely defenceless under Nietzsche's unforgiving microscope. My reason for saying this goes back to something we touched on – and promised to return to – in the closing

---

[4]Alasdair MacIntyre, *After Virtue: A Study in Moral Theory* (1981: 2013 edn: Duckworth, London), 1–2.

paragraph of the chapter on Rorty. That chapter ended with the claim that Berlin's moral and political theory invites us to reimagine the basis of our allegiance to liberalism, not as something that must derive its appeal from some irrefutable and absolute moral foundation but as an honest acknowledgement that, even though liberalism only arose yesterday and may end up being forgotten tomorrow, its value is not necessarily diminished by the inescapable contingency and likely transience of its existence. While the sentiment underlying this claim is not necessarily unsound, it doesn't say enough to allay the suspicion that it amounts to little more than mere gesturing. For even if we accept that truth and contingency do not necessarily resist one another (and that is a big, controversial assumption in itself), why should we think that this is germane to, let alone good news for, liberalism? Framed in more Nietzschean terms, why should we think that the problem of morality is solved by liberalism?

A possible answer begins with something we mentioned at the end of the previous chapter. There it was argued that Berlin's defence of liberalism is at once epistemological and ethical: it combines the meta-ethical claim that our values and conceptions of the good life conflict in principle, and not merely in practice, with the normative claim that a more humane and tolerant society is one that acknowledges and respects the rich plurality of competing yet objective values and ways of life. There is more packed into this thesis than I intimated in the last chapter. Unpacking it will help mark the first step in helping us to determine if Berlin can provide a response to Nietzsche's challenge.

Let's begin with the nature and scope of the meta-ethical thesis of value pluralism. The first crucial thing to recognize about this thesis is that it is not merely, or even primarily, a factual or descriptive one. Berlin is not just saying that the plurality of competing and incommensurable values and ways of life is a social fact or datum of modern Western culture. If that was all he was claiming, there would be little to distinguish his central claim to fame from the sociological observations found in Max Weber's *Politics as a Vocation*. The critical difference is that Berlin wants to make the separate and philosophically more fundamental claim that value pluralism is true. What crucially differentiates this deeper claim from the purely descriptive thesis is that value pluralism is now elevated to something that captures an essential, as distinct from an arbitrary, aspect of contemporary human experience. The nature and significance of this distinction emerge when we begin to consider the various ways of responding to the two different versions of value pluralism, that is, the fact of value pluralism and the truth of value pluralism. If we judge that the plurality of diverse and conflicting ways of living is a pervasive and, to all intents and purposes, an ineliminable fact of contemporary life, we may choose to adopt something like Rawls' solution and propose a purely political – as distinct from a metaphysical – theory of justice, with its reliance on the idea of an overlapping consensus. We could, of course, also opt for a more self-consciously postmodern and ethnocentric theory of political justice along Rortian lines, or, indeed, a more egalitarian arrangement than Rawls's 'justice as fairness' solution, with the assumption in either case that no draconian changes are going to be made to basic civil and political liberties. All realistic solutions will end up having to treat the existing diverse ways of life and schemes of value as a currently unavoidable social phenomenon that requires a morally neutral liberal state. But the landscape changes somewhat when we view value pluralism not just as a fact but as a truth of contemporary life. For we are now arguing that an undeniable and pervasive fact of human experience is underpinned by a significant and striking meta-ethical truth, that value pluralism reflects something epistemologically and morally compelling and not merely historically and sociologically arbitrary about our moral experience. This opens up the de facto possibility or, rather, the necessity of providing a principled rather than a merely pragmatic or modus vivendi defence of liberal toleration. The pragmatic defence of liberalism can derive its legitimacy only from the impossibility of agreement in a morally heterogeneous society. However, Berlin is required to defend his liberal pluralism on the principle of truth. Where someone like Rawls must be metaphysically agnostic with regard to his justification of political liberalism and someone like Rorty has no option but to treat the truth as irrelevant to his own non-foundational defence of postmodern bourgeois liberalism, Berlin can provide a distinctly ground-level or philosophical basis for his advocacy of liberalism.[5] But are we really saying that Berlin's pluralist justification of liberalism is ultimately based on truth? I believe we are. Bernard Williams came to much the same conclusion in his Introduction to Berlin's *Concepts and Categories* when he observed:

> Berlin – in the last analysis, as thinkers of a rather different tendency put it – finds value in knowledge and true understanding themselves, and regards it as itself an argument for the liberal society that that society expresses more than any other does a true understanding of the pluralistic nature of values. (CC2 vii–viii)

But the very idea that truth justifies liberalism is likely to make liberals uncomfortable and leave its critics stunned. For, surely, liberalism's quintessential virtue or vice – depending on which side of the fence you stand – is that it keeps a respectful or, alternatively, unacceptable distance from the truth, that its principled defence of itself is that it doesn't suffer from the bias of committing itself to any strong moral principle. Typically, liberals are far more anxious to be epistemologically abstinent when it comes to truth's place in the moral and political sphere. And their reasons

---

[5] For an acute if strongly analytic article on how value pluralism differs from Rawls's intuitionism or 'deontological pluralism', see John Skorupski, 'Value Pluralism', in his *Ethical Explorations* (1999: Oxford University Press, Oxford), 65–81.

are not unreasonable. They fear that once truth-claims are permitted to justify or even enter the political sphere, it is a slippery slope to moral absolutism and political authoritarianism. But, of course, a commitment to the truth of value pluralism should not be confused with a commitment to moral absolutism or its close companion, moral perfectionism. The former recognizes the compatibility of moral objectivity and ineliminable moral conflict while the latter typically identifies truth and goodness in terms of moral uniformity. Moreover, someone who genuinely recognizes the truth of value pluralism has a particularly gripping reason – though not, needless to say, a logically necessary one – to resist all forms of moral homogeneity and authoritarianism. From a pluralist perspective, the more objective values and conceptions of the good life that a society can accommodate the better, even if this means that certain values and ways of life will inevitably become more bleached in such ethically heterogeneous and crowded company.

It might be objected at this point that we have moved a little too quickly and easily in connecting the dots between Berlin's meta-ethical thesis of value pluralism and his normative belief in liberalism. For, surely, it cannot be taken for granted that the recognition of value pluralism entails the advocacy of liberalism? This is a reasonable objection that deserves a response but not for the reasons the logic-choppers claim. The answer lies in acknowledging that meta-ethics is not a purely value-free epistemological enquiry, or at least not in the way that Berlin conducted it. The very idea that one could engage in a value-neutral analysis of morality struck Berlin as absurd and futile. Asking someone to carry out a value-neutral analysis of ethics is akin to asking someone to go for a swim without getting wet. Anyone carrying out a serious and honest study of ethics quickly realizes that, given the nature of the domain being investigated, value-laden analysis and judgement are both necessary and inescapable. Berlin recognized that the very categories and concepts of thought that are presupposed by and make possible normative enquiry and moral experience are themselves ethically charged. Saying this, of course, is not to assert that meta-ethical enquiry is necessarily indistinguishable from normative ethics but only to affirm that neither can be pursued in an evaluatively innocent way. The very possibility of carrying out a genuine investigation into the ethics of human existence presupposes a number of normative commitments and epistemological values, including those of intellectual curiosity, the search for truth and knowledge, a commitment to go where the argument may lead, fidelity to the facts, acknowledgement of what other scholars have said or discovered on the topic and so forth. What this helps show is that our epistemological concepts and ideals such as truth, knowledge, curiosity, objectivity, open-mindedness, impartiality are themselves inescapably value-laden. So even before one starts one's enquiry, a whole series of epistemological principles and norms have been either presupposed or consciously committed to. Genuine meta-ethical discourse and debate necessarily occupies the inherently complex and shifting liminal zone surrounded by the distinct and often rival concerns and constraints of epistemology, ethics, history, literature, politics, anthropology and so forth. This is important to highlight because meta-ethical enquiry has implications which derive not only from whatever specific understanding or findings our enquiries arrive at but also from the very act of engaging in such enquiry itself. If epistemological concepts such as truth, knowledge and objectivity were not considered valuable in the first place, the point of conducting an enquiry into anything would make little or no sense.

So far, so obvious, one might say. But truth really matters and without it much of how we think about and live our lives would never get off the ground. So when Berlin discovers what he believes is an important truth about our moral experience, this type of discovery has the potential to carry some weight. Its authority depends not just on the extent to which we consider his discovery true but also on the degree to which we find it important and relevant. The problem with so much of the meta-ethical enquiry that was carried out during and since Berlin's lifetime is that its practitioners kept on focusing on matters that were, for the most part, either trivially true or, worse still, trivially false. But there is nothing frivolous about Berlin's discovery of the putative truth of value pluralism. And one of the ways we recognize its non-trifling importance is that it helps us to make a great deal more sense of our moral experience than rival meta-ethical perspectives do, including utilitarianism and deontology. Berlin's meta-ethical thesis has real implications for how we choose to conduct our lives as individuals and, more generally, for why and how society chooses to accommodate and preserve human diversity. One of the criteria for a substantial insight having authority is whether we find it difficult to deny or repress the particular insight after we have grasped its meaning and implications. Once we discover something to be true we cannot *undiscover* it or *unknow* it or at least not without a great deal of nostalgic effort and wilful denial. Truth and knowledge matter and together they form the principal ground upon which Berlin rests his pluralist defence of liberalism.

Another implication that follows from his meta-ethically based pluralism is a concern with the conditions of truth-telling, which a liberal society is more committed to promoting and protecting than rival ideologies. Nobody, not even Berlin, has more eloquently and accurately conveyed the epistemological and moral significance of grasping the truth of his account of value pluralism better than Bernard Williams:

> What truth is it that is known to someone who recognises the ultimate plurality of values? In philosophical abstraction, it will be that there are such values, and, put in that blank way, it can be taken to speak for an objective order of values which some forms of consciousness (notably the liberal form) are better than others at recognising. But that way of putting it is very blank indeed. It is more characteristic of Berlin's outlook, and more illuminating in itself, to say that one who properly recognises the plurality of values is one who understands the deep and creative role that these various values can play in human life. In that

perspective, the correctness of the liberal consciousness is better expressed, not so much in terms of truth – that it recognises the values which indeed there are – but in terms of truthfulness. It is prepared to try to build a life round the recognition that these different values do each have a real and intelligible human significance, and are not just errors, misdirections or poor expressions of human nature. To try to build life in any other way would now be an evasion, of something which by now we understand to be true. What we understand is a truth about human nature as it has been revealed – revealed in the only way in which it could be revealed, historically. The truthfulness that is required is a truthfulness to that historical experience of human nature. (CC2 xxxviii)

But even though Berlin may convince us that we do not have to forsake truth to provide a plausible defence of liberalism, we are still left with the serious challenge of contingency. In fact, it might now appear that by positing the centrality of truth in politics, we have loaded the dice even more unfavourably against a self-consciously historicist justification of liberalism. For if we are saying that liberalism embodies the truth of value pluralism, where does this leave us with the recognition of the historical contingency of liberalism? Do we not find ourselves committed to the hopelessly naive view that history is somehow on our side in some teleological or Hegelian sense? Or, alternatively, are we inverting the postmodern solution by purchasing truth at the cost of the recognition of contingency. Neither option is attractive. It is a little too late in the day for us to be swallowing some self-fulfilling but incredible story that we are magically riding history's progressive wave. And the difficulty with separating truth from contingency is that you end up with a pretty thin and anaemic version of truth. Where Rorty was prepared to let truth be the victim of the consciousness of contingency, we would be committing the opposite sacrilege by demanding that the truth appropriate or displace the undeniable verdict of history. There is, I think, a way out of this quandary but it is not very clean and on the face of it not particularly thrilling either. But, then again, Berlin, paraphrasing C. I. Lewis, was fond of saying that 'there is no *a priori* reason for supposing that the truth, when it is discovered, will prove interesting' (CC2 293).[6] At any rate, it requires us to weave a thread through truth, history and liberalism. Let me conclude this part of the book by adumbrating a possible connection between them.

---

[6] C. I. Lewis's exact words were 'If the truth should be complex and somewhat disillusioning, it would still not be a merit to substitute for it some more dramatic and comforting simplicity. C. I. Lewis, *Mind and the World-Order: Outline of a Theory of Knowledge* (1929: Scribner, New York), 339.

13 REASON, HISTORY AND LIBERALISM

In his 1983 book, *Reason, Truth and History* Hilary Putnam wrote:

> With the rise of science has come the realisation that many questions cannot be settled by the methods of the exact sciences, ideological and ethical questions being the most obvious examples. And with the increase in our admiration and respect for the physicist, the cosmologist, the molecular biologist, has come a decrease in our respect and trust for the political thinker, the moralist, the economist, the musician, the psychiatrist, etc.[1]

With the possible exception of economists, little has changed in the intervening years to undermine Putnam's diagnosis of the situation. Putnam's book gives us reasons for increasing our respect and trust for the kinds of thinkers he lists. He achieves this by seeking to break the grip that certain deep-rooted and unhelpful dichotomies of thought have in defining what are acceptable solutions to genuinely philosophical problems. One of these rigid dichotomies is of particular relevance to our discussion. It concerns the seemingly fixed category of thought which leads us to think that when it comes to assessing the possibility of objective knowledge, there exist three mutually exclusive and essentially exhaustive options: either we adopt some form of positivism or materialism and deny that normative discussion has any cognitive content, or we adopt some form of cognitive and ethical relativism and simply give up on the possibility of objective knowledge or, finally, we indulge in what Putnam calls 'double-entry book-keeping', which involves assigning technical or specialist questions to the exact sciences and moral and political thinking to 'a different tribunal: the Party, the Utopian future, the

---

[1] Hilary Putnam, *Reason, Truth and History* (1983: Cambridge University Press, Cambridge), 150. Hereafter referred to as RTH.

Church' (RTH 150). The great virtue of Putnam's book is to reveal that none of these options is either inevitable or desirable and, more positively, that there is a way beyond such a seemingly unavoidable and constricting trichotomy. The relevance of Putnam's approach for our purposes emerges most clearly in his critique of Foucault's view of history. Putnam argues that when you pull away the layers and get to the bedrock of Foucault's attitude to the past, you find that his

> real point is that ideological perspectives of the past were not foolish or irrational at all, but rather that all ideology in the very wide sense in which we use the term, including our present ideology, is culture-relative. He is trying to show us how every culture lives, thinks, sees, makes love, by a set of unconscious guiding assumptions with non-rational determinants. If previous ideologies now seem 'irrational' it is because we judge them by our culture-bound notion of rationality. (RTH 160)

Such a view of history and of the totalizing power of ideology is, as Putnam rightly remarks, internally incoherent and ultimately self-defeating. For if, like Foucault, we are content to launch a wholesale assault on our own notion of rationality from within then there is nothing left to distinguish between rational argument and mere rationalization. Giving up on our principled preparedness to objectively examine aspects of our beliefs, even our most precious beliefs, that may well turn out to be irrational for the thesis that all our beliefs including our beliefs regarding rationality and truth are ideological through and through is hardly an enticing suggestion.

Putnam then makes another crucial point. He imagines a sceptical voice on his shoulder arguing that, even if we accept his critique of Foucault, it 'does not get us very far' because it remains the case that 'we still do not have a way of resolving normative questions and disputes to everyone's satisfaction' (RTH 163). His response to the sceptic is that the fact that we cannot make everyone happy when it comes to our considered response to normative questions and disputes does not mean that there are not better and worse arguments or resolutions in such cases. As he states:

> It is not true that we would be just as well off in the long run if we abandoned the idea that there really are such things as impartiality, consistency and reasonableness, even if we only approximate them in our lives and practice, and come to the view that there are only subjective beliefs about these things, and no fact of the matter as to which of these 'subjective beliefs' is right. (RTH 163–4)

Putnam seeks to justify his rejection of value subjectivism by refuting the Benthamite claim that the trivial game of push-pin is as good as poetry (RTH 152). It is interesting that Berlin takes on a similar, if more morally dramatic, challenge by seeking to justify the view that we can show there is something objectively wrong and not merely subjectively or emotively eccentric in relation to sadistic behaviour. Both thinkers are committed to the idea that values are capable of being rationally argued for and against.

In the case of sadism, Berlin imagines confronting 'a man who is in the habit of pushing pins into other people' (CC2 315). He cross-examines the pin-pusher, asking him why he is drawn to this habit to which the pin-pusher eventually admits it is for his own gratification. He then asks the pin-pusher whether he would be equally happy to push pins into tennis balls instead, to which the man responds that he would. Then Berlin makes the following argument:

> At this point, I begin to suspect that he [the pin-pusher] is in some way deranged. I do not say (with Hume), 'Here is a man with a very different scale of moral values from my own. Values are not susceptible to argument. I can disagree but not reason with him', as I should be inclined to say of a man who believes in hara-kiri or genocide. I rather incline to the belief that the pin-pusher who is puzzled by my questions is to be classified with homicidal lunatics and should be confined in an asylum and not in an ordinary prison. I do this because a man who cannot see that the suffering of pain is an issue of major importance in human life – that it matters at all – who cannot see why anyone should wish to know – still less mind – whether pain is caused or not, provided he does not suffer it himself, is virtually beyond the reach of communication from the world occupied by me and my fellow men. ... This seems to me to show that the recognition of some values – however general and however few – enters into the normal definition of what constitutes a sane human being. We may find that these ends do not remain constant if we look far enough in time and space; yet this does not alter the fact that beings totally lacking such ends can scarcely be described as human; still less as rational. In this sense, then, pursuit of, or failure to pursue, certain ends can be regarded as evidence of – and in extreme cases part of the definition of – irrationality. (CC2 316–17)[2]

What Putnam's and Berlin's similar-type arguments help reveal is the way in which normative considerations can enter into both our defence of reason and the justifiability of our moral and political beliefs. In this way they also suggest that the need to choose between a cognitively principled but dogmatically ahistorical defence of political liberalism or a self-consciously contingent yet relativist account of pluralistic liberalism is a false dichotomy. There appears to be at least one other

---

[2] From Isaiah Berlin, 'The Rationality of Value Judgements', first published in *Nomos* 7 [Carl Friedrich ed. *Rational Decision* (1964: New York, Atherton Press, London; 1964: Prentice-Hall International], reprinted in CC2.

option which holds out the possibility of connecting history, truth and liberalism in a way that is historically self-aware and yet rationally feasible. In respect of Berlin's vision, it runs along the following lines in my view.

The truth of value pluralism is not equivalent to the type of truth found in Euclid's theorem that the sum of the angles of a triangle is always 180 degrees or to the truth that the earth orbits the sun. And the difference is not just that it is neither a mathematical nor an empirical truth. It is also a truth that requires a unique set of circumstances to permit its development and recognition to take shape. This is not to say, of course, that there is anything inevitable or non-contingent about Euclid's and Kepler's scientific discoveries, or that they could have happened anywhere or at any time, or even that once they were made their general acceptance was a relatively straightforward matter. But it is to suggest that their discovery, and subsequent widespread acceptance and internalization, were less reliant on historical and psychological contingencies than the emergence and recognition of value pluralism.

The reality as well as the recognition of the truth of value pluralism crucially rely on the convergence of a particular set of contingent circumstances. The circumstances I am referring to are, of course, more commonly known as Western modernity. In other words, value pluralism only became a relevant and assertible truth in the wake of a series of historical events that just as easily might not have occurred. In addition, as we saw in the previous section, value pluralism is unlike mathematical and empirical truths in that there is an important distinction to be made between its 'truth' and its mere sociological 'fact'. So even the contingent emergence of modernity itself is no guarantee that the truth of value pluralism will be generally recognized as such. In fact, it is perhaps more likely that value pluralism is viewed by most modern or postmodern people as a fact rather than a truth, as something that is purely a function of avoidable moral and political disagreement rather than an inherently true and valuable aspect of human experience.

For those of us who perceive and treasure the truth of value pluralism, the self-conscious awareness of its truth is something that is profoundly more than of passing interest. Our belief that liberalism represents something uniquely noble and true about humanity may turn out to be untrue and forgotten about but it nonetheless remains unavoidably objective and urgent in its intent. And this is what makes Berlin's pluralist defence of liberalism so compulsive and compelling. For his justification of liberalism is an epistemologically and morally principled one precisely because it rests its case on what he believes is a central truth about our lives. This is an insight that has emerged as part of our historical development and it is also one that reflects something authentic and pervasive about the fabric of our contemporary human experience. Hence value pluralism does manage to link, in a necessarily tentative and provisional way, the historical and the normative. It also makes a connection to liberalism. Those of us who recognize the historical, epistemological and normative links between value pluralism and liberalism are likely to have a perspective very different from those who see moral diversity as an inconvenient or morally deplorable fact of private and public life. The former are prone to observing the decline and destruction of objective ethical variety as utterly disastrous and unbearably sad whereas the latter tend to view its disappearance as a necessary and unqualified moral triumph. Again, this is not to claim that the legitimacy and appeal of liberalism derive from some teleological view of history. It is too late in the day for us to pin our hopes on Hegelianism or some similar-type grand theory of historical inevitabilism. Nor is it to suggest that value pluralism provides the only viable cement to keep a liberal society together. There are, of course, other compelling sources of liberal solidarity. But it is to claim that the historical, epistemological and moral record would suggest that liberalism has been well served by a commitment to the value of truth, even when or, rather, especially when, it leads us to be sceptical of the very foundations on which it rests. Such truthful scepticism reminds us that when it comes to trying to discover a philosophically and morally undeluded defence of liberalism, there is a thin line between whistling in the wind and producing a compelling tune. Berlin's account of liberalism suggests that it might well be a veritable instance of the latter, that it may even show signs of the kind of truth that the philosopher C.S Peirce (1839–1914) referred to when he talked about 'opinion which is fated to be ultimately agreed to by all who investigate'.[3]

Being conscious of the historical accident that gave rise to liberalism and the absence of any guarantee that it will last forever can hardly be described as a naive or complacent stance, even in the presence of a philosophical bullshit detector such as Nietzsche. Nor does a preference for a liberal, open society require us to deny that liberal modernity has its own peculiar myths, some of which we seem only dimly aware of: our habit, for example, of using 'we' and 'us' in the universal sense, or of believing that democracy really is deep down the only legitimate form of government or our assumption that we will one day transcend our finitude, are just some of the more obvious ones. But a genuinely pluralist liberal is more likely to be more conscious of such fictions and therefore less blind to the spell of myths and myth-making. His or her commitment to the values of truth and truthfulness are likely to be informed by a conviction that does not claim that liberalism enjoys any kind of metaphysically privileged status or the blessing of some ineffable will. Another way of articulating this might be to say that a philosophically honest defence of liberalism is informed by a recognition that historical forces have the power to be both its friend

---

[3] C. S. Peirce, 'How To Make Our Ideas Clear', in *Charles S. Peirce: Selected Writings*, ed. By Philip Wiener (1958: Dover, New York).

and its foe, its vindication and its downfall, that the triumph of liberalism is ultimately a contingent affair but not necessarily an epistemologically or morally arbitrary one.

Registering the very fine and precarious thread that runs through truth, history and liberal toleration shows that we may have a genuine alternative to either adopting an absurd view of life in the manner of post-war existentialism or being relentlessly ironic in the way Rortian postmodernists appear to demand. In fact, absurdity or irony must surely strike us as a distinctly misplaced and immature response. Why be absurd or ironic in any kind of unnaturally determined and sustained way about something that is precious and fragile and, above all, based on our best approximation of a central truth about our lives? A sense of vigilant gratitude would seem a more apt response, rooted in an honest and undeluded appreciation of the incorrigibly imperfect, frequently cruel, often wilfully destructive, yet infinitely unpredictable, occasionally exquisite and not entirely unhopeful world many of us still find ourselves occupying. The fact that we may not converge on the truth of liberalism in the same way that we find it easier to agree on the truths of science is not necessarily a reason to dismiss the former as capricious and ungroundable. That liberalism and the pluralism on which it rests may end up being ephemeral phenomena does not invalidate them. We don't have to believe – and have no reason to, at any rate – that the world is the cosmically natural home of liberalism to regard a liberal society as a morally decent and politically un-encroaching setting for human beings or rather those inhabiting the modern world. This is what Berlin ultimately meant when he referred to our un-metaphysical faith in a tolerant, free, sceptical, open and decent society in the closing and justly celebrated paragraph of *Two Concepts of Liberty* (L 217). It is a sentiment which he was to reiterate eight years later in a less well-known lecture he gave at Columbia University on 'The Lessons of History':

> The most noble and moving of democrats, Condorcet, was sure that the day would arrive at last: the day on which mankind will be happy, free and wise. But this is not very likely, because it is an *a priori* truth that one cannot have everything. Herder said long ago that we cannot recapture that which made the ancient Greeks or Jews or Indians wise or happy or great. That is gone for ever. This truism – that we build for our time, and then we shall see – is the strongest argument for what must be called a rather untidy liberalism. Values are not less sacred because they are not eternal. This is a liberalism in which one is not over-excited by any solution claiming finality or any single answer; where, above all, one is not deluded by the thought that one is called upon to remove the terrible obstacles that are the last great stones that stand before the doors of perfection, and that the destruction of entire

societies is not too high a price to pay for victory in the war to end all wars, the overcoming of the last great obstacle, after which prehistory ends and true history begins.[4]

It is now time that we turn our attention to a central article on Berlin's faith in liberalism, that is, his conviction that the hallmark of a liberal and civilized society is the freedom to be free.

---

[4]Isaiah Berlin 'The Lessons of History' is available online at http://berlin.wolf.ox.ac.uk/lists/nachlass/lesshist.pdf. It is also published in Joshua Cherniss and Steven Smith eds., *The Cambridge Companion to Isaiah Berlin* (2018: Cambridge University Press, Cambridge), 276.

PART FOUR

FREEDOM

14 THEORY VERSUS PRACTICE

In his tribute to his colleague and friend, the English philosopher J. L. Austin, Berlin recounts the following anecdote. During one of the weekly philosophical meetings that were held before the war with their fellow Oxford philosophers A. J. Ayer, Stuart Hampshire (1914–2004), Donald MacKinnon (1913–94) and others, Austin whispered the following remark to Berlin:

> They all *talk* about determinism and *say* they believe in it: I have never met a determinist in my life, I mean a man who really did believe in it as you and I believe that men are mortal. Have you? (PI3 174)

Austin's comment is noteworthy for a number of reasons. It shows that one of the most distinguished analytic philosophers of his day was prepared to raise serious doubts that a person could sincerely believe in the putative truth of determinism in the same way that he or she could believe in other kinds of truths such as our own mortality, although it is not entirely clear in what sense Austin is referring to the concept of determinism.[1] The episode also reveals that a philosopher who even in academic circles had a reputation for being rather dessicated, detached and pedantic felt that the matter of the correspondence – or, in this case, of the stark lack of one – between one's philosophical ideas and one's ordinary, practical beliefs was not a trivial one. And a final point worth mentioning about this episode is that it further endeared him to his colleague, providing Berlin with even more evidence that Austin was someone who genuinely understood the nature and point of

---

[1] It is possible that Austin is referring to determinism in the literal sense that everything is determined. But it is more likely that he referring to compatibilist theories of freedom. If it is the latter then it would seem that he judged compatibilism as an evasion of rather than a serious response to the problem of free will.

philosophy. Berlin would aver later in his life that Austin 'probably had a greater influence on me, at least on what I believed as a philosopher, than anybody else in Oxford at the time' (CC2 286–7).

The concern of this chapter is Berlin's understanding of freedom and its place in his liberal political philosophy. By freedom, I mean free will as distinct from his celebrated conception of negative and positive liberty, which are essentially political ideas. One of the more conspicuous anomalies of recent scholarly commentary on Berlin is the virtually complete absence of any mention, let alone serious treatment, of this more fundamental aspect of his thought.[2] This is odd for the obvious reason that freedom is central to his defence of liberalism. Moreover, Berlin has some extremely interesting things to say about freedom that are of general philosophical importance independently of their place in his justification of a liberal society. The aim of what follows is to show that freedom forms a foundational element of Berlin's political philosophy and to explain why he thought that free will, or at least our continuing belief in free will, was so important not just for liberalism but also for who we are as human agents.

It is no exaggeration to state that among the initiated within analytic philosophy the acceptance of compatibilism is virtually de rigueur. Compatibilism can be defined as the view that freedom is reconcilable with determinism since being free is essentially the ability to do what you want to do given the desires, goals, values and personality that you happen to have. The prevailing view is that compatibilism is true or, at the very least, truth's leading candidate. The equally dominant view among the majority of professional philosophers is that given the validity of compatibilism, we should cease believing in free will in the libertarian sense, that is, that we are, in some ultimate way, responsible for what we are and what we do. The only freedom that is possible and therefore worth considering, according to compatibilists, is the freedom that is reconcilable with determinism. Though hard determinists, fatalists, libertarians, free will sceptics and no doubt other exotic forms of non-compatibilist life continue to be found within the philosophical community (and outside it), more often than not their ideas are dismissed by the currently orthodox wisdom as unduly pessimistic, hopelessly opaque, scientifically illiterate or just plain mad and bad. The confident attitude and strident tone of the compatibilist perspective is expressed eloquently by the contemporary American philosopher, Daniel Dennett:

> People care deeply about having free will, but they also seem to have misguided ideas about what free will is or could be (like their misguided ideas about colour

---

[2]There are a few exceptions, the most impressive being Mark Bode's article 'Everything is What It Is and Not Another Thing: Knowledge and Freedom in Berlin's Political Thought', *British Journal for the History of Philosophy* 19 no. 2 (2011): 305–26.

or consciousness). Our decisions are not little miracles in the brain that violate the physics and chemistry that account for the rest of our bodies' processes, even if many folk think this must be what happens if our decisions are to be truly free. We can't conclude from this, however, that we *don't* have free will, because free will in this bonkers sense is not the only concept of free will. The law, according to the common sense, contrasts signing a contract 'of your own free will' with signing a contract under duress or under the influence of an hallucination or other mental derangement. Here is a perfectly familiar sense of free will, a distinction presupposed by many of the practices and attitudes that comprise our manifest image, that has no demonstrated dependence on the bonkers sense.[3]

Dennett takes the view that those who deny the validity of compatibilism are with the fairies. The attitude of most mainstream academic philosophers, like Dennett, to those who continue to believe in the libertarian or 'bonkers' version of free will is analogous to the rather patronizing attitude adopted by certain secularists towards religious believers; atheism is true but accepting the truth that God does not exist should not be thought to endanger our inherited moral norms. What rarely gets a mention in such deplorably optimistic assertions is the not unimportant fact that a great deal of our moral heritage is derived from a Christian world view.

Nonetheless, the compatibilist thesis raises a major problem for Berlin. For he wishes to retain a sense of free will that is irreconcilable with determinism or, at least, with the belief that determinism is true. A basic feature of the self-image and appeal of Berlin's pluralist theory of liberalism is that we enjoy genuine freedom of choice to ultimately decide our way of life and to make our own decisions in the face of fundamental and pervasive moral diversity and disagreement. The type of freedom that Berlin considers vital to liberalism and, more generally, to our strongly held sense of humanity, is significantly and crucially more demanding than the compatibilist-type freedom, which is generally thought to be available in a causally determined world. So is Berlin complicit in fuelling the illusion of ultimate human freedom in a self-evidently determined world? And, if so, are we to conclude that Berlin's political thought is fatally flawed given its dependence on a conception of freedom that is considered untenable by mainstream philosophical and scientific opinion? The short answer is, I suggest, not necessarily.

Fortunately, justifying this qualified response does not require us to prove that determinism is false or that libertarian or ultimate free will is true. The notorious problem of free will has defeated infinitely greater minds than mine and I'm under

---

[3]Daniel Dennett, *Intuition Pumps* (2014: Penguin, London), 406. Dennett first articulated his compatibilist view in *Elbow Room* (1984: MIT Press, Cambridge, Mass) before developing it further in *Freedom Evolves* (2004: Penguin, London).

no illusions that I have something profoundly original or important to contribute to this fiendishly complex and seemingly intractable question. Nor will the justification of my response proceed on the basis that Berlin finally resolved the problem of free will in favour of his own preferred libertarian view of freedom. While Berlin is relatively clear where he stands in relation to the problem of free will, he doesn't make any immodest claims to have solved the free will question or to have come up with anything close to a final word on the matter. In fact, Berlin explicitly acknowledges that the free will problem remains one of the most insoluble philosophical questions of all and conceded that he lacked the insight of genius to make a meaningful contribution to solving it. Rather, we shall follow Berlin's lead by approaching the problem of free will from a less foundational but no less important perspective.

As indicated already, Berlin doesn't believe that determinism has been shown to be demonstrably true. Nor does he claim that we have conclusive proof for the existence of ultimate or libertarian free will. What he is more certain about, however, is that the compatibilist versions of freedom fall decisively short of what we intuitively understand freedom to mean and entail. Moreover, he is also convinced that it would be immeasurably unwise, even reckless, to abandon our everyday, firmly held notion of freedom in the absence of knowing for sure that determinism is true and, more pressingly, what its truth would require in terms of our own self-understanding and our interpersonal relations. The question of how he arrives at this diagnosis as well as the extent to which it coheres with his pluralist defence of liberalism, especially his commitment to reason and truth, will be the main focus of what follows. But before we delve into these substantive issues, it is worth stating briefly how the question of free will became so central to Berlin's outlook in the first place.

When Berlin published his most influential work *Four Essays on Liberty* in 1969 he took the opportunity to address the various comments and objections raised by critics in response to his four previously published essays. The two essays which had provoked most philosophical interest and debate were his Auguste Comte Memorial Trust Lecture delivered in 1953 and his inaugural lecture as Chichele Professor of Political Theory at Oxford University five years later. The first of these lectures is entitled *Historical Inevitability* and it is concerned with mounting a sustained attack upon the various forms of historical determinism or historicism as it was commonly referred to at the time. The second and most famous of Berlin's essays is, of course, 'Two Concepts of Liberty', which constitutes his most influential statement of the doctrine of value pluralism and its relation to the concept of negative or liberal freedom. Berlin tells us in the introduction to his *Four Essays on Liberty* that the scholarly criticism prompted by these essays fell into four main categories. The issue of determinism and its relevance to our notions of who we are accounted for the first of these four categories and it is on this specific topic that Berlin dedicates more than half of his introduction. While I will be referring to Berlin's two essays as well as his introduction, the principal and less renowned essay I shall be relying on is one that was published in 1964.[4] The essay is *From Hope and Fear Set Free* and it constitutes Berlin's most sustained and most compelling reflection on the theme of free will and its relation to liberalism. Unlike his essays in *Four Essays on Liberty*, it also contains his most systematic effort to discuss the problem of free will independently of its particular relevance to theories of causality and teleology in history.

---

[4]'From Hope and Fear Set Free' originally published in *Proceedings of the Aristotelian Society*, Vol. 64 (1964) and later published in CC. Interestingly, Berlin was uncharacteristically pushy with his editor, Jon Stallworthy, to include this essay in *Four Essays on Liberty* (1969: Oxford University Press, Oxford) and was prepared even to let it replace the less philosophically substantial 'Political Ideas in the Twentieth Century' if required. He lost this particular battle and it is arguable that a proper understanding of the nature and significance of his political philosophy was the chief casualty. For an authoritative account of this episode, see Henry Hardy's 'An Editor's Tale' in *Liberty*, ix–xxxiii. Hardy rights the wrong by including the paper and much else besides in his edition of *Liberty* or 'Five Essays on Liberty'.

15 THE CENTRAL PROBLEM OF FREEDOM

The philosophical problem of freedom or free will (I will use these terms interchangeably throughout this chapter), as far as Berlin is concerned, can be stated relatively clearly and straightforwardly. According to Berlin, our everyday, common-sense notion of freedom and moral responsibility is incompatible with the alleged truth of determinism. While he acknowledges that he himself cannot know for certain whether determinism is true or false, and while he is open to the distinct possibility that determinism may well end up being shown to be demonstrably true in the future, he is certain that our ordinary understanding of free will is incompatible with it. As he states near the beginning of his introduction to *Four Essays of Liberty*, 'free will and determinism cannot both be correct' (L 6).

Our ordinary, day-to-day understanding of and commitment to freedom, Berlin claims, is based on the intuitively pervasive and robustly held belief that we are ultimately free to choose between different courses of action. More specifically, he tells us that our common notion of choice is made up of two dimensions: namely, that we are free to choose in the sense of being able to do what we choose to do and because we choose to do it, and secondly and much more controversially, in the sense of not being determined to choose what we choose by causes outside of our control. It is this second, more demanding dimension of freedom, the notion that I am in some way non-causally free, that I could have acted otherwise, which Berlin argues makes our ordinary understanding of freedom basically and irrefragably at odds with the idea or reality of determinism. But it is Berlin's next move that makes his understanding of the free will debate stand out as a particularly distinctive contribution; for many philosophers before and since Berlin have argued in favour of libertarianism but what sets his position apart is his essentially phenomenological – as distinct from metaphysical – account of what would happen, not so much if determinism were true, but if it was generally believed by humankind to be true. His assessment is that the outcome would be so devastating as to result in a virtual annihilation of our existing concepts and categories of thought regarding freedom and moral responsibility and, arguably, much else.

For Berlin, therefore, the central problem of freedom is the challenge posed by the impact that believing in determinism (whether or not it happens to be true) would have upon our implicitly Kantian or libertarian understanding of ourselves as non-causally, freely choosing agents. It is a challenge that he believes compatibilists have misunderstood and grossly underestimated. For it is not just that determinism is incompatible with free will or libertarianism, but also that we cannot seem to give up the truth or conviction that we have ultimate free will. Berlin also suspects that self-proclaimed compatibilists would find it extremely difficult, if not impossible, to live their lives based on a belief in the truth of determinism. In any case, like Austin, he sees no evidence of their living the putative truth of determinism in their actual, diurnal lives. For Berlin, if ever there was a clear and manifest instance of a lack of correspondence between a philosophical doctrine and an everyday conviction, the case of the compatibilist could scarcely be more conspicuous: one is to be committed to the truth of something that strikes us as literally unbelievable and unliveable the perspective of one's ordinary, practical life.

Knowledge and Freedom

In his essay 'From Hope and Fear Set Free', Berlin gives his view of freedom an original gloss by approaching the question of free will and determinism from the perspective of knowledge. His starting point is to question the veracity of the old biblical bromide, 'And ye shall know the truth, and the truth shall make you free'. The assumption informing this axiom from *St John's Gospel* is one that has proved remarkably influential among philosophers as well as the laity. In essence, it is the idea that knowledge brings freedom, that the more knowledgeable we are, the more free we become. It also happens to be a truism that Berlin is deeply sceptical of. He has two major reasons for thinking that if determinism is true or at least is believed to be true, then the idea that knowledge increases freedom is blown out of the water since believing that determinism is true would radically diminish rather than preserve the reality of our everyday sense of freedom and responsibility.

The first of these reasons centres on his claim that the type of freedom that most philosophers have defended as reconcilable with determinism, that is, compatibilist freedom, is but a pale, evasive shadow of our ordinary, libertarian notion of freedom. And by our ordinary, libertarian view of free will, Berlin means that we have genuine options available to us and that what we choose is to some extent ultimately or non-causally up to us. Greater knowledge in a world where determinism is true, or rather is taken to be true, does not bring greater freedom of the kind Berlin thinks is indispensable to our conception of moral agency and, more broadly, to our self-understanding as autonomous human beings. His second argument revolves around his more general pluralist belief that we have no reason for assuming that knowledge and freedom are always compatible, let alone indissolubly connected. The way this second claim operates in the context of his discussion regarding free will and determinism is quite complicated and cannot be addressed properly until we examine the nature and plausibility of Berlin's first reason in some detail.

Beginning with the ancient Stoic, Chrysippus, who is arguably the first thinker to offer a deliberate, self-consciously compatibilist solution to the enduring problem of free will, many philosophers have tended to argue in favour of the truth of determinism in some form or other or at least have felt an obligation to incorporate its implications into their idea of freedom. And they have typically interpreted determinism to mean some variant of the basic notion that every act of will is determined by its respective antecedents with the result that nothing could ever happen other than it actually does. Berlin is primarily interested in the ingenious ways that thinkers have attempted to accommodate the alleged fact of determinism rather than focusing directly on the question of the truth or falsity of determinism itself. But either way, he considers that all such attempts have proved unsuccessful in showing that the acceptance of the truth of determinism is compatible with our day-to-day, strong understanding and felt experience of freedom.

One of the principal philosophical strategies that have been used in an effort to reconcile determinism and freedom is through knowledge. Chrysippus again appears to be the first in a long line of thinkers, which includes Hobbes, Locke, Hume, Mill, Russell, Ayer and, of course, most of today's analytic philosophers, to pioneer this strategy: he produced a solution known as self-determination, which is the idea that my knowledge or awareness of 'being acted upon by outside forces without being able to resist them' still leaves sufficient freedom or 'elbow room', as Dennett calls it, for me to bend my will in such a way that by doing so I can claim that it played a necessary part in the overall outcome. As Berlin says:

> Chrysippus' answer, that all that I can reasonably ask for is that my own character should be among the factors influencing behaviour, is the central core of the classical doctrine of freedom as self-determination. (CC2 237)

Berlin then quickly reminds us that the ancient Cynic, Oenamaus, described Chrysippus's attempt to reconcile determinism or self-determination with freedom as *hemidoulia* or 'half-slavery' on the grounds that:

> I am only half free if I can correctly maintain that I should not have done x if I had not chosen it, but add that I could not have chosen differently. Given that I have decided on x, my action has a motive but not merely a cause: my 'volition' is itself among the causes – indeed one of the necessary conditions – of my

behaviour, and it is this that is meant by calling me or it free. But if the choice or decision is itself determined, and cannot, causally, be other than what it is, then the chain of causality remains unbroken, and, the critics asserted, I should be no more truly free than I am on the most rigidly determinist assumptions. (CC2 237)

Since Oenamaus's verdict, other libertarian thinkers have followed suit and none more decisively than Kant, who for similar reasons famously dismissed compatibilism as 'a wretched subterfuge'. Berlin is largely in agreement with this libertarian or incompatibilist response arguing that 'the half-loaf' offered by self-determinism 'is not the bread the libertarians crave' even if it is not as unpalatable as the harder forms of determinism. In other words, being aware or 'knowledgeable' that I can do what I choose, but I cannot choose otherwise than I do, is a long way short of our ordinary and more robust sense of freedom to non-causally choose between alternatives or consider myself the ultimate source of my beliefs and actions – Berlin oscillates between a leeway conception of free will and a source conception of free will but both are incompatible with determinism. The fact that I may know the world or my personality is a prison does not make the world or my personality any less a prison. And no level of knowledge, according to Berlin, can plausibly claim that the bleached, exiguous version of freedom put forward by compatibilism either bears any meaningful resemblance to what we understand by real freedom or could possibly compensate for the loss of such contra-causal freedom:

> If classical determinism is a true view (and the fact that it does not square with our present usage is no argument against it), knowledge of it will not increase liberty – if liberty does not exist, the discovery that it does not exist will not create it. This goes for self-determinism no less than for its most full-blown mechanistic-behaviourist variety. (CC2 241)

But does determinism require us to give up everyday freedom?

Two years before Berlin delivered 'From Hope and Fear Set Free', one of the most impressive figures in British analytic philosophy, Peter Strawson (1919–2006), presented seminal paper on the free will debate to the British Academy in 1961.[1]

---

[1] P.F. Strawson, 'Freedom and Resentment', in *Proceedings of the British Academy*, Vol. XLVIII (1962) and later republished in his *Freedom and Resentment and Other Essays* (1974: Methuen, London), 1–25. Hereafter referred to as FR.

Strawson wrote his essay from the perspective of someone who strongly suspects that determinism is true, or at least, is far more likely to be true than not. But in his paper he is officially agnostic on the question of the truth or falsity of determinism since he claims that, practically speaking, it is and should remain irrelevant to our everyday sense of freedom and moral responsibility. Indeed, the main point of his paper is to question the significance of determinism with regard to our ordinary, common-sense notion of freedom and morality. What makes his contribution relevant to our discussion is its suggestion that the type of objection raised by Berlin can be accommodated without having to resort to, what he calls, 'the obscure and panicky metaphysics of libertarianism' (FR 25).

Strawson sets out to defuse the libertarian, or what he regards as the pessimistic fear that determinism threatens our day-to-day notions and practices of freedom and moral responsibility. In contrast to Berlin, Strawson argues that we do not have to accept the libertarian or pessimistic view that our everyday reactive attitudes such as gratitude, resentment, blame, forgiveness and so forth and the moral practices upon which they rely must perish or radically alter as a consequence of determinism. The chief burden of his article is to show how determinism is *practically* benign with regard to our common experience of freedom and morality.

Strawson rests his deflationary thesis on two distinct but related arguments. The first centres on his view that determinism is essentially silent or innocuous with regard to what he calls our 'participant' attitudes that make up our understanding of ourselves as free, responsible and morally engaged individuals. What he means by this is that whether determinism is true or false – it is clear, by the way, that Strawson believes that the overwhelming evidence lies on the side of determinism being true but he does not let this prompt him to sell our everyday notion of freedom short by thinking it can be unproblematically replaced by some compatibilist or optimistic (as Strawson refers to such arguments) notion of freedom – does not threaten or imply that nobody is ever responsible for his or her actions.

His second and more fundamental point is that we should not feel the need to abandon our 'participant' or internal attitudes even if we accept determinism since doing so would involve an unnecessary and unacceptably costly denial of our humanity. In fact, he claims that the option to give up our commitment to freedom and morality is more of a notional than a real one since it is already too deeply and ubiquitously embedded in our individual psyche and societal practices. He adds that it would also be irrational to do so even if we managed *per impossibile* to suspend our deeply ingrained moral attitudes since whatever benefits might ensue from such a 'rational' step would pale into insignificance compared with the devastating human cost of abandoning our everyday moral practices and attitudes. He suggests that the libertarian rejection and compatibilist acceptance of determinism reflect a common short-sightedness. They share a failure to appreciate the irrationality of the 'rational' impulse to either insist on or reject our everyday, moral attitudes in the face of determinism. Strawson suggests that this error has its source in their over-intellectualization of the problem of free will. He seeks to amplify this last point by contrasting our response to the separate problem of induction, which has not resulted in anything like the same kind of hyper-intellectualism and excessive anxiety that the problem of free will has caused:

> Compare the question of the justification of induction. The human commitment to inductive belief formation is original, natural and non-rational (not irrational), in no way something we choose or could give up. Yet rational criticism and reflection can refine standards and their application, supply 'rules for judging of cause and effect'. Ever since the facts were made clear by Hume, people have been resisting acceptance of them. (FR 23)

The premise of Strawson's justification of the above claim rests largely on his view of how our reactive attitudes operate. These are attitudes we typically have and show towards other people based on their attitudes to us. So, for example, if someone shows generosity towards me, I will typically react to that person with gratitude. Conversely, if someone shows aggression towards me, then I will typically convey a reactive attitude of resentment. But, and this is a crucial part of Strawson's paper, there are occasions when we inhibit or even suspend our reactive attitudes. These occasions or circumstances might occur when we say 'He didn't mean to' or 'She was pushed' or alternatively 'She's only a child' or 'He's a hopeless schizophrenic'. The way we inhibit or moderate our normal reactive attitude, of, say, resentment, in the first two statements suggests reasons for not feeling resentment about a particular action of someone towards us whereas the latter two statements suggest reasons for not feeling resentment towards a particular person at all. In the latter two cases, we adopt what Strawson calls an 'objective attitude' towards another human being, which means that we suspend our normal reactive attitudes. Strawson then raises what he considers is the decisive question: If we believed that determinism is true, would it mean that we would regard everyone with the same objective attitude? His answer is an emphatic 'No'. He argues that determinism would not give us a reason for abandoning our reactive attitudes, or by extension our moral reactive attitudes, which he describes as 'vicarious analogues' of our basic reactive attitudes. Having such attitudes is just a brute fact of our human situation and nothing about determinism could or should fundamentally threaten or change it. In response to his quasi-rhetorical question of whether the acceptance of determinism could lead to the destruction of our participative reactive attitudes, he says:

> It does not seem to be self-contradictory to suppose that this might happen. So I suppose we must say that it is not absolutely inconceivable that it should

happen. But I am strongly inclined to think that it is, for us as we are, practically inconceivable. The human commitment to participation in ordinary inter-personal relationships is, I think, too thoroughgoing and deeply rooted for us to take seriously the thought that a general theoretical conviction might so change our world that, in it, there were no longer any such things as inter-personal relationships as we normally understand them; and being involved in inter-personal relationships as we normally understand them precisely is being exposed to the range of reactive attitudes and feelings that is in question. (FR 11)

The intended effect of Strawson's paper is to convince pessimistic libertarians to stop worrying about determinism as there's *practically* nothing to worry about. It is also intended to dissuade compatibilists or optimists from radically redefining our understanding of freedom on the basis that determinism obliges such a move, that is, to come up with a new version of freedom that is compatible with determinism. Whether determinism is true or not, life goes on largely unchanged, as indeed it should, in Strawson's view. He ends his paper by concluding that, having defused the alleged threat of determinism to freedom and morality, 'in return we must now demand of the pessimist a surrender of his metaphysics' (FR 23).

Strawson's justly acclaimed article remains one of the more impressive counterarguments to libertarianism (and the cruder forms of compatibilism). It is also especially germane to our current discussion because it operates on roughly the same humanistic level as Berlin's rejection of compatibilism, that is, allowing for the fact that there appears to be no conclusive and universally accepted proof of the truth or falsity of determinism, would believing in determinism entail the loss of our everyday notion of freedom and moral responsibility? So the next obvious question is: Does Strawson's argument manage to refute, or at least disarm, Berlin's libertarian or 'pessimistic' challenge?

16 IS BELIEF IN DETERMINISM LIVEABLE?

As we have seen, Berlin and Strawson analyse the problem of freedom on a fundamentally humanistic and phenomenological as distinct from a naturalistic and ultra-rationalist level. Strawson supposes that, regardless of whether determinism is true or false, we can and should go on living as we do without feeling the necessity to radically revise our deep-seated moral practices whereas Berlin is much more sceptical of such a strategy. But, who is more right? There's a possibility that they may both be partly right and partly wrong. There is also the distinct possibility that neither of them is right at all. We'll begin by looking at where Berlin may be on thinner ice.

It is clear from reading Strawson's essay that, while he says he is non-committal or agnostic for the purposes of his argument about the matter of the truth or otherwise of determinism, he is incredulous about the metaphysical claims of libertarianism. His main issue is with 'the contra-causal' element of libertarianism, which he clearly finds barmy (FR 24). Strawson is hardly alone in this regard. The libertarian insistence on some kind of 'contra-causal' or 'non-causal' or sui generis freedom is generally recognized as its Achilles heel. And we have no special reason to think that Berlin's libertarianism is or should be immune to this potentially crippling weakness.

Berlin himself tends to shift his position on this core aspect of his libertarianism, perhaps reflecting his own philosophical discomfort. There are times when he is stern in his affirmation of 'non-causal' or 'ultimate' freedom and others when his avowal is more vague and equivocal (CC2, compare 240 with 248). But his bottom line doesn't really falter – he believes that unless we retain the idea that freedom includes a source conception of free will, a conviction that I am the source of my choices in some ultimate or deep way, then we have lost the freedom that is crucial to our sense of who we are. And it is this version of free will that compatibilists find incoherent and therefore unacceptable. They argue that what makes the libertarian notion of free will invalid or unintelligible is that it is in flagrant conflict with the truth of determinism, with the ways things just are: For how can we even make sense, they argue quite reasonably, of human actions being 'uncaused' or 'contra-causal' in the context of a determined world? Accordingly, compatibilists defend a less demanding version of free will, which seeks to reconcile the truth of determinism with the sense that we remain free in a way that retains significance and meaning. So, unlike Berlin, they deny that freedom has to be the price of accepting determinism and, instead, claim that we can still salvage a scientifically valid yet psychologically and morally plausible concept of freedom even in the context of a determined world, a world in which every event, including every human choice and action, is always and everywhere answerable to the binding laws of determinism.

There are, of course, a large variety of compatibilist conceptions of freedom. Strawson's nuanced and even elusive position looks at freedom in terms of our susceptibility to reactive attitudes. The nature and possibility of our freedom and moral responsibility consists in our holding these reactive attitudes (including moral reactive attitudes) such as friendship and antipathy, gratitude and resentment, etc. towards one another. But the crucial point here is Strawson's claim that our reactive attitudes exist whether determinism is true or not, that the possible or probable truth of determinism neither does nor should obviate or undermine our participative reactive attitudes. According to Strawson's stance, Berlin is tilting at windmills when he opposes determinism: the freedom we need and enjoy every day does not require us to believe in any kind of metaphysically strange and hopelessly ambitious version of free will. Nor does it demand that we need to reject determinism since it is practically innocuous anyway. Determinism is therefore eminently liveable in a practical sense since the type of freedom and moral responsibility that we exercise in our day-to-day lives carries on independently of it in splendid and blithe indifference. In short, determinism is effectively irrelevant to our everyday sense of freedom. This looks like bad news for Berlin; not merely because his version of freedom is threatened but because of his insistence that its sustenance relies on an implausible libertarian version of free will. But before we are tempted to conclude that Strawson's argument renders Berlin's version or, rather, justification of libertarianism untenable and unnecessary, we need to dig a little a deeper. Once we do, things are not as straightforwardly obvious as they may at first seem.

The principal problem with Strawson's solution is that it underestimates the genuine instability and tension that exist between taking a scientific or naturalistic view of the world (a world that he clearly thinks is universally determined) and, at the same time, retaining a 'participative' or internal perspective that allows us to interpret and experience our moral attitudes as if they were entirely unaffected by determinism. He thinks the fear that we cannot hold these two distinct and incompatible perspectives simultaneously is a symptom of excessive theoretical fastidiousness and that, therefore, engaging in an 'intellectualist' preoccupation about it should not be encouraged. Where Strawson is optimistic that determinism doesn't pose any practical threat to our everyday understanding of freedom, Berlin seems to find such nonchalance unpersuasive and unsustainable. There is an unmistakable impression that Strawson wishes to have his cake and eat it, that he wants to claim that our everyday belief in freedom is unaffected by determinism while also implicitly claiming that the exercise of these same everyday beliefs remains reconcilable with conceding that everything that happens has an explanation in terms of causally sufficient conditions, that our practical conviction of free will can be squared with our naturalistically generated insight that determinism is true. In fact, it might be more accurate to say that Strawson's reconciliation is more apparent than real since it rests less on seeking to integrate determinism and everyday freedom than it does on trying to show that they can coexist unproblematically by exposing their mutual irrelevance.

There are three principal reasons why Berlin has a problem with the type of insouciant solution advocated by Strawson. The first is that it would, in his view, lead us almost unavoidably to equate or assimilate our current moral attitudes with something akin to aesthetic attitudes. This would effectively mean treating virtues like honesty or justice or, indeed, vices like cruelty or snobbery as we do natural traits like beauty or cleverness or ugliness or feeble-mindedness. The crucial difference, as Berlin sees it, is that 'we praise or congratulate the possessors of the latter qualities with no implication that they could have chosen to own a different set of characteristics' (CC2 240). If we had to make such an equation, which he believes accepting the truth of determinism would require, then we would have to abandon the basic categories and concepts that shape our existing moral and legal outlook and replace them with radically new ones that

> will substitute knowledge and understanding for attribution of responsibility; it will render indignation, and the kind of admiration that is its opposite, irrational and obsolete; it will expose such notions as desert, merit responsibility, remorse, and perhaps right and wrong too, as incoherent, or at the very least, inapplicable. (CC2 240)

This objection may not be particularly troubling to Strawson since he makes the not implausible claim that our existing moral reactive attitudes already incorporate the sort of objective insights that Berlin highlights and that they achieve this without any need to transform our everyday moral attitudes. If Strawson is right here then it looks like Berlin may be guilty of exaggerating his case about the need to aestheticize or in some way transform our ideas of freedom and moral responsibility in the absence of a belief in ultimate freedom.

The second problem, hinted at in the passage above, is that Strawson can only ever give the misleading appearance of defusing the libertarian's concerns with determinism. Berlin would argue that since it is precisely the intuitive or libertarian conception of free will that underlies and informs our everyday notion of freedom and moral responsibility, that if we accept, or it was conclusively shown, that the objective, naturalistic world does not possess the sort of libertarian freedom or moral responsibility that we can't help ourselves believing in, we are still left with a monumental and perhaps unassailable challenge. And the challenge is not just psychological as someone like Strawson seems to assume. What Berlin's analysis of the matter brings out is that even if we managed to overcome the obvious and by no means easily surmountable psychological obstacles required of believing in the truth of determinism, we are still left with the even more fundamental difficulty of coherently thinking of a world in which our ordinary notion of freedom and the ubiquitous moral, legal and political world view on which it depends is an illusion. It is one thing to confront the problem that living the truth of determinism may be psychologically impossible but it is quite another to face the challenge that our underlying patterns of thought, which our everyday notions of freedom and morality presuppose and rely on, are conceptually incoherent.

It is important to clarify at this point that Berlin is not primarily claiming that it is impossible to think that we could internalize a drastically attenuated notion of freedom that is compatible with determinism. Rather, what he is arguing is that there is no way of conceptually reconciling a genuine belief in determinism with our existing understanding of free will, the essence of which he believes is 'the freedom to make an unforced choice' or, put slightly differently, the notion that 'I could have done otherwise' in some ultimate, 'the buck stops here' way. To assume or suggest otherwise, he argues, is to spectacularly misjudge the nature and scale of the transformation needed to overturn our evolved and embedded conceptual framework. Berlin forcefully and eloquently articulates the scenario we would find ourselves in by imagining we had received conclusive proof of the truth of determinism:

> The principal difference, however, between previous advances and this imaginary breakthrough (and it is with this surmise that most of my critics have disagreed) is that besides effecting a vast alteration in our empirical knowledge, it would alter our conceptual framework far more radically than the discoveries of the physicists of the seventeenth or twentieth century, or the biologists of the nineteenth, have changed it. Such a break with the past, in psychology alone, would do great violence to our present concepts and usages. The entire vocabulary of human relations would suffer radical change. Such expressions as 'I should not have done x,' 'How could you have chosen x?' and so on, indeed the entire language of the criticism and assessment of one's own and others' conduct, would undergo a sharp transformation, and the expression we needed for descriptive and for practical-corrective, deterrent, hortatory, etc. purposes (what others would be open to a consistent determinist?) would necessarily be vastly different from the language we now use. It seems to be that we should be unwise to underestimate the effect of robbing praise, blame, a good many

counterfactual propositions, and the entire network of concepts concerned with freedom, choice, responsibility, of much of their present function and meaning. (CC2 246-47)

This brings us to the third major difficulty that Berlin has with the typical philosophical response to determinism. This difficulty is perhaps far more applicable to conventional compatibilism of the kind put forward by Dennett than it is to the more subtle version held by Strawson. This is his view that even if we grant the possibility that a belief in determinism is sustainable, it is clear that the notion of freedom we would be left with would barely qualify as even a radically bleached version of what most people at most times have understood by the term. This may be Berlin's most effective argument against compatibilism. It hinges on the possibility that knowledge or a certain type of knowledge may diminish rather than enlarge our intuitive understanding of and belief in freedom, that the more informed and rational we become about the world and ourselves the less we may be able to indulge our long-held, cherished convictions about our possession of ultimate, libertarian-style freedom.

In making this claim Berlin is, of course, aware that he is taking on one of the more sacred truths of philosophy. This is the alleged axiom that knowledge brings greater freedom on the basis that it is only by becoming more knowledgeable that we can become more rational and perhaps even more autonomous agents in the world. Berlin has serious doubts about the absolute validity of this philosophical tenet, at least in the context of our understanding of freedom. His initial reservation rests on the claim that compatibilists tend to fall into the trap of committing what looks like a basic category error; in their craving to show that granting the truth of determinism does not spell the end of freedom, they end up labelling whatever is compatible with determinism as freedom even though it may bear little or no resemblance to our common, everyday notion of freedom. The obvious reply to Berlin is to argue that libertarians do not have a monopoly on defining the meaning of freedom, especially if their understanding of freedom is naturalistically unfounded.

Closely related to this point is his view that compatibilists are prone to conflating what might well be an increase in truth or knowledge or rationality as an increase in freedom and moral autonomy. For example, the discovery that I may enjoy a degree of freedom that is itself no less determined than other phenomena but is necessarily incompatible with our ordinary, participative idea of freedom may render me more free from illusion but could not be described as an increase in my level of freedom. The fact that I may be entirely aware that I am a 'prisoner in my own personality' does not make me any more free than I was before I became conscious of my relatively unfree state. It just means I am less deluded. Here again, Berlin may appear straightforwardly vulnerable to the charge of declaring a preference for a life of blissful ignorance over one based on an honestly naturalistic understanding of and adjustment to the way of the world. But this objection, I think, would be wide of the mark. For he is not so much defending the superiority of the unexamined or illusory life as he is emphasizing that knowledge and freedom are distinct concepts and values with irreducibly separate meanings that cannot be conflated without violating their true nature and significance. We are witnessing again an example of Berlin's insistence on Bishop Butler's maxim that our most basic concepts and categories have their own enduring intellectual, normative and historical identity, which no amount of clever, *a priori* reasoning or naturalistic reductionism can obviate. Berlin articulates this point with the following rhetorical question:

> The advance of knowledge stops men from wasting their resources upon delusive projects. It has stopped us from burning witches or flogging lunatics or predicting the future by listening to oracles or looking at the entrails of animals or the flight of birds. It may yet render many institutions & decisions of the present – legal political moral social – obsolete, by showing them to be as cruel and stupid and incompatible with the pursuit of justice or reason or happiness or truth, as we now think the burning of widows or eating the flesh of an enemy to acquire his skills. If our powers of prediction and so our knowledge of the future become much greater, even if they are never complete, this may radically alter our view of what constitutes a person, an act, a choice: and *eo ipso* our language & our picture of the world. This may make our conduct more rational, perhaps more tolerant, charitable, civilised, it may improve it in many ways but will it increase the area of free choice? For individuals or groups? It will certainly kill some realms of the imagination founded upon non rational beliefs, and for this it may compensate by making some of our ends more easily or harmoniously obtainable. But who shall say if the balance will necessarily be on the side of wider freedom, unless someone establishes large equivalences between the notions of freedom, self-determination & self-knowledge by some *a priori* fashion – as Spinoza and Hegel and their modern followers seek to do – why this need be true? (CC2 257)

We shall return to this specific theme of the tension between knowledge and freedom in more detail towards the end of this chapter. Suffice to say for now that Berlin is deeply sceptical of the idea that freedom somehow consists in the recognition of necessity.

Internal and External Perspectives

I now wish to examine where Berlin may be even more vulnerable than I have described his position so far. Let's recall Strawson's central claim that it is possible and preferable to bracket the 'objective' or external view of the world, which is suggestive of determinism's truth, from the 'participative' or internal view, which is composed of a 'web of human attitudes and feelings' that rest on a non-determinist notion of freedom and responsibility. One of the key problems with Strawson's viewpoint is that it demands a degree of discontinuity between our objective and participative perspectives which, at best, looks unstable and, at worst, entirely unviable. The philosophical work of Thomas Nagel (1937–), a notable philosopher who has dedicated much of his professional life to exploring the character and significance of the relation between impersonal and personal standpoints, is instructive here. He argues that 'there is no way of preventing the slide from internal to external criticism once we are capable of an external view'.[1] He suggests that we would need to become psychological, moral and even epistemological schizophrenics if we were to consciously and consistently put Strawson's recommendation into practice. For it is far from clear how we could combine for more than a flickering moment, let alone sustain over a lifetime, the objective detachment and participative engagement implicit in Strawson's solution to the problem of freedom. And yet none of this should obviate the more crucial point that we can and do take an objective view of things and that it can and does affect our internal view of the world. In other words, Strawson's paper may have exaggerated our ability and desire to compartmentalize these different and often competing perspectives – the practical or participative and the objective or absolute. But surely none of this renders Berlin's position any less vulnerable since he appears to be guilty of preferring freedom to knowledge, of favouring our parochial and consoling preferences over the objective truth when it comes to free will. In short, where Strawson seems to be guilty of the charge of exaggerating the extent to which the truths of the natural world and our ordinary, everyday beliefs can coexist in relatively harmless harmony, Berlin would appear to be culpable of the far more egregious charge of privileging the concerns of a determinedly delusional view of the world over the apparent truths (many would say, obvious truths) of a naturalistic one.

Most philosophers who have reflected on the problem of free will from an objective or external vantage point have concluded that either some form of determinism is likely to be true or, at the very least, that our everyday, pre-theoretical notion of uncaused or non-antecedent freedom of choice – the incompatibilist notion of freedom that Berlin believes in and wishes to preserve – is not backed up by science.[2] Indeed, the prevailing wisdom of the philosophical literature would

---

[1] Thomas Nagel, *The View from Nowhere* (1986: Oxford University Press, Oxford), 125.
[2] There are, of course, exceptions including in more recent times Peter van Inwagen, *An Essay on Free Will* (1983: Oxford University Press, Oxford & New York) and Robert Kane, *Free Will and Values* (1985: Albany, New York), several of the essays in Timothy O'Connor ed. *Agents, Causes, Events* (1995: Oxford University Press, Oxford). One of the most philosophically sophisticated treatments of the problem of free will, and one that I am much indebted to, is David Wiggins's 'Towards a Reasonable Libertarianism' originally published in, *Essays on Freedom of Action*, ed. Ted Honderich (1973: Routledge & Kegan

suggest that the more objective or naturalistic we become about this particular matter, the less plausible and coherent our common, pre-reflective intuitions of freedom are rendered. It is precisely this so-called objectivist perspective that informs Strawson's dismissal of the metaphysics of libertarianism as 'obscure and panicky'.

So is Berlin's position guilty of the philosophical equivalent of bad faith, that is, of prioritizing our wishful thinking regarding freedom over what the cold light of truth reveals and demands? Put more pointedly, is his defence of freedom vulnerable to the charge of being culpably superficial, of betraying the findings of science for the sake of protecting and perpetuating the self-fulfilling fiction of libertarianism? I think there is a sense in which Berlin is vulnerable to this type of objection and a deeper sense in which he may transcend it.

There is no doubt that the external perspective does not get the hearing it perhaps deserves from Berlin on the topic of determinism. There is a defensive unpreparedness to acknowledge, internalize and modify our thoughts in accordance with the relevant insights of naturalism. And one of the things that is likely to result from the human power to seek and gain some level of naturalistic objectivity is a serious doubt about the tenability or even coherence of ultimate free will, a doubt that is likely to undermine rather than underwrite our common understanding of freedom and moral responsibility. One does not have to accept Dennett's barely concealed philosophical contempt for libertarians to acknowledge that there is at the very least a deep and perhaps unavoidable gulf in our understanding of freedom between, on the one hand, the external or objective perspective that argues incompatibilist freedom is an illusion and, on the other hand, the humanistic or perhaps subjectivist perspective that believes we can't and shouldn't do without it.

Thomas Nagel and another eminent philosopher, Barry Stroud, have been reminding us for some time that a central characteristic of human understanding is our unquenchable striving for an objective account of the world and our place in it and the equally powerful pull of our subjective intuitions and commitments.[3] Indeed, a view shared by both Stroud and Nagel is that a reconciliation between the separate and often rival demands of objectivity and subjectivity may not be possible. Moreover, they are both convinced that a certain tension between these two perspectives is more likely to form part of the human condition and that our natural temptation to make one perspective replace or eclipse the other

---

Paul, London) and later reprinted in David Wiggins, *Needs, Values, Truth* (1998: Oxford University Press, Oxford).

[3]See Thomas Nagel, *The View from Nowhere* (1986: Oxford University Press, Oxford) and Barry Stroud, 'The Study of Human Nature and the Subjectivity of Value', in *The Tanner Lectures on Human Values*, ed. G. Peterson, Vol. X (1989: Salt Lake City, Utah), 213–59 and his later book *Engagement and Metaphysical Detachment: Modality and Value* (2011: Oxford University Press, Oxford).

would be potentially ruinous to our sense of ourselves as ethically engaged, truth-seeking human beings. Berlin may not be necessarily guilty of seeking to subordinate 'the view from nowhere' to 'the view from here and now' but there are times when he comes perilously close. One suspects that he is tipping the scales a little too heavily in favour of the latter standpoint, albeit to redress the imbalance caused by the preponderance of the former one, a preponderance that continues to this day especially among scientistically inclined thinkers. This reaction on Berlin's part may be understandable but it can leave him exposed to the charge that he is favouring one partial view of philosophy over another one-sided view of the subject. Indeed, there is an unerring sense that Berlin is prioritizing a version of what Kant referred to as the *Weltbegriff* (world or universal view of philosophy) over the *Schulbegriff* (scholastic or logical view of philosophy), even though both conceptions of philosophy undoubtedly have legitimate claims to our attention.[4]

At this juncture it might help to introduce the ideas of Galen Strawson (1952– and P. F. Strawson's philosopher son) into the discussion. His contribution to the question of free will is particularly instructive in showing that the main weakness of Berlin's commitment to libertarianism may not be located in his rejection of compatibilism.

There are three core strands in Galen Strawson's essentially a priori critique of libertarianism that are noteworthy and possibly decisive.[5] The first and most general feature of his position is that it operates independently of the alleged truth or falsity of determinism. The second and main thrust of his argument is that the whole notion of being ultimately morally responsible for our actions is impossible since 'the way you are is, ultimately, in every last detail, a matter of luck, good or

---

[4]Kant distinguishes between these two aspects or aspirations of philosophy in his *Critique of Pure Reason*:

> If the receptivity of our mind, its power of receiving representations in so far as it is in any wise affected, is to be entitled sensibility, then the mind's power of producing representations from itself, the spontaneity of knowledge, should be called the understanding. Our nature is so constituted that our intuition can never be other than sensible; that is, it contains only the mode in which we are affected by objects. The faculty, on the other hand, that enables us to think the object of sensible intuition is the understanding. To neither of these powers may a preference be given over the other. Without sensibility no object would be given to us, without understanding no object would be thought. Thoughts without content are empty, intuitions without concepts are blind. *Critique of Pure Reason*, trans. Norman Kemp Smith (1933: MacMillan, London) A51/B76.

[5]Galen Strawson has written extensively on the subject of free will, most notably in his book *Freedom and Belief* (1986: Oxford University Press, Oxford). My synopsis of his position above is based mainly on his more recent paper 'The Bounds of Sense', in *The Oxford Handbook of Free Will*, ed. Robert Kane (2002: Oxford University Press, Oxford and New York), 441–60, henceforth referred to as BOS. Incidentally, Strawson does not think there are only a priori reasons for denying the truth of libertarianism: he also thinks there are a posteriori arguments against libertarianism too, a leading one being that based on the evidence of Einstein's theory of special relativity. 441.

bad' (BOS 449). He gives a brief but ingenious argument that claims to show the impossibility of being ultimately morally responsible for our actions in the way libertarianism seems to demand. His argument goes as follows:

- When you act, you do what you do, in the situation in which you find yourself, because of the way you are.

It seems to follow that

- to be truly or ultimately morally responsible for what you do, you must be truly or ultimately morally responsible for the way you are, at least in certain crucial mental respects.

But

- You can't be ultimately responsible for the way you are in any respect at all, so you can't be ultimately morally responsible for what you do.

Why can't you be ultimately responsible for the way you are? Because

- To be ultimately responsible for the way you are, you would have to have intentionally brought it about that you are the way you are, in a way that's impossible.

A third element of Galen Strawson's critique of libertarianism is his arresting claim that while ultimate, 'heaven or hell, buck stopping, up-to-me-ness moral responsibility' – the type of freedom that Berlin is committed to defending – is impossible and can be shown *a priori* to be incoherent, it is not meaningless in the same way that the concept of a round square is not straightforwardly meaningless:

> Some say that they don't really know what the content of this notion [of a round square] is, but it is easy to specify. A round square is an equiangular, equilateral, rectilinear, quadrilateral closed plane figure every point on the periphery of which is equidistant from the single point within its periphery. It is because we know the content of the notion that we know that there cannot be such a thing as a round square and the same is true of URD [the idea that we are ultimately responsible for our actions and deserving of praise or blame, etc.]. Many say that statements or concepts that are self-contradictory are meaningless, but meaningfulness is a necessary condition of contradictoriness. (BOS 452)

My reason for highlighting Galen Strawson's objections to libertarianism is to show that there are non-compatibilist grounds for rejecting Berlin's view of freedom. In fact, Strawson's *a priori* assault on libertarianism may be more fatal than the more common objections raised by compatibilists. There is something puzzling and perhaps even impossible about the idea of deep and ultimate responsibility even if we grant that it coheres with our ordinary notion of freedom. As Strawson himself states, the fact that we may not be ultimately responsible for our actions may be 'a bewildering fact, but it's a fact nonetheless' (BOS 457).

In his paper 'The Bounds of Sense' Galen Strawson acknowledges that while there are cogent reasons for saying that libertarianism is impossible, there are also powerful reasons for supposing the opposite. He adds that 'there are frames in which the answer is yes [that we do possess ultimate moral responsibility] and there are frames in which the answer is no' (BOS 441). I suggest that Berlin provides a compelling frame for saying the answer is yes.

The deeper sense in which Berlin's treatment of freedom may transcend the charge of philosophical incoherence or bad faith is precisely because it is deliberately, even deeply, superficial. More specifically, Berlin's defence of libertarianism is superficial for philosophical reasons as opposed to anything based on mere bias or some kind of anti-philosophical or anti-scientific denial of the truth. One way of elucidating this aspect of his libertarianism is by contrasting it with the spurious depth and candidness of so many compatibilist responses to the problem of free will.

One of the long-standing reasons for the recalcitrance of the problem of free will centres on the failure of compatibilism to provide libertarians with what they want, or more accurately, with what they are not prepared to forsake. It may well be the case that in the final analysis, libertarianism is indefensible but compatibilism is unlikely to become a universally accepted or even credible fact or belief in our lives until it finds a way of rescuing 'the truth' or insight of libertarianism that seems inseparable from our sense of who we are as human beings. The putative truth of determinism may be a necessary condition for us to wave goodbye to free will but it is a long way short of being a sufficient one. And what Berlin's contribution to the debate achieves in this context is a reminder of how much we would lose if we prematurely and unimaginatively embraced a belief in determinism tomorrow. His opposition to abandoning our common and incompatibilist notion of freedom is largely based on a refusal to accept that the possible truth of determinism alone is enough to prompt us to let go of our commitment to freedom and all that would result from this. Berlin exposes the simple-minded depth and self-assuredness of the various compatibilist arguments by showing that they grossly underestimate or remain blissfully unaware of what would happen if we abandoned our belief in libertarian freedom for a compatibilist version of freedom. As he states himself:

> Knowledge we are told extends the bounds of freedom, and this is *a priori* proposition. Is it inconceivable that the growth of knowledge will attend more and more successfully to establish the determinists thesis as an empirical truth, and explain our thoughts and feelings wishes and decisions, or actions and choices, in terms of invariant, regular, natural successions, to seek to

alter which will seem almost as irrational as entertaining a logical fallacy? This was the programme and the belief that many respected philosophers, as different in their outlooks as Spinoza, Holbach, Schopenhauer, Comte and the behaviourists. Would such a consummation extend the area of freedom in what sense would it not rather render this notion, for want of a contrasting one altogether otiose and would this not constitute a novel situation? The 'dissolution' of the concept of freedom would be accompanied by the demise by that sense of 'know' in which we speak, not of knowing that, but of knowing what to do; ... for if all is determined there is nothing to choose between, and so nothing to decide. Perhaps those who have said of freedom that it is the recognition of necessity were contemplating this very situation. If so, their notion of freedom is radically different from those who define it in terms of conscious choice and decision.' (CC2 258)

What should be clear by now is that identifying Berlin's resistance to determinism as a form of quietism or pre-theoretical bias misses the point. Rather, he is opposed to a distinctly impoverished type of philosophical blindness or blitheness regarding the implications of the immense transformation and loss arising from something as seismic as a universal conversion to a compatibilist conception of freedom. According to Berlin, it is as if philosophers have judged the establishment of the alleged truth of determinism as their primary or exclusive concern and then treated its normative and practical consequences as a mere afterthought. It is precisely this combination of philosophical arrogance and complacency that he is so critical of. His own treatment of free will is deliberately superficial in the sense that it stays on the phenomenological surface where human beings actually live and breathe their freedom and avoids the putatively deep reasoning that philosophers are perpetually prone to when it comes to this topic. It would seem that, sometimes, genuine depth is found on the surface of life. In this context, one is reminded of Kant's famous statement in the Preface to the second edition of the *Critique of Pure Reason* where he claims that it is necessary to deny speculative reason or knowledge to accommodate faith or what he refers to as 'the supersensible'.

> But, after we have thus denied the power of speculative reason to make any progress in the sphere of the supersensible, it still remains for our consideration whether data do not exist in practical knowledge, which may enable us to determine the transcendent concept of the unconditioned, to rise beyond the limits of all possible experience from a practical point of view, and thus to satisfy the great ends of metaphysics. Speculative reason has thus, at least, to make room for such an extension of our knowledge; and it must leave this space vacant, still does not rob us of the liberty to fill it up, if we can, by means of practical data – nay, it even challenges us to make the attempt. (CPR, B xx)

For Kant, the fact that God's existence as well as our free will cannot be demonstrably proven does not show that they are unreal or disproven: both are indispensable presuppositions of our moral lives. This prompts the obvious and not uninteresting reflection (but one we do not have the room to discuss here) of whether or to what extent the belief in ultimate or libertarian freedom is analogous to the belief in God?

Does this mean that Berlin's defence of free will operates within the sphere of intuitive belief rather than scientific truth? Is Galen Strawson correct in his assessment that the absence of ultimate free will and moral responsibility is a deeply perplexing but nonetheless true fact of life? Perhaps. But Berlin gives us grounds for suspecting that such a diagnosis may fail to do justice to the reality of human life, that there is a perspective from which the human world may be entitled to truths that do not readily line up with our physicalist view of the world. There may be a growing consensus among naturalistically inclined philosophers that determinism is true but that has not diminished the common conviction that we possess ultimate free will. Put differently, free will may be considered a universal or near universal illusion from a particular perspective but it is one we seem incapable of living without; hence the quip, *of course I believe in freedom, what choice do I have!* And one of the components of our resistance to believing in determinism and accepting compatibilism is that we appear to hold the belief that libertarian-style freedom is true and not just convenient to believe, that it is so embedded in our sense of ourselves to be unalterable, and its denial of or blindness to the findings of science is a vice of its virtue. This may be far from satisfactory but its unsatisfactoriness is not necessarily a sufficient reason to reject it. One might rework Pascal's famous adage to capture the paradox we appear to be left with by saying that: *everyday, libertarian-style freedom possesses non-scientific reasons that naturalistic reason seems incapable of fathoming.*

17 TRUTH, FREEDOM AND VALUE PLURALISM

Berlin's analysis of the problem of freedom serves to reveal an intriguing and radical strand of his theory of pluralism. His claim that knowledge does not necessarily set us free, that truth may well disabuse us of our belief in freedom opens up a genuinely unsettling but fascinating vista. For we are now left with the paradox that truth itself can be in conflict with the ideal of freedom, an ideal that not only undergirds but is crucial to the very integrity and appeal of Berlin's defence of a liberal, tolerant society. On one level, this outcome is entirely in line with Berlin's version of value pluralism, which consistently and explicitly argues that there exists no hierarchy among objective human values, including epistemological ones, and that our values themselves compete and conflict with each other. Nonetheless, it is undeniable that there's something deeply precarious and maybe even self-defeating about an admission that the truth itself can be in conflict with the very ideal that is at the heart of the political philosophy being defended. It is one thing to say that justice can conflict with compassion or liberty with equality but quite a different matter to concede that truth or knowledge may be incompatible with freedom. Are we facing the possibility that Berlin's version of value pluralism leads us down the path of epistemological incoherence or even chaos? Or is there a way of defusing Berlin's latest paradox?

One way of answering this question is by acknowledging that Berlin's admission that some of our most precious beliefs and practices may not have truth on their side is not unprecedented in the Western philosophical tradition. There have been occasions when the truth, or what is perceived as true, has been considered unliveable. Moreover, the verdict that certain alleged truths or insights may be intolerable has also been the outcome of serious philosophical rumination rather than unreflective or irrational prejudice. The recent contribution of Saul Smilansky to the free will debate is a good example; Smilansky provides a very sophisticated defence of the need for illusion in the absence of libertarian free will. Interestingly, he does not regard what he calls 'illusionism' (living an illusory life) as a regrettable or embarrassing fact of human life. Rather, he claims that 'humanity is fortunately deceived on the free will issue, and this seems to be a condition of civilized morality and personal value'[1]. While Smilansky's argument is interesting, raising as it does the distinct possibility that although libertarian free will may well be untrue, our believing in it may be unavoidable, I wish to examine a different example in which we find truth's liveability problematic. I think this different and older case brings out more clearly the very real possibility that our resistance or, in some cases, inability to accept and/or live certain truths may be based on more than merely psychological factors, that there may also be philosophically or, at least, phenomenologically generated limitations to what we can endorse and carry out in our day-to-day lives.[2]

The example I have in mind is provided by pure or Pyrrhonian scepticism. The Pyrrhonian version of ancient scepticism was rediscovered in the sixteenth century following the publication of the writings of the ancient Greek philosopher, Sextus Empiricus. In the words of an eminent contemporary scholar in this area, Pyrrhonian scepticism adds up to 'the only serious attempt in Western thought to carry scepticism to its furthest limits and live by its result'.[3] The Pyrrhonian brand of ancient scepticism claimed that the only form of true happiness was possible through being in a constant state of *ataraxia* or tranquillity from disturbance, which was achieved through *epoché* or the suspension of judgement. The most perceptive analysis and assessment of the philosophical challenge presented by pure scepticism in this context remains that of Hume. Hume gave what many regard as the best reason for why a genuinely consistent sceptic cannot live his scepticism even if such scepticism may well be true. His argument is formulated in Book XII of his *An Enquiry Concerning Human Understanding* as follows:

> A Stoic or Epicurean displays principles, which may not only be endurable, but which have an effect on conduct and behaviour. But a Pyrrhonian cannot

---

[1]Saul Smilansky, 'Free Will, Fundamental Dualism, and the Centrality of Illusion' in *The Oxford Handbook of Free Will*, op.cit, 500. It is important to highlight that Smilansky considers determinism true and libertarian free will untrue. But he also thinks that a life based on belief in the truth of determinism is unliveable. See also Saul Smilansky, *Free Will and Illusion* (2000: Clarendon Press, Oxford).

[2]It is also tempting in this context to compare this aspect of the free will debate with confronting someone, usually a hard-boiled scientist, who says that from the point of view of the universe, everything we do is meaningless. Working out where such a statement goes wrong is not dissimilar from working out where hard and soft determinists (and compatibilists) may be going wrong.

[3]Myles Burnyeat, 'Can the Sceptic Live His Scepticism?', in *The Original Sceptics: A Controversy*, eds. Myles Burnyeat and Michael Frede (1997: Hackett, UK), 26. Incidentally, Burnyeat's paper is one of the best proofs, if one were needed, of the enduring philosophical interest of the ideas of long-dead thinkers.

expect his philosophy will have any constant influence on the mind: or if it had, that its influence would be beneficial to society. On the contrary, he must acknowledge, if he will acknowledge anything, that all human life must perish, were his principles universally and steadily to prevail. All discourse, all action would immediately cease; and men remain in total lethargy, till the necessities of nature, unsatisfied, put an end to their miserable existence. It is true; so fatal an event is very little to be dreaded. Nature is always too strong for principle. And though a Pyrrhonian may throw himself or others into a momentary amazement and confusion by his profound reasonings, the first and most trivial event in life will put to flight all his doubts and scruples, and leave him the same, in every point of action and speculation, with the philosophers of every other sect, or with those who never concerned themselves in any philosophical researches. When he awakes from his dream, he will be the first to join in the laugh against himself, and to confess, that all his objections are mere amusement, and can have no other tendency than to show the whimsical condition of mankind, who must act and reason and believe; though they are not able, by their most diligent enquiry, to satisfy themselves concerning the foundation of these operations, or to remove the objections, which may be raised against them.[4]

The parallels between the issue raised by Pyrrhonian scepticism and compatibilism are both structurally and substantively analogous. Like compatibilism, Pyrrhonian scepticism may well have more truth or, at least, more reason on its side. And like compatibilism, radical or Pyrrhonian scepticism claims that its philosophical outlook is not only liveable but also the only rationally defensible way of life available to us (even if, strictly speaking, Pyrrhonianism ultimately eschews any form of knowledge or belief, albeit on the back of the exercise of reason!). Similarly, Hume's rejection of Pyrrhonian scepticism as a reasonable and practicable way of life is, I believe, as pertinent to compatibilism. As Hume argues in the passage quoted above, what renders it impossible to sustain unadulterated scepticism as a way of life is that 'mankind ... must act and reason and believe'. As Myles Burnyeat reminds us, we must recognize that Hume's rejection of Pyrrhonianism is not so much based on any opposition to its knowledge, or truth claim (e.g. he does not try to invalidate the perhaps warranted sceptical objections to our everyday inferences such as our belief in causality) as it is on the matter of whether a sceptic like Sextus Empiricus can stop holding the beliefs that his arguments show to be rationally unwarranted. Hume argues that it is impossible for a sceptic to live his scepticism as it would entail living without belief and without the type of reason

---

[4] David Hume, *An Enquiry Concerning Human Understanding* (2008 edn: Oxford University Press, Oxford), Book XII, 116–17.

that accompanies and nourishes our everyday beliefs. The fact that there may exist well-founded sceptical arguments against the rationality of our everyday beliefs and inferences is not necessarily enough to prompt us to give them up. As Hume remarks, 'nature is always too strong for principle', with the result that we go on believing in the things we must, independently of and even in spite of the insights and conclusions of more speculative reason. As an ad hominem aside, it is interesting to note that even Pyrrho himself found it impossible to practise the very scepticism he preached: for he reportedly admitted that it is difficult to divest oneself completely of one's humanity after he had let it be shown he became frightened by the bark of a dog. This telling anecdote offers further vindication of Hume's more general thesis that a sceptic cannot realistically live his scepticism.

Berlin's problem with compatibilism is not dissimilar to Hume's problem with wholesale scepticism. Moreover, his reason for rejecting compatibilism as a possible or even notionally coherent position may be as valid, mutatis mutandis, as Hume's objections to Pyrrhonianism as an endurable way of life. Let's recall that the focus of Berlin's main difficulty with compatibilism is not so much its alleged embrace of determinism as its notion of freedom. Like Hume, Berlin is prepared to admit that determinism may well be true and he even indulges the possibility that its truth may become more widely or even universally accepted in the future. However, what he does have a major problem with is the cost of our giving up our belief in libertarian freedom and confronting the unendurable shortcomings of the type of freedom that compatibilists wish to replace it with. Mirroring Hume's argument, therefore, Berlin thinks that we would need to divest ourselves of much of our humanity in order to keep up the kind of limited and bleached version of freedom typically advocated by compatibilists. In other words, he doesn't think that a life without the kind of freedom we commonly believe in, a type of freedom that is incompatible with a belief in the truth of determinism, is a possible life for us in the sense of our current understanding of what's vital to our understanding of who we are as free and morally responsible human beings. Berlin also makes the under-appreciated and perhaps crucial point that it is not even clear whether the question of determinism being true is ultimately or exclusively an empirical question given that our existing concepts and categories are so invested in its denial (CC2 247-48).

This, at least, is one possible way of partially defusing the paradox we sighted above. But, at best, it only manages to mitigate rather than resolve the tension between the admission that determinism is or may be true and the refusal to forsake libertarian free will. Berlin's position remains precarious for at least two reasons. Firstly, it is not sufficiently clear that compatibilist freedom would be as difficult to live as a way of life as the sceptical way of life advocated by Pyrrho. Pyrrhonianism as a liveable form of life looks like a non-starter both on a notional and on a real level whereas it is not as obvious that the same applies to compatiblilist freedom. No doubt there would be a massive cost in relinquishing our common belief in free will, a cost that Berlin conveys in a convincing and moving way, but it remains far from clear-cut that the abandonment of our belief in libertarian free will would be as conclusively devastating or even as inconceivable as Berlin suggests. In this vein one is reminded of a particularly vivid passage at the end of *War and Peace*. In the final chapter of the Epilogue, Tolstoy likens the conflict between his belief in free will and in determinism with that of the earlier disagreement that he speculates must have existed in people's minds between the existing Ptolemaic or earth-centred view of the solar system versus the emerging heliocentric or sun-centred view:

> Just as in astronomy the problem of recognising of the world's motion lay in the difficulty of getting away from a direct sensation of the earth's immobility and a similar sensation of the planets' motion, so in history the problem of recognizing the dependence of personality on the laws of space, time and causation lies in the difficulty of getting away from the direct sensation of one's own personal independence. But just as in astronomy the new attitude was 'No, we cannot feel the earth's movement, but if we accept its immobility we are reduced to absurdity, whereas if we accept the movement we cannot feel we arrive at laws,' so in history the new attitude is 'No, we cannot feel our dependence, but if we accept free will we are reduced to absurdity, whereas if we accept dependence on the external world, time and causation, we arrive at laws.'

Tolstoy then ends his novel with the following final two sentences:

> In the first case we had to get away from a false sensation of immobility in space and accept movement that we could not feel. In the present case it is no less essential to get away from a false sensation of freedom and accept a dependence we cannot feel.[5]

It is interesting to note Ludwig Wittgenstein's view (as told by his pupil Elizabeth Anscombe) on the same theme:

> He (Ludwig Wittgenstein) once greeted me with the question: 'Why do people say that it was natural to think that the sun went round the earth rather than that the earth turned on its axis?' I replied: 'I suppose, because it looked as if the sun went round the earth.' 'Well, he asked, 'what would it have looked like if it had looked as if the earth turned on its axis?'[6]

---

[5] L. Tolstoy, *War and Peace*, Epilogue, Chapter 12 (2007: Penguin, London), 1358.
[6] Elizabeth Anscombe, *An introduction to Wittgenstein's Tractatus* (1959: Routledge & Kegan Paul, London), 151.

What Tolstoy reminds us of, and what Berlin seems unwilling to concede in this case, is that even our most entrenched and precious personal feelings about matters that are deeply important to us can be given up in the face of conflicting but undeniable evidence.[7] This is not to suggest that the cost of such a sacrifice is painless, for it would require of us that we abandon the deeply rooted and ubiquitous belief that *I could have done otherwise*. But it is to claim that we have managed to let go of similar, seemingly inescapable beliefs down the ages, beliefs that may be considered on a par with the loss of faith in libertarian free will. The obvious examples are the gradual loss of faith in God, and the related assumption that planet Earth and the human beings who inhabit it possess some unique cosmic significance. To a greater or lesser extent, we have managed over time to find a way of living without these beliefs, albeit not without a great deal of dismay, resentment and what Weber (1864–1920) famously called *disenchantment*. This is reflected also in the way our basic concepts and categories have evolved, the more transcendent-inclined ones giving way to more naturalistic and secular patterns of thought. The one major caveat to add at this juncture is that, compared with the heliocentric view of the solar system or even Nietzsche's belated announcement that 'God is dead',[8] the idea of determinism hardly offers either clarity of meaning or clearly defined ethical implications. It was not for nothing that J. L. Austin referred to determinism as 'a name for nothing clear, that has been argued for only incoherently'.[9] This caveat bolsters Berlin's resistance to waving farewell to libertarian freedom. It may even be one of his strongest reasons for rejecting compatibilism.

Secondly, as has been noted, Berlin's commitment to free will comes at a cost. While we may be prepared to agree with his view that compatibilism would shatter the basis of our existing conceptual framework, his defence of an incompatibilist conception of freedom against the background of the probable, if not certain, truth of determinism remains deeply problematic. We are left with the seemingly inexorable predicament that compatibilist freedom is unliveable but determinism is undeniable, neither of which should be viewed as reassuring news for libertarianism. Berlin's fundamental Kantianism with regard to free will

---

[7]Berlin stresses that Tolstoy the hedgehog was in unavoidable conflict with Tolstoy the fox on the question of determinism and freedom. Berlin portrays Tolstoy's deep ambiguity in the following terms:

'The unresolved conflicts between Tolstoy's belief that the attributes of personal life alone are real and his doctrine that analysis of them is insufficient to explain the course of history (that is, the behaviour of societies) is paralleled, at a profounder and more personal level, by the conflict between, on the one hand, his own gifts as both a writer and as a man and, on the other, his ideals – that which he sometimes believed himself to be, and at all times profoundly believed in, and wished to be.' (HF2 43).

[8]Friedrich Nietzsche, *Thus Spoke Zarathustra*, part 1, *Zarathustra's Prologue* (1883), end of § 2; and elsewhere.

[9]J. L. Austin, 'Ifs and Cans', *Philosophical Papers* (1979: Oxford University Press, Oxford), 231. It is not clear in this instance if Austin is referring to determinism or compatibilism.

commits him to asserting that the price of compatibilism is not worth the sacrifice. Put metaphorically, the putative truth of determinism resembles an unwelcome and inassimilable guest from the *noumenal* world who is a destructive, even fatal, presence in the phenomenal world of free will and morality. Unless we manage to develop a form of dual-aspect realism where the objects of experience can make coherent sense from both a *noumenal* and a phenomenal perspective, or, alternatively, succumb to some form of objectivist or subjectivist one-sidedness or dogmatism, the precariousness caused by this discrepancy in our thought may well be an unalterable part of our lives. This can leave one speculating with regard to the intended or possible meaning(s) of Quine's memorable remark that 'the Humean condition is also the human condition'.[10]

My own reading of Hume on this matter is coloured by Barry Stroud's (1935) masterful paper 'The Study of Human Nature and the Subjectivity of Value'.[11] Stroud argues persuasively that our more detached and reflective self cannot escape the view that our values are subjective and yet, at the same time, our more engaged self cannot accept or at least live with the view of the world that behoves us to believe that our values are merely subjective. He also thinks that the tension between these two perspectives is as fundamental as it is unsettling. And crucially, Stroud, like Berlin, emphasizes that this tension cannot be understood or be reduced to a purely psychological affair. As he states:

> But it is not just a matter of psychological instability, or oscillation. It is a question of whether that restricted view of the fully 'objective' world can even be reached ... . Can we coherently think of a world in which all our valuings are exposed as purely 'subjective'? Could we then continue to understand ourselves to be making any evaluations at all? I think neither defenders nor opponents of 'subjectivism' have taken this question seriously enough. (HNSV 71–2)

One of the more interesting aspects of Stroud's analysis is that it does not end up embracing moral objectivism in the wake of its analysis of the evident shortcomings of moral subjectivism. His subsequent work in this area, which in many ways builds on the rich vein of the central idea discussed in his 1989 Tanner Lectures, reveals the fascinating philosophical avenues and insights that emerge once we stop letting ourselves fall into the trap of adopting a conventionally binary approach to the basic and recurring question of morality – of assuming, in other words, that either moral objectivism or moral subjectivism, and their respective variants, exhaust the valid

---

[10] W. V. O. Quine, *Ontological Relativity and Other Essays* (1969: Columbia University Press, New York), 72.

[11] G. Peterson ed. *The Tanner Lectures on Human Values*, Vol. x (1989: Salt Lake City, Utah). Hereafter referred to as HNSV.

options available. The real value of this feature of Stroud's work is his suggestion that the shrewdest way of treating the central philosophical question of morality may lie in keeping one's gaze firmly fixed on what makes it such an intractable and central problem rather than succumbing to the habitual temptation of resorting to one of the established and tired theoretical isms for a 'solution'.

However, we are still left with a more general paradox raised by Berlin's analysis and assessment of the problem of free will, a paradox that has its source in his pluralist and phenomenological conception of philosophy. If truth is ultimately one value among other values, and since value pluralism holds that all genuine values (including epistemological ones) are not only incommensurable but can and do compete and conflict with each other, it would seem we may be facing the rather disturbing outcome that truth itself cannot enjoy any kind of privileged status if value pluralism is itself a veridical characterization of our moral experience. Berlin himself confirms this unstable state of affairs in the final paragraph of his paper 'From Hope and Fear Set Free':

> I wish to make no judgement of value: only to suggest that to say that knowledge is a good is one thing; to say that it is necessarily, in all situations, compatible with, still more that it is on terms of mutual entailment with (or even, as some seem to suppose, is literally identical with), freedom, in most of the senses in which this word is used, is something very different. Perhaps the second assertion is rooted in the optimistic view – which seems to be at the heart of much metaphysical rationalism – that all good things must be compatible, and that therefore freedom, order, knowledge, happiness, a closed future (and an open one?) must be at least compatible, and perhaps even entail one another in a systematic fashion. But this proposition is not self-evidently true, if only on empirical grounds. Indeed, it is perhaps one of the least plausible beliefs ever entertained by profound and influential thinkers. (CC2 258–9)

Berlin's response to the idea that knowledge can and does conflict with other values is in a way a confirmation, perhaps even a vindication, of the truth of value pluralism. But, of course, saying that the truth can conflict with other values is not to undermine or deny its importance. To think otherwise would merely reveal that one is either a consistency fundamentalist or is still under the spell of the spurious rationalism which assumes that unless the truth is compatible with all other genuine values then one may as well give up on the truth and consign it to the dustbin of dead ideas.[12] In this respect too, there's a deep similarity between

---

[12] The work of Jon Elster is relevant here, especially his *Reason and Rationality* (2009: Princeton University Press, Princeton, NJ). Elster highlights the various ways in which hyper-rational appeals to reason can undermine reason itself.

Hume's outlook and Berlin's. Both accept that even the truth is not sovereign in all areas of life, and both are aware that to acknowledge the limits of truth's sovereignty is itself a recognition of a deep and precious truth. Reflection can weaken, or at least render problematic, the supposed absoluteness of truth's hold over us just as it can cast doubt on the supposed bindingness of many of our moral commitments. This seems both reasonable and realistic.

But it is possible to bring things a step further. Berlin's pluralism helps us make better sense of our situation than even Hume came up with. And a major part of Berlin's advancement on Hume is that it serves to remind us that we cannot necessarily extricate ourselves from the Humean problematic. Where Hume was prepared only to go so far as to claim that the ideal of human perfection is pragmatically impossible, Berlin provides us with grounds for believing that the ideal of human perfectibility is conceptually and experientially incoherent too. Berlin formulates this crucial distinction most clearly in his essay, 'The End of the Ideal of a Perfect Society':

> But if in fact the thinkers whom I am thinking of, the German Romantic thinkers, have anything in them at all, if not all virtues are compatible with each other, if in fact you cannot have both efficiency and spontaneity, if in fact you cannot have knowledge, necessarily, and happiness, if you cannot have equality and liberty, and similarly with many other virtues, then you must make choices, and whichever choices you make you will lose something. But this, if true, certainly undermines the idea of a perfect society, not just in practice – because men are stupid or because men are inefficient – or because they do not have divine grace, or because they do not know what the answer is, or because they do not know how to get there, or because they are going along the wrong path, which is the old view – but in principle, logically, the notion of a perfect universe is not coherent, if different ideals are of equal validity, which is what Herder said, and if different virtues are not compatible with each other, and that is why tragedy happens. If Antigone has to choose between love and honour there is no solution; whichever she does, she loses something. You cannot say love is inferior to honour, and you do not want to say honour is inferior to love. Both these are ultimate values, and there is no way of settling the issue: you must just plump in some sort of way. (EIPS 46, 48)

So where does this leave our discussion of Berlin's understanding of freedom? We can summarize his position as follows. Berlin thinks that:

1. the argument for determinism is unclear.
2. our belief in the truth or reality of free will in the deep or ultimate or libertarian sense should be maintained unless or until the truth of determinism is conclusively proven and its meaning, scope and implications made clear.

3 compatibilism is essentially a poorly conceived, implausible and destructive evasion.

4 our intuitive belief in libertarianism operates primarily within a phenomenological rather than a metaphysical sphere.

5 our belief in real or ultimate or libertarian freedom should not be characterized as or reduced to a purely psychological affair.

6 our very concepts and categories of thought would need to undergo a massive and perhaps even unimaginable transformation to adjust to the alleged truth of determinism.

7 the onus of proof lies with those who claim that determinism is true rather than with those who defend libertarianism or ultimate free will and moral responsibility.

One might be tempted to think that the best way of reconstructing Berlin's view of freedom is to interpret it in terms close to what Galen Strawson has described as 'a subjectivist commitment theory of freedom'.[13] This is a theory of freedom which claims that we are free (in the libertarian sense) not just because we subjectively believe we are free but because we also cannot help being committed to the belief that we are. In other words, it is the inescapabilty of our feeling of being free combined with the felt experience of being free that gives the impression that we are dealing with an objective phenomenon rather than merely a subjective experience. The advantage of seeing Berlin's viewpoint in such a light is that it helps take the edge off the contrast between his faith in libertarian-style freedom and what strike many of us as the undeniable insights of naturalism. If we accept that determinism is simply the view that everything is determined and has nothing intrinsically to do with free will, we become more open to viewing the so-called problem of free will in primarily psychological terms. Indeed, the logical next step might seem to be to hand over the problem of free will to the psychologists so that it can be treated as a case of motivated irrationality – there is the distinct possibility that a major part of the free will problem may simply be rooted more in our overriding desire for libertarian-style free will than in our belief in its truth. But, of course, even if we were prepared to take this step, we couldn't realistically restrict the implications of naturalism to the matter of free will. Accepting the naturalistic view of the world creates a hornets' nest for many more of our most cherished everyday phenomenological assumptions and convictions. Samuel Beckett's memorable line about the 'issueless predicament of existence' gives us a flavour of what might be involved or required in taking on

---

[13]Galen Strawson, *Freedom and Belief* (1986: Clarendon Press, Oxford), chapter 3.

board genuine naturalism.[14] Indeed, one can be left thinking that compatiblism takes a remarkably optimistic view of freedom in the context of an entirely indifferent world. There is an unerring sense that the naturalistic or objective perspective asks too much – and too little – of us mere mortals, even when we acknowledge that our impulse for a thoroughly naturalistic account of the world is itself implacably human.

But it is likely that Berlin would resist such a subjectivist theory of freedom and that his reasons for resistance would not be unfounded. No doubt he would have a difficulty with the inescapability prong of the argument, which would have struck him as a psychological variation of the anti-libertarian position that we inevitably choose because of who we causally happen to be. I suspect that he would also have rejected the theory on the more general grounds that it reflects a commitment to an excessively naturalistic attitude about something that is simply too deep and precious in relation to our own human-centred view of things. For even if we were to accept that the putative truth of determinism is incompatible with the perspective that informs our intuitive sense of ultimate, libertarian freedom, we are still left with the seemingly insurmountable challenge of the extent to which we are required to reconcile these compelling perspectives. Holding both perspectives would seem to require a psychologically unfeasible cognitive dissonance. In the end, one suspects that there is something deeply Kantian about Berlin's commitment to free will, a conviction that our sense of ourselves as genuinely free agents is sacred and should not be annihilated by a recognition of the inexorable laws of natural science.

So while Berlin's position is not what could be described as anywhere near a complete or particularly satisfactory theory of free will, it does succeed in giving us a deeper understanding of this possibly intractable question. He admitted that he didn't have the perception of genius to contribute something of permanent value to the free will problem but he suggests that even if our everyday, incompatabilist notion of freedom may end up being exposed as illusory the inescapability of our belief in the truth of such freedom suggests that it is far from an illusion in the ordinary sense of the word. It might even be the case that if the 'illusion' of free will is so necessary and ultimately unavoidable it is idle to describe it as untrue. In the end, one is left with the impression, yet again, that Berlin is primarily concerned with reminding us of the scope and significance of a serious and seemingly insoluble philosophical question than he is with seeking to produce a conclusive solution to the recalcitrant problem

---

[14]From Samuel Beckett's review of Thomas MacGreevey, *Jack B Yeats: An Appreciation and an Interpretation* (1945) and quoted in Dermot Moran 'Beckett and Philosophy', in *Samuel Beckett: Playwright & Poet*, ed. Christopher Murray (2009: Pegasus Press, New York), 94.

itself. The closing paragraph of his essay, 'John Stuart Mill and the Ends of Life', seems quite apt at this point:

> He [J. S. Mill] broke with the pseudo-scientific model, inherited from the classical world and the age of reason, of a determined human nature, endowed at all times, everywhere, with the same unaltering needs, emotions, motives, responding differently only to differences of situation and stimulus, or evolving according to some unaltering pattern. For this he substituted (not altogether consciously) the image of man as creative, incapable of self-completion, and therefore never wholly predictable: fallible, a complex combination of opposites, some reconcilable, others incapable of being resolved or harmonised; unable to cease from his search for truth, happiness, novelty, freedom but with no guarantee, theological or logical or scientific, of being able to attain them; a free, imperfect being, capable of determining his own destiny in circumstances favourable to the development of his reason and his gifts. He was tormented by the problem of free will, and found no better solution for it than anyone else, though at times he thought he had solved it. He believed that it is neither rational thought, nor domination over nature, but freedom to choose and to experiment that distinguishes men from the rest of nature; of all his ideas it is this view that has ensured his lasting fame. By freedom he meant the condition in which men were not prevented from choosing both the object and manner of their worship. For him only a society in which this condition was realised could be called fully human. Its realisation was an ideal which Mill regarded as more precious than life itself. (L 250-51)

18 REIMAGINING THE NATURE AND AUTHORITY OF PHILOSOPHY

One of main reasons Berlin gave for rejecting the compatibilist solution to the problem of free will centres on the human cost that he felt would result from giving up our normal, libertarian sense of freedom. Yet surely couldn't the same kind of argument be used against value pluralism? At first glance, value pluralism would seem to share compatibilism's radically destabilizing effect on our everyday moral ideas and practices. Like compatibilism, value pluralism asks us to give up the influential and implicitly monistic idea that there is a unified and correct answer to normative questions and that the whole point of sedulously and imaginatively reflecting on such questions is precisely to arrive at a determination of the uniquely right thing to do or be. However, the impression of such an affinity between a belief in value pluralism and a belief in compatibilism is more apparent than real. While both beliefs are radically subversive of conventional thinking and practice, the source and implications of their heterodoxy are worlds apart. They also generate vastly different expectations of humanity. Compatibilism claims to reconcile us with a truth about the external or natural world, whereas value pluralism justifies itself on the internal or phenomenological grounds that it reflects a truth about the reality of our own lived, everyday human experience. Compatibilism requires that we abandon our ordinary, implicitly libertarian notion of freedom for a comparatively anaemic version of freedom that would radically transform how we make sense of ourselves and society, not just psychologically but conceptually. Value pluralism, on the other hand, invites us to replace a unified and absolutist conception of morality with a perspective that perceives ethical diversity and conflict as an inherently unavoidable and infinitely precious feature of life.

The difference between the two beliefs raises all sorts of interesting and important questions. An obvious one concerns the tension between the insights that derive from a purely naturalistic view of the world and those that have their source in a more anthropological understanding of the world of humanity. Our belief that the sciences can and should provide objective, all-embracing and measurable solutions to all genuine questions, including human-centred ones, is one that has become deeply attractive in our culture since the Enlightenment. As we saw in Part Two, it is also an impulse that Berlin exposed as at best one-sided since the natural and social sciences lack the intellectual and evaluative resources needed to comprehend and address many of the deepest and most urgent questions of human life. Notwithstanding the fact that the sciences play a vital role in the explanation of the natural world, including, of course, features of human nature, there remain vast and significant elements of our lives that also require a more philosophically imaginative and historically informed sensibility which one associates with the humanities and the arts. The indispensability of such subjects as history, anthropology, psychology and literature that inform a more anthropocentrically minded – as distinct from a naturalistically focused – philosophy for deepening our understanding of ourselves and others can hardly be overstated. But this is easier said than done for two major reasons. The analytic tradition finds strength and solace in its austere, impersonal self-image as a self-styled scientific enterprise and is therefore reluctant to indulge in what it sees as a heightened form of belles-lettrism or self-fulfilling rhetoric. The second and more telling reason is that pursuing the kind of creatively ambitious and nuanced philosophy that Berlin engages in is far more difficult than the predominantly formal, abstruse and largely unreadable work in which the vast majority of academic moral and political theorists routinely and rather mechanically engage.[1]

Another related and important question concerns the less obvious matter of the authority of philosophy. Put bluntly, why should we take any notice of what philosophy says on such humanly important topics as freedom and morality? This point becomes even more pressing if we reflect on the fact that some of the things philosophy would dissuade us from are themselves a product of philosophical speculation: Would anyone, for example, have believed in what Berlin refers to as the Ionian fallacy of moral monism if it had not been created and sustained by Western philosophy (including religious philosophy and theology) in the first place?[2] And should we jeopardize our existing sense of freedom and much else

---

[1] Alasdair MacIntyre argues that the skills required of an outstanding political philosopher are virtually superhuman: 'Political theory is an oddity among academic subjects, a kind of no man's land between philosophy, history and empirical political science. ... The political theorist is this summoned to be a kind of academic superman synthesizing the skills of the historian and the philosopher, quite apart from mobilizing the relevant pieces of knowledge provided by such kindred disciplines as law, anthropology and economics.' From his review of John Dunn, *Western Political Theory in the Face of the Future* in the *London Review of Books, 20 December 1979*. Incidentally, MacIntyre counts Berlin among the 'superhuman' political theorists who have answered this summons.

[2] I owe this salutary point to Henry Hardy.

besides on the basis of a philosophical theory that claims to be the only rational response to the putative truth of determinism?

One way of responding to these questions is to deny that philosophy has any genuine authority or relevance in our day-to-day lives and that our relationship with it should follow the advice of George Gerswhin's song, 'Let's call the whole thing off'. But such a response tends either to miss the point of philosophy or to signify a cynical and even sinister disregard of critical thought in general. Another way of treating the matter is to view philosophy and especially practical philosophy with a severe dose of informed scepticism. Berlin's colleague and friend Bernard Williams was perhaps the most acute, if devastating, voice of radical philosophical scepticism about philosophy's traditional claims in the sphere of ethics. His critique of the weirdly formal and systematic moral theorizing that is still dominant among analytical philosophers, especially in North America, remains largely justified and necessary. But he was perhaps too unqualified and extreme in his rejection of virtually all philosophical theorizing about ethics. It is, at times, hard to determine what role, if any, philosophy could perform in helping us make sense of how we ought to live our own lives in the wake of William's radical demolition of ethical theory.[3]

A more balanced response to these central questions is the type of middle-ground answer that Simon Blackburn canvasses in his philosophical primer *Think*, and which was touched on earlier in the book. He intimates that the authority of philosophy should reside in the space where reflection is continuous with practice. The relationship between society and reflection ought to be a symbiotic affair: the independent interests of thought should be as responsive to the more day-to-day, unreflective beliefs and practices of the community as the other way around. This goes back to something we mentioned briefly at the beginning of the book regarding the effect of Berlin's outlook in changing the dynamic of the relationship between human life and practical philosophy. He thinks that philosophical reflection must treat the messy stuff of life as its raw material and not as something that is or ought to be answerable to some artificially tidy and absolute rational principles.

Berlin's conception of humanistic philosophy has more in common with literature than science. This reveals itself not merely in the way Berlin perceives the world but also in the way Berlin views the history of philosophy. The interest

---

[3] In his defence, Williams may have felt that there was no hope of producing a philosophically credible and humanly valuable account of ethics until the ground was cleared of theoretically inspired nonsense. There is also the point or principle – which Williams consistently exemplified in his writings – that a key virtue of serious and truthful reflection is its refusal to confuse helping us make sense of our lives with providing us with false but seductive forms of consolation. Moreover, there is typically far more substance in his critique of moral philosophy than there exists in the vast and largely undifferentiated sea of academic ethical theory.

and relevance of the ideas of Plato, Descartes and Kant do not necessarily expire with the passage of time just like the works of Homer, Shakespeare and Goethe have not lost their appeal. The nature of the relationship between the humanities (including philosophy) and their history is different to that which holds between the sciences and their history. This isn't to suggest that philosophy can regard its past as eternally relevant and revelatory: there are several ways in which that rather naive view of philosophy's past is no longer an option. But it is to affirm that how philosophy treats the past remains a crucially important philosophical question in a way that does not apply to the natural and exact sciences.

Given the distinct and competing interests and priorities of society and philosophy there will always be a genuine tension between the two. The tension is likely to be most evident and pronounced in those areas where the insights of philosophy threaten or undermine the complacent consensus or vested interests of the community, or alternatively where the community, or more narrowly the state, may gain from an ignorant and supine citizenship.[4] This may be starting to sound more like a fairly commonplace defence of free speech rather than a justification of philosophy's role in society. That impression would not be entirely mistaken, not because it is not a distinctive reflective activity but because philosophy, like any other reflective discipline, must be able to give a credible and compelling account of its raison d'être in the *agora* to which it necessarily belongs. There is no reason why philosophy should think of itself as being entitled to a privileged place within society's marketplace of ideas. It should feel the same pressure (no more and no less) to compete for its space as any other intellectual or humanistic discipline. It must explain what special role it can perform in society and on what authority it rests its unique claim to our attention. This explanation would include specifying the tasks of helping us to make sense of the world we live in and of helping us to determine how best to live our lives within that world. Some aspects of philosophy, of course, will fulfil these tasks more directly than others, but again it must fall on philosophy's shoulders to convince us that its more esoteric and abstract domains contribute to the intellectual health of the subject (humanistically and non-humanistically conceived) as a whole. Fulfilling this role provides it with the best chance it has of establishing its own credentials. And it is likely that its distinctive integrity and force will end up residing where it has always resided, that is, in supplying us with a viewpoint or set of viewpoints about the world that could only have been produced by the sort of genuinely sceptical, difficult, promiscuous, abstract, precise, systematic, curious, self-conscious, parasitical, open, honest and, above all, truth-seeking activity that philosophy is, and has always been, at

---

[4] Of course, the nature and scope of the ignorance of the electorate is often far from random in the sense that it may non-accidentally yet unconsciously serve the interests of either the state and/or other powerful corporate interests. See Steven Lukes *Power: A Radical View (1974: Macmillan, London)*.

its best. It is the kind of enquiry Stanley Cavell was referring to when he defined philosophy as 'education for grown-ups'.[5]

But how does this connect with our specific question about the separate claims of compatibilism and value pluralism? The simple and, no doubt, frustrating reply is that this question itself cannot be answered without philosophical reflection. And that is because it is an irreducibly philosophical question. But the more we are open to reflecting on this question the more likely we are to arrive at a more enlightened if non-definitive, view of the matter. And this is precisely where Berlin's thought distinguishes itself. His approach to the big and possibly unanswerable questions of life is not unlike that of Socrates. He shares with Socrates a preoccupation with the questions that most impinge on our sense of who we are rather than on our understanding of the natural world, vital though the latter is. As one commentator aptly put it: 'Berlin loves the human world in a way that philosophers of another age loved the natural world.'[6] There are of course risks associated with adopting a more humanistic conception of philosophy, not least that we make the subject more responsive to our own parochial concerns rather than the dictates of truth and objectivity. Bertrand Russell highlighted this danger, arguing that 'those philosophies which assimilate the universe to man' end up with an utterly distorted version of knowledge that 'is not a union with the not-Self, but a set of prejudices, habits, and desires, making an impenetrable veil between us and the world beyond'.[7] One can accept Russell's basic point without having to deny or lessen the validity of Berlin's philosophic outlook. The subject of philosophy should be a broad church, eminently capable of accommodating inherently different and rival conceptions of its purpose. Berlin's understanding of philosophy therefore should not be seen as a uniquely correct account of the subject but rather as an alternative to the still prevailing view that a naturalistic conception of philosophy is the one and only legitimate and respectable form of the discipline and its scientific standards of truth and objectivity the only ones available.

Like Socrates and indeed Russell, Berlin has more faith in the big questions themselves than in their alleged answers, and in not losing sight of why these questions have resisted final and infallible solutions. What emerges from reading Berlin is not merely a different conception of the scope and purpose of philosophy, but one that changes our understanding of life's big questions too. It is virtually impossible to read Berlin without being intellectually changed by the experience. He prompts you to think more imaginatively, more historically, more

---

[5]Stanley Cavell, *The Claim of Reason: Wittgenstein, Skepticism, Morality and Tragedy* (1982 edn: Oxford University Press, Oxford & New York), 125.

[6]Leon Wieseltier, 'Two Concepts of Secularism', in *Isaiah Berlin: A Celebration*, eds. Edna and Avishai Margalit (1991: Hogarth Press, London), 81.

[7]Bertrand Russell, *The Problems of Philosophy* (1912: 1998 edn: Oxford University Press, Oxford), 92–3.

sceptically and, above all, more urgently about whatever intellectual topic he may be discussing. You may agree or disagree with him, you may find his approach edifying or misguided, he may inspire praise or derision, but it is most unlikely you will be left cold or unaffected by what he has to say. And whether you admire or disapprove of his work, several important insights emerge: that a question can be meaningful without being conclusively answerable, that the absence of an Archimedean perspective does not mean there cannot be rationally better and worse ways of thinking about the important things in life, that there is at least one genuine and arresting alternative to positivism and relativism and that genuine philosophy requires a creative, multi-disciplinary ambition, a willingness to go out on a limb rather than play it safe by seeking refuge in some pre-defined and over-specialized sub-branch of professional philosophy. All of these considerations inform his silence with regard to prescribing a certain way of life or conception of the good. According to Berlin, this is not something that philosophy ought in good conscience to provide since how we conduct our lives is a process that each of us should experience and shape according to our own lights. Indeed if we were to imagine Berlin breaking his pluralist reticence on the matter it would no doubt be to remind us that a true and truthful life is not one that is compatible with the desire to deny or avoid the opportunity of freely choosing how to live one's own individual life. But, of course, the deeper reason is that the complexity and unpredictability of human experience is not something that naturally lends itself to simple questions and neat solutions. As Clifford Geertz remarked:

> Isaiah's great strength was his ability to get deeply enough into views foreign to his own, even antipathetic to them, to appreciate their force. ... Berlin is for that reason for me a much more shaking thinker: one who makes things harder, not easier. ... Isaiah's arguments are not fully adequate, as he himself insisted they could not be in the nature of the case. But they take us into the heart of the matter: how to decide and act when there are no answers in the back of the book.[8]

Another intimately related lesson that readers are likely to take from reading Berlin is the idea that philosophy should matter to our lives. And by matter I don't mean in the sense of expecting that philosophical reflection can or ought to provide us with a metaphysically grand and detailed blueprint of how we should conduct our lives or about how society should be governed – as Geertz indicates above, Berlin's philosophy is the great antidote to harbouring such naively sanguine expectations. Rather I mean in the sense that we are less likely to be wandering in the dark and,

---

[8] Richard Shweder and Byron Good eds. *Clifford Geertz by his colleagues* (2005: Chicago University Press, Chicago, Ill), 110.

as a result, will be better placed to make up our own informed and independent view about the deeper questions of life, questions that are vital to the philosopher in all of us. In this vein, one imagines that Berlin would have been sympathetic to the spirit of Rorty's recommendation that analytic philosophers should start to 'think of themselves as taking part in a conversation rather than as practising a quasi-scientific discipline'.[9] In the meantime, one suspects that if academic philosophy ends up withering on the vine as a result of state under-funding or from sheer irrelevance, it will not have to look too far to find who to blame. For it to possess any chance of converting the laity to its almost infinite intellectual charms and insights, it needs to begin by reimagining its purpose(s), which in turn might prompt it to recognize that its current state of largely sterile detachment and ossifying specialization is neither inevitable nor useful.

This brings us back to something we have touched on a number of times throughout this book, namely, the matter of style and its integral importance to philosophy. Yet again Berlin is instructive here. The manner of his writing corresponds in an revealing way with his subject matter. His style is characterized more by exploration and allusion than by demonstration and proof, while his arguments rely on the accretion of shrewdly chosen historical and imaginative examples and less on formal and abstract analysis. There is very little that is dry and detached about his writings, as befits the vital and often urgent themes they are concerned with. They are driven by the goal of deepening our understanding and widening our moral sensibility as opposed to winning arguments in some tendentiously value-free and demonstrable manner. In many ways he combines the best aspects of analytic philosophy – rigour, clarity, suppleness and a commitment to follow the argument wherever it leads – with the scepticism and irreverence for disciplinary boundaries characteristic of his great hero Alexander Herzen. Indeed the following tribute he pays to Herzen could just as accurately be applied to himself:

> Herzen was not, and had no desire to be, an impartial observer. No less than the poets and the novelists of his nation, he created a style, an outlook, and, in the words of Gorky's tribute to him, 'an entire province, a country astonishingly rich in ideas',[10] where everything is immediately recognisable as being his and his alone, a country into which he transplants all that he touches, in which things, sensations, feelings, persons, ideas, private and public events, institutions, entire cultures are given shape and life by his powerful and coherent historical imagination, and have stood up against the forces of decay in the solid world

---

[9] Richard Rorty, 'Analytic and conversational philosophy' in his *Philosophy as Cultural Politics: Philosophical Papers*, Vol. 4 (2007: Cambridge University Press, Cambridge), 126.
[10] M. Gorky, *Istoriya Rrusskoi Literatury* (1939: Goslitizdat, Moscow), 206.

which his memory, his intelligence and his artistic genius recovered and reconstructed. (AC2 266)[11]

But there is a more substantial point at play here about Berlin's distinctive philosophical approach. By taking a more synoptic view of human thought, his lens is sufficiently capacious to spot the underlying patterns of human understanding without losing sight of the telling detail of a specific historical thinker or cultural setting. The ability to combine both macroscopic and microscopic perspectives, as well as a historical and analytic viewpoint brings with it uniquely valuable insights that are not obvious or even recognizable to the specialist who is prone to mistaking the wood for the trees. A better way of describing his characteristic approach might be via the analogy of a flea busily working its patch and comparing its perspective with that of a photograph of the elephant whose flesh it is living off. It is not that the wider perspective invalidates or trivializes the more local and specialized under-labourer of philosophy; for there are discoveries that only the philosophical specialist will be in a position to discover. But it is inadvisable for the specialist, even a very clever and eloquent one, to dominate the philosophical scene quite so overwhelmingly at the cost of more inclusive and wide-ranging minds. The deleterious effect of such a narrow and specialized approach to philosophy is exemplified in the recent fortunes of the free will debate we have discussed in this chapter. Very few professional philosophers are willing even to entertain the idea that anything other than compatibilism is the rational response to the free will/determinism debate. Perhaps they are all right, as Berlin is prepared to admit, but the fact that such a large and important philosophical question can elicit a response that secures such overwhelming consensus among the professional philosophical community should give us pause for concern, and not just for the reason that J. L Austin shared with Berlin sotto voce, that no self-declared determinists or rather compatibilists seem to practice what they philosophically preach.

It is more to do with the deeper misgiving that philosophy itself is being sold short, that it has allowed itself be relegated to occupying an unnecessarily remote and recondite presence in society by identifying itself too closely with science or at the very least with a severely naturalistic mindset. One of the things that Berlin's conception of philosophy helps reveal is just how humanly impoverished and historically unself-conscious so much contemporary analytic philosophy is. The extent and depth of the contrast between Berlin's way of doing philosophy and the default approach within the academic analytic tradition is so pronounced that one could be forgiven for thinking that they are pursuing entirely different disciplines.

---

[11]This aspect of Herzen's life and writings is brought out by Aileen Kelly in her recent *The Discovery of Chance: The Life and Thought of Alexander Herzen* (2016: Harvard University Press, Cambridge, Mass).

Berlin reminds us of the need to rebalance the philosophical scales so that the subject can regain its more soulful (though far from sentimental) side without of course denying the legitimate sphere and role of its distinctly naturalistic concerns and hopes. He was fond of reminding us of Herder's observation that 'we live in a world we ourselves create' and that the central world is the human one.[12] Berlin's writings reflect a deep-rooted fidelity to this internalist perspective, a perspective that mines and amplifies the anthropocentric yet undeniably authoritative sources of human understanding. Berlin's attitude to philosophy and more broadly to human experience rests at least partly on the idea that *there must be something more* than what science tells us about ourselves.

Even if we restrict ourselves to Berlin's contribution to the question of free will, what stands out is his insistence that we understand the problem in a more imaginatively honest and inclusive manner. In other words, this is not a topic that can be grasped in primarily non-anthropocentric terms or spuriously analysed in moral isolation as if we were looking at a translucent and inanimate object through a microscope. At the very least Berlin shows that even if we grant the truth of determinism, our currently undeveloped compatibilist notions of freedom fall ludicrously short of providing us with anything near a convincing normative compass to navigate our way in a putatively determined world. His treatment of the topic coheres with that of William James (1842–1910) who insisted that 'the issue is decided nowhere else than *here* and *now*' since '*that* is what gives the palpitating reality to our moral life and makes it tingle'.[13] In Berlin's hands we get a much greater imaginative appreciation of the here and nowness of the matter or, more negatively, of the harmful limits that compatibilism imposes on what we believe the will can choose to do. His treatment of the topic also suggests that the hard or genuine problem of free will is not what scientifically minded philosophers think it is, that is, the challenge of persuading unscientifically minded people that compatibilism is the path of truth and wisdom. Rather he insists that it is the far more profound and difficult problem of acknowledging that we are confronted with at least two different and conflicting ways of describing and understanding the world and ourselves, each of which has a real and authoritative claim on us. In short, we are faced with a genuine paradox and one that Berlin helps us to recognize and value. In fact, it is precisely this kind of 'philosophical imagination' that Berlin felt is vital to making any real sense and perhaps even progress concerning he seemingly intractable problem(s) of free will (L 29). Berlin's recognition of this paradox also confirms the deeper philosophical pluralism underpinning his more celebrated

---

[12]*Herders sämmtliche Werke*, ed. Bernhard Suphan and others (1877–1913: Berlin, Weidmann), Vol. viii, 252.

[13]William James, 'The Dilemma of Determinism', in *The Heart of William James*, ed. Robert Richardson (2012: Harvard University Press, Cambridge, Mass), 45.

theory of value pluralism. His underlying philosophical - as distinct from value - pluralism is one which insists that the scientific world view can ever tell us only so much much about the world, that it can never tell us everything that is known or understandable about it. Of course, most scientists and scientifically minded philosophers might happily agree with Berlin's viewpoint to the extent that they would readily concede that science, including the human sciences, do not tell us everything about the world that we care about. But where they diverge from Berlin, or rather where Berlin diverges from them, is that those parts of the world or of human experience that are neither explained nor even acknowledged by science should not be disqualified willy-nilly from the status of objective understanding. He is adamant that the rich domains of human life that are typically explored by the non-sciences, especially history and literature, generate forms of human understanding and indeed knowledge that have every right to be described as objective and true. To suggest that science is the only source of genuine truth and knowledge is to remain in the grip of a narrow and constricting (though, highly attractive and widespread) delusion. In this regard, Berlin's effort to reframe and reinvigorate philosophy as primarily a humanistic discipline has a great deal in common the the twentieth-century phenomenological turn to recapture the Life-world or Lebenswelt, the intelligible field of our common subjective experience.[14] Indeed, both Berlin and the phenomenologists share a refusal to accept that the scientific perspective has the capacity to account for everything of objective meaning in human life as well as a commitment to the idea that the humanities, especially history, are indispensable to enabling us to accurately describe and more fully comprehend the world of meaning – the Lebenswelt – which we inhabit in our day-to-day lives. And, finally, where the phenomenologists exploited the ancient concept of epoché (withdrawal of assent) as a way of setting aside certain biases and beliefs, especially scientific ones, to allow a phenomenon to be understood in terms of its own inherent meaning and significance, Berlin used the technique of *Einfühlung* to access the concepts and categories of an alien culture or the mindset and ideas of a past thinker as a way of (re)presenting the distinctive world of human consciousness and reality in an authentic and arresting light.

---

[14]Edmund Husserl, *The Crisis of European Sciences and Transcendental Phenomenology* (1936, 1970: Northwestern University Press, Evanston, Ill).

PART FIVE

AUTHENTICITY

19 FRAMING THE DEBATE

A customary feature of commentaries on Isaiah Berlin is a consideration of his famous distinction between two concepts of political liberty. Typically, scholars discuss and evaluate this aspect of his thought in one of three ways. Admirers of Berlin's liberalism defend his account of negative liberty, a concept which, as we saw in Chapter 1, stands for freedom from political or state interference. They also tend to applaud Berlin's insistence on prioritizing a minimum degree of negative liberty as the right response to a morally diverse world, in which everyone should enjoy the right to pursue their own chosen way of life. Opponents of Berlin's liberalism, on the other hand, characteristically criticize his elevation of negative liberty over positive liberty – the latter of which stands for the freedom to be someone or do something in the political sphere – either because it sells positive notions of liberty short or because the privileging of negative liberty is based on nothing more than a theoretically confused, morally bereft and politically naive assessment of our social reality. And, finally, those unwilling to take either of the above sides are likely to have mixed views about the matter. Typically, they are impressed with the historical range of Berlin's analysis of liberty but are also likely to be puzzled by how his theory of value pluralism coheres with his defence of a tolerant society.

What follows does not take this well-trodden path. The world hardly needs another analysis of Berlin's two concepts of liberty. It has already been done many times and, in some cases, extremely well.[1] Moreover, few are better at critiquing Berlin on liberty than Berlin himself. Rather I shall be concerned with another

---

[1] The following includes a selection of some of the best critical analyses of Berlin's seminal essay: L. J. MacFarlane, 'On Two Concepts of Liberty', *Political Studies* 14 (1966): 77–81; G. C. McCallum, 'Negative and Positive Liberty', *Philosophy, Politics and Society*, eds. Laslett, W. G. Runciman and Q. kinner 4th series (1972: Oxford University Press, Oxford), 174–193; Charles Taylor, 'What's Wrong with Negative Liberty', in *The Idea of Freedom*, ed. A. Ryan (1979: Oxford University Press, Oxford); John Gray, 'On Negative and Positive Liberty', *Political Studies* 28 (1980): 507–26; Quentin Skinner, 'The Idea of Negative Liberty: Philosophical and Historical Perspectives', in *Philosophy in History: Essays in the*

aspect of Berlin's liberalism that rarely gets much mention. The feature of his thought I am referring to is romanticism. The burden of this chapter is to show that it provides the key to understanding why Berlin felt that the preservation of negative liberty is such an indispensable element of a tolerant and civilized society. Indeed, my thesis is that Berlin's understanding and defence of negative freedom make little sense without romanticism, that without romanticism negative freedom loses much, if not all, of its appeal as a moral, intellectual and political ideal.

Our starting point is not Berlin but a brilliant little book by the Canadian philosopher Charles Taylor (1931), a thinker who also held the Chichele Chair in Social and Political Theory following Berlin's immediate successor, John Plamenatz (1912-75). There is no better work than Taylor's *The Ethics of Authenticity* to set the scene for an appreciation of the nature and importance of romanticism in Berlin's political philosophy.[2] Taylor's book is about modernity. More specifically, it is concerned with the question of working out what, if any, is the moral core of modernity. Taylor takes this question seriously. He reveals the earnestness of his investigation early on by refusing to play the tired intellectual game that clouds so much discussion and debate concerning modern identity and culture. This game is played between what he calls 'the boosters' and 'the knockers'. The boosters view the rise of modernity in unambiguously laudatory terms, highlighting, in particular, people's freedom to choose their own way of life and to express their own individuality. The rise of the modern state which derives its legitimacy from being neutral with regard to the various ways of life that pervade contemporary society is also interpreted in unequivocally positive terms. Knockers, on the other hand, see things differently. For them, the modern ideal of being free to be ourselves has come at too high a cost: it has resulted in a crippling erosion of meaning in our lives and to an all-pervasive culture of seemingly limitless atomism, materialism and narcissism. It has also led to the withdrawal of the individual from the public sphere leaving us vulnerable to all kinds of political manipulation and thought control, not to mention the loss of the meaning in our lives that can derive from active participation in the public arena.

According to Taylor, it is not so much that the boosters and knockers are wrong as that their respective perspectives are so incurably one-sided. The chief virtue of Taylor's critique of modernity is that it sees beyond the half-truths of both irredeemably partisan perspectives. What the boosters get correct is that

---

Historiography of Philosophy, ed. R. Rorty, B. Schneewind and Q. Skinner (1984: Cambridge University Press, Cambridge), 193-22.

[2]Charles Taylor's *The Ethics of Authenticity* (1991: Harvard University Press, Cambridge, Mass) (hereafter EA), is a concise and accessible distillation of his earlier and much longer work *The Sources of the Self* (1989: Cambridge University Press, Cambridge) hereafter TSS. Taylor would later return to the same territory in his even more monumental, *A Secular Age* (2007: Harvard University Press, Cambridge, Mass).

there is something admirable about the idea that people have the right to make up their own mind about what kind of life to live. Similarly, the knockers are onto something when they perceive a loss of meaning in people's lives, a sense that negative freedom has had the effect of leaving our own lives less meaningful and the lives of others less important to us. But where the boosters go astray, Taylor argues, is in failing to see just how vulnerable the ideal of personal autonomy is to debased forms of individualism. And where the knockers go off the rails, he claims, is by conflating self-fulfilment and egotism.

But it is with Taylor's next move that things start getting more original and deeply perceptive. For he suspects that there is a way beyond the ultimately unproductive debate between the boosters and the knockers. He bases his case on the premise that there is a genuine and important moral ideal informing modernity, an ideal which has become increasingly obscured by unceasing and sharply polarized debate. As he puts it:

> The moral ideal behind self-fulfilment is that of being true to oneself, in a specifically modern understanding of that term. … What we need to explain is what is peculiar to our time. It's not just that people sacrifice their love relationships, and the care of their children, to pursue their careers. Something like this has perhaps always existed. The point is that today many people feel *called* to do this, feel they ought to do this, feel their lives would be somehow wasted or unfulfilled if they did not do it. (EA 15, 17)

Having registered that there is a genuine moral ideal at play here and, crucially, that the form of this ideal is historically and culturally peculiar to modernity, Taylor proceeds to say something even more striking. He argues that the modern ideal of being true to ourselves, what he calls 'the ethics of authenticity', is one that dares not declare its name. For a variety of complex reasons this ethical value has got itself tangled up in all sorts of other preoccupations and polemics with the result that it has almost suffocated itself. Taylor argues convincingly that the main cause of its virtual asphyxiation is that it has allowed itself to become indistinguishable from a permissive but corrosive form of moral subjectivism or relativism. The genuine ethical ideal of authenticity has let itself be subsumed into 'a species of moral laxism', a kind of uncritical yet dogmatic You're ok, I'm ok attitude (EA 16). The upshot is that we are left with a value that has sunk 'to the level of an axiom, something one does not challenge but also never expounds' (EA 17). This explains, Taylor contends, why we find it so difficult to engage in any kind of explicit justification of the substantive foundations of liberal freedom. There exists a deep-seated and pervasive fear that any attempt to do so will end up endangering the very thing we value and need. And so we are left with an 'extraordinary inarticulacy about one of the constitutive ideals of modern culture' (EA, 18).

It should be said that Taylor identifies more than one malaise at the heart of our modern disenchantment of the world. Alongside the debasement of the aspiration of authenticity there exist two other major malaises: the prevalence and primacy of instrumental reason in our culture as well as our estrangement from the public sphere and the consequent loss of political participation and control by the citizenry. While Taylor discusses these 'three malaises of modernity' coherently and concisely in *The Ethics of Authenticity*, his more detailed treatment of the theme of modernity in *Sources of the Self* is understandably more nuanced, especially Part One, Chapters 1 to 4. The following passage from *Sources of the Self* provides an illuminating gloss on what has been discussed above:

> The more one examines the motives – what Nietzsche would call the 'genealogy' – of these theories of obligatory action [Kantianism, utilitarianism], the stranger they appear. It seems that they are motivated by the strongest moral ideals, such as freedom, altruism and universalism. These are among the central moral aspirations of modern culture, the hypergoods that are distinctive to it. And yet what these ideals drive the theorists towards is a denial of all such goods. They are caught in a strange pragmatic contradiction, whereby the very goods which move them push them to deny or denature all such goods. They are constitutionally incapable of coming clean about the deeper sources of their own thinking. Their thought is inescapably cramped. (TSS 88)

Incidentally, Taylor states in a tribute to Berlin that his principal legacy rests on the refusal to side with 'the unruffled boosters of the Enlightenment' or 'its irreconcilable enemies' and, more positively, on teaching us 'that the best way to further the cause of the Enlightenment was to understand more fully what its critics have been saying'. (BI 37-38)

The sources and nature of romanticism

The relevance and value of Taylor's work for our purposes is that it highlights something which we take for granted or have perhaps even forgotten. I am referring, of course, to the moral basis of living a life that is true to our own lights, of the life of a person who, in Iris Murdoch's (1919–99) memorable words, 'confronted even with Christ turns away to consider the judgement of his own conscience and to hear the voice of his own reason'.[3] Our complacency or obliviousness about the moral source of modernity is not something restricted to everyday debate. One could read through reams of scholarly commentary on Berlin's concept of negative

---

[3]Iris Murdoch, *The Sovereignty of the Good* (1970: Routledge & Kegan Paul, London), 80.

liberty and be none the wiser about the moral grounding of this pivotal political concept. In fact, the impression that such commentaries often leave us with is a sense of deep puzzlement: for they fail to say why Berlin felt so strongly that we need an area within which we 'can act unobstructed by others' in the first place (L, 169). This is a travesty since Berlin has robust reasons for arguing that

> pluralism, with the measure of 'negative' liberty that it entails, seems to me a truer and more humane ideal than the goals of those who seek in the great, disciplined, authoritarian structures the ideal of positive 'self-mastery' by classes, or peoples, or the whole of mankind. (L 216)

So the obvious questions must be: Why does Berlin believe this? What is the source of his belief that we should have the space to freely choose and pursue our own way of life? What is the unarticulated core of the modern ideal of individual freedom and authenticity? The answer, in a word, is romanticism. The rest of this chapter will focus on Berlin's conception of this rich and enormously influential idea.

Berlin is too knowledgeable and sophisticated a thinker to even try to give a definitive account of something as protean and promiscuous as the idea of romanticism. But rather than despair of finding the holy grail of romanticism – as the renowned critic, A. O. Lovejoy, ended up doing – Berlin approaches the matter more obliquely by seeking, Wittgenstein-style, to identify certain similarities or *family resemblances* that romantic thought, music and art appear to share. He begins this task by dramatizing the difference between a conversation one might have had with someone in the 1820s – say an avant-garde young man in France or an enthusiast of the Schlegel brothers of Germany or a convert to Coleridge in England, compared to a dialogue one might have had with someone in the sixteenth century (RR2 8-9). It is worth quoting Berlin at some length since nobody can reconstruct more vividly than him the difference between these two imagined but credible encounters:

> You would have found that their [in the 1820s] ideal of life was approximately of the following kind.
>
> The values to which they attached the highest importance were such values as integrity, sincerity, readiness to sacrifice one's life to some inner light, dedication to some ideal for which it is worth sacrificing all that one is, for which it is worth both living and dying. You would have found that they were not primarily interested in knowledge, or in the advance of science, not interested in political power, not interested in happiness, not interested, above all, in adjustment to life, in finding your place in society, in living at peace with your government, even in loyalty to your king, or to your republic. You would have found that common sense, moderation, was very far from their thoughts.

You would have found that they believed in the necessity of fighting for your beliefs to the last breath in your body, and you would have found that they believed in the value of martyrdom as such, no matter what the martyrdom was martyrdom for. You would have found that they believed that minorities were more holy than majorities, that failure was nobler than success, which had something shoddy and something vulgar about it. The very notion of idealism, not in its philosophical sense, but in the ordinary sense in which we use it, that is to say the state of mind of a man who is prepared to sacrifice a great deal for principles or for some conviction, who is not prepared to sell out, who is prepared to go to the stake for something which he believes, because he believes in it – this attitude was relatively new. What people admired was wholeheartedness, sincerity, purity of soul, the ability and readiness to dedicate yourself to your ideal, no matter what it was.

No matter what it was: that is the important thing. Suppose you had a conversation in the sixteenth century with somebody fighting in the great religious wars which tore Europe apart at that period, and suppose you said to a Catholic of that period, engaged in hostilities, 'Of course these Protestants believe what is false; of course to believe what they believe is to court perdition; of course they are dangerous to the salvation of human souls, than which there is nothing more important; but they are so sincere, they die so readily for their cause, their integrity is so splendid, one must yield a certain meed of admiration for the moral dignity and sublimity of people who are prepared to do that.' Such a sentiment would have been unintelligible. (RR2 10–11)

By asking the correct questions and engaging in the right kind of imaginative and historical empathy Berlin manages to find a way of telling the story of something as eclectic and elusive as romanticism, a movement which he claims had its roots in Germany during the latter half of the eighteenth century. He identifies three thinkers from this period whom he describes as 'the true fathers of Romanticism'. The following chapter sets out to give a very brief summary of the romanticism of each of these thinkers' thought.

20 THREE ROMANTIC THINKERS

Hamann

The first of these figures, Johann Hamann, is perhaps the one most closely associated with the *Sturm und Drang* ('Storm and Stress') movement that immediately preceded romanticism's official emergence in Germany. While Berlin does not rate this proto-romantic movement that highly – he judges that its only work of genius was Goethe's (1749–1832) *The Sorrows of Young Werther* – nonetheless he contends that it did introduce a new and destabilizing consciousness into the world by re-orientating the nature and meaning of people's lives. And the reason why Berlin felt that Hamann stood out from the *Sturm and Drang* crowd and deserves special attention is that he was the first thinker to resist the Enlightenment at its root. Hamann saw himself as Socrates in modern garb, a gadfly whose role was to oppose and, if possible, destroy the prevailing false wisdom of his age. For Hamann, this meant waging war against two foes: the first was the establishment, by which he meant the Church of Rome and the governing monarchies of Europe, which he referred to collectively as 'the Pharisees', and the second were the so-called freethinkers and philosophers of Paris, Edinburgh and Berlin, whom he called 'the Sadducees' (TCE2, 342). It is his opposition to the 'Sadducees' that is most relevant to our discussion.

The Sadducees shared three basic beliefs: faith in the cold but impartial light of reason, the existence of an essential human nature and of universal human goals, and finally the idea that the discovery and pursuit of these universal goals can only be achieved through unaided reason. Hamann, or the 'Magus of the North' as he liked to call himself, attacked all three of these pillars of the Enlightenment with an unreserved and relentless ferocity. Without getting into the intricate and frequently obscure details of Hamann's thought, we can summarize his antagonism towards the 'newtonized' perspective of the world as follows.

Hamann was among the first thinkers to question the whole basis and point of the Enlightenment project by arguing that it had misunderstood the nature of the world and of our place in it. He sought to replace its mechanistic and quantified view of human nature, the view held by what Burke would subsequently call 'sophisters, economists, and calculators', with a picture of what real, living, breathing people are like in all their glorious, imperfect and incorrigible individuality.[1] Hamann is above all the champion of the individual. He is adamant that the abstract and necessary laws of metaphysics and science invented by the Sadducees not only violate everything that is sacred and integral to us as concrete and unique beings. More fundamentally, he is convinced that such a rationalistic but blind conception of the world traduces the inescapably contingent, free and chaotic world we actually inhabit. To paraphrase Pascal's famous maxim (again!), the world has reasons which Enlightenment rationality itself cannot fathom. Berlin conveys the essence of Hamann's rejection of scientific and metaphysical knowledge in a crucial passage which I have already quoted, and which bears repetition:

> No bridge is needed between necessary and contingent truths because the laws of the world in which man lives are as contingent as the 'facts' in it. All that exists could have been otherwise if God had so chosen, and that can be so still. God's creative powers are unlimited, man's are limited; nothing is eternally fixed, at least nothing in the human world – outside it we know nothing, at any rate in this life. The 'necessary' is relatively stable, the 'contingent' is relatively changing, but this is a matter of degree, not kind. (TCE, 363)

Apart from being in many ways an accurate description of Berlin's own conception of knowledge (especially if we are willing to replace 'God' with 'Archimedean perspective'), this passage helps reveal why Hamann's theory of knowledge was so liberating. For it invites us to view the world as basically contingent not necessary, empirical not rationalist, one in which human experience in all its palpable, unregenerate and individualistic dimensions takes centre stage, albeit (for Hamann) in a way that includes a relationship with God. Notwithstanding Hamann's religious beliefs, which are integral to his thought, the crucial point is that the Enlightenment is challenged, for the first time, with the uncompromising claim that it is infected with an incurably flawed notion of the nature of the world and of man's place in it. According to Berlin, Hamann lights the initial fuse that will end up not so much exploding the Enlightenment but, at the very least, opening up a radically new and competing conception of how we should make sense of the world. It is a conception that has a decidedly mixed set of blessings.

---

[1] Edmund Burke, *Reflections on the Revolution in France* (1790): *The Writings and Speeches of Edmund Burke*, Vol. 8, *The French Revolution*, ed. L. G. Mitchell (1979: Oxford University Press, Oxford), 127.

On the one hand, it offers a refreshing antidote to the soulless generalizations and severely homogenizing strain intrinsic to Enlightenment thought by offering a diametrically opposed understanding of the inextinguishable uniqueness of human beings. On the other hand, it is irrationally hostile to any attempt to comprehend the world and humanity in objective and all-encompassing terms. It also prides itself in its warm and wilful embrace of 'the inarticulate, the mystical, the demonic, the dark reaches and mysterious depths' (TCE2 431). In this respect, Hamann's major legacy is to have opened a veritable Pandora's box, one that exposed modern Western culture to forces, at once intensely individualistic and irrepressibly primal, that both the Enlightenment and indeed Christianity had led us to believe we had outgrown or at least successfully suppressed. Moreover, once the lid was lifted it proved impossible to put back on.

Herder

According to Berlin, the second major thinker to deliver an unrecoverable shock to the Enlightenment system was Johann Herder, a contemporary and friend of Hamann. Herder distinguished himself, according to Berlin, as the next of the 'true fathers of Romanticism', by deploying three distinct but overlapping ideas: expressionism, belonging and pluralism. Let's look briefly at each of these.

The idea of expressionism may be explained as follows. The language we start using from childhood to express ourselves is not created by us from nowhere or from nothing. Rather it is made up of words we have inherited from our predecessors. And the words our ancestors have bequeathed us are specific to us and do not form part of some universal, undifferentiated Esperanto. They are primarily the product of our own group or culture. The critical point here is that the words we use and indeed all the other artefacts we make are constitutively the product of the concrete culture or group of which each of us is a member. There is no way of truly understanding the nature of ancient democracy or of a miller's life in the sixteenth century independently of the ethos of ancient Athenian society or of popular and learned culture in Reformation Italy respectively.[2] The key insight of expressionism is that what differentiates cultures both spatially and temporally is far more tangible and meaningful than anything they may have in common.

This brings us to Herder's second major romantic theme – the notion of belonging. This notion is closely connected with expressionism. It centres on

---

[2] For example, the imaginative and empathic historical scholarship of historians such as Moses Finley on the Greek Dark Ages and Carlo Ginzburg on sixteenth-century Reformation Italy offers powerful reminders of this truth. See M. I. Finley, *The World of Odysseus* (1962: Penguin, London) and Carlo Ginzburg, *The Cheese and the Worms – The Cosmos of a Sixteenth-Century Miller* (1980: Routledge & Kegan Paul, London).

the idea that what makes us who we are is a function of the specific community to which we belong. This notion should not be confused with the platitude that we are all children of our time and place. Rather its claim is that we are essentially rooted beings who derive our identity and who can only comprehend our lives from within our local community. Herder's notion of belonging is the complete opposite of the Enlightenment ideal of the cosmopolitan citizen. One of the more salient aspects of Herder's notion is that past and present cultures have their own identities, values and ways of life which are unique to them. As a result, there is no Archimedean perspective, no transcendent view from nowhere, from which we can survey and judge 'humanity'. We are products of our own culture all the way through. In addition, our identities and values are historically and culturally specific. We cannot turn the clock back and transfer or restore ancient or Renaissance ways of life to the contemporary world. Those societies had their own inimitable and incommensurable notions of identity and belonging just like we have our own today. Nor can we naively assume that imposing our own historically conditioned judgements on the past tells us much or anything of substance about previous societies. This does not necessarily mean that cultures beyond our own are hermetically sealed bubbles that resist our understanding. Herder was no relativist, according to Berlin. But it does stop us in our Enlightenment tracks by forcing us to question the twin axioms that all cultures are ultimately commensurable and that there exist objective, ahistorical answers to the so-called perennial and universal questions facing us. Herder upturns this central tenet of Western thought by arguing that it is, strictly speaking, unintelligible.

It is at this point that Herder's notion of belonging melds with his cultural pluralism. He believed that every culture has its own centre of gravity, its *Schwerpunkt*, and that no two centres of gravity were or are or can be the same. I will leave the description of the pluralist element of Herder's romanticism to Berlin himself:

> He [Herder] believes in objective standards of judgement that are derived from understanding the life and purposes of individual societies, and are themselves objective historical structures, and require, on the part of the student, wide and scrupulous scholarship as well as sympathetic imagination. What he rejects is the single overarching standard of values, in terms of which all cultures, characters and acts can be evaluated. Each phenomenon to be investigated presents its own measuring-rod, its own internal constellation of values in the light of which alone 'the facts' can be truly understood. This is much more thoroughgoing than the realisation that man is incapable of complete perfection. … For what is here entailed is that the highest ends for which men have rightly striven and sometimes died are strictly incompatible with one another. Even if it were possible to revive the glories of the past, as those pre-historicist thinkers

(Machiavelli or Mably, for instance) thought who called for a return to the heroic virtues of Greece or Rome, we could not revive and unite them all. If we choose to emulate the Greeks, we cannot also emulate the Hebrews; if we model ourselves on the Chinese, whether as they are in reality, or in Voltaire's *opéra bouffe* version, we cannot also be the Florentines of the Renaissance, or the innocent, serene, hospitable savages of eighteenth-century imagination. Even if, *per impossible*, we could choose among these ideals, which should we select? Since there is no common standard in terms of which to grade them, there can be no final solution to the problem of what men as such should aim at. (TCE2 293–4)

What is emerging so far from Berlin's account of German romanticism is an outlook that is both emphatically subjective and individualistic and almost allergic to the scientific world view of Enlightenment rationalism. We are also seeing why Berlin was so fascinated with this radically anti-Enlightenment strain in modern thought. For what is particularly impressive about his perspective is how it brings out both the edifying and not so edifying sides of romanticism. There is a clear and vivid recognition that the romantic movement captures features of the modern soul that the mainstream Enlightenment thinkers had either neglected or supressed. More specifically, it was thinkers like Hamann and Herder, and after them Schiller and Fichte, who were responsible for creating our idea of the sacred importance of the individual and, more generally, of modern subjectivism. Moreover, they were also responsible for amplifying and, in many cases, glorifying the darker but no less objective aspects of our nature – this is true of the less restrained or 'unbridled' members of the romantic movement such as Fichte and Schlegel, if we limit ourselves to Germany. These are the unethical, unregenerate aspects of our nature that reason or rather rationalism cannot seem to reach but which, at the same time, are also inherently bound up with the modern notion of individual, authentic consciousness. The subtext of Berlin's account of the German Romantics is never too far beneath the surface: that they chose to pay witness to and develop a vital and undeniable side of our humanity, a side that Enlightenment rationalism denied at its peril.

Kant

Finally, we come to Kant, perhaps the most fascinating member of the trio who, Berlin claims, was instrumental in making romanticism the formidable force it became. Berlin is, of course, aware that Kant will strike us as a distinctly unlikely romantic bedfellow: for surely his philosophical ideas and normative preferences belong unambiguously to the Enlightenment project. Berlin resolves this paradox by claiming that, notwithstanding the fact that Kant despised what he saw as the wilful ignorance of the Romantics towards the sciences, he shared their estimation of the pre-eminence of the individual will. For Berlin, Kant's metaphysics and epistemology fit squarely within the Enlightenment world view but his moral philosophy belongs resolutely within the romantic family.

Why and how did Kant come to hold the view that the main distinguishing feature of human beings is our capacity to exercise our own individual will and secondly, and crucially, that we actually enjoy free will? For Kant, the unique capacity of human beings to choose freely is what gives our lives meaning. Unless we have the freedom to choose between right and wrong, good and evil – notions that he felt we ourselves have freely created – morality simply makes no sense. As Berlin remarks, 'Man is man, for Kant, only because he chooses.' Coupled with his belief that enlightenment or civilization rests on the capacity of human beings to determine their own lives, and not be at the benign or malign behest of anyone else, is his conviction that we possess free will. Kant's view of free will is remarkably similar to Berlin's notion of freedom, discussed in the previous chapter. Like Berlin, Kant is opposed to both hard and soft forms of determinism – wholesale mechanical determinism and the less absolute form of determinism that permits compatibilist notions of freedom, the latter of which, as we have seen, Kant rejected outright. He believed that we possess free will in the only sense that really mattered, the sense that is incompatible with both hard and soft determinism.

Berlin then draws on an intriguing aspect of Kant's conception of freedom. It centres on his innovative refusal to accept the traditionally positive view of man's place in nature, the view that man is or ought to be essentially at one with the natural world. Kant was keen to differentiate man from the natural world since he felt that the latter conforms entirely to causal laws while the former's unique glory is defined by our freedom. Berlin articulates this deeply original aspect of Kant's moral philosophy as follows:

> The notion of Mistress Nature, Dame Nature, something benevolent, something you worshipped, something which art ought to imitate, something which morals ought to derive from, something which politics are founded upon, as Montesquieu said – this derogates from man's inborn liberty of choice, because nature is mechanical, or even if not mechanical, even if it is organic, at any rate every event in nature follows by a rigorous necessity from every other; and therefore, if man is part of nature, then he is determined, and morality is a hideous illusion. Therefore nature in Kant becomes at worst an enemy, at best simply neutral stuff which one moulds. Man is conceived of as in part a natural object: plainly his body is in nature; his emotions are in nature; all the various things which are capable of making him heteronomous, or depend upon something other than his true self, are natural; but when he is at his freest, when he is at his most human, when he rises to his noblest heights, then he dominates nature, that is to say he moulds her, he breaks her, he imposes his personality

upon her, he does that which he chooses, because he commits himself to certain ideals; and by committing himself to these ideals he imposes his seal upon nature, and nature therefore becomes plastic stuff. Some bits of nature are more plastic than others, but all nature must be presented to man as something with which or upon which or at which he does something not something to which he – not the whole of him, at any rate – belongs. (RR2 88–9)

Kant's emphasis on man's separateness from the natural world – what the German thinkers referred to as Innerlichkeit, the tendency to withdraw from the empirical world and create a new inner world by an act of free will – is a crucial move since it further establishes the notion of the primacy of man's autonomy. We are seeing here the early shoots of what would become an increasingly important phenomenon in Western thought: the sense that we are alone in an indifferent and meaningless world, which can be both liberating and alienating. The more unbridled members of the romantic movement, including Fichte, Schelling and, later on, Schopenhauer and Nietzsche, embraced this strain of thought, which is made up of two fundamental elements: a belief in the pre-eminence of the indomitable, unfettered individual will and the conviction that the world does not possess any cosmic pattern or grand scheme that we can latch on to give our lives meaning. In essence, it is the freedom that results from the realization that if God is dead, everything is permitted. Kant, of course, could never have foreseen such developments, and certainly would not have endorsed them, but he did inadvertently prepare the ground that made them possible.

Bernard Williams reminds us of the continuing relevance of this perspective in his paper, 'The Human Prejudice'. After highlighting in a typically amusing, if caustic, way that our place in the galaxy 'seems almost extravagantly non-committal', he adds:

If there is no such thing as the cosmic point of view, if the idea of the absolute importance in the scheme of things is an illusion, a relic of a world not yet thoroughly disenchanted, then there is no point of view except ours in which our activities can have or lack a significance. Perhaps, in a way, that is what Russell wanted to say, but his journey through the pathos of loneliness and insignificance as experienced from a non-existent point of view could only generate the kind of muddle that is called sentimentality. Nietzsche by contrast got it right when he said that once upon a time there was star in the corner of the universe, and a planet circling that star, and on it very clever creatures who invented knowledge; and then they died, and the star went out, and it was as though nothing had happened.[3]

---

[3]Bernard Williams, *Philosophy as a Humanistic Discipline* (2006: Princeton University Press, Princeton, NJ), 137–8. For a more optimistic yet sophisticated treatment of the human condition that attempts to

Berlin, however, is careful to insist that Kant's notion of freedom was in other ways typical of its time. This emerges most tellingly in the conventionalism of his monistic belief that if men exercise their freedom in the light of reason then they will all arrive at the same moral determination concerning how best to live their lives. In other words, he remained true to the rationalist article of faith that knowledge is virtue, that if or when we choose to reason properly, when we apply the categorical imperative, we will inevitably end up in the same promised and harmonious moral universe. It was left to Kant's disciple, the playwright Friedrich Schiller (1759–1805), who would end up cutting the Gordian knot tying individualism to some pre-ordained or, at least, excessively uniform moral identity. Schiller refused to accept that the unfettered but rational will would necessarily choose the narrow moral path defined by Kant. In a way, Schiller's own outlook proved in the end more faithful to the spirit of Kant's famous adage: 'Out of the crooked timber of humanity nothing straight was ever made.'[4] For Berlin, it was Schiller who through his dramatic works articulated a far more radical embrace of the individual will and its essential opposition to the more causal or empirical aspects of our nature. This laid the final piece of groundwork which enabled:

> a crucial note in the history of human thought, namely that ideals, ends, objectives are not to be discovered by intuition, by scientific means, by reading sacred texts, by listening to experts or to authoritative persons; that ideals are not to be discovered at all, they are to be invented; not to be found but to be generated, generated as art is generated. ...
>
> There he leaves it. That is the heritage of Schiller, which afterwards entered very deeply into the souls of the Romantics, who abandoned the notion of harmony, who abandoned the notion of reason, and who became, as I said earlier, somewhat unbridled. (RR2 100–1)

The final two words in the above passage could hardly be more understated. The three 'Fathers of Romanticism', with the help of Schiller, had sparked a fuse that paved the way for some of the greatest intellectual explosions of the next hundred years or so and arguably contributed to several of the most real and atrocious ones in the twentieth century. I do not propose to discuss the details of the more radical manifestations of romanticism that would emerge during the nineteenth century. Suffice to say that, in the hands of thinkers like Fichte, Schelling and Goethe, not to mention those beyond Germany such as Shelley, Byron, Victor Hugo and Lamartine, far more 'unbridled' forms of romanticism emerged, culminating in

---

confront the challenge of contingency without embracing moral nihilism, see John Kekes, *The Human Condition* (2010: Oxford University Press, Oxford).

[4]Immanuel Kant, *Kant's gesammelte Schriften* (1990: Berlin), Vol. 8, 23, line 22.

Nietzsche, who would claim that art rather morality reveals the quintessential activity of man. Nor will I add my own speculations on the question of whether twentieth-century totalitarianism and the horrors committed under its various forms – whether communism or fascism – had its roots in romanticism. Rather we shall move onto a consideration of Richard Rorty's fascinating thoughts on Isaiah Berlin's *The Roots of Romanticism*.

21 SMASHING THE JIGSAW

In his paper 'Grandeur, Profundity and Finitude', Rorty discusses what he considers are the two outstanding philosophical quarrels that remain with us since they were first introduced by Plato. The first of these is the quarrel between poetry and philosophy, and the second is the continuing dispute between the philosophers and the sophists.[1] Rorty argues that Berlin's book on romanticism helps us get beyond the first of these quarrels, which he believes is preoccupied with 'whether human beings are at their best – realise their special powers to the fullest – when they use reason to discover how things really are, or when they use imagination to transform themselves' (GPF 74). By bravely insisting, *contra* scholars like Lovejoy, that there was a phenomenon we can refer to as romanticism and, more significantly, by identifying its main opponent as universalism – universalism, in Rorty's view, is equivalent to Platonic and Enlightenment rationalism, both of which adhere in some shape or form to the three articles of reason that we have already touched upon in our discussion of Hamann – Berlin has helped us transform the age-old quarrel in a very interesting and constructive way. He does this, according to Rorty, by first of all detecting that all forms of universalistic or Enlightenment grand theories operate on the basis that the problems of human knowledge and of human life can be solved by adopting a jigsaw puzzle approach to the questions of life, an approach that is defined by Berlin in the following passage:

> We lie among the disjected fragments of this puzzle. There must be some way of putting these pieces together. The all-wise man, the omniscient being, whether God or an omniscient earthly creature – whichever way you like to conceive

---

[1]'Grandeur, 'Profundity and Finitude' in Richard Rorty, *Philosophy as Cultural Politics: Philosophical Papers*, Vol. 4 (2007: Cambridge University Press, Cambridge), 73–88 (hereafter GPF).

it – is in principle capable of fitting all the various pieces together into one coherent pattern. Anyone who does this will know what the world is like: what things are, what they have been, what they will be, what the laws are that govern them, what man is, what the relation of man is to things, and therefore what man needs, what he desires, and how to obtain it. (RR2 28)

The second virtue of Berlin's book rests, for Rorty, on revealing how romanticism literally shattered the philosophical pretensions of universalism (or, alternatively, of Enlightenment rationalism) by showing that the various pieces of human knowledge and indeed of human nature do not form part of some grand conceptual pattern or system. As Berlin himself says:

Previous generations supposed that all good things could be reconciled. This is true no longer. If you read Büchner's tragedy *The Death of Danton*, in which Robespierre finally causes the deaths of Danton and Desmoulins in the course of the Revolution, and you ask, 'Was Robespierre wrong to do this?', the answer is no; the tragedy is such that Danton, although he was a sincere revolutionary who committed certain errors, did not deserve to die, and yet Robespierre was perfectly right in putting him to death. There is a collision here of what Hegel afterwards called 'good with good'. It is due not to error, but to some kind of conflict of an unavoidable kind, of loose elements wandering about the earth, of values which cannot be reconciled. What matters is that people should dedicate themselves to these values with all that is in them. If they do that, they are suitable heroes for tragedy. If they do not do so, then they are philistines, then they are members of the bourgeoisie, then they are no good and not worth writing about. (RR2 14–15)

According to Rorty, the outcome of Berlin's treatment of romanticism is that it helps justify our willingness 'to admit that enquiry need have no higher goal than the solving of problems when they arise' (GPF 83). In other words, Rorty sees Berlin's account of romanticism's opposition to universalism as a further endorsement of his own kind of postmodern or post-philosophical bourgeois liberalism. While Rorty's identification of Berlin as among the 'commonsensical finitists' has a certain plausibility and appeal, it is doubtful that Berlin would have been prepared to have gone as far as Rorty in 'becoming content to see ourselves as a species of animal that makes itself up as it goes along' (GPF 88). Rorty suggests that the philosophical grandeur of universalism and the profundity (or infinity) of romanticism have ended up cancelling each other out and that what we are left with is an undeluded and un-metaphysical residue of modus vivendi political pragmatism. Berlin's response to the conflict between Enlightenment rationalism and romantic expressionism is very different. Rather than seeing it as a quarrel that can be overcome or simply dispensed with, his entire oeuvre can be read as a sustained, anti-reductionist effort to keep the central quarrel alive. Berlin sees deep truths (and enduring falsehoods) in both the Enlightenment and Counter-Enlightenment movements, truths that are peculiarly germane to and valued by modernity, even if certain aspects of them can be detected in or were anticipated by earlier ages. So while he would not disagree with Rorty that one of the hallmarks of living in a civilized and compassionate society is a commitment to mitigating the sharpness and frequency of the various conflicts between the values and ideals associated, respectively, with universalism and romanticism, Berlin does not see this endeavour as part of a larger cooling off of the conflict between these forces. On the contrary, he argues that one of the main aims of philosophy is to keep alive and vindicate the very different and competing values and conceptions of the good that are associated with both of these intellectual crusades. As he observes, 'we are children of both worlds' and, therefore, only a vision that embraces both can remain credible and secure our allegiance (RR2, 163). In this way, Berlin resembles Mill who showed a similar impulse to emphasize the existence and insights of dissenting perspectives and views. The spirit informing Mill's wonderful essay on Coleridge resonates with that of Berlin's writings on various Counter-Enlightenment thinkers. It would seem that both thinkers were reminding us that liberalism is at its best when it is not the sole landlord of human thought.

22 THE LIBERALISM OF ROMANTICISM

Having discussed the nature of Berlin's understanding of Romanticism, we are now left with the matter of the political implications of this movement. This chapter, therefore, will seek to address the question with which we began this final part of the book, namely, why does Berlin believe that it is critical we have negative liberty in the first place? What is it that makes freedom from interference such an indispensable feature of a free and civilized society? In the closing paragraph of *The Roots of Romanticism,* Berlin makes the following startling claim:

> The result of Romanticism, then, is liberalism, toleration, decency and the appreciation of the imperfections of life; some degree of increased rational self-understanding. This was very far from the intentions of the Romantics. But at the same time – and to this extent the Romantic doctrine is true – they are the persons who most strongly emphasised the unpredictability of all human activities. They were hoist by their own petard. Aiming at one thing, they produced, fortunately for us all, almost the exact opposite. (RR2 170)

How are we to make sense of this statement, conceptually, let alone historically? For surely, as Berlin himself intimates, do Romanticism and liberalism not pull in opposite directions? How can Romanticism be both a friend and a foe of liberal freedom? It would seem that Berlin is rather perversely asking us to believe something that cannot be true or, at least, coherent. And yet it is only by addressing this paradox that we get to the heart of his defence of negative freedom. The key to unlocking the paradox is to be found not in the well-known essay 'Two Concepts of Liberty' of 1958 but in the Flexner Lectures that Berlin delivered six years earlier. Although these lectures were not published until 2006, under the title *Political Ideas in the Romantic Age,* they constitute the central core or, as Henry Hardy aptly put it, the *Grundrisse* (foundations) of his thought (PIRA2 xxv). The specific lecture that we shall be concerned with is 'The Idea of Freedom'.

'The Idea of Freedom' supplies a solution to the above paradox. On one level, this lecture prefigures Berlin's enduring conviction that since liberty is essentially freedom from interference, the essence of political liberty is freedom from state interference. But, on another level, it articulates a more substantial notion of freedom that, for some reason, Berlin chose not to maintain to when it came to preparing his much more famous 'Two Concepts of Liberty'. Joshua Cherniss, a scholar who has done a peerless job of analysing the evolution of Berlin's political thought, is no doubt right to see this discontinuity as a 'complication' rather than a contradiction in Berlin's thought (PIRA2 lvi). Indeed, I would go a little further than Cherniss and argue that Berlin did not so much change his understanding of liberty as convey his view of its intrinsic value in more guarded and implicit terms.

In his earlier lecture Berlin formulates and defends a more explicitly full-blooded conception of freedom than the negative concept of liberty he ended up justifying in 'Two Concepts of Liberty'. The basic difference between the two can be summarized in one word, Kant. But before we discuss Kant, let me first sketch the kernel of his view of liberty up to the point where he incorporates the Kantian or quasi-Kantian dimension of freedom.

'The Idea of Freedom' starts by defining what Berlin claims is the core meaning or essence of liberty. While recognizing that large and contested concepts such as 'liberty' change over time and between cultures, he argues that the basic desire for political freedom boils down to 'the desire on the part of individuals or groups not to be interfered with by other individuals or groups' (PIRA 112). He clarifies the meaning and range of this notion of political freedom negatively by saying that 'when we speak of the lack of social or political freedom, we imply that somebody, rather than something, is preventing us from doing or being something we wish to do or be' (PIRA2 113). This helps Berlin differentiate political freedom from psychological and physical constraints that can too often muddy the waters in both academic and everyday debate about this concept. He also makes the point that historically the story of liberty from, say, Bodin onwards consisted of variations on the relatively fixed theme of finding a workable compromise between individual freedom and political authority, between granting the right of civil liberty and preserving the stability of the state – the degree of variation tending to depend on whether the particular political thinker held a negative or positive view of human nature.

This remained the standard problematic of political discourse, especially within the social contract tradition, until Rousseau (1712–1778). According to Berlin, Rousseau solved the long-standing problem of modern political theory by denying its reality. Heavily influenced (in spite of his best efforts) by the Enlightenment idea that in the wake of the unstoppable progress being achieved by the natural and formal sciences, it was only a matter of time before the same conclusive success would be reproduced in the emerging field of the science of man, Rousseau introduced the notion that there is no real conflict between man and the state. He squared this particular circle by identifying individual liberty and the (in)famous general will. His formulation of the latter is notoriously elusive (and many have since argued, ultimately vacuous), but one way of grasping it, at least at an abstract level, is by comparing it with the religious doctrine that by voluntarily submitting one's free will to God's purpose one becomes truly free. So for Rousseau, our liberty not only remains whole but only becomes capable of achieving itself when, and only when, the 'great coincidence' of all individual wills conjoin to create the single, general (PIRA2 149).

If we leave aside the obvious ways in which such a conception of freedom opens the door to totalitarianism, what is centrally relevant for our purposes is the emergence of the idea of the real self as a crucial part of this idea of freedom. It helped fuel the idea that it is illusory to think that there is a conflict between personal autonomy and political authority reveals itself when we understand our true selves, when we look into our innermost souls and recognize that our own true self is the same as that of our fellow human beings. Once we perceive our true selves, the possibility of genuine social harmony arises, and the seemingly inescapable strain between individual and society, the personal and the political, vanishes. Rousseau's way of discovering our true or authentic self does not follow the route of observing our empirical selves and seeking to derive general insights and features about our actual desires. He approaches the matter the other way around, by defining what is true and good about human nature and then arguing that this real self is or should be the object of our desires, whether we know it or not. The details of Rousseau's quasi-spiritual concept of what constitutes the true self need not detain us here. The critical point to note, for Berlin, is that he introduced three key innovative notions that would leave an indelible imprint on modern consciousness:

> (1) that freedom is an absolute value and may not be curtailed, for there is no morality without it; (2) that morality is discoverable not in the de facto activities of men in accordance with this or that pattern ... but in conscious acts of will whereby men dedicate themselves to this or that goal independently of and, if need be, against other 'pulls' and 'pushes' exercised by their physical nature ...; and finally (3) the uniqueness of the right rule, distinguishable from mere inclination by the fact that a man can discover it only when he is in the special state of mind in which the truth is revealed to him .... Following such truths, obtained in this semi-mystical condition, on the part of the individual cannot conceivably bring him into conflict with other individuals following similar rules, since the following of the rules is automatically a self-adjustment to the goal of the universe, which is one of harmonious development, involving no collisions. (PIRA2 182–3)

Rousseau's brand of iconoclasm paved the way for the far more formidable intellectual figure of Kant, who delivered the equivalent of another Copernican revolution in normative thought. 'The Idea of Freedom' includes Berlin's most detailed and explicitly positive recognition of Kant's achievement and legacy in the sphere of moral and political philosophy. As we have already discussed above, the central nerve of Kant's normative theory revolves around his notion of individual freedom. Berlin elucidates the nature and importance of Kant's understanding of freedom by highlighting two key principles that he added to Rousseau's concept of liberty, namely, the universalism of the true self and the essential rationality of human nature, which in turn enables us to discover true and universal moral rules. But it was three separate though intimately related elements of Kant's moral philosophy that Berlin considers most worthy of our attention.

The first of these is his dualistic view of human nature. It is a metaphysical view of man which sees two sides to our nature, the empirical self, which like all other material objects is affected, if not determined, by the independent workings of the physical world, and the non-empirical or transcendent self that operates and expresses itself through the autonomous acts of its own will. It is this latter self that Kant largely derives from Romanticism. While it is clear that Berlin is sceptical of the ontological and theological aspects of this construct, he is not shy about declaring that Kant:

> said something which no one has since altogether wished to deny ...; namely, that to conceive something as one's duty is not the same as merely to wish it, however strongly, or to think it likely to lead to pleasure or to happiness or to avoidance of pain, or to a strengthening of some natural or social pattern whose value resides in some psychologically identifiable satisfaction which men find themselves naturally pursuing. (PRIA2 187)

The other important element of Kant's thought which 'impressed upon the consciousness of his generation and posterity' centres on what Berlin identifies as his 'disinterestedness' (PIRA2 189). This is the idea that a distinctly human life or project or act has a certain value and nobility independently of any impact (good, bad or indifferent) it may have on anything or anyone else. As Berlin says, this core aspect of Kant's moral theory informed much of the following century's 'concept of integrity, purity of heart, moral independence' (PIRA2 189).

The final feature of Kant's thought that proved to be of permanent significance is his idea of individuals as ends in themselves, possessing absolute and inviolable value in virtue of being the sole authors of their moral identity and of their own moral destiny. It is the absolute non-negotiability of the value of human beings as 'sources of acts of will, creators of values' that would become the moral DNA of modernity. Together these elements formed a potent and progressive mix which has left a large imprint on our understanding of the ethical preciousness of all human beings. Berlin sums up the import of Kant's doctrines in the final page of his lecture:

> The whole ethical content of nineteenth-century democratic doctrine is here: the emphasis on the preservation of the right to develop one's individual capacity, the hatred of anything likely to derogate from it, to lower human dignity; the liberal protest against any form of despotism, however benevolent and rational, not because it diminishes human happiness but because it is intrinsically degrading, a falsification of what human relationships between equal and independent (and ideal-pursuing) beings ought to be, a betrayal of the ideal which humanity exists to fulfil; the notion of humanity as something in the name of which rights can be claimed, crimes punished, revolutions made – this complex of values is inspired not by the utilitarian considerations or the empirical sociology of the eighteenth century but by the humanist idealism of Kant and his successors. (PIRA2 193–4)

This ringing endorsement of Kant suggests that, at least at the time of writing this lecture in the early 1950s, he was prepared to defend a notion of negative liberty that went beyond a purely instrumental justification, that he was willing to champion the claim that freedom is intrinsically valuable since it is good to be free. As Joshua Cherniss says, 'In seeking to combine a "negative" conception of liberty with a non-instrumentalist understanding of liberty's value, Berlin placed himself between the liberal and Romantic camps he portrayed as irreconcilably opposed' (PIRA lviii). This prompts the question: Which Berlin are we to believe? Should we identify Berlin's apparent commitment to more than an instrumental defence of negative liberty as a temporary flirtation that he grew out of by the late 1950s? Or did this commitment persist, albeit more implicitly? Arguments can be marshalled in favour of both a negative and a positive response to this question. While Berlin is perhaps more consistently explicit in his instrumental defence of negative liberty, it is also clear that he did not limit himself to a purely instrumental view of liberty. The fundamentally bivalent (intrinsic and instrumental) nature of Berlin's conception of liberal freedom is exemplified in his seminal essay 'Two Concepts of Liberty': within the nine pages of his discussion of the notion of negative freedom it is abundantly clear that the intrinsic value of freedom is essentially presupposed by the instrumental importance of freedom. Moreover, the symbiotic relationship between the two dimensions of negative liberty is reinforced later in the same essay when Berlin highlights the connections between value pluralism and negative freedom (L169–78 and 212–17 respectively).

It is also worth highlighting the following excerpt from Berlin's Introduction to 'Four [now Five] Essays on Liberty', where he states: 'If it is maintained that the identification of the value of liberty with the value of a field of free choice amounts to a doctrine of self-realisation, whether for good or evil ends, and that this is closer to positive than to negative liberty, I shall offer no great objection' (L 53). He is very explicit in his defence of the intrinsic value of freedom in this essay, and in 'The End of the Ideal of the Perfect Society':

> But suppose I say: Here is a pill; if you swallow it I promise that you will never feel remorse again; I promise you that you will never want to do anything other than what will make you happy, and what may make other people happy as well. ... If you ask people whether they will take a pill like that, and deprive themselves of what they imagine, anyhow, to be liberty, not very many people would accept this advice. The French philosophes, and maybe Professor Skinner [B. F. Skinner], would say that this was due to the illusion that they were free, to the bad way in which they were educated, but in fact it is possible to take another line and to say that people regard choice, will, as a central human faculty; to be deprived of it for any reason whatever they would regard as some kind of dehumanisation, and this is one of the reasons why we speak about human rights at all – all this talk about degradation, dehumanisation and so forth, exploitation of human beings, presupposes that you think that the important thing is that people should choose, or at any rate have some area in which they can at least choose their own lives and not be chosen for, in which they can act freely and not be acted upon, or acted for; that paternalism is not a virtue, necessarily, though perhaps in some cases it has to be employed. (EIPS 62, 64)

But it is important we don't let ourselves get too preoccupied with the nature and consequences of this largely procedural and pernickety distinction. Otherwise we run the risk of engaging in precisely the type of arid conceptual logic-chopping that saps Berlin's philosophy of its creative and moral force. In this respect, we would do well to keep in mind Berlin's own advice that 'the central issue of all philosophy [is] the distinction between words (or thoughts) that are about words, and words (or thoughts) that are about things' (L 95). We should also recall his approval of Bertrand Russell's remark that 'the deepest convictions of philosophers are rarely found in their formal arguments since this would leave the inner citadel of their fundamental beliefs vulnerable to the enemy' (L 245-46). Having said that, I think we can safely say that for Berlin negative freedom is not essentially valuable in itself: its principal value lies in being a political precondition for people to exercise their own free and spontaneous choice.

A different and more fruitful way of treating this aspect of Berlin's political philosophy is to consider it in the light of Alexander Herzen's view of freedom. Berlin's hero occupied a refreshingly realistic position on the nature and importance of freedom. Like Berlin, he never allowed his understanding of liberty to be obscured or trivialized by the abstractions of theoretical debate.

What distinguishes Herzen's thoughts on liberty is a quality that Berlin believed he shared with Tolstoy, the unpindownable but still unmistakable *sense of reality*. This defining trait of Herzen's outlook manifests itself in a number of ways. First, there is his unwavering opposition, almost allergy, to all forms of moral, political and religious utopianism. He had read about or observed at first-hand enough instances of the Church or the state or the revolutionary leader claiming that the promised land lay around the corner – in this world or the next – to see through the intellectual fraud and practical dangers of such otherworldly theories. They all shared the idea that history possesses some discoverable meaning, and that all we have to do is fall in line with its progressive and inevitable unfolding. Those who fail to see the underlying goal of history or the party or the nation are either ignorant, irrational or morally bereft. Herzen had the bracing intellect, moral courage and rhetorical flair to call out such totalitarian ideologies for what they were; philosophically empty and morally pernicious:

> If progress is the goal, for whom are we working? Who is this Moloch who, as the toilers approach him, instead of rewarding them, draws back; and as a consolation to the exhausted and doomed multitudes, shouting 'morituri te salutant', can only give the … mocking answer that after their death all will be beautiful on earth. Do you truly wish to condemn the human beings alive today to the sad role of caryatids supporting a floor for others some day to dance on …?
>
> If humanity marched straight towards some result, there would be no history, only logic … . Reason develops slowly, painfully, *it does not exist* in nature, nor outside nature … . One has to arrange life with it as best one can, because there is no libretto. If history followed a set libretto it would lose all interest, become unnecessary, boring, ludicrous … . History is all improvisation, all will, all extempore – there are no frontiers, no itineraries.[1]

Herzen also emphasizes the absolute priority of the individual and, as Berlin reminds us, 'without a trace of Byronic or Nietzschean hyperbole' (RT2 108). His passion for individual freedom does not come loaded with some grand metaphysical theory. He was sufficiently ahead of his time to see that no such theories are available or needed. And yet he does not conclude in any kind of melodramatic or cynical manner that life is therefore rendered meaningless. The meaninglessness of the world does not mean that our individual lives are worthless. For Herzen, as Berlin eloquently puts it:

---

[1] Alexander Herzen, *From the Other Shore*, trans. Moura Budberg and *The Russian People and Socialism*, trans. Richard Wollheim, with an introduction by Isaiah Berlin (1956: Weidenfeld and Nicolson, London), 36–7, 38–9.

> The purpose of life is life itself, the purpose of the struggle for liberty is the liberty here, today, of living individuals, each with his own individual ends, for the sake of which they move and fight and suffer, ends which are sacred for them; to crush their freedom, stop their pursuits, to ruin their ends for the sake of some ineffable felicity of the future, is blind, because it outrages the only values we know, tramples on real human lives and needs, and in the name of what? Of freedom, of happiness, justice – fanatical generalisations, mystical sounds, abstractions. Why is personal freedom worth pursuing? Only for what it is in itself, because it is what it is, not because the majority desires freedom. (RT2 107)

Note the final remark. According to Herzen and Berlin, the value of individual freedom is not something that can safely rely on the endorsement of the majority which is always prone to what Mill called 'the despotism of custom'. Neither thinker was naive enough to believe that human beings are born with an inbuilt will or preference to be paragons of cultivated individuality – the stubborn conformity of the majority was and remains a daily reminder of our indifference or blindness to the noble aspiration and expression of our individual selves. Does this render the pursuit of individual liberty a distinctly elitist preference? Hardly. All it shows is that people do not exercise their individual liberty to the extent that they might and, more often than not, find greater solace in 'the deep slumber of decided opinion'.[2] But notwithstanding this fact what crucially differentiates open from closed societies, tolerant states from oppressive ones, liberal regimes from their totalitarian opposites is that the former recognize the preciousness of the right of people to be left alone to do as they freely wish, whether they decide to pursue their own creative path or not. One of the tragedies of liberal societies is that their distinctive liberties are rarely appreciated by their members unless or until they are curtailed or removed. The centrality and fragility of our individual freedom have not diminished with time. As Berlin writes in his essay 'Herzen and Bakunin on Individual Liberty',

> Unless a minimum area is guaranteed to all men within which they can act as they wish, the only principles and values left will be those guaranteed by theological or metaphysical or scientific systems claiming to know the final truth about man's place in the universe, and his functions and goals therein. And these claims Herzen regarded as fraudulent, one and all. (RT2 128)

The experience of reading Herzen mirrors that of reading Berlin. Both authors leave us with the distinct impression that they are writing for grown-ups.

---

[2] John Stuart Mill, 'On Liberty', in *On Liberty and other essays*, ed. John Gray (1991: Oxford World Classics, Oxford), 49. The phrase is not Mill's but is quoted by him without specifying its source.

The effect of being in their company is a heightened impulse to stay true to the empiricist conviction that 'every belief must be tested at the bar of human experience'.³ Another edifying effect of reading their respective writings is a judicious bias against the excessive abstractions and remoteness of philosophical debate, such as an undue interest in the distinction between instrumental and intrinsic justifications of negative freedom that can threaten to obscure the far more important matter of 'the specific ends of specific human beings in specific situations' (RT2 128). In this respect, their shared sensibility has a great deal in common with that of another thinker for grown-ups, William James. In his very fine essay, 'On a Certain Blindness in Human Beings', James makes the following pertinent observation:

> And now what is the result of all these considerations and quotations? It is negative in one sense, but positive in another. It absolutely forbids us to be forward in pronouncing on the meaninglessness of forms of existence other than our own; and it commands us to tolerate, respect, and indulge those whom we see harmlessly interested and happy in their own ways, however unintelligible these may be to us. Hands off; neither the whole of truth nor the whole of good is revealed to any single observer, although each observer gains a partial superiority of insight from the peculiar position in which he stands. Even prisons and sick-rooms have their special revelations. It is enough to ask of each of us that he should be faithful to his own opportunities and to make the most of his own blessings, without presuming to regulate the rest of the vast field.⁴

Regrettably, there is growing tendency within contemporary academic scholarship on Berlin to argue that the only way to defend the Enlightenment is to sing its exclusive praises. Aside from the fact that the most eloquent and acute defenders of the Enlightenment were diffident about it – Hume, Diderot, Kant, Goethe – this narrow-minded contemporary perspective ends up missing the central lesson of their ideas. Both the Enlightenment and the Counter-Enlightenment enshrine the central traits of modernity, traits that inform and define the morally diverse and conflictual inheritance of our present situation. The most perceptive modern commentators have recognized and celebrated the inescapable tensions and oppositions of the modern condition without denying the dark side of both formative movements, whether it's the arid scientism and cold, insipid

---

³John Gray, *Seven Types of Atheism* (2018: Allen Lane, London), 37. See also Aileen Kelly's 'The European Nanny: Herzen and Mill on Liberty' in her *Views from the other Shore* (1999: Yale University Press, New Haven), 114–138. Gray is more philosophically engaging than Kelly but the latter gives a more reliable account of Herzen's understanding of liberty.

⁴William James, *Pragmatism and Other Essays* (2000: Penguin, London), 284–85.

instrumentalism of Enlightenment rationalism or the often destructive and unrestrained irrationalism of Romanticism.[5]

Like his other great hero, Ivan Turgenev (1818–83), Berlin is a passionate moderate, not out of some bland and complacent allegiance to the middle road but because, in most cases, it is where the messy truth lies. It is also where the affirming flame of humane reason and individual conscience is more likely to be found. Berlin was loath to choose between sides, especially if the choice was between the Enlightenment and Counter-Enlightenment, rationalism and romanticism, hedgehogs and foxes. He had the moral intelligence to see that these distinct and rival intellectual movements and outlooks had their bright and sinister sides, and the wisdom to realize that the choice should never be either-or, but always both. For Berlin, the personal and political spheres of life should be seen as arenas of inevitable and extensive ethical disagreement giving rise to the need for humane toleration and principled compromise and reform. To demand otherwise is to fall victim to some form of intellectual myopia or moral dogmatism, to expect more from the world than it can reasonably deliver. In this regard, he never forgot the truth of Herzen's cautionary observation:

> People love a neat outward appearance. When it comes to truth, they see only one striking aspect and do not want to see grass growing round the back. But real truths come only in three dimensions, all of which are essential.[6]

---

[5] The latest example of this blinkered critique of Berlin's thought is found in T. J. Reed's 'Sympathy and Empathy: Isaiah's dilemma, or How He Let the Enlightenment Down', in *Isaiah Berlin and the Enlightenment*, eds. Laurence Brockliss and Ritchie Robertson (2016: Oxford University Press, Oxford), 113–20.

[6] 'Kaprizy I pazdum'' ('Whims and Thoughts', 1846): A. I. Gertsen [Herzen], *Sobranie sochinenii v tridsati tomakh,* Vol. 2 (1954–66: Moscow), 101.

EPILOGUE

In the Preface I referred to a work of genius to which Berlin was deeply attracted. The writing in question is Diderot's satirical dialogue, *Rameau's Nephew*. I shall end this chapter and indeed the book by discussing it in the light of Isaiah Berlin's deeply ambivalent attitude towards the Enlightenment and its critics. But first a brief word about Diderot himself.

As principal editor of *The Encyclopaedia of the Arts and Sciences,* Denis Diderot (1713–84) had an enormous influence on his own century and the ones that followed. He devoted his life to promoting the idea that the main hope of human progress lay in following the path of science and secularism and to in opposing all forms of ignorance and superstition, which he believed were largely the product of clerical authority and dogmatic religious belief. The son of a cutler from the provincial town of Langres, Diderot rejected from an early age the ubiquitous and oppressive power of both the Church and the monarchy. Due to the intolerance of his time, and given his virtually lifelong commitment to subverting the tyranny of controlled and conventional opinion, he was forced to walk a tightrope restraining himself and his like-minded contributors to the *Encyclopaedia* from being too blatant in their anti-establishment views while remaining true to the radical Enlightenment programme of demystification and evidence-based, secular enquiry. Diderot frequently failed in this regard, with the result that he was in constant trouble with the authorities and even ended up spending time incarcerated. His spell in prison had the effect of making him less flagrantly careless in declaring his iconoclastic convictions; although he continued with his tireless work of editing the *Encyclopaedia* (which eventually filled seventeen volumes), he chose to leave much of his more radical writings unpublished in his lifetime. Never allowing his various brushes with the authorities undermine his restless, independent spirit, Diderot established himself as the truest and bravest *philosophe* of his generation. He remained until the end of his life a free thinker devoted to the noble task of encouraging and empowering others to follow the light of secular reason.

The tale of the survival of *Rameau's Nephew* is almost as fascinating as the ideas it contains. Following Diderot's death in 1784, the book, which remained unpublished during his lifetime, was left with the rest of his estate to his daughter, Mme de Vandeul, and her strait-laced husband. Shocked by its contents, Diderot's son-in-law felt obliged to purge the work of its obscenities. Fortunately, another manuscript of *Rameau's Nephew*, or *The Second Satire* as it was also called, had been sent to Catherine the Great of Russia. She had arranged at an earlier date to purchase Diderot's library and his own papers in return for an annual salary of 1,000 *livres* and to let him be caretaker of it until his death. The Empress Catherine's manuscript eventually found its way, via the German writers Klinger and Schiller, into the possession of Goethe who translated it into his native language, and published it for the first time in 1805, under the German title *Rameaus Neffe*. It was not until 1821 that the book was published in French, but this edition was a corrupted retranslation of the original German publication. Another French edition of the work was published two years later, but again this edition was based on the heavily censored Vandeul version. Then, no less than seventy-seven years later, a remarkable event occurred. One day in 1890, a librarian by the name of Georges Monval was browsing the second-hand bookstalls along the Quai de Voltaire in Paris and happened upon a manuscript titled *The Second Satire*. Fortunately, he appreciated the significance of his find, and consequently the only untranslated and unadulterated version that had originally been sent to Catherine the Great was miraculously saved for posterity. How it ended up in one of the *bouquinistes* of the left bank of Paris remains one of the unsolved mysteries of the past.[1]

Yet it is the unique treasure that lies inside this book that overshadows everything else, even its unlikely reappearance. The dramatic work centres around a conversation in a Paris café between two characters; one is called 'Me' (*Moi*) or the philosopher (henceforth referred to as 'the philosopher') and the other 'Him' (*Lui*) or Rameau's nephew (henceforth referred to as 'the nephew'). While the philosopher may appear, to all intents and purposes, to represent the views of its author, Diderot is careful to distance himself somewhat from this character by using a narrator who occasionally comments on the ideas and conduct of both dramatic figures. What is instantly and enduringly impressive about this play is its uncanniness. And the reason for this is largely the presence of the nephew, an all-round decadent scoundrel who holds centre stage from start to finish. The nephew without a proper name even gets to speak the immortal last line of the book: 'He that laughs last, laughs best' (RN 89).

---

[1]The remarkable story of the trials, tribulations and reappearance of Diderot's work, which is the stuff of fiction, is told by Nicholas Cronk in his introduction to Denis Diderot, *Rameau's Nephew and First Satire*, trans. Margaret Mauldon (2006: Oxford University Press, Oxford). Hereafter referred to RN.

We are introduced to the nephew in the first page of the play:

> While I was there [the Café de la Régence] one evening, watching everything, not saying much and listening as little as possible, I was accosted by one of the most bizarre characters in this country, to which God has granted its fair share. He is a composite of nobility and baseness, good sense and irrationality. The concepts of honour and dishonour must surely be strangely jumbled in his head, for he makes no parade of the good qualities which nature has given him, and, for the bad, evinces no shame. He is, what's more, endowed with a strong constitution, an exceptionally vivid imagination, and an uncommonly powerful pair of lungs. If ever you meet him, and are not stopped in your tracks by his singularity, then either you will stick your fingers in your ears or you will take to your heels. (RN 3)

Those of us who are not tempted to block our ears (or eyes) end up utterly and unforgettably stopped in our tracks by this mercurial and subversive character. Hegel was one of the first readers to appreciate the originality of the nephew, of the significance of his uncompromisable sense of individuality.[2] In his *Phenomenology of Spirit* (1807), he contrasts what he calls 'the honest soul' and 'the distraught and disintegrated consciousness'.[3] Hegel identifies the figure of the philosopher as the embodiment of the honest man. The honest soul is essentially the person of sincerity, a person who not only tells the truth but can be relied on to tell the truth because of his integrity. While sincerity is very much a modern virtue – it is possible to discern its emergence in certain of Shakespeare's characters, such as Horatio in *Hamlet*, and its development in the dramatic works of Molière, especially in a rather extreme and pure form in the character of Alceste in *The Misanthrope*, as well as in Rousseau's *Confessions* – Hegel felt it had become a distinctly naive or outdated ideal by the end of the eighteenth century. For the *honnête homme* was still under the illusion that a life of frictionless honour, peace and contentment is, in principle, possible for the individual within society. The innocence of the placid soul also betrays itself in its uncultivated understanding of music with its jejune fondness for simple melodies and excessively uniform tones. Hegel shows far more interest in the morally disaffected but aesthetically sophisticated figure of the nephew. For Hegel, the nephew exposes and amplifies the latent conflict between sincerity and authenticity, between the conventions of telling the truth and the demands of being true to oneself. He is the first genuine instance of the fragmented but self-conscious soul who possesses no self to be true to and who, in Hegel's teleological theory of history, exemplifies Geist estranged from itself. The nephew is clearly superior to the philosopher,

---

[2] Lionel Trilling, *Sincerity and Authenticity* (1971: Harvard University Press, Cambridge, Mass), ch 2.
[3] G. W. F. Hegel, *The Phenomenology of Mind*, trans. and ed. by J. B. Ballie (1931: London), 543.

Hegel argues, since he represents the latest and necessary stage in the gradual and inevitable emergence of Geist or Spirit, the disintegrated, unhappy consciousness intensely aware of both its own alienated yet authentic condition as well as the obsolete form of good-natured but naive sincerity that precedes it. While '*Moi*' personifies a commitment to ethical ideals that may still enjoy the official blessing of society, '*Lui*' reflects a need to break free from what he regards as civilization's artificial and corrosive moral ties and its all too obvious hypocrisy and absurdity.

A thumbnail sketch of Hegel's theory of world history might be helpful at this point. Hegel believed that there is meaning to history, that it was not simply one random event succeeded by another or a tale told by an idiot. In the *Introduction to the Lectures on The Philosophy of History* he famously claims that 'the history of the world is none other than the progress of the consciousness of freedom'.[4] He also put forward a very distinctive account of how such progress occurs; he saw that history as in a near perpetual state of flux but gradually moving towards its ultimate resolution. He called this process of change *the dialectic*. Every historical period has tensions and conflicts within itself which prove destabilizing of the status quo and end up precipitating further change which in turn introduces a new historical epoch which contains new fundamental disagreements which prompt yet another societal transformation. In more abstract terms, this can be described as a thesis confronting its antithesis, which in turn generates a synthesis. As indicated, this dialectical process does not go on arbitrarily and in perpetuity as history does have a meaningful pattern and ultimate goal which consists in the ineluctable unfolding and realization via human consciousness of what Hegel refers to as *Geist* (variously translated as 'Mind', 'Spirit' and 'Reality'), which represents final and perfect consummation of knowledge and freedom.

According to Hegel, the nephew's sincerity is more genuine because he is his own man, accountable to nobody except his own autonomous if decadent self. We have here the initial stirrings of the radical idea that the authentic human soul is an unfettered one, free to explore whatever path(s) it chooses, even if that path leads to depravity, disintegration and negation. This is also the germ of the idea that Nietzsche would later latch onto in highly original and subversive ways in his own philosophy and that novelists like Fyodor Dostoyevsky, Joseph Conrad and Hugo von Hofmannsthal have explored in gripping and disturbing ways.[5]

---

[4]G. V. W. Hegel, *Introduction to the Lectures on the History of Philosophy*, trans. by T. M. Knox and A.V. Miller (1837: 1994 edn: Oxford University Press, Oxford), no. 21.

[5]This theme is pertinent to virtually all of Nietzsche's works but especially *Thus Spoke Zarathustra* and *Ecce Homo*. With regard to the works of novelists and poets, I am referring chiefly to Fyodor Dostoyevsky's *Notes from the Underground* (1864) and *Crime and Punishment* (1866); Joseph Conrad's *Heart of Darkness* (1899) and the less well-known but remarkable *The Lord Chandos Letter* (1902) by Hugo von Hofmannsthal.

In the context of French literature and society, the nephew can be viewed as a forerunner of the Sartrean ideal of sincerity, that is, of being faithful to the emptiness of existence as well as a prototype of the asocial, bohemian nihilist portrayed by Jean Genet in his life and writings.

While Hegel's interpretation of *Rameau's Nephew* is highly perceptive and deserves more credit and less defensive condescension than it typically receives from Anglophone critics, I wish to put forward a different way of reading Diderot's dramatic work, one that I believe Berlin invites us to adopt. Unlike Hegel's reading of the satire, the following view of *Rameau's Nephew* does not require us to see its two central characters and their respective ideas as mutually exclusive (as 'thesis' and 'antithesis', in Hegelian terms) and, more fundamentally, as mere actors in the unfolding of *Geist*. Rather it sees the play as a genuinely two-way and open-ended conversation between two very credible, if antithetical, characters.

What is clear even within the first few pages of the narrative is that the philosopher is intrigued by and not a little attracted to the nephew:

> He's like a grain of yeast that ferments, and restores to each of us his natural individuality. He shocks us, he stirs us up; he forces us to praise or blame; he brings out the truth; he identifies honourable men and unmasks scoundrels; it is then that the man of good sense keeps his ears open, and takes the measure of his companions. (RN 4)

The underlying fondness of the philosopher for the swaggering, shameless nephew is sustained throughout the play, even if he is frequently appalled, embarrassed or exasperated by his interlocutor's seedy and unblushing delight in defying social etiquette and conventional morality. And the philosopher's basic affection is not unreciprocated by the vagabond nephew, who warmly welcomes the company of his earnest friend from the start. Highlighting the conviviality between these two characters is not intended in any way to belittle the differences between them and their ideas which are irreconcilable; indeed any attempt to domesticate or resolve the various quarrels between the two is not only doomed to failure but misses the whole point of the satire. Rather it is to suggest that Diderot is asking us to recognize the distinct and opposing traits and ideas embodied in both. There is a clear impression that no matter how shocking and unregenerate the nephew may be, the philosopher can neither ignore him nor disown him. He is simply too irresistibly fascinating as well as all too human. The play therefore encourages us to challenge our habitual reactions, broaden our moral imagination and explore the depths of our internally divided and contradictory selves. Indeed one of its more unsettling (and liberating) aspects is the suggestion that our notions of reason, truth and virtue do not possess stable and uncontested meanings with the highly subversive implication that nothing is sacred and everything can be questioned.

There are a series of revealing moments in the narrative that highlight the ambivalence of the relationship between the philosopher and the nephew, and indeed the underlying scepticism of the narrator himself. One of these moments happens when the protagonists find themselves talking about philosophy. The nephew does an inspired job of puncturing the pretensions of the subject by making fun of the intellectualist fantasies and falsehoods that philosophers typically indulge in, such as the laughable idea that all men 'seek the same kind of happiness'. He also adds that philosophers are welcome to follow their own effete thoughts about virtue and happiness, but that it is all vanity compared with 'Drinking fine wines, eating one's fill of choice dishes, tumbling pretty girls, sleeping on soft beds' (RN 32). But just before they had discussed the topic of philosophy, the nephew had unintentionally revealed that even his blithe spirit is not as careless as he may wish us to assume. After overtly pimping himself among the affluent echelons of Paris society in return for all the creature comforts of life, it turns out that even he cannot go on living such a parasitical life. It would appear that even the nephew is not without the need for some form of dignity, that even his devil-may-care attitude and seemingly unbridled decadence have their limits. As he concedes himself: 'Let's get this clear: there's kissing arses literally, and kissing arses figuratively. Ask that fat Bergier, who kisses Madame de La Marck's arse both literally and figuratively; and, upon my word! in that particular case I should find both equally unpleasant' (RN 17).

Shortly after this admission, the nephew launches into one of his characteristically ironic and self-critical soliloquies on which the narrator comments:

> As I listened to him describing the scene of the procurer seducing the young girl, I found myself torn between two conflicting emotions, between a powerful desire to laugh and an overwhelming surge of indignation. I was in agony. Again and again a roar of laughter prevented my rage bursting forth; again and again the rage rising in my heart became a roar of laughter. I was dumbfounded by such shrewdness and such depravity; by such soundness of ideas alternating with such falseness; by so general a perversity of feeling, so total a corruption, and so exceptional a candour. (RN 19–20)

The book is replete with such instances of the ambivalent feelings not just on the part of the narrator but of 'Me' and 'Him' too.

Another episode worth highlighting comes nearer the end of the book, when the nephew spontaneously launches into performing a highly discordant musical composition of his own:

> Now he was muddling and mixing some thirty airs of every style – Italian, French, tragic, comic; sometimes, singing a bass part, he'd descend into the

depths of hell; sometimes, straining at the notes as he imitated a falsetto, he'd tear at the upper registers, all the while imitating, with gait, carriage and gestures, the different characters singing; by turns furious, mollified, imperious, derisive. Now he's a young girl in tears, mimicking all her simpering ways; now he's a priest, a king, a tyrant, threatening, commanding, raging; now he's a slave, obeying. ... The roars of laughter [from the crowd] were loud enough to open cracks in the ceiling. He noticed nothing of this; he just went on with his performance, transported by passion, an enthusiasm so akin to madness that it was not clear whether he'd ever recover from it, or whether he should not be flung into a carriage and taken straight to the madhouse, still singing a fragment from Jommelli's *Lamentations*. (RN 68)

Again, the narrator responds to the nephew's mesmerizing performance almost helplessly: 'Was I filled with admiration? Yes, I was. Was I moved to pity? Yes, I was' (RN 68).

What we seem to be confronted with here is an unerring sense that there is no uniquely right way of adjudicating, let alone resolving, the tensions that occupy the very heart of Diderot's dialogue. It is as if human life is simply too capricious, variegated and primal to be contained by something as relatively pure, principled and paltry as philosophy and the vainly neat moral theories which its practitioners have come up with over the ages. The dialectical clash between the two characters and everything they hold dear remains unresolved and unresolvable and, in part, disquietingly so. Many of us may find ourselves feeling a certain moral duty to side with *Moi* or the philosopher, but in the end this can only be achieved by disowning, wittingly or not, our own irrepressible, individual contrariness which the nephew embodies par excellence. Others may wish to align themselves with the uber-sophisticated, authentic and scandalous nephew, but again only at the cost of denying many of our most rational and morally decent, if often narrow and levelling, ideals and dispositions. What the play would appear to be insinuating is that there is no way of reconciling or transcending the deep and unbridgeable differences that fall within 'the human horizon' without denying vital and indisputable human traits. *Rameau's Nephew* remains the great, indestructible antidote to narrow-mindedness and moralism. More fundamentally and positively, it also reminds us of the sublime pleasure to be derived from observing or taking part in conversation among genuinely free-thinking and open-minded companions.

But why should this be germane to Berlin's thought? Well, my suggestion is that the spirit of human complexity informing Diderot's satire is emblematic of Berlin's richly pluralistic vision of the world. One can almost hear the voice of Berlin's imaginative sensibility as much as that of Diderot's in the dialogue between '*Moi*' and '*Lui*'. More generally, Berlin's fox-like credentials show themselves most conspicuously in his handling of the matter of 'the' Enlightenment and its main detractors. He recognizes that *les lumières* and their most intransigent opponents capture different if often conflicting traits of our nature. One has only to consider that other miniature masterpiece of subversive scepticism and ambivalence, Heinrich von Kleist's *On the Marionette Theatre*, to see through the superficiality of regarding the Enlightenment as an unalloyed blessing or its enemies as inveterate irrationalists. The chief critics of the Enlightenment represent widely divergent and incommensurable values and ideals, not all of which could be described as straightforwardly ethical but none of which could be denied as genuinely human. Where the Enlightenment accentuates the centrality of rationality, empiricism, toleration, universalism and progressivism, its rivals tend to underline the primacy of subjectivity, individualism, variety, ethnocentricity, alienation and authenticity. Both ways of looking at the world have, of course, their dark sides, whether, it is the cool and dehumanizing instrumental reason that dominates so much of modern life or the kind of atavistic impulses that fuelled many of the most atrocious acts of man's inhumanity to man in the last century and continues to do so to this day. Berlin's equivocation and ambivalence, his intimation that, to paraphrase Auden on poetry, philosophy 'might be defined as the clear expression of mixed ideas' is captured in the following passage which comes near the end of his extended essay 'Herder and the Enlightenment'[6]:

> The French Revolution was founded on the notion of timeless truths given to the faculty of reason with which all men are endowed. It was dedicated to the creation or restoration of a static and harmonious society, founded on unalterable principles, a dream of classical perfection, or, at least, the closest approximation to it feasible on earth. It preached a peaceful universalism and a rational humanitarianism. But its consequences threw into relief the precariousness of human institutions; the disturbing phenomenon of apparently irresistible change; the clash of irreconcilable values and ideas; the insufficiency of simple formulae; the complexity of men and societies; the poetry of action, destruction, heroism, war; the effectiveness of mobs and of great men; the crucial role played by chance; the feebleness of reason before the power of fanatically believed doctrines; the unpredictability of events; the part played in history by unintended consequences; the ignorance of the workings of the sunken two-thirds of the great human iceberg, of which only the visible portion had been studied by scientists and taken into account by the ideologists of the great Revolution. (PSM2 434)

The key thing is that we must try not to lose sight of the 'the complexity of men and societies', that we resist the simplifying, unsceptical urge to deride or neglect

---

[6] W. H. Auden, *New Year Letter* (1941: Faber, London) 119.

the irreducibly different yet legitimate outlooks proclaimed by the Enlightenment thinkers and their sternest critics. Isaiah Berlin provides us with a uniquely true and truthful picture of our complexity, of the wondrous variety of human life. The undogmatic authority and moral charm of his writings are infused with a clear-eyed, imaginative awareness of our diversity and imperfectibility as well as an unflinching affirmation of the spontaneity and preciousness of the individual human conscience. As he wrote in a letter near the end of his eventful and exemplary life:

> But when you say that I am not sure that I know where I myself stand – that I oscillate, as it were, between the Enlightenment and the Counter-Enlightenment – I know what you mean. What I truly believe is that we are children of two traditions, which we have not reconciled in our own breasts – not merely my own breast, but most people's. ... In the end I come down on the side of the Enlightenment, but the other side should be listened to: they have identified grave flaws, they have a vision too. (A 477–78)[7]

---

[7] Earlier in the same letter to the scholar, Mark Lilla, Berlin states that his two favourite thinkers of the eighteenth century are Lessing and Diderot. Incidentally, in an excellent review of Berlin's study of Hamann, Lilla suggests that:

> If anything (and this may be the key), Berlin is an ultra-liberal frustrated by the internal limits of the Enlightenment itself: what he sees as its blind spots and intolerances, its all too quick willingness to see in its critics l'infâme rather than dissenters wishing to live differently. What Berlin appears to want is not the contrary of the Enlightenment, but what the Germans call *ein Aufklärung über die Aufklärung*. Mark Lilla, 'The trouble with the Enlightenment' in the *London Review of Books*. (6 January 1994)

BIBLIOGRAPHY

Isaiah Berlin's Writings

Karl Marx: His Life and Environment, Henry Hardy, ed. (1939: 5th edn. 2013: Princeton University Press, Princeton, NJ).

The Hedgehog and the Fox: An Essay on Tolstoy's View of History, Henry Hardy, ed. (1953: 2nd edn. 2013: Princeton University Press, Princeton, NJ).

The Age of Enlightenment: The Eighteenth-Century Philosophers: Selected with an Introduction and Commentary by Isaiah Berlin (1956, 2nd edn. 1979: Oxford University Press, Oxford).

Russian Thinkers, Aileen Kelly and Henry Hardy, eds. (1978; 2nd edn. 2008: Penguin, London).

Concepts and Categories: Philosophical Essays, Henry Hardy, ed. (1978: 2nd edn. 2013: Princeton University Press, Princeton, NJ).

Against the Current: Essays in the History of Ideas, Henry Hardy, ed. (1979: 2nd edn. 2013: Princeton University Press, Princeton, NJ).

Personal Impressions, Henry Hardy, ed. (1980: 3rd edn. 2014: Princeton University Press, Princeton, NJ).

The Crooked Timber of Humanity: Chapters in the History of Ideas, Henry Hardy, ed. (1990: 2nd edn. 2013: Princeton University Press, Princeton, NJ).

The Magus of the North: J. G. Hamann and the Origins of Modern Irrationalism, Henry Hardy, ed. (1993: John Murray, London).

The Sense of Reality: Studies in Ideas and Their History, Henry Hardy, ed. (1996: Pimlico, London).

The First and the Last (1999: New York Review of Books, New York).

The Roots of Romanticism, Henry Hardy, ed. (1999: 2nd edn. 2013: Princeton University Press, Princeton, NJ).

The Power of Ideas, Henry Hardy, ed. (2000: 2nd edn. 2013: Princeton University Press, Princeton, NJ).

Three Critics of the Enlightenment: Vico, Herder Hamann and Henry Hardy, eds. (2000: 2nd edn. 2013: Princeton University Press, Princeton, NJ).

Freedom and Its Betrayal: Six Enemies of Human Liberty, Henry Hardy, ed. (2002: 2nd edn. 2014: Princeton University Press, Princeton, NJ).

Liberty, Incorporating Four Essays on Liberty (1969), Henry Hardy, ed. (2002: Oxford University Press, Oxford).

The Soviet Mind: Russian Culture under Communism, Henry Hardy, ed. (2004: 2nd edn. Brookings Classics, Washington DC).

Political Ideas in the Romantic Age: Their Rise and Influence on Modern Thought,
   Henry Hardy, ed. (2006: 2nd edn. 2014: Princeton University Press, Princeton, NJ).

Isaiah Berlin's Letters

Flourishing: Letters 1928–1946, Henry Hardy, ed. (2004: Chatto & Windus, London).
Enlightening: Letters 1946–1960, Henry Hardy and Mark Pottle, eds. (2009: Chatto & Windus, London).
Building: Letters 1960–1975, Henry Hardy and Jennifer Holmes, eds. (2013: Chatto & Windus, London).
Affirming: Letters 1975–1997, Henry Hardy and Mark Pottle, eds. (2015: Chatto & Windus, London).

Anthology of Isaiah Berlin's Writings

The Proper Study of Mankind: An Anthology of Essays, Henry Hardy and Roger Hausheer, eds. (1997: 2nd edn. 2013: Vintage, London).

Dialogues and Interviews

Isaiah Berlin, Anthony Quinton, 'Iris Murdoch and Stuart Hampshire', *The Twentieth Century* CLVII (January–June, 1955), 495–521.
'The Lessons of History', *Columbia University*, 1966. http://berlin.wolf.ox.ac.uk/lists/nachlass/lesshist.pdf
Ramin Jahanbegloo, *Conversations with Isaiah Berlin* (1992: Halban, London).
Steven Lukes, 'Isaiah Berlin: In Conversation with Steven Lukes', *Salmagundi* (Fall, 1998).
With Bryan Magee, 'An Introduction to Philosophy', in Bryan Magee, *Men of Ideas* (1978: BBC Publications, London), subsequently published as *Talking Philosophy* (2001: Oxford University Press, Oxford).
Beata Polanowska-Sygulska, *Unfinished Dialogue* (2006: Prometheus, New York).
'Synthetic *A Priori* Propositions', Reply to Sellars, *APA*, Bryn Mawr, 1951. 3 (*IBVL*).

A selection of unpublished and published papers and replies by Isaiah Berlin

'The End of the Ideal of the Perfect Society', University of New South Wales, 1975.
   Available on the Isaiah Berlin Virtual Library (IBVL), http://berlin.wolf.ox.ac.uk/index.html
'Reply to Robert Kocis', *Political Studies* 31 (1983), 388–93.
'Reply to Ronald H. McKinney, "Towards a Postmodern Ethics: Sir Isaiah Berlin and John Caputo"', *Journal of Value Inquiry* 26 (1992), 557–60.

Selected books, articles and reviews on Isaiah Berlin

Anderson, Perry, 'England's Isaiah', a review of Isaiah Berlin, *The Crooked Timber of Humanity* in the *London Review of Books*, 20 December 1990, 3–7.

Annan, Noel, 'The Don as Magus – Isaiah Berlin', in *The Dons: Mentors, Eccentrics and Geniuses* (1999: HarperCollins, London), 209–32.

Archard, David, ed. *Philosophy and Pluralism* (1996: Cambridge University Press, Cambridge).

Barry, Brian, 'Isaiah, Israel and Tribal Realism', *Times Literary Supplement*, 9 November 2001.

Baum, Bruce and Robert Nichols, eds. *Isaiah Berlin and the Politics of Freedom: 'Two Concepts of Liberty' 50 Years Later* (2013: Routledge, London and New York).

Berlin, Isaiah, Edna Ullmann-Margalit and Avishai Margalit, eds. *Isaiah Berlin: A Celebration* (1991: Hogarth Press, London).

Brockliss, Laurence and Richie Robertson, eds. *Isaiah Berlin and the Enlightenment* (2016: Oxford University Press, Oxford).

Cherniss, Joshua, *A Mind and Its Time the Development of Isaiah Berlin's Political Thought* (2013: Oxford University Press, Oxford).

Cherniss, Joshua and Henry Hardy, 'Isaiah Berlin', Stanford Encyclopedia of Philosophy (online).

Cherniss, Joshua and Steven Smith, eds., *The Cambridge Companion to Isaiah Berlin* (2018: Cambridge University Press, Cambridge).

Cohen, Marshall, 'Berlin and the Liberal Tradition', *Philosophical Quarterly* 10 (1960), 216–27.

Collini, Stefan, 'Liberal Mind; Isaiah Berlin', in *English Pasts: Essays in History and Culture* (1999: Oxford University Press, Oxford).

Crick, Bernard, 'On Isaiah Berlin', in *Crossing Borders: Political Essays* (2001: Continuum, London), 163–73.

Crowder, George, 'Isaiah Berlin and Bernard Williams, "Pluralism and Liberalism: A Reply"', *Political Studies* 44 (1996), 649–51.

Crowder, George, *Isaiah Berlin: Liberty and Pluralism* (2004: Polity Press, Cambridge).

Crowder, George, *Liberalism and Value Pluralism* (2002: Continuum, London and New York).

Crowder, George, 'Negative and Positive Liberty', *Political Science* 40 (1988), 57–83.

Crowder, G., 'Pluralism and Liberalism', *Political Studies* 42 (1994), 293–305 (reply by IB and Bernard Williams, *Political Studies* 42 (1992), 306–9.

Crowder, George, 'Two Concepts of Liberal Pluralism', *Political Theory* 35 (2) (April 2007), 121–46.

Crowder, George and Henry Hardy, eds. *The One and the Many; Reading Isaiah Berlin* (2007: Prometheus Books, New York).

Dworkin, Ronald, Mark Lilla and Robert Silvers, eds. *The Legacy of Isaiah Berlin* (2001: New York Review of Books, New York).

Ferrell, Jason, 'Isaiah Berlin: Pluralism and Liberalism in Theory and Practice', *Contemporary Political Theory* 8 (3) (2008), 295–316.

Galipeau, Claude, *Isaiah Berlin's Liberalism* (1994: Clarendon Press, Oxford).

Galston, William, *Liberal Pluralism: The Implications of Value Pluralism for Political Theory and Practice* (2002: Cambridge University Press, Cambridge).

Geerken, John H., 'Machiavelli Studies since 1969', *Journal of the History of Ideas* 37 (1976), 351–68.
Gellner, Ernest, 'Sauce for the Liberal Goose' review of J. Gray, *Prospect* (November 1995), 56–61.
Gray, John, *Isaiah Berlin* (1995: 2013 edn. Princeton University Press, Princeton, NJ).
Hardy, Henry, ed. *The Book of Isaiah: Personal Impressions* (2009: The Boydell Press, Woodbridge).
Hardy, Henry, 'A Huge Unsorted Heap', *Oxford Today* 14 (2) (Hilary 2002), 51.
Hardy, Henry, *In Search of Isaiah Berlin: A Literary Adventure* (2018: I.B Tauris, London).
Hardy, Henry, 'Isaiah Berlin: Against dogma' from 'Footnotes to Plato' series (digital version only) in the *Times Literary Supplement*, 17 October 2018.
Hardy, Henry, 'Skeptical Isaiah Berlin' (Letter), *New York Review of Books*, 8 April 2010.
Hardy, Henry, Kei Hiruta and Jennifer Holmes eds. *Isaiah Berlin & Wolfson College* (2009: Wolfson College, Oxford).
Harris, Ian, 'Berlin and His Critics', in Isaiah Berlin, *Liberty*, ed. Henry Hardy (2002: Oxford University Press, Oxford), 349–66.
Ignatieff, Michael, *Isaiah Berlin: A Life* (1998: Chatto & Windus, London).
Katznelson, Ira, *Liberalism's Crooked Circle: Letters to Adam Michnik* (1996: Princeton University Press, Princeton, NJ).
Kaufman, A. S., 'Professor Berlin on "Negative Freedom"', *Mind* 71 (1962), 241–43.
Kekes, John, *The Morality of Liberalism* (1993: Princeton University Press, Princeton, NJ).
Kocis, Robert, *A Critical Appraisal of Sir Isaiah Berlin's Political Philosophy* (1989: Edwin Mellon Press, New York).
Kocis, Robert, 'Toward a Coherent Theory of Human Moral Development: Beyond Sir Isaiah Berlin's Vision of Human Nature', *Political Studies* 31 (1983), 370–87.
Lilla, Mark, 'The Trouble with the Enlightenment', a review of Isaiah Berlin *The Magus of the North*, in the *London Review of Books*, 6 January 1994.
Llosa, Mario Vargas, 'Isaiah Berlin: A Hero of Our Time', in *Making Waves* (1996: Faber, London), 144–7.
Lukes, Steven, 'Berlin's Dilemma', *Times Literary Supplement*, 27 March 1998.
Lukes, Steven, *Liberals and Cannibals: The Implications of Diversity* (2003: Verso, London).
MacCallum, Gerald C., 'Berlin on the Compatibility of Values, Ideals, and "Ends"', *Ethics* 77 (1966–7), 139–45.
MacCallum, Gerald C., 'Negative and Positive Freedom', *Philosophical Review* 76 (1967), 312–34; repr. as 'Negative and Positive Liberty', in Peter Laslett, W. G. Runciman and Quentin Skinner, eds. *Philosophy, Politics and Society*, 4th Series (1972: Blackwell, Oxford).
MacFarlane, L. J., 'On Two Concepts of Liberty', *Political Studies* 14 (1966), 77–8.
Mali, Joseph, *The Legacy of Vico in Modern Cultural History* (2012: Cambridge University Press, Cambridge), 195–256.
Margalit, Avishai, 'The Philosopher of Sympathy: Isaiah Berlin and the Fate of Humanism', *New Republic* 20 (February 1995), 31–7.
McKinney, Ronald, 'Towards a Postmodern Ethics: Sir Isaiah Berlin and John Caputo', *Journal of Value Inquiry* 26 (1992), 395–407.
Miller, David, 'Crooked Timber or Bent Twig? Isaiah Berlin's Nationalism', *Political Studies* 53 (2005), 100–23.

Momigliano, Arnaldo, 'On the Pioneer Trail', *New York Review of Books*, 11 November 1976.

Parekh, Bhikhu, 'Isaiah Berlin', Chapter 2 in his *Contemporary Political Thinkers* (1982: Martin Robertson, Oxford) repr. as 'Review Article: The Political Thought of Sir Isaiah Berlin', *British Journal of Political Science* 12 (1982), 201–26.

Plaw, Avery, 'Why Monist Critiques Feed Value Pluralism: Ronald Dworkin's Critique of Isaiah Berlin', *Social Theory and Practice* 30 (1) (January 2004), 105–26.

Pompa, Leon, 'Isaiah Berlin: 1909–1997', *New Vico Studies* 16 (1998), 129–36.

Putnam, Hilary, 'Pragmatism and Relativism: Universal Values and Traditional Ways of Life', in James Conant, ed. *Words and Life* (1995: Harvard University Press, Cambridge, Mass), 182–97.

Quinton, Anthony, ed. *Political Philosophy* (1967: Oxford University Press, Oxford).

Riley, Jonathan, 'Isaiah Berlin's "Minimum of Common Moral Ground"', *Political Theory* 41 (1) (2013), 61–89.

Rorty, Richard, *Contingency, Irony and Solidarity* (1989: Cambridge University Press, Cambridge), chapter 3.

Rorty, Richard, *Philosophy & Cultural Politics: Philosophical Papers IV* (2007: Cambridge University Press, Cambridge), chapters 5 and 7.

Rorty, Richard, *Philosophy as Poetry* (2016: University of Virginia Press, Charlottesville), chapter 3.

Ryan, Alan, *The Idea of Freedom: Essays in Honour of Isaiah Berlin* (1979: Oxford University Press, Oxford).

Ryan, Alan, 'Isaiah Berlin, 1909–1997', *Proceedings of the British Academy* 130 (2005), 3–20.

Ryan, Alan, 'Wise Man', *New York Review of Books*, 17 December 1998.

Sandel, Michael, 'Introduction', in *Liberalism and Its Critics* (1984: Blackwell, Oxford), 1–11.

Shklar, Judith, 'The Liberalism of Fear', in Nancy Rosenblum, ed. *Liberalism and the Moral Life* (1984: Harvard University Press, Cambridge, Mass), 21–38.

Siedentop, Larry, 'The Ionian Fallacy: Isaiah Berlin's Singlemindedness', *Times Literary Supplement* 23 (September 1994).

Siedentop, Larry, 'What Are We to Make of Isaiah Berlin?' in William Roger Louis, ed. *Still More Adventures with Britannia: Personalities, Politics and Culture in Britain* (2003: I.B. Tauris, London: Harry Ransom Humanities Research Center), 175–94.

Skinner, Quentin, 'A Third Concept of Liberty', the British Academy's Inaugural Isaiah Berlin Lecture, *Proceedings of the British Academy* 117, 2001. Lectures (2002); shortened version, *London Review of Books*, 4 April 2002, 16–18.

Talisse, R. B., 'Does Value Pluralism Entail Liberalism?' *Journal of Moral Philosophy* 7 (3) (2010), 303–20.

Taylor, Charles, 'What's Wrong with Negative Liberty', in *Philosophy and Human Agency: Philosophical Papers* 2 (1985: Cambridge University Press, Cambridge), 211–29.

Walzer, Michael, 'Are There Limits to Liberalism?' *New York Review of Books*, 19 October 1995.

Weinstock, Daniel, 'The Graying of Berlin', *Critical Review* 11 (1998), 481–501.

Wieseltier, Leon, 'Two Concepts of Secularism', in Edna Ullmann-Margalit and Avishai Margalit, eds. *Isaiah Berlin: A Celebration* (1991: Hogarth Press, London), 80–99.

Other Selected Books and Articles

Anscombe, G. E. M., 'Modern Moral Philosophy', *Philosophy* 33 (1958), 1–19.
Anscombe, G. E. M., 'On Brute Facts', *Analysis* 18 (1958), 69–72.
Aristotle, *Ethica Nicomachea*, Vol. 9 of *The Works of Aristotle Translated into* English, ed. W. D. Ross (1910–52: Oxford University Press, Oxford).
Austin, J. L., *Philosophical Papers*, J. O. Urmson and G. Warnock, eds. (1979: Oxford University Press, Oxford).
Austin, J. L., *Sense and Sensibilia* (1962: Oxford University Press, Oxford).
Ayer, A. J., *Language, Truth and Logic* (1936: Gollancz, London).
Baier, Annette, 'Extending the Limits of Moral Theory', *Journal of Philosophy* 83 (10) (October 1986), 538–45.
Barrett, William, *Irrational Man: A Study in Existential Philosophy* (1958: Doubleday, New York).
Barry, Brian, 'Introduction' and 'The Strange Death of Political Philosophy', in *Democracy and Power: Essays in Political Theory 1* (1991: Clarendon Press, Oxford), 1–9 and 11–23.
Blackburn, Simon, Think (1999: Oxford University Press, Oxford).
Blumenberg, Hans, *The Legitimacy of the Modern Age* (1982: MIT Press, Cambridge, Mass).
Bourke, Richard and Raymond Geuss, eds. *Political Judgement: Essays for John Dunn* (2009: Cambridge University Press, Cambridge).
Burke, Edmund, 'Reflections on the Revolution in *France*' (1790): *The Writings and Speeches of Edmund Burke*, Vol. 8, *The French Revolution*, L. G. Mitchell, ed. (1979: Oxford University Press, Oxford).
Burke, Peter, Vico (1985: Oxford University Press, Oxford).
Burnyeat, Myles, 'Can the Sceptic Live His Scepticism', in Myles Burnyeat and Michael Frede, eds. *The Original Sceptics: A Controversy* (1997: Hackett, Indianapolis), 25–57.
Campbell, Richard, *Truth and Historicity* (1992: Clarendon Press, Oxford).
Cassam, Quassim, *Vices of the Mind: From the Intellectual to the Political* (2018: Oxford University Press, Oxford).
Cavell, Stanley, *The Claim of Reason: Wittgenstein, Skepticism, Morality and Tragedy* (1979: Oxford University Press, Oxford).
Cicero, Marcus Tullius, *On Duties*, trans. Walter Miller (1913: Loeb Classical Library, Harvard University Press, Cambridge, Mass).
Colish, Marcia, 'Cicero's *De officiis* and Machiavelli's *The Prince*', *Sixteenth Century Journal* 9 (4) (1978), 81–93.
Collingwood, R. J., *An Autobiography* (1939: Oxford University Press, Oxford).
Critchley, Simon, *Very Little ... Almost Nothing: Death, Philosophy and Literature* (2004: Routledge, London).
D'Ancona, Matthew, Post-Truth (2017: Penguin, London).
Davidson, Donald, 'On the Very Idea of a Conceptual Scheme', *Inquiries into Truth and Interpretation* (1984: Oxford University Press, Oxford).
Dennett, Daniel, *Freedom Evolves* (2003: Allen Lane, London).
Dennett, Daniel, *Elbow Room: The Varieties of Free Will Worth Wanting* (1984: MIT Press, Cambridge, Mass).
Diderot, Denis, *Rameau's Nephew and First Satire*, trans. Margaret Mauldon (2008 edn: Oxford University Press, Oxford).
Dummett, Michael, *Frege: Philosophy of Mathematics* (1991: Duckworth, London).

Dunn, John, *Western Political Theory in the Face of the Future* (1979: Cambridge University Press, Cambridge).
Dworkin, Ronald, 'Do Liberal Values Conflict', in Dworkin, et al., eds. *The Legacy of Isaiah Berlin* (2001: New York Review of Books, New York), 73–90.
Dworkin, Ronald, *Justice for Hedgehogs* (2011: Harvard University Press, Cambridge, Mass).
Dworkin, Ronald, 'Objectivity and Truth: You'd Better Believe It', in *Philosophy and Public Affairs* 25 (2) (Spring 1996), 87–139.
Elster, John, *Reason and Rationality* (2009: Princeton University Press, Princeton, NJ).
Fish, Stanley, 'Antifoundationalism, Theory Hope and the Teaching of Composition', in *Doing What Comes Naturally* (1989: Oxford University Press, Oxford),
Frankfurt, Harry, *On Bullshit* (2005: Princeton University Press, Princeton, NJ).
Gallie, W. B., 'Essentially Contested Concepts', in *Philosophy and Historical Understanding* (1964: Chatto & Windus, London), 157–91.
Gardbaum, Stephen, 'Why the Liberal State Can Promote Moral Ideals after All', *Harvard Law Review* 104 (1991), 1350–71.
Geertz, Clifford, 'Anti Anti-Relativism', in *Available Light: Anthropological Reflections on Philosophical Topics* (2000: Princeton University Press, NJ), 42–67.
Geertz, Clifford, *The Interpretation of Cultures* (1993: Fontana, London).
Geuss, Raymond, *Philosophy and Real Politics* (2008: Princeton University Press, Princeton, NJ).
Graham, Gordon, *The Shape of the Past: A Philosophical Approach to History* (1997: Oxford University Press, Oxford).
Gertsen, A. I., *Sobranie sochinenii v tridstati tomakh* (1954–66: Moscow).
Gray, John, *Two Faces of Liberalism* (2000: Polity Press, Cambridge).
Gutting, Gary, *What Philosophers Know: Case Studies in Recent Analytic Philosophy* (2009: Cambridge University Press, Cambridge).
Hacking, Ian, 'Five Parables', in *Historical Ontology* (2003: Harvard University Press, Cambridge, Mass).
Hampshire, Stuart, *Innocence and Experience* (1989: Allen Lane, London).
Hart, H. L. A., *The Concept of Law* (1961: Clarendon Press, Oxford).
Hegel, G. W. F., *On Art, Religion, and the History of Philosophy*, ed. J. Glenn Gray and intro. Tom Rockmore (1970: Hackett Publishing, Indianapolis).
Hegel, G. W. F., *The Phenomenology of Mind*, trans. and ed. J. B. Ballie (1931: George Allen and Unwin, London).
Herzen, Alexander, *Childhood, Youth and Exile*, trans. J. D. Duff (1980: Oxford University Press, Oxford).
Herzen, Alexander, *My Past and Thoughts: The Memoirs of Alexander Herzen*, trans. Contance Garnett, 4 vols. (1968: Chatto & Windus, London).
Honderich, Ted, ed. *The Oxford Companion to Philosophy* (1995: Oxford University Press, Oxford).
Hulliung, Mark, *Citizen Machiavelli* (1983: Princeton University Press, Princeton, NJ).
Hume, David, *An Enquiry Concerning Human Understanding* (2008 edn: Oxford University Press, Oxford).
Hume, David, *Essays and Treatises on Several Subjects* Vol. II (1779 edn: J. Williams, Dublin).
Husserl, Edmund, *The Crisis of European Sciences and Transcendental Phenomenology* (1970 ed.: Northwestern University Press, Evanston, Ill).
Hyland, James, *Democratic Theory: The Philosophical Foundations* (1995: Manchester University Press, Manchester).

James, William, 'The Dilemma of Determinism', in Robert Richardson, ed. *The Heart of William James* (2012: Harvard University Press, Cambridge), 20–45.
James, William, *Pragmatism and Other Writings* (2000: Penguin, London).
Kane, Robert, ed. *The Oxford Handbook of Free Will* (2002: Oxford University Press, Oxford), especially essays by G. Strawson and S. Smilansky.
Kant, Immanuel, *The Critique of Pure Reason*, trans. Norman Kemp Smith (1929 edn: Macmillan, London).
Kekes, John, *The Human Condition* (2010: Oxford University Press, Oxford).
Kekes, John, *Pluralism and Philosophy: Changing the Subject* (2000: Cornell University Press, Ithaca, NY).
Kelly, Aileen, *The Discovery of Chance: The Life and Thought of Alexander Herzen* (2016: Harvard University Press, Cambridge, Mass.).
Kołakowski, Leszek, *Metaphysical Horror* (2001 edn: Penguin, London).
Kripke, Saul, *Naming and Necessity* (1980 edn: Blackwell, Oxford).
Lear, Jonathan, 'Leaving the World Alone', *The Journal of Philosophy* 79 (7) (July 1982), 382–403.
Lear, Jonathan, 'Moral Objectivity', in S. C. Browne, ed. *Objectivity and Cultural Divergence* (1984: Cambridge University Press, Cambridge).
Leslie, Margaret, 'In Defence of Anachronism', *Political Studies* 18 (4) (1970), 433–47.
Lewis, C. I., *Mind and the World-Order: Outline of a Theory of Knowledge* (1929: Scribner, New York).
Lieberson, Jonathan, *Varieties* (1998: Weidenfeld & Nicolson, New York).
Lukes, Steven, *Moral Conflict and Politics* (1991: Clarendon Press, Oxford), Part One.
Lynch, Michael, *True to Life: Why Truth Matters* (2004: MIT Press, Cambridge, Mass.).
Lyons, Johnny, 'The hegemony of history' in *Dublin Review of Books*, Issue 114, September 2019.
MacDonald, Margaret, 'The Language of Political Theory', in A. Flew, ed. *Logic and Language*, First Series (1951: Oxford University Press, Oxford).
Machiavelli, Niccolò, *The Prince*, trans. Peter Bondanella and Intro. Maurizio Viroli (2005: Oxford University Press, Oxford).
MacIntyre, Alasdair, *A Short History of Ethics* (1967: Routledge & Kegan Paul, London).
MacIntyre, Alasdair, *After Virtue* (1981: Duckworth, London).
MacIntyre, Alasdair, *The Tasks of Philosophy: Selected Essays*, Vol. 1 (2006: Cambridge University Press, Cambridge).
Miller, David, 'Linguistic Philosophy and Political Theory', in David Miller and Larry Siedentop, eds. *The Nature of Political Theory* (1983: Oxford University Press, Oxford), 35–51.
Monk, Ray, *Ludwig Wittgenstein: The Duty of Genius* (1989: Chatto & Windus, London).
Moran, Dermot, 'Beckett and Philosophy', in Christopher Murray, ed. *Samuel Beckett: Playwright & Poet* (2009: Pegasus Press, New York), 93–110.
Murdoch, Iris, 'Against Dryness', *Encounter* 16 (1) repr. in Stanley Hauerwas and Alasdair MacIntrye, eds. *Revisions: Changing Perspectives in Moral Philosophy* (1983: University of Notre Dame Press, Indiana), 43–50.
Murdoch, Iris, *The Sovereignty of Good* (1970: Routledge and Kegan Paul, London).
Nabokov, Vladimir, *Lectures on Russian Literature*, ed. Fredson Bowers (1981: Harcourt, New York).
Nagel, Thomas, *The Last Word* (1997: Oxford University Press, Oxford).
Nagel, Thomas, *Other Minds: Critical Essays 1969–1994* (1995: Oxford University Press).
Nagel, Thomas, *The View from Nowhere* (1986: Oxford University Press, Oxford).
Nietzsche, Friedrich, *The Portable Nietzsche* (1952: Viking, New York).

O'Grady, Jane, 'David Hume: Natural, Comfortable Thinking' part of the 'Footnotes to Plato' series in the *Times Literary Supplement*, 24 September 2018.
Parfit, Derek, *Reasons and Persons* (1984: Oxford University Press, Oxford).
Peirce, C. S. 'How to Make Our Ideas Clear', in *Charles S. Peirce: Selected Writings*, ed. Philip Wiener (1958: Dover, New York).
Piercey, Robert, *The Uses of the Past from Heidegger to Rorty: Doing Philosophy Historically* (2009: Cambridge University Press, Cambridge).
Priest, Graham, 'Why It's Irrational to Believe in Consistency', in Berit Brogaard and Barry Smith, eds. *Rationality and Irrationality: Proceedings of the 23rd International Wittgenstein Symposium* (2001: Verlagsgesellschaft, Vienna), 284–93.
Putnam, Hilary, 'Beyond Historicism', in *Realism and Reason: Philosophical Papers Vol. 3* (1981: Cambridge University Press, Cambridge), 287–303.
Putnam, Hilary, *The Collapse of the Fact/Value Dichotomy and Other Essays* (2002: Harvard University Press, Cambridge, Mass).
Putnam, Hilary, *Realism with a Human Face*, ed. James Conant (1990: Harvard University Press, Cambridge, Mass).
Putnam, Hilary, *Reason, Truth and History* (1983: Cambridge University Press, Cambridge).
Quine, Willard van Orman, 'Two Dogmas of Empircism', in His *From a Logical Point of View* (1963: Harper, New York), 20–46.
Rawls, John, *A Theory of Justice* (1973 edn: Oxford University Press, Oxford).
Raz, Joseph, 'Facing Diversity: The Case of Epistemic Abstinence', in *Ethics in the Public Domain* (1994: Clarendon Press, Oxford), 60–96.
Reeder, John P., 'Foundations without Foundationalism', in Gene Outka and John P. Reeder, eds. *Prospects for a Common Morality* (1993: Princeton University Press, Princeton, NJ), 191–214.
Rohr, Michael David, entry on 'Richard Rorty', in Edward Craig, ed. *The Routledge Encylopedia of Philosophy*, Vol. 8 (1998: Routledge, London and New York), 352–6.
Rorty, Richard, *Objectivity, Relativism and Truth: Philosophical Papers*, Vol. 1 (1991: Cambridge University Press, Cambridge).
Rorty, Richard, 'Trotsky and the Wild Orchids', in *Philosophy and Social Hope* (1999: Penguin, London), 3–20.
Runciman, W. G., *Great Books, Band Arguments* (2010: Princeton University Press, Princeton, NJ).
Runciman, W. G., *Social Science and Political Theory* (1963: 1971 edn. Cambridge University Press, Cambridge).
Russell, Bertrand, *The Problems of Philosophy* (1912: 1998 edn. Oxford University Press, Oxford).
Scanlon, Tim, 'The Aims and Authority of Moral Theory', *The Oxford Journal of Legal Studies* 12 (1992), 1–23.
Schochet, Gordon, 'Quentin Skinner's Method', *Political Theory* 2 (3) (1974), 261–76.
Scruton, Roger, *On Human Nature* (2017: Princeton University Press, Princeton, NJ).
Shklovsky, Viktor, 'Art as Technique' (1917) in Lee T. Lemon and Marion J. Reis (trans.), *Russian Formalist Criticism* (1965: University of Nebraska Press, Lincoln, Nebr).
Shweder, Richard and Byron Good, eds. *Clifford Geertz by His Colleagues* (2005: Chicago University Press, Chicago, IL).
Skinner, Quentin, *The Foundations of Modern Political Thought*, Vol. 1 (1978: Cambridge University Press, Cambridge).

Skinner, Quentin, 'The Idea of Negative Liberty: Philosophical and Historical Perspectives', in R. Rorty, J. B. Schneewind and Q. Skinner, eds. *Philosophy in History* (1984: Cambridge University Press, Cambridge), 193–221.
Skinner, Quentin, *Liberty before Liberalism* (2001: Cambridge University Press, Cambridge).
Skinner, Quentin, *Machiavelli* (1981: Oxford University Press, Oxford).
Skorupski, John, 'Value Pluralism', in *Ethical Explorations* (1999: Oxford University press, Oxford), 65–81.
Smilansky, Saul, *Free Will and Illusion* (2000: Clarendon Press, Oxford).
Snyder, Timothy, *On Tyranny* (2017: Bodley Head, London).
Snyder, Timothy, *The Road to Unfreedom* (2018: Bodley Head, London).
Sorell, Tom, *Moral Theory and Anomaly* (2000: Blackwell, Oxford).
Sorell, Tom, 'On Saying No to History of Philosophy', in Tom Sorell and G. A. J. Rogers, eds. *Analytic Philosophy and History of Philosophy* (2005: Clarendon Press, Oxford), 43–59.
Strawson, Galen, *Freedom and Belief* (1986: Clarendon Press, Oxford).
Strawson, P. F., 'Freedom and Resentment', in *Freedom and Resentment and Other Essays* (1974: Methuen, London), 1–25.
Strawson, P. F., *Analysis and Metaphysics: An Introduction to Philosophy* (1995: Oxford University Press, Oxford).
Stroud, Barry, 'The Study of Human Nature and the Subjectivity of Value', in *Philosophers Past and Present* (2011: Oxford University Press, Oxford), 65–102.
Stroud, Barry, 'Transcendental Arguments', *Journal of Philosophy* 1968 repr. in his *Understanding Human Knowledge* (2000: Oxford University Press, Oxford), 9–25.
Tanner, Michael, Nietzsche (1994: Oxford University Press, Oxford).
Taylor, Charles, *The Sources of the Self: The Making of Modern Identity* (1989: Cambridge University Press, Cambridge).
Taylor, Charles, *The Ethics of Authenticity* (1991: Harvard University Press, Cambridge, Mass).
Thucydides, *History of The Peloponnesian War*, trans. by Rex Warner and Intro. by M. I. Finley (2000 edn: Penguin, London).
Tolstoy, Leo, *A Critical Anthology*, ed. Henry Gifford (1971: Penguin, London).
Trilling, Lionel, *Sincerity and Authenticity* (1972: Harvard University Press, Cambridge, Mass).
Tuck, Richard, 'Humanism and Political Thought', in Anthony Goodman and Angus MacKay, eds., *The Impact of Humanism on Western Europe* (1990: Longman, London), 43–65.
Tully, James, ed. *Meaning and Context: Quentin Skinner and His Critics* (1988: Polity, Cambridge).
Vico, Giambattista, *New Science: Principles of the New Science Concerning the Common Nature of Nations*, trans. David Marsh and Intro. Anthony Grafton (1999 edn: Penguin, London).
Warner, Martin, *Philosophical Finesse: Studies in the Art of Rational Persuasion* (1989: Clarendon Press, Oxford).
Weber, Max, 'The Politics of Vocation', in W. G. Runciman, ed. *Weber Selections in Translation* (1978: Cambridge University Press, Cambridge), 209–25.
White, Hayden, 'The Aims of Interpretation Is to Create Perplexity in the Face of the Real: Hayden White in conversation with Erlend Rogne', *History and Theory* 48 (2009), 63–75.
White, Morton, 'Tolstoy and the Empirical Fox', *Raritan* 22 (2003), 110–26.

Wiggins, David, 'Truth, Invention and the Meaning of Life' and 'Towards a Reasonable Libertarianism', in *Needs, Values, Truth* (1987: Oxford University Press, Oxford) 87–137 and 269–302.
Williams, Bernard, *Morality* (1972: Cambridge University Press, Cambridge).
Williams, Bernard, 'Conflict of Values', in *Moral Luck* (1981: Cambridge University Press, Cambridge), 71–83.
Williams, Bernard, *Essays and Reviews: 1959–2002* (2014: Princeton University Press, Princeton, NJ).
Williams, Bernard, *Ethics and the Limits of Philosophy* (1985: Harvard University Press, Cambridge, Mass).
Williams, Bernard, 'The Human Prejudice' and 'Philosophy as a Humanistic Discipline', in *Philosophy as a Humanistic Discipline* (2006: Princeton University Press, Princeton, NJ), 135–52 and 180–99.
Wolf, Susan, 'Two Levels of Pluralism', *Ethics* 102 (July, 1992), 785–98.
Wollheim, Richard, 'Modern Philosophy and Unreason', *Political Quarterly*, XXVII (1953), 246–57.
Wood, James, 'Tolstoy's *War and Peace*', in *The Fun Stuff* (2012: Farrar, Strauss & Giroux, New York), 145–61.

INDEX

analytic political theory 8, 13, 25–31, 118–22, 212–17
Anderson, Perry 84 n.5, 91 n.13
Anscombe, Elizabeth 158–9
Archilochus xv
Aristotle 119–20, 143
Augustine, St. 55
Austin, J. L. 33, 83, 131–2, 156–7, 175–6, 205, 219
authenticity 225–39
Ayer, A. J. 27, 175, 182

Baier, Annette 14 n.11
Bakunin, Mikhail 250
Banville, John xxi
Barrett, William 106 n.4
Barry, Brian 9 n.4, 26
Beckett, Samuel 209
Berkeley, George 38
Berlin, Irving xii
Berlin, Isaiah
    conception of philosophy 31–5, 41–52, 79–100
    contingency 12, 45, 48–52, 60–4, 75–7, 83–100, 107–8, 111–12, 118, 123–38, 155–7, 158–65, 169–72, 215–21, 240–2
    Enlightenment and Counter-Enlightenment 10–14, 228–52, 257–61
    free will 18, 175–221
    human nature 82–7
    liberalism 3–7, 111, 158–65, 169–72, 243–52
    personal freedom 243–51
    political liberty 3–5, 225–6
    sense of reality 101–10

style of philosophy xii–xvii, 7–10, 13–15, 19, 25, 101–7, 212–21, 261
value pluralism 5–7, 66–78, 98–100, 149–57, 161–5
Blackburn, Simon 113–15, 214
Bloch, Marc 57
Blumenberg, Hans 99–100
Bode, Mark 176 n.2
Bodin, Jean 244
Boucher, David 90 n.12
Bourke, Richard 89 n.9
Broad, C. D. 112
Brodsky, Joseph 9
Burke, Edmund 232 n.1
Burke, Peter 91 n.13
Burnyeat, Myles 201 n.3, 202
Butler, Bishop 192
Byron, Lord 238

Campbell, Richard 136–7
Cavell, Stanley 216
Chekhov, Anton 107
Cherniss, Joshua 244, 247
Chrysippus, of Elis 182–3
Churchill, Winston xii
Cicero, Marcus Tullius 3, 71–2
Coleridge, Samuel Taylor 229, 242
Colish, Marcia 70 n.5
Collingwood, R. G. 89, 97
Conrad, Joseph 256
Cronk, Nicholas 254 n.1
Crowder, George 9 n.4, 84 n.5, 118 n.1, 121

d'Ancona, Matthew 114 n.5
Davidson, Donald 95 n.19, 127
Dennett, Daniel 126, 176–7, 182, 191

Descartes, René   98, 215
Diderot, Denis   xiii, 251, 253–61
Dilthey, Wilhelm   57
Dostoevsky, Fyodor   103, 256
Drury, Maurice   103
Dummett, Michael   10
Dunn, John   89 n.9, 90, 213 n.1
Dworkin, Ronald   139–57

einfühlung   57, 221, *see also fantasia*
Elster, Jon   207 n.12
Empiricus, Sextus   201–3
epoché   201, 221
Euclid   169

family resemblances (Wittgenstein)
    84–6
fantasia   17, 57–8, *see also einfühlung*
Ferrell, Jason   118 n.1
Fichte   235, 237
Finley, M. I.   233 n.2
Fish, Stanley   115 n.6
Foucault, Michel   167
Frankfurt, Harry   114

Galipeau, Claude   9 n.4, 84 n.5
Galston, William   118 n.1
Geerken, John   72–3
Geertz, Clifford   61–2, 131–2, 217
Gellner, Ernest   73 n.8
Genet, Jean   257
Gerswhin, George   214
Geuss, Raymond   89 n.9
Gilbert, Felix   69
Ginzburg, Carlo   233 n.2
Goethe, Johann Wolfgang von   215, 231,
    251, 254
Gorky, Maxim   218 n.10
Graham, Gordon   90 n.10
Gray, John   6 n.2, 10 n.6, 84 n.5, 129,
    225 n.1, 251 n.3

Hacking, Ian   91 n.14
Hamann   88–9, 91, 231–3
Hampshire, Stuart   72 n.7, 146 n.4, 175
Hand, Learned   100
Hardy, Henry, IV, Foreword by   ix–xi,
    xxi, 86 n.7, 179 n.4, 213 n.2, 243
Harman, Gilbert   154
Hart, Herbert   8, 46–7

Hausheer, Roger   10 n.6, 95 n.18
Hegel, G. W. F.   53, 136–7, 255–7
Herder, Gottfried   57, 233–5
Herzen, Alexander   97, 218–19, 248–52
Hobbes, Thomas   3, 81, 182
Hofmannsthal, Hugo von   256
Homer   59
Honderich, Ted   26 n.4, 31 n.12
Hugo, Victor   238
Hulliung, Mark   73 n.8, 91 n.13
Hume, David   xiv, 14–15, 27, 38, 66, 144,
    182, 201–3, 206, 208, 251
Husserl, Joseph   221 n.14
Hyland, James   xx, 84

Ignatieff, Michael   xii, 14
Innerlichkeit   237
Inwagan, Peter van   193 n.2

Jahanbegloo, Ramin   119 n.2
James, William   220, 251

Kane, Robert   193 n.2
Kant, Immanuel   xiv, 13, 17, 35, 37–52,
    127, 145, 195, 198, 214, 235–8,
    246–7, 251
Kekes, John   118 n.1, 238 n.3
Kelly, Aileen   219 n.11, 251 n.3
Kepler, Johannes   169
Kleist, Heinrich von   260
Klinger, Friedrich   254
Kocis, Robert   84 n.5
Kolakowski, Leszek   123
Korda, Alexander   xii
Kripke, Saul   94 n.17, 112 n.2

Laslett, Peter   82
Lear, Jonathan   32 n.13
Lebenswelt   221
Leibniz, G. W.   7, 38
Leslie, Margaret   96
Lessing, Gottfried   261 n.8
Lewis, C. I.   165
Lichtenberg, Georg Christoph   15, 44 n.6
Lieberson, Jonathan   10 n.6, 118 n.1
Lilla, Mark   261 n.8
Llosa, Mario Vargas   12 n.8
Locke, John   182
logical positivism   8, 26–9
logic-choppers   17, 118–22

Lovejoy, A. O.   229, 240
Lukes, Steven   84 n.5, 129 n.10, 215 n.4

McCallum, G. C.   225
MacDonald, Margaret   28 n.8
MacFarlane, L. J.   225 n.1
Machiavelli, Niccolò   3, 64, 66–77
MacIntrye, Alasdair   65 n.1, 89 n.8
MacKinnon, Donald   175
Magee, Bryan   107 n.6
Mali, Joseph   58 n.2
Mannheim, Karl   130
Maslow, Abraham   10
meta-ethics   26–31, 111–13, 168–72
Mill, J. S.   6, 127, 242, 250
Molière, Jean-Baptiste Poquelin   255
Monk, Ray   124
Monval, George   254
moral or value monism   4–6, 11–12, 17–18, 54, 59–62, 66–8, 82, 87, 139–57
moral or value pluralism   22–3, 162–4, 166–71, 191–4, 236–7
Morgenbesser, Sidney   10 n.6, 118 n.1
Murdoch, Iris   146 n.4, 228 n.3

Nabokov, Vladimir   104 n.3
Nagel, Thomas   xiv, xx, 112, 124 n.2, 193–4
Nietzsche, Friedrich   125, 159–61, 170, 205, 237, 256
Nozick, Robert   9, 30

Obama, Barack   31
O'Connor, Timothy   193 n.2
Oenamaus   182–3

Pascal, Blaise   199, 232
Pasternak, Boris   123
Pauli, Wolfgang   120
Pears, David   81
Peirce, C. S.   170
Plato   xiv, 3, 23–5, 81, 82, 98, 127, 143, 214, 240
Pocock, John   90
Polanowska-Sygulska, Beata   84
Popper, Karl   3
Priest, Graham   122 n.5

Putnam, Hilary   xiv, 53 n.1, 132, 166–8
Pyrrho, of Elis   202–4

Quine, Willard van Orman   65, 82, 206
Quinton, Anthony   29, 31 n.12, 146 n.4

Rawls, John   9, 30, 131, 135–6, 161–2
Rée, Jonathan   133 n.16
Reed, T. J.   252 n.5
Riley, John   84 n.5
romanticism   228–52
Rorty, Richard   xiv, 84 n.5, 123–38, 155, 218, 239, 240–2
Rousseau, Jean-Jacques   244–7, 255
Runciman, W. G.   47 n.7, 72 n.6
Russell, Bertrand   182, 216, 248
Ryan, Alan   69 n.3
Ryle, Gilbert   58

Sandel, Michael   116–17, 123–4, 137, 139
Sartre, J-P.   257
Scanlon, Tim   112, 113 n.2
Schelling, Friedrich   238, 260
Schiller, Friedrich   235, 238, 254
Schlegel, Friedrich   229
Schochet, Gordon   93 n.16, 96 n.20
Schopenhauer, Arthur   181, 237
Sellars, Wilfred   39
Sen, Amartya   13 n.13
Shakespeare, William   215, 255
Shelley, Percy, Bysshe   125 n.4, 238
Shklovsky, Viktor   106 n.5
Siedentop, Larry   9 n.4
Sisyphus, myth of   152
Skinner, Quentin   xxi, 64, 70–2, 90–5, 225 n.1
Skorupski, John   162 n.5
Slote, Michael   72 n.6
Smilansky, Saul   200–1
Snyder, Timothy   114 n.5
Socrates   216, 231
Sophocles   162
Sorrell, Tom   154 n.7
Spender, Stephen   x
Stallworthy, Jon   179 n.4
Stevens, Wallace   39 n.3
Stowe, Harriet Beecher   127
Strawson, Galen   xxi, 195–9, 209–10
Strawson, P. F.   xv, 18, 37, 183–95
Stroud, Barry   xx, 42, 194, 206–7

Talisse, Robert   118 n.1
Tanner, Michael   159 n.3
Taylor, Charles   225 n.1, 226–8
Thucydides   30
Tocqueville, Alexis de   3
Tolstoy, Leo   xv–xvi, 101–6, 204–5
transcendental argument   58–66
Trilling, Lionel   xiii, 7, 255 n.2
Tuck, Richard   70 n.5, 71, 72
Turgenev, Ivan   97, 99–100, 252

Valery, Paul   xv
verstehen   57
Vico, Giambattista   17, 53–64, 92, 131
Vienna Circle   98
Voltaire   60 n.4

Walzer, Michael   47 n.8, 118 n.1
Weber, Max   72, 161
White, Hayden   52
White, Morton   91 n.13
Whitehead, A. N.   23
Wieseltier, Leon   216 n.6
Wiggins, David   150–2, 193 n.2
Williams, Bernard   xiv, 8, 10 n.6, 119–20, 145, 162, 214, 237
Wilson, Edmund   xvi
Wittgenstein, Ludwig   32, 84–6, 204
Wolf, Susan   149–50
Wollheim, Richard   30 n.10, 86
Wood, James   104 n.3

Yeats, W. B.   114